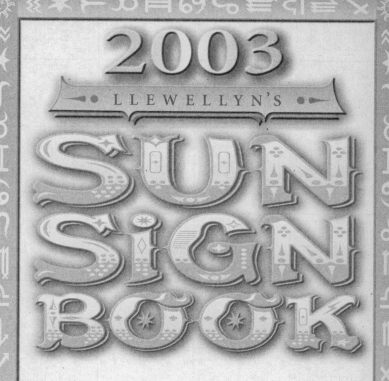

2003

LLEWELLYN'S

SUN SIGN BOOK

Forecasts by
Terry Lamb

Book Editing and Design: K. M. Brielmaier
Cover Art: Wendy Froshay
Cover Design: Kevin R. Brown
Copyright 2002

Llewellyn Publications
A Division of Llewellyn Worldwide, Ltd.
P.O. Box 64383 Dept. 0-7387-0071-1 St. Paul, MN 55164-0383

2002

JANUARY
S	M	T	W	T	F	S
		1	2	3	4	5
6	7	8	9	10	11	12
13	14	15	16	17	18	19
20	21	22	23	24	25	26
27	28	29	30	31		

FEBRUARY
S	M	T	W	T	F	S
					1	2
3	4	5	6	7	8	9
10	11	12	13	14	15	16
17	18	19	20	21	22	23
24	25	26	27	28		

MARCH
S	M	T	W	T	F	S
					1	2
3	4	5	6	7	8	9
10	11	12	13	14	15	16
17	18	19	20	21	22	23
24	25	26	27	28	29	30
31						

APRIL
S	M	T	W	T	F	S
	1	2	3	4	5	6
7	8	9	10	11	12	13
14	15	16	17	18	19	20
21	22	23	24	25	26	27
28	29	30				

MAY
S	M	T	W	T	F	S
			1	2	3	4
5	6	7	8	9	10	11
12	13	14	15	16	17	18
19	20	21	22	23	24	25
26	27	28	29	30	31	

JUNE
S	M	T	W	T	F	S
						1
2	3	4	5	6	7	8
9	10	11	12	13	14	15
16	17	18	19	20	21	22
23	24	25	26	27	28	29
30						

JULY
S	M	T	W	T	F	S
	1	2	3	4	5	6
7	8	9	10	11	12	13
14	15	16	17	18	19	20
21	22	23	24	25	26	27
28	29	30	31			

AUGUST
S	M	T	W	T	F	S
				1	2	3
4	5	6	7	8	9	10
11	12	13	14	15	16	17
18	19	20	21	22	23	24
25	26	27	28	29	30	31

SEPTEMBER
S	M	T	W	T	F	S
1	2	3	4	5	6	7
8	9	10	11	12	13	14
15	16	17	18	19	20	21
22	23	24	25	26	27	28
29	30					

OCTOBER
S	M	T	W	T	F	S
		1	2	3	4	5
6	7	8	9	10	11	12
13	14	15	16	17	18	19
20	21	22	23	24	25	26
27	28	29	30	31		

NOVEMBER
S	M	T	W	T	F	S
					1	2
3	4	5	6	7	8	9
10	11	12	13	14	15	16
17	18	19	20	21	22	23
24	25	26	27	28	29	30

DECEMBER
S	M	T	W	T	F	S
1	2	3	4	5	6	7
8	9	10	11	12	13	14
15	16	17	18	19	20	21
22	23	24	25	26	27	28
29	30	31				

2003

JANUARY
S	M	T	W	T	F	S
			1	2	3	4
5	6	7	8	9	10	11
12	13	14	15	16	17	18
19	20	21	22	23	24	25
26	27	28	29	30	31	

FEBRUARY
S	M	T	W	T	F	S
						1
2	3	4	5	6	7	8
9	10	11	12	13	14	15
16	17	18	19	20	21	22
23	24	25	26	27	28	

MARCH
S	M	T	W	T	F	S
						1
2	3	4	5	6	7	8
9	10	11	12	13	14	15
16	17	18	19	20	21	22
23	24	25	26	27	28	29
30	31					

APRIL
S	M	T	W	T	F	S
		1	2	3	4	5
6	7	8	9	10	11	12
13	14	15	16	17	18	19
20	21	22	23	24	25	26
27	28	29	30			

MAY
S	M	T	W	T	F	S
				1	2	3
4	5	6	7	8	9	10
11	12	13	14	15	16	17
18	19	20	21	22	23	24
25	26	27	28	29	30	31

JUNE
S	M	T	W	T	F	S
1	2	3	4	5	6	7
8	9	10	11	12	13	14
15	16	17	18	19	20	21
22	23	24	25	26	27	28
29	30					

JULY
S	M	T	W	T	F	S
		1	2	3	4	5
6	7	8	9	10	11	12
13	14	15	16	17	18	19
20	21	22	23	24	25	26
27	28	29	30	31		

AUGUST
S	M	T	W	T	F	S
					1	2
3	4	5	6	7	8	9
10	11	12	13	14	15	16
17	18	19	20	21	22	23
24	25	26	27	28	29	30
31						

SEPTEMBER
S	M	T	W	T	F	S
	1	2	3	4	5	6
7	8	9	10	11	12	13
14	15	16	17	18	19	20
21	22	23	24	25	26	27
28	29	30				

OCTOBER
S	M	T	W	T	F	S
			1	2	3	4
5	6	7	8	9	10	11
12	13	14	15	16	17	18
19	20	21	22	23	24	25
26	27	28	29	30	31	

NOVEMBER
S	M	T	W	T	F	S
						1
2	3	4	5	6	7	8
9	10	11	12	13	14	15
16	17	18	19	20	21	22
23	24	25	26	27	28	29
30						

DECEMBER
S	M	T	W	T	F	S
	1	2	3	4	5	6
7	8	9	10	11	12	13
14	15	16	17	18	19	20
21	22	23	24	25	26	27
28	29	30	31			

2004

JANUARY
S	M	T	W	T	F	S
				1	2	3
4	5	6	7	8	9	10
11	12	13	14	15	16	17
18	19	20	21	22	23	24
25	26	27	28	29	30	31

FEBRUARY
S	M	T	W	T	F	S
1	2	3	4	5	6	7
8	9	10	11	12	13	14
15	16	17	18	19	20	21
22	23	24	25	26	27	28
29						

MARCH
S	M	T	W	T	F	S
	1	2	3	4	5	6
7	8	9	10	11	12	13
14	15	16	17	18	19	20
21	22	23	24	25	26	27
28	29	30	31			

APRIL
S	M	T	W	T	F	S
				1	2	3
4	5	6	7	8	9	10
11	12	13	14	15	16	17
18	19	20	21	22	23	24
25	26	27	28	29	30	

MAY
S	M	T	W	T	F	S
						1
2	3	4	5	6	7	8
9	10	11	12	13	14	15
16	17	18	19	20	21	22
23	24	25	26	27	28	29
30	31					

JUNE
S	M	T	W	T	F	S
		1	2	3	4	5
6	7	8	9	10	11	12
13	14	15	16	17	18	19
20	21	22	23	24	25	26
27	28	29	30			

JULY
S	M	T	W	T	F	S
				1	2	3
4	5	6	7	8	9	10
11	12	13	14	15	16	17
18	19	20	21	22	23	24
25	26	27	28	29	30	31

AUGUST
S	M	T	W	T	F	S
1	2	3	4	5	6	7
8	9	10	11	12	13	14
15	16	17	18	19	20	21
22	23	24	25	26	27	28
29	30	31				

SEPTEMBER
S	M	T	W	T	F	S
			1	2	3	4
5	6	7	8	9	10	11
12	13	14	15	16	17	18
19	20	21	22	23	24	25
26	27	28	29	30		

OCTOBER
S	M	T	W	T	F	S
					1	2
3	4	5	6	7	8	9
10	11	12	13	14	15	16
17	18	19	20	21	22	23
24	25	26	27	28	29	30
31						

NOVEMBER
S	M	T	W	T	F	S
	1	2	3	4	5	6
7	8	9	10	11	12	13
14	15	16	17	18	19	20
21	22	23	24	25	26	27
28	29	30				

DECEMBER
S	M	T	W	T	F	S
			1	2	3	4
5	6	7	8	9	10	11
12	13	14	15	16	17	18
19	20	21	22	23	24	25
26	27	28	29	30	31	

Table of Contents

Meet Terry Lamb 5
New Concepts for Signs of the Zodiac 6
Understanding the Basics of Astrology 8
Signs of the Zodiac 9
The Planets 10
Using this Book 11
2003 at a Glance 12
Ascendant Table 14
Astrological Glossary 16
Meanings of the Planets 22

2003 Sun Sign Forecasts
Aries 28
Taurus 52
Gemini 76
Cancer 100
Leo 125
Virgo 149
Libra 172
Scorpio 196
Sagittarius 220
Capricorn 244
Aquarius 268
Pisces 292

2003 Sun Sign Articles

Meet Terry Lamb

A ll horoscopes and sign descriptions for this book were written by Terry Lamb. A counselor, instructor, and healer using a spiritually oriented approach to astrology and healing, Terry specializes in electional astrology (choosing the right day for an event according to planetary influences), as well as family and relationship matters as they influence our personal fulfillment. She is the

author of *Born To Be Together: Love Relationships, Astrology, and the Soul*, and is a contributing author to Llewellyn's *Moon Sign Book*. She has also been published in *Cosmos*, the *NCGR Journal*, and the *Mountain Astrologer*, and has written a monograph on her research into planetary cycles and childhood called *The Cycles of Childhood*. In addition, her publications have appeared on various websites, including StarIQ.com, and her own site, www.terrylamb.net.

Terry is also director of the Astrological Certification Program, a two-year course of study designed to provide professional-level skills that may be used to gain certification and success in an astrological career. Fourth-level certified by the National Council for Geocosmic Research (NCGR), she is an instructor in the NCGR Online College, and serves on their Board of Examiners. She is also NCGR's Executive Secretary, the president of the San Diego chapter of NCGR, and a past board member of the San Diego Astrological Society. Terry is a faculty member of the United Astrology Congress and has been a featured speaker at the ASTRO 2000 Conference, NCGR Education Conferences, and regional conferences and seminars. She currently resides in Spring Valley, California.

New Concepts for Signs of the Zodiac

The signs of the zodiac represent characteristics and traits that indicate how energy operates within our lives. The signs tell the story of human evolution and development, and all are necessary to form the continuum of whole life experience. In fact, all twelve signs are represented within your astrological chart.

Although the traditional metaphors for the twelve signs (such as Aries, the Ram) are always functional, these alternative concepts for each of the twelve signs also describe the gradual unfolding of the human spirit.

Aries: The Initiator is the first sign of the zodiac and encompasses the primary concept of getting things started. This fiery ignition and bright beginning can prove to be the thrust necessary for new life, but the Initiator also can appear before a situation is ready for change and create disruption.

Taurus: The Maintainer sustains what Aries has begun and brings stability and focus into the picture, yet there also can be a tendency to try to maintain something in its current state without allowing for new growth.

Gemini: The Questioner seeks to determine whether alternatives are possible and offers diversity to the processes Taurus has brought into stability. Yet questioning can also lead to distraction, subsequently scattering energy and diffusing focus.

Cancer: The Nurturer provides the qualities necessary for growth and security, and encourages a deepening awareness of emotional needs. Yet this same nurturing can stifle individuation if it becomes too smothering.

Leo: The Loyalist directs and centralizes the experiences Cancer feeds. This quality is powerfully targeted toward self-awareness, but can be shortsighted. Hence, the Loyalist can hold steadfastly to viewpoints or feelings that inhibit new experiences.

Virgo: The Modifier analyzes the situations Leo brings to light and determines possibilities for change. Even though this change may be in the name of improvement, it can lead to dissatisfaction with the self if not directed in harmony with higher needs.

Libra: The Judge is constantly comparing everything to be sure that a certain level of rightness and perfection is presented. However, the Judge can also present possibilities that are harsh and seem to be cold or without feeling.

Scorpio: The Catalyst steps into the play of life to provide the quality of alchemical transformation. The Catalyst can stir the brew just enough to create a healing potion, or may get things going to such a powerful extent that they boil out of control.

Sagittarius: The Adventurer moves away from Scorpio's dimension to seek what lies beyond the horizon. The Adventurer continually looks for possibilities that answer the ultimate questions, but may forget the pathway back home.

Capricorn: The Pragmatist attempts to put everything into its rightful place and find ways to make life work out right. The Pragmatist can teach lessons of practicality and determination, but can become highly self-righteous when shortsighted.

Aquarius: The Reformer looks for ways to take what Capricorn has built and bring it up to date. Yet there is also a tendency to scrap the original in favor of a new plan that may not have the stable foundation necessary to operate effectively.

Pisces: The Visionary brings mysticism and imagination, and challenges the soul to move beyond the physical plane, into the realm of what might be. The Visionary can pierce the veil, returning enlightened to the physical world. The challenge is to avoid getting lost within the illusion of an alternate reality.

Understanding the Basics of Astrology

Astrology is an ancient and continually evolving system used to clarify your identity and your needs. An astrological chart—which is calculated using the date, time, and place of birth—contains many factors which symbolically represent the needs, expressions, and experiences that make up the whole person. A professional astrologer interprets this symbolic picture, offering you an accurate portrait of your personality.

The chart itself—the horoscope—is a portrait of an individual. Generally, a natal (or birth) horoscope is drawn on a circular wheel. The wheel is divided into twelve segments, called houses. Each of the twelve houses represents a different aspect of the individual, much like the facets of a brilliantly cut stone. The houses depict different environments, such as home, school, and work. The houses also represent roles and relationships: parents, friends, lovers, children, partners. In each environment, individuals show a different side of their personality. At home, you may represent yourself quite differently than you do on the job. Additionally, in each relationship you will project a different image of yourself. Your parents rarely see the side you show to intimate friends.

Symbols for the planets, the Sun, and the Moon are drawn inside the houses. Each planet represents a separate kind of energy. You experience and express that energy in specific ways. (For a complete list, refer to the table on the next page.) The way you use each of these energies is up to you. The planets in your chart do not make you do anything!

The twelve signs of the zodiac indicate characteristics and traits that further define your personality. Each sign can be expressed in positive and negative ways. (The basic meaning of each of the signs is explained in the corresponding sections ahead.) What's more, you have all twelve signs somewhere in your chart. Signs that are strongly emphasized by the planets have greater force. The Sun, Moon, and planets are placed on the chart according to their position at the time of birth. The qualities of a sign, combined with the

Signs of the Zodiac

Aries	♈	The Initiator
Taurus	♉	The Maintainer
Gemini	♊	The Questioner
Cancer	♋	The Nurturer
Leo	♌	The Loyalist
Virgo	♍	The Modifier
Libra	♎	The Judge
Scorpio	♏	The Catalyst
Sagittarius	♐	The Adventurer
Capricorn	♑	The Pragmatist
Aquarius	♒	The Reformer
Pisces	♓	The Visionary

energy of a planet, indicate how you might be most likely to use that energy and the best ways to develop that energy. The signs add color, emphasis, and dimension to the personality.

Signs are also placed at the cusps, or dividing lines, of each of the houses. The influence of the signs on the houses is much the same as their influence on the Sun, Moon, and planets. Each house is shaped by the sign on its cusp.

When you view a horoscope, you will notice that there appear to be four distinctive angles dividing the wheel of the chart. The line that divides the chart into a top and bottom half represents the horizon. In most cases, the left side of the horizon is called the Ascendant. The zodiac sign on the Ascendant is your rising sign. The Ascendant indicates the way others are likely to view you.

The Sun, Moon, or planet can be compared to an actor in a play. The sign shows how the energy works, like the role the actor plays in a drama. The house indicates where the energy operates, like the setting of a play. On a psychological level, the Sun represents who

The Planets

Sun	☉	The ego, self, willpower
Moon	☽	The subconscious self, habits
Mercury	☿	Communication, the intellect
Venus	♀	Emotional expression, love, appreciation, artistry
Mars	♂	Physical drive, assertiveness, anger
Jupiter	♃	Philosophy, ethics, generosity
Saturn	♄	Discipline, focus, responsibility
Uranus	♅	Individuality, rebelliousness
Neptune	♆	Imagination, sensitivity, compassion
Pluto	♇	Transformation, healing, regeneration

you think you are. The Ascendant describes who others think you are, and the Moon reflects your inner self.

Astrologers also study the geometric relationships between the Sun, Moon, and planets. These geometric angles are called aspects. Aspects further define the strengths, weaknesses, and challenges within your physical, mental, emotional, and spiritual self. Sometimes, patterns also appear in an astrological chart. These patterns have meaning.

To understand cycles for any given point in time, astrologers study several factors. Many use transits, which refer to the movement and positions of the planets. When astrologers compare those positions to the birth horoscope, the transits indicate activity in particular areas of the chart. The *Sun Sign Book* uses transits.

As you can see, your Sun sign is just one of many factors that describes who you are—but it is a powerful one! As the symbol of the ego, the Sun in your chart reflects your drive to be noticed. Most people can easily relate to the concepts associated with their Sun sign, since it is tied to their sense of personal identity.

Using this Book

This book contains what is called "Sun sign astrology." That is, astrology based on the sign that your Sun was in at the time of your birth. It can be surprisingly accurate, in spite of the fact that there are at least eight other bodies in the heavens that astrologers typically use when interpreting your chart. The technique has its foundation in ancient Greek astrology, in which the Sun was one of five points in the chart that was used as a focal point for delineation. Since the Sun represents your overall life purpose and deepest sense of identity, you are likely to find the descriptions under your sign helpful.

The most effective way to use astrology, however, is through one-on-one work with a professional astrologer, who can integrate the eight or so other bodies into his or her interpretation to provide you with guidance. There are factors related to the year and time of day you were born that are highly significant in the way you approach life and vital to making wise choices. In addition, there are ways of using astrology that aren't addressed here, such as compatibility between two specific individuals, discovering family patterns, or picking a day for a wedding or grand opening.

I've described the year's major challenges and opportunities for every Sun sign in the "Year Ahead" section. The first part of each section applies to all individuals born under the sign. I've also included information for specific birth dates that will help you understand the inner changes you'll experience during 2002. The section illustrates your fundamental themes for the year ahead. They will be the underlying principles present throughout the year. These cycles comprise your major challenges and opportunities relating to your personal identity. Blend these ideas with the information you find in the monthly forecast section for your Sun sign and Ascendant.

To best use the information in the monthly forecasts, you'll want to determine your Ascendant, or rising sign. If you don't know your Ascendant, the tables following this description will help you determine your rising sign. They are most accurate for those born in the continental United States. They're only an approximation, but they can be used as a good rule of thumb. Your exact Ascendant may vary from the tables according to your time and place of birth. Once you've approximated your ascending sign using the tables or determined your Ascendant by having your chart calculated, you'll know two significant factors in your chart. Read the monthly forecast sections for both your Sun and Ascendant to gain the most useful information.

Your "Rewarding and Challenging Days" sections indicate times when you'll feel either more centered or more out of balance. The rewarding days are not the only times you can perform well, but the times you're likely to feel better integrated! During challenging days, take extra time to center yourself by meditating or using other techniques that help you feel more objective.

The Action Table found at the end of each sign's section offers general guidelines for the best time to take a particular action. Please note, however, that your whole chart will provide more accurate guidelines for the best time to do something. Therefore, use this table with a grain of salt, and never let it stop you from taking an action you feel compelled to take.

These guidelines, although highly useful, cannot incorporate all the factors influencing your current life situation. However, you can use this information for an objective awareness about the way the current cycles are affecting you. Realize that the power of astrology is even more useful when you have a complete chart and professional guidance.

2003 at a Glance

The power struggles and political standoffs of the past two years will be put behind us in 2003, and a renewed cooperative spirit will shine through, as Saturn finally leaves its opposition to Pluto and makes a more harmonious water trine to Uranus in Pisces. This lays the groundwork for the dissipation of some of the tensions felt around the world because of rigid differences in political systems.

There will be a high level of idealism, as some groups which have been recently disenfranchised or out of power begin to regain a voice. It will be a good year for the entertainment industry in general, but especially for film during the first half of the year. There may be quite a sensation in the entertainment world from February through April.

The challenges we will face will be expressed in terms of care and relief for those in distress. It will be as if the lights have come on and suddenly the leaders of the world can see the plight of disadvantaged people. At the same time, those who have been victims show signs of rising up against their oppressors. There will be increased concern about human rights and conditions of life, especially by nations toward their own peoples. At first this concern is only to quell unrest, but as the benefits accrue, nations see a chance to create genuine peace.

Education will continue to be an issue this year, and there will be some breakthroughs in techniques and approaches. There may be a return of interest in the arts and their role in the schools as a form of therapy and a curb to violence, as well as a support for mental development. New, more global ways of evaluating students will be suggested, and some of the old standards, which have given skewed results for minority groups, will be set aside. Standardized testing, which has received a high degree of emphasis in recent years, may fall off in some areas, as the negative effects of this view emerge.

Unexpected events of unknown origin may occur during the late summer, which could destabilize the economy—particularly the stock market—especially at the end of August. The experience will build throughout the summer, and its effects will be felt into the fall and early winter. This could be an event or extreme weather pattern that challenges the existence of a nation somewhere in the world, or it could be an act of violence that will tie in with the political issues of our era. However, there is relief in the form of assistance and the resourcefulness of the people who are affected.

All of the issues of today are challenges associated with globalism. As we become increasingly more like one worldwide family, it is inevitable that dysfunctions come to the surface. It takes time, patience, and wisdom to outlast the difficulties, but in 2003 we have the chance to make visible progress.

Ascendant Table

Your Time of Birth

Your Sun Sign	6–8 am	8–10 am	10 am–Noon	Noon–2 pm	2–4 pm	4–6 pm
Aries	Taurus	Gemini	Cancer	Leo	Virgo	Libra
Taurus	Gemini	Cancer	Leo	Virgo	Libra	Scorpio
Gemini	Cancer	Leo	Virgo	Libra	Scorpio	Sagittarius
Cancer	Leo	Virgo	Libra	Scorpio	Sagittarius	Capricorn
Leo	Virgo	Libra	Scorpio	Sagittarius	Capricorn	Aquarius
Virgo	Libra	Scorpio	Sagittarius	Capricorn	Aquarius	Pisces
Libra	Scorpio	Sagittarius	Capricorn	Aquarius	Pisces	Aries
Scorpio	Sagittarius	Capricorn	Aquarius	Pisces	Aries	Taurus
Sagittarius	Capricorn	Aquarius	Pisces	Aries	Taurus	Gemini
Capricorn	Aquarius	Pisces	Aries	Taurus	Gemini	Cancer
Aquarius	Pisces	Aries	Taurus	Gemini	Cancer	Leo
Pisces	Aries	Taurus	Gemini	Cancer	Leo	Virgo

Your Time of Birth

Your Sun Sign	6–8 pm	8–10 pm	10 pm–Midnight	Midnight–2 am	2–4 am	4–6 am
Aries	Scorpio	Sagittarius	Capricorn	Aquarius	Pisces	Aries
Taurus	Sagittarius	Capricorn	Aquarius	Pisces	Aries	Taurus
Gemini	Capricorn	Aquarius	Pisces	Aries	Taurus	Gemini
Cancer	Aquarius	Pisces	Aries	Taurus	Gemini	Cancer
Leo	Pisces	Aries	Taurus	Gemini	Cancer	Leo
Virgo	Aries	Taurus	Gemini	Cancer	Leo	Virgo
Libra	Taurus	Gemini	Cancer	Leo	Virgo	Libra
Scorpio	Gemini	Cancer	Leo	Virgo	Libra	Scorpio
Sagittarius	Cancer	Leo	Virgo	Libra	Scorpio	Sagittarius
Capricorn	Leo	Virgo	Libra	Scorpio	Sagittarius	Capricorn
Aquarius	Virgo	Libra	Scorpio	Sagittarius	Capricorn	Aquarius
Pisces	Libra	Scorpio	Sagittarius	Capricorn	Aquarius	Pisces

How to use this table: 1. Find your Sun sign in the left column.
2. Find your approximate birth time in a vertical column.
3. Line up your Sun sign and birth time to find your Ascendant.

This table will give you an approximation of your Ascendant. If you feel that the sign listed as your Ascendant is incorrect, try the one either before or after the listed sign. It is difficult to determine your exact Ascendant without a complete natal chart.

Astrological Glossary

Air—One of the four basic elements. The air signs are Gemini, Libra, and Aquarius.

Angles—The four points of the chart that divide it into quadrants. The angles are sensitive areas that lend emphasis to planets located near them. These points are located on the cusps of the First, Fourth, Seventh, and Tenth Houses in a chart.

Ascendant—Rising sign. The degree of the zodiac on the eastern horizon at the time and place for which the horoscope is calculated. It can indicate the image or physical appearance you project to the world. The cusp of the First House.

Aspect—The angular relationship between planets, sensitive points, or house cusps in a horoscope. Lines drawn between the two points and the center of the chart, representing the Earth, form the angle of the aspect. Astrological aspects include conjunction (two points that are 0 degrees apart), opposition (two points, 180 degrees apart), square (two points, 90 degrees apart), sextile (two points, 60 degrees apart), and trine (two points, 120 degrees apart). Aspects can indicate harmony or challenge.

Cardinal Sign—One of the three qualities, or categories, that describe how a sign expresses itself. Aries, Cancer, Libra, and Capricorn are the cardinal signs, believed to initiate activity.

Chiron—Chiron is a comet traveling in orbit between Saturn and Uranus. Although research on its effect on natal charts is not yet complete, it is believed to represent a key or doorway, healing, ecology, and a bridge between traditional and modern methods.

Conjunction—An aspect or angle between two points in a chart where the two points are close enough so that the energies join. Can be considered either harmonious or challenging, depending on the planets involved and their placement.

Cusp—A dividing line between signs or houses in a chart.

Degree—Degree of arc. One of 360 divisions of a circle. The circle of the zodiac is divided into twelve astrological signs of 30 degrees each. Each degree is made up of 60 minutes, and each minute is made up of 60 seconds of zodiacal longitude.

Earth—One of the four basic elements. The earth signs are Taurus, Virgo, and Capricorn.

Eclipse—A solar eclipse is the full or partial covering of the Sun by the Moon (as viewed from Earth), and a lunar eclipse is the full or partial covering of the Moon by the Earth's own shadow.

Ecliptic—The Sun's apparent path around the Earth, which is actually the plane of the Earth's orbit extended out into space. The ecliptic forms the center of the zodiac.

Electional Astrology—A branch of astrology concerned with choosing the best time to initiate an activity.

Elements—The signs of the zodiac are divided into four groups of three zodiacal signs, each symbolized by one of the four elements of the ancients: fire, earth, air, and water. The element of a sign is said to express its essential nature.

Ephemeris—A listing of the Sun, Moon, and planets' positions and related information for astrological purposes.

Equinox—Equal night. The point in the Earth's orbit around the Sun at which the day and night are equal in length.

Feminine Signs—Each zodiac sign is either masculine or feminine. Earth signs (Taurus, Virgo, and Capricorn) and water signs (Cancer, Scorpio, and Pisces) are feminine.

Fire—One of the four basic elements. The fire signs are Aries, Leo, and Sagittarius.

Fixed Signs—Fixed is one of the three qualities, or categories, that describe how a sign expresses itself. The fixed signs are Taurus, Leo, Scorpio, and Aquarius. Fixed signs are said to be predisposed to existing patterns and somewhat resistant to change.

Hard Aspects—Hard aspects are those aspects in a chart that astrologers believe to represent difficulty or challenges. Among the hard aspects are the square, the opposition, and the conjunction (depending on which planets are conjunct).

Horizon—The word "horizon" is used in astrology in a manner similar to its common usage, except that only the eastern and western horizons are considered useful. The eastern horizon at the point of birth is the Ascendant, or First House cusp, of a natal chart, and the western horizon at the point of birth is the Descendant, or Seventh House cusp.

Houses—Division of the horoscope into twelve segments, beginning with the Ascendant. The dividing line between the houses are called house cusps. Each house corresponds to certain aspects of daily living, and is ruled by the astrological sign that governs the cusp, or dividing line between the house and the one previous.

Ingress—The point of entry of a planet into a sign.

Lagna—A term used in Hindu or Vedic astrology for Ascendant, the degree of the zodiac on the eastern horizon at the time of birth.

Masculine Signs—Each of the twelve signs of the zodiac is either "masculine" or "feminine." The fire signs (Aries, Leo, and Sagittarius) and the air signs (Gemini, Libra, and Aquarius) are masculine.

Midheaven—The highest point on the ecliptic, where it intersects the meridian that passes directly above the place for which the horoscope is cast; the southern point of the horoscope.

Midpoint—A point equally distant to two planets or house cusps. Midpoints are considered by some astrologers to be sensitive points in a person's chart.

Mundane Astrology—Mundane astrology is the branch of astrology generally concerned with political and economic events, and the nations involved in these events.

Mutable Signs—Mutable is one of the three qualities, or categories, that describe how a sign expresses itself. Mutable signs are Gemini, Virgo, Sagittarius, and Pisces. Mutable signs are said to be very adaptable and sometimes changeable.

Natal Chart—A person's birth chart. A natal chart is essentially a "snapshot" showing the placement of each of the planets at the exact time of a person's birth.

Node—The point where the planets cross the ecliptic, or the Earth's apparent path around the Sun. The North Node is the point where a planet moves northward, from the Earth's perspective, as it crosses the ecliptic; the South Node is where it moves south.

Opposition—Two points in a chart that are 180 degrees apart.

Orb—A small degree of margin used when calculating aspects in a chart. For example, although 180 degrees form an exact opposition, an astrologer might consider an aspect within 3 or 4 degrees on either side of 180 degrees to be an opposition, as the impact of the aspect can still be felt within this range. The less orb on an aspect, the stronger the aspect. Astrologers' opinions vary on how many degrees of orb to allow for each aspect.

Outer Planets—Uranus, Neptune, and Pluto are known as the outer planets. Because of their distance from the Sun, they take a long time to complete a single rotation. Everyone born within a few years on either side of a given date will have similar placements of these planets.

Planets—The planets used in astrology are Mercury, Venus, Mars, Jupiter, Saturn, Uranus, Neptune, and Pluto. For astrological purposes, the Sun and Moon are also considered planets. A natal or birth chart lists planetary placement at the moment of birth.

Planetary Rulership—The sign in which a planet is most harmoniously placed. Examples are the Sun in Leo, Jupiter in Sagittarius, and the Moon in Cancer.

Precession of Equinoxes—The gradual movement of the point of the Spring Equinox, located at 0 degrees Aries. This point marks the beginning of the tropical zodiac. The point moves slowly backward through the constellations of the zodiac, so that about every 2,000 years the equinox begins in an earlier constellation

Qualities—In addition to categorizing the signs by element, astrologers place the twelve signs of the zodiac into three additional categories, or qualities: cardinal, mutable, or fixed. Each sign is considered to be a combination of its element and quality. Where the element of a sign describes its basic nature, the quality describes its mode of expression.

Retrograde Motion—Apparent backward motion of a planet. This is an illusion caused by the relative motion of the Earth and other planets in their elliptical orbits.

Sextile—Two points in a chart that are 60 degrees apart.

Sidereal Zodiac—Generally used by Hindu or Vedic astrologers. The sidereal zodiac is located where the constellations are actually positioned in the sky.

Soft Aspects—Soft aspects indicate good fortune or an easy relationship in the chart. Among the soft aspects are the trine, the sextile, and the conjunction (depending on which planets are conjunct each other).

Square—Two points in a chart that are 90 degrees apart.

Sun Sign—The sign of the zodiac in which the Sun is located at any given time.

Synodic Cycle—The time between conjunctions of two planets.

Trine—Two points in a chart that are 120 degrees apart.

Tropical Zodiac—The tropical zodiac begins at 0 degrees Aries, where the Sun is located during the Spring Equinox. This system is used by most Western astrologers and throughout this book.

Void-of-Course—A planet is void-of-course after it has made its last aspect within a sign, but before it has entered a new sign.

Water—One of the four basic elements. Water signs are Cancer, Scorpio, and Pisces.

Meanings of the Planets

The Sun

The Sun indicates the psychological bias that will dominate your actions. What you see, and why, is told in the reading for your Sun. The Sun also shows the basic energy patterns of your body and psyche. In many ways, the Sun is the dominant force in your horoscope and your life. Other influences, especially that of the Moon, may modify the Sun's influence, but nothing will cause you to depart very far from the basic solar pattern. Always keep in mind the basic influence of the Sun and remember all other influences must be interpreted in terms of it, especially insofar as they play a visible role in your life. You may think, dream, imagine, and hope a thousand things, according to your Moon and your other planets, but the Sun is what you are. To be your best self in terms of your Sun is to cause your energies to work along the path in which they will have maximum help from planetary vibrations.

The Moon

The Moon tells the desire of your life. When you know what you mean but can't verbalize it, it is your Moon that knows it and your Sun that can't say it. The wordless ecstasy, the mute sorrow, the secret dream, the esoteric picture of yourself that you can't get across to the world, or that the world doesn't comprehend or value—these are the products of the Moon. When you are misunderstood, it is your Moon nature, expressed imperfectly through the Sun sign, that feels betrayed. Things you know without thought—intuitions, hunches, instincts—are the products of the Moon. Modes of expression that you feel truly reflect your deepest self belong to the Moon: art, letters, creative work of any kind; sometimes love; sometimes business. Whatever you feel to be most deeply yourself is the product of your Moon and of the sign your Moon occupies at birth.

Mercury

Mercury is the sensory antenna of your horoscope. Its position by sign indicates your reactions to sights, sounds, odors, tastes, and touch impressions, affording a key to the attitude you have toward the physical world around you. Mercury is the messenger through which your physical body and brain (ruled by the Sun) and your inner nature (ruled by the Moon) are kept in contact with the outer world, which will appear to you according to the index of Mercury's position by sign in the horoscope. Mercury rules your rational mind.

Venus

Venus is the emotional antenna of your horoscope. Through Venus, impressions come to you from the outer world, to which you react emotionally. The position of Venus by sign at the time of your birth determines your attitude toward these experiences. As Mercury is the messenger linking sense impressions (sight, smell, etc.) to the basic nature of your Sun and Moon, so Venus is the messenger linking emotional impressions. If Venus is found in the same sign as the Sun, emotions gain importance in your life, and have a direct bearing on your actions. If Venus is in the same sign as the Moon, emotions bear directly on your inner nature, add self-confidence, make you sensitive to emotional impressions, and frequently indicate that you have more love in your heart than you are able to express. If Venus is in the same sign as Mercury, emotional impressions and sense impressions work together; you tend to idealize the world of the senses and sensualize the world of the emotions to interpret emotionally what you see and hear.

Mars

Mars is the energy principle in the horoscope. Its position indicates the channels into which energy will most easily be directed. It is the planet through which the activities of the Sun and the desires of the Moon express themselves in action. In the same sign as the Sun, Mars gives abundant energy, sometimes misdirected in temper, temperament, and quarrels. In the same sign as the Moon, it gives a great capacity to make use of the innermost aims, and to make the inner desires articulate and practical. In the same sign as Venus, it quickens emotional reactions and causes you to act on them, makes for ardor and passion in love, and fosters an earthly awareness of emotional realities.

Jupiter

Jupiter is the feeler for opportunity that you have out in the world. It passes along chances of a lifetime for consideration according to the basic nature of your Sun and Moon. Jupiter's sign position indicates the places where you will look for opportunity, the uses to which you wish to put it, and the capacity you have to react and profit by it. Jupiter is ordinarily, and erroneously, called the planet of luck. It is "luck" insofar as it is the index of opportunity, but your luck depends less on what comes to you than on what you do with what comes to you. In the same sign as the Sun or Moon, Jupiter gives a direct, and generally effective, response to opportunity and is likely to show forth at its "luckiest." If Jupiter is in the same sign as Mercury, sense impressions are interpreted opportunistically. If Jupiter is in the same sign as Venus, you interpret emotions in such a way as to turn them to your advantage; your feelings work harmoniously with the chances for progress that the world has to offer. If Jupiter is in the same sign as Mars, you follow opportunity with energy, dash, enthusiasm, and courage; take long chances; and play your cards wide open.

Saturn

Saturn indicates the direction that will be taken in life by the self-preservative principle that, in its highest manifestation, ceases to be purely defensive and becomes ambitious and aspiring. Your defense or attack against the world is shown by the sign position of Saturn in the horoscope of birth. If Saturn is in the same sign as the Sun or Moon, defense predominates, and there is danger of introversion. The farther Saturn is from the Sun, Moon, and Ascendant, the better for objectivity and extroversion. If Saturn is in the same sign as Mercury, there is a profound and serious reaction to sense impressions; this position generally accompanies a deep and efficient mind. If Saturn is in the same sign as Venus, a defensive attitude toward emotional experience makes for apparent coolness in love and difficulty with the emotions and human relations. If Saturn is in the same sign as Mars, confusion between defensive and aggressive urges can make an indecisive person—or, if the Sun and Moon are strong and the total personality well developed, a balanced, peaceful, and calm individual of sober judgment and moderate actions may be indicated. If Saturn is in the same sign as Jupiter, the reaction to opportunity is sober and balanced.

Uranus

Uranus in a general way relates to creativity, originality, or individuality, and its position by sign in the horoscope tells the direction in which you will seek to express yourself. In the same sign as Mercury or the Moon, Uranus suggests acute awareness, a quick reaction to sense impressions and experiences, or a hair-trigger mind. In the same sign as the Sun, it points to great nervous activity, a high-strung nature, and an original, creative, or eccentric personality. In the same sign as Mars, Uranus indicates high-speed activity, love of swift motion, and perhaps love of danger. In the same sign as Venus, it suggests an unusual reaction to emotional experience, idealism, sensuality, and original ideas about love and human relations. In the same sign as Saturn, Uranus points to good sense; this can be a practical, creative position, but, more often than not, it sets up a destructive conflict between practicality and originality that can result in a stalemate. In the same sign as Jupiter, Uranus makes opportunity, creates wealth and the means of getting it, and is conducive to the inventive, executive, and daring.

Neptune

Neptune relates to the deepest wells of the subconscious, inherited mentality, and spirituality, indicating what you take for granted in life. Neptune in the same sign as the Sun or Moon indicates that intuitions and hunches—or delusions—dominate; there is a need for rigidly holding to reality. In the same sign as Mercury, Neptune indicates sharp sensory perceptions, a sensitive and perhaps creative mind, and a quivering intensity of reaction to sensory experience. In the same sign as Venus, it reveals idealistic and romantic (or sentimental) reaction to emotional experience, as well as the danger of sensationalism and a love of strange pleasures. In the same sign as Mars, Neptune indicates energy and intuition that work together to make mastery of life—one of the signs of having angels (or devils) on your side. In the same sign as Jupiter, Neptune describes intuitive response to opportunity generally along practical and money-making lines; one of the signs of security if not indeed of wealth. In the same sign as Saturn, Neptune indicates intuitive defense and attack on the world, generally successful unless Saturn is polarized on the negative side; then there is danger of unhappiness.

Pluto

Pluto is a planet of extremes—from the lowest criminal and violent level of our society to the heights people can attain when they realize their significance in the collectivity of humanity. Pluto also rules three important mysteries of life—sex, death, and rebirth—and links them to each other. One level of death symbolized by Pluto is the physical death of an individual, which occurs so that a person can be reborn into another body to further his or her spiritual development. On another level, individuals can experience a "death" of their old self when they realize the deeper significance of life; thus they become one of the "second born." In a natal horoscope, Pluto signifies our perspective on the world, our conscious and subconscious. Since so many of Pluto's qualities are centered on the deeper mysteries of life, the house position of Pluto, and aspects to it, can show you how to attain a deeper understanding of the importance of the spiritual in your life.

2003
Sun Sign Book
Forecasts

By Terry Lamb

ARIES

The Ram
March 20 to April 20

♈

Element:	Fire
Quality:	Cardinal
Polarity:	Yang/Masculine
Planetary Ruler:	Mars
Meditation:	I build upon my strengths.
Gemstone:	Diamond
Power Stones:	Bloodstone, carnelian, ruby
Key Phrase:	I am
Glyph:	Ram's head
Anatomy:	Head, face, throat
Color:	Red, white
Animal:	Ram
Myths/Legends:	Artemis, Jason and the Golden Fleece
House:	First
Opposite Sign:	Libra
Flower:	Geranium
Key Word:	Initiative

Positive Expression:	Misuse of Energy:
Courageous	Impatient
Innovative	Blunt
Confident	Abrasive
Self-reliant	Impetuous
Energetic	Belligerent
Independent	Reckless

Aries

Your Ego's Strengths and Shortcomings

With your keen mind and fiery enthusiasm, you're always ready to go, Aries! You are a fire-starter, igniting the fuel of others' ideas (or your own) and giving them life. You enjoy being in the middle of the action, where new sod is being turned. There's nothing like a start-up to set your heart singing and your mind to work.

This is because you like what's new, what's never been done before. You are a true pioneer, and even in these days of "ho-hum, nothing new under the Sun," you can find plenty to be excited about. While there are no undiscovered countries on Earth, there are in the mind, in the heart, in business, and in the realms of knowledge, so this is where you may find the untrodden soil that you seek. Actually, the danger is not that you will run out of new things, but that you'll run out of time to do them all—and end up leaving some of them undone.

Take care, though, that you are not the only one in your life story. We all need other people, and you can lose sight of this in your singular focus on your latest project. The joy of union with others, whether intimates or acquaintances, gives us fulfillment and provides us with intangible resources, because adult life is about interdependence. It's a fact that we must rely on each other, and you may at times forget those who helped you get to your present position, or fail to appreciate how those around you now may help you to your next one.

Although you sometimes have a steep learning curve when it comes to interpersonal relations, no one can fault you for your courage and sincerity. Your high energy is infectious and your joy and "can-do" attitude is an asset to any project or venture. If people want to hook their wagons to a star, all they have to do is to find you, Aries!

Shining Your Love Light

The newness in a relationship is what thrills and entices you. You love finding out more about yourself through the other person, just as you delight in exploring what makes him or her tick. You may not prefer to stay with a single partner for a long time, although that does not mean that you make a poor long-term partner. When you find the right person with whom you can explore your inner and outer worlds, you will be content to stay with one person.

As a fire sign, your energies flow most easily with the other fire signs, Leo and Sagittarius, although all that flame can be too much of a good thing. You will share an enthusiasm for life but may lack the practicality to lead a stable material existence. A relationship with another Aries may have the allure of someone who really understands you, but your inborn competitive spirit can divide you in the long run. Taurus will stabilize you and challenge you to incorporate sensibility and groundedness into your nature, but may appear too slow for you. Gemini is more your style, with the speed and social skills to match your zest for life. Cancer's watery ways feel nurturing, but you may not understand the emotional world Cancers live in. You hit a natural groove with Leo, whose love of life and generosity flow with your innate sincerity to recreate the world. Virgo is your complement in some ways, bringing analysis to your action and making a combination no one can stop. Libra is your strength if you accept your need to let others in your life, but could be your nemesis if you cannot see the value of cooperative ways. Scorpio can be the fuel to your flame, providing strength of will to match your boldness, but the emotional depths may tire you. Sagittarius's high-flying ways send you into the stratosphere, uplifting you with a vision of what can be. Capricorn may seem a cold competitor, but a level-headed entrepreneurial spirit could spark your interest. Aquarius's dry humor and camaraderie appeal, and this sign's airy intellectualism supports your drive to action. While you may feel stifled by sensitivity, Pisces touches the soft, shy inner you.

Making Your Place in the World

You are an enterprising type, and you love covering new ground, creating a new business, starting a project, or inventing a career no one has ever thought of before. You are very much self-made and may find it easier to work alone—not because you dislike people, but because you feel they get in your way, impeding your progress. However, you must discover their importance, as they give you the feedback you need to make your efforts relevant to others. If you view their insights as intrusions, your efforts will end up dangerously irrelevant to the rest of the population.

You may find it easiest to work for yourself in your own business or to lead a team that does not rely heavily on closely coordinated teamwork. You're great at outside sales, project management, field training, and troubleshooting, because each of these skills requires self-reliance and independent thinking—both strong suits for you. You also have a rough-and-ready attitude toward life. You think quickly and are often at your best under pressure. This makes you ideal for emergency services and law enforcement. You may find yourself drawn to work as an emergency medical technician, police officer, dispatcher, or any other position that requires you to think on your feet. No matter what you choose, you bring initiative, drive, and a can-do attitude to your career.

Power Plays

When you are in your element, you exude a demonstrable force—the power of initiative. You're best at the beginning of something, when pioneering ideas and actions are needed. You love the opportunity to take on a task that has never been done before. You're also good in emergency situations and physical or athletic activities, where fast thinking and prompt action put your reflexes to the test.

The source for all this vitality is self-knowledge. When you are in command of a situation and able to remain larger than your circumstances, it is because you are in command of yourself. You are not caught in ego or selfishness, and you can focus outward on the situation without prejudices that jeopardize the outcome. If you get caught in narrow self-interest or petty principles, you will lose your edge and begin to deplete your own personal energy store. You will become tired, then burned out, and you will lose your spontaneous good judgment. As long as you stay in touch with the big picture, you recognize your relative importance and you draw upon limitless strength that comes from the spiritual level of your being.

Famous Aries

Patricia Arquette, Tracy Chapman, Howard Cosell, Claire Danes, Sarah Michelle Gellar, Herbie Hancock, Eric Idle, Erica Jong, Lucy Lawless, Spike Lee, Elizabeth Montgomery, Rosie O'Donnell

The Year Ahead for Aries

After a time of ease, opportunity—even play—it's time to come down to earth and work toward your goals, Aries. As Jupiter, Saturn, and Uranus shift signs, you will notice a comparable shift in emphasis into areas of your chart that bring out the deeper sides of your nature. Now that you've had your fun, you're probably aching for some new initiatives—new projects to stimulate your entrepreneurial spirit.

Jupiter has been in the Aries-friendly sign of Leo since mid-2002. This has added spark to your naturally fun-loving approach to life. You may be particularly satisfied with the higher level of creativity that fills your work and play. You may also have had the best-ever romance or vacation—something to remember fondly for years to come. In August, Jupiter's move into Virgo signals a time to get more serious and think about the accomplishments you want to create in the future. This is also a time to look at your lifestyle and health routines. A past lack of discipline may suggest establishing some new patterns. An active response—a new exercise routine— rather than a completely new regimen is likely to fit Jupiter's nature better and be easier to stick with. Allow the joys of the last year to fill you with enthusiasm for a new phase, not to engender resentment for the "get back to work" mood.

Saturn in Gemini has been relatively good for you. It has lent structure to your studies and steadiness to your serious activities. It has led you to think about long-term goals, maybe even what you want to be when you grow up. More than anything, it has schooled your attitudes and allowed you to see how your thoughts influence the outcomes you experience. Starting in June, Saturn in Cancer may lead you to think even more soberly about life, especially your past. You may find that your home, or someone in the home, becomes a burden somehow, or you may begin to question the influences of your family in some way. This is a time of differentiating yourself from the world around you. You may discover ways to make your home more comfortable and want to embark on a home-improvement project. You may also uncover emotional sensitivities or just feel like spending more time in private.

Chiron in Capricorn for another year highlights the ways in which you can improve your character to make you more "executive material." You may also find yourself interested in bringing more care and healing into what you already do. Uranus's move into Pisces in March signals a shift in focus from social to spiritual change in your life. In your solar Twelfth House there are hidden, unconscious factors which will come to the surface over the next seven years. Although unexpected and sometimes challenging, this is good, because it helps to identify stumbling blocks you've always had to deal with but now can eradicate. Neptune is still lending a spiritual cast to your circle of acquaintances and influencing the way others see your influence on groups. This can suggest popularity among the masses, but it is more likely to involve you in groups that share an interest in spiritual, religious, or artistic activities, goals, and ideals. Pluto has been transforming your goals with a mostly subtle hand. You may be dreaming of a personal power that you would not have thought yourself capable of in years past. Take care to find the larger service you wish to fulfill and measure out two doses of compassion for each dose of power, and you will have the recipe for success.

The eclipses since mid-2002 have made you aware of some practical limitations that you must resolve before you can fulfill your dreams. The eclipses this year will make it possible—even necessary—for you to enact those changes. They will come in the form of financially motivated adjustments so that you have more strength in your resources for future endeavors.

If you were born from March 21 to 24, Uranus will enter Pisces and your solar Twelfth House from March 11 to September 15. This signals the beginning of a long period when you will be drawn inside yourself to connect more deeply with your sense of purpose and direction in this lifetime. Since Uranus will return to Aquarius for one last hurrah from September 15 to December 30, you may only be able to guess at what these new issues may be rather than actually grappling with them. Since Uranus's transit through this house will last seven years, there's plenty of time to get in touch with this part of your nature, so take your time. You may find yourself exploring spirituality in a different way or having new spiritual experiences.

You may even change your spiritual or religious path or affiliation. You may be drawn to explore unexplained or mysterious areas of your past in an effort to satisfy your longings for greater fulfillment. You could also find yourself doing more quiet, background work in support of others. Unexpected events may highlight your life over the coming seven years as Uranus makes its way through this house—events that sometimes have the feel of "karma." It's sure to enrich you in unaccustomed ways and bring the renewal of life and energy that you so enjoy.

If you were born from March 21 to April 3, when Saturn enters Cancer on June 4 it will square your Sun from your solar Fourth House. How you experience this depends on how well you deal with the need for long-term efforts in your life. If you are good at applying yourself vigorously and steadily to a large project or long-range goal, you will find this time easier to handle and ultimately quite rewarding. Saturn brings to us robust, sustainable rewards through our own hard work and self-discipline. If we cannot put in the effort essential to our goals, the rewards of Saturn will pass us by. This year, Saturn's position will draw your attention to things in the home, family, and your private life. You may decide to explore your past, change your relationships with your family, or remodel your home. Saturn suggests that we look at our structures in these areas and decide if they are what we want. If not, we will want to change them. You may decide to put more effort into some family relationships and less into others. You may set boundaries with relatives who have taken advantage of you in the past, or you may decide to stand on your own feet instead of relying so much on those close to you. This can bring periods of aloneness, which may be industrious or idle. Either way, your mind is likely to be busy working out what you want from this transit and making the most of it.

If you were born from March 30 to April 3, Neptune in Aquarius will make a sextile from your solar Eleventh House to your Sun. You may have felt this coming for about a year in the form of an interest in developing relationships with people who have more in common with you spiritually. You may decide to join a group, or you could just follow an attraction to people who share your spiritual goals and interests. Either way, your social milieu is bound to go through a subtle shift in interest and activity. You may also find that your interest in groups or group activities in general is waning because you are pursuing more personal goals or individual relationships, so this may be a time of more selectivity as well. Although generally this is a harmonious aspect, there is the danger, caused by Neptune, of being subtly drawn into experiences that are not good for you. There may be an insidious quality that does not at first display itself, but which emerges as harmful to you. Neptune can obscure such factors because we are paying attention to other things, like our pleasures and fantasies. If you do not let the allure of Neptune consume you, this should not be difficult to overcome.

If you were born from April 7 to 11, Pluto is trining your Sun, giving support from your solar Ninth House. This long-term transit has been affecting you for the past two or three years in subtle ways, but for the next year it will be more prominent. Although Pluto is known for its powerful transformative effects, its current relationship with your Sun is very harmonious. This means that you are likely to be able to very effectively channel its power into positive and long-sought changes. Its influence will be felt in your goals, aspirations, and pursuits such as philosophy and higher education. Don't be surprised if you are inspired to take up a profound study or delve into an arcane work of philosophy or spiritual inquiry. You may also find this a pleasant time to travel to places you've never been before. Foreign countries, languages, and cultures may call to you now. This transit will work best for you if you can use it to support the other initiatives in your life. For instance, if you can make your travel experiences a part of your current career or personal development, you will be able to tap the greatest potential that Pluto has to offer.

If you were born from April 12 to 21, Saturn will sextile your Sun, lending a hand from your solar Third House until it leaves Gemini on June 4. By now, you should be aware of areas where greater broad-mindedness and tolerance may be desirable. However, you may not have felt as though you really wanted to change. Now you may find it to your advantage to do so. This may come about as a conscious realization that you are limiting your own potential with old ways of thinking, or it may come as the opening of the mind that occurs when you pursue knowledge through classroom study or come into contact with new ideas. No matter what, this represents an opportunity for growth that you will want to take advantage of—so you can maximize your own potential for future successes. This may also be a time of directed self-study, such as the research often required before we share information with others. Whether it is in the classroom, through publication, or just in the daily commerce of life, the more you can expand your base of knowledge this year, the more profitable the future will be for you.

If you were born from April 16 to 21, Uranus in Aquarius will provide an opportunity to grow when it sextiles your Sun this year. During this time you are likely to want to change the way you relate to the groups to which you belong, or to drop some groups and find others, or even drop out altogether. This can include ethnic groups and your broader circle of friends, as well as membership organizations. You may find yourself called upon to take up a leadership role, or you may decide to free yourself of some responsibilities related to such a position. You may also find yourself developing a deeper sense of what it means to be affiliated with groups and to become more conscious of their politics. This will allow you to discover whether your goals really align with these groups or not. You may want to free yourself from some of the restrictions you associate with a particular group, even if that only means cutting your hair unconventionally, going out less often with "the crowd," or attending fewer meetings. Ultimately, our sense of freedom comes from within, but we often need to assert it externally in order to discover how to be inwardly free. You should be able to assert your freedom, whether externally or internally, rather harmoniously this year, as you will likely find ways to do so that do not ruffle others' feathers.

Tools for Change

With Mars and Uranus sashaying into your solar Twelfth House this year, it is a good time to address the inner you. Although you are not usually focused on what goes on inside—you're too busy with external activities—there are elements of a successful and fulfilling life that you are not tapping if you don't learn to know the real you, the eternal part of yourself that transcends physical life, your self.

There are many ways of contacting your self, but the bottom line is that they must be chosen by you alone. If you are accident-prone, as some Aries are, you may not be completely grounded in your physical body. Some of the ways this can be remedied are through athletics, especially those emphasizing individual performance and whole-body involvement. Those which may be particularly suited to your Mars-ruled nature are fencing, archery, and the martial arts. Body-oriented therapies are uniquely equipped to give you an awareness of your physical body. For instance, massage therapies differentiate each part of the musculature and release trauma, whether physical or emotional, that has created blockages in your body.

Acupuncture, because it uses needles, is also specifically Mars-ruled, and so would be of great benefit to you—and probably to your liking. Acupuncture can put you in touch with the energetic level of who you are. Psychology is another invaluable tool in learning about yourself, because it teaches you about human nature. And psychologically based therapies give you that all-important mirror: another person to reflect who you are.

Don't forget the spiritual part of who you are. The other tools will help you integrate this greater part of yourself into your awareness and help you make use of it in fulfilling your path, but they aren't usually enough. Meditation and spiritual practices are key to plumbing your vast spiritual nature. It doesn't matter which spiritual path (if any) you choose, just that it be meaningful to you. One of the many forms of yoga may also be uniquely suited to your nature, since it "yokes" the body and spirit. Kundalini yoga may appeal to you, with its breath of fire and power-building asanas.

The true purpose of Aries is to learn to embody the true self in living form. This self is the spirit-soul complex that forms 90 percent of who you are. Anchoring this part of you into your conscious mind-body will provide you with guidance and fulfillment beyond any expectation.

♈

Affirmation for the Year

My true self is anchored in me and guides my every action.

Aries/January

In the Spotlight

You're out there, doing what you love. Your career is at a yearly peak of activity, and lots of people are looking to you for leadership. But Mercury retrograde is going to slow down the responses you receive from others, and maybe even your own ability to act. Don't expect straightforward motion until after January 23.

Wellness and Keeping Fit

In your eagerness to fulfill the energy of the moment, you could overdo it. Injuries, illness, or just a general malaise could be the result. These are most likely to occur when you are distracted from the immediate circumstances of the moment, so pay attention.

Love and Life Connections

Your charisma quotient is on the rise, and you'll see increased focus naturally flowing your way, especially after January 17. Venus and Mars are making everyone feel more adventurous, and this is just your cup of tea. Your relationships and social life can be a breath of fresh air during what could be an otherwise frustrating month, if you give them some time, energy, and attention.

Finance and Success

While Mercury is retrograde from January 2 to 23, it is advisable not to make major decisions, in spite of fluctuations in the markets or the whims of those you are dealing with. This is a good time to reorganize your office, catch up on filing, and up-end your priority list, so some of those things you never get around to are accomplished.

Cosmic Insider Tip

Whenever we go through the retrograde dance with Mercury, there are changes in plan due to the emergence of new information. Exercising patience and being flexible will go a long way toward making this month effective for you.

Rewarding Days 1, 4, 5, 9, 10, 14, 15, 18, 19, 20, 27, 28, 31

Challenging Days 2, 3, 16, 17, 23, 24, 29, 30

Affirmation of the Month I can wait for the right time to act.

Aries/February

In the Spotlight
Your star continues to rise as Mercury, Venus, and Mars soar in your solar chart. Social interactions will be especially fruitful, and you'll receive extra attention—perhaps even official recognition.

Wellness and Keeping Fit
The way is clear, your body is back in balance, and you're in a mood to relate. Put these together and find a sociable sport—do tennis, golf, basketball, hockey, or go to the spa at peak hours. It's a good way to make friends or business contacts and handle your health at the same time.

Love and Life Connections
This is a great time for you with people that you know through business—colleagues and acquaintances—and your business affairs will soon show it. However, don't forget about the people in your private life who provide quiet background support. You don't want to exhaust your emotional bank account.

Finance and Success
Networking is your power activity in February, especially if your business or career depends on interchange with others. Even if it doesn't, this is a great time to heighten your profile. This is also a good time to close deals, as others will be naturally more generous, since they see you as a powerful person now. However, there are still some transactions which may not be "ripe" yet. These will either bear fruit or fall from the tree in April.

Cosmic Insider Tip
Enjoy the good times when you have them. While we don't want to anticipate worse periods, we know that they occur. There's no sense in marring a period free from difficulty with fear or negative expectations about what hasn't happened yet.

Rewarding Days 1, 2, 5, 6, 7, 10, 11, 12, 15, 16, 23, 24, 28

Challenging Days 13, 14, 19, 20, 25, 26, 27

Affirmation of the Month I enjoy whatever I do.

Aries/March

In the Spotlight
It's time to go inside, just for a month, to replenish and recharge. This is an important "path correction" period, when you can get insights to what has happened over the past year and what you want to create in the new one starting at your birthday.

Wellness and Keeping Fit
You are likely to want to get away from it all for your daily constitutional during March, especially from March 1 to 21. This may mean using your own fitness equipment or aerobics tape at home, doing some cross-country skiing, or going on a hike with a friend.

Love and Life Connections
There may be a stark contrast between your daytime activities, which are likely to be very social, and your evening activities, which will probably be spent mostly at home. This is a good time to talk over the future with your partner and family. Their input can be valuable in casting your new fate.

Finance and Success
It seems you are leading a charmed existence, with several months of expansion under your belt. Yet, there's still one area, one project perhaps, that just hasn't yet come through. Don't trick yourself into thinking that you have to push it through. Stay in touch with the interested parties as a way of expressing your continued intentions, but don't rush anyone.

Cosmic Insider Tip
It's important to allow yourself some downtime, even if you can't completely retreat from the world. This feeds the creative side of you that makes your work exciting and increases its quality. Your inner self is your fountain of creativity.

Rewarding Days 1, 4, 5, 6, 9, 10, 11, 14, 15, 22, 23, 24, 27, 28

Challenging Days 12, 13, 18, 19, 25, 26

Affirmation of the Month I listen to my inner self.

Aries/April

In the Spotlight

From your birthday, you will feel your energy rebound and your attention turn outward. Mercury and Mars support your activities before April 26, Venus after April 21. This means that people will help you make the connections and follow through on your ideas.

Wellness and Keeping Fit

You may be thinking more about body shape now than any other aspect of your wellness program. What better time to begin (or strengthen) your routine? You may also want to watch your meal portions as Mercury enters the self-indulgent sign of Taurus.

Love and Life Connections

You may feel especially dreamy and romantic while Venus is in Pisces until April 21. You may even want to take your honey away to someplace special for some tender moments. After April 21, you'll be more sociable, interested in enjoying everyone's company. Misunderstandings could arise after April 25, so be prepared to forgive, but also to cop to your own mistakes.

Finance and Success

Ah! Another month of great prospects and solid leads, and that big one is finally on the hook. When it's good, it's important to remember that the wheel turns. You'll fare better if you'll just set some of your assets aside for a rainy day. Until April 26, take any action you want, but you'll find that as you approach that date, things seem to slow down of their own accord. Yep, it's Mercury retrograde again.

Cosmic Insider Tip

You're in your element now, with activities all over the map. You love the excitement, but it may be difficult to follow up if you say yes to everything. By the end of the month you'll know by your stress level whether you tempered your eagerness enough.

Rewarding Days 1, 2, 6 7, 11, 12, 19, 20, 23, 24, 28, 29

Challenging Days 8, 9, 10, 15, 16, 21, 22

Affirmation of the Month I can take time for tender moments.

Aries/May

In the Spotlight

Finances may be about to boil over as Mercury retrograde influences your money and resources. Other areas continue to bring you prosperity and loads of new opportunities, as the Sun, Venus, and Mars are in a friendlier space.

Wellness and Keeping Fit

Even though you are tempted, this is not the right time to ignore your well-being. Naturally, it's best if you can do something good for your body, even if it's not up to your normal standards. Keep it simple, but keep it up, and you'll find yourself calmer and more capable.

Love and Life Connections

May will find you focused on things other than romance and relationships, but if you pay attention you'll find that others are favorably inclined toward you. You are probably meeting lots of new people, and will continue to do so through mid-June. If you're looking for a new date, it should be easy to find now. However, they'll be better suited to you after May 20.

Finance and Success

Oops! Maybe you overspent somewhere, or maybe you just have a cash flow shortage as your business expansion begins to take shape. Whatever its source, you may have less cash available right now, and it feels uncomfortable. But if you hang in there until May 20 both the markets and your cash flow will improve.

Cosmic Insider Tip

You want to focus on one thing at a time, but it doesn't work very well when you do. It helps to let your peripheral vision operate periodically to avoid nasty surprises. Still, the glitches this month are not serious.

Rewarding Days 3, 4, 8, 9, 16, 17, 21, 22, 25, 26, 27, 30, 31

Challenging Days 5, 6, 7, 12, 13, 18, 19, 20

Affirmation of the Month I can be patient until the right time.

Aries/June

In the Spotlight

You get to quench your curiosity and explore new thoughts as a part of the new initiatives you've taken on this year. As Saturn enters Cancer, you may find that family and emotional issues arise. Still, affairs in the outer world are going well, fueling your ability to deal with events at home.

Wellness and Keeping Fit

Your standard plans and practices go well until after June 16, when Mars enters your solar Twelfth House. You may then start to feel as if the Earth is shifting out from under you—tired, unmotivated, and as if it takes extra effort just to walk. Your energies are internalizing, and it's best to bend like a willow with the changes.

Love and Life Connections

Your direction with relationships is turning inward right now, toward your emotional nature and events on the home front. These responsibilities do have to be attended to periodically—as a part of the cycle. This is a long one, as you can probably see. It gives you the opportunity to get in touch with your roots and perhaps repay others for their past support.

Finance and Success

You've got time to make plans and execute them carefully, so don't rush anything right now. You may be clear to take your first actions after June 20, but you have almost three years to work things out. Your business activity level may drop somewhat now, as the fast planets move below the horizon.

Cosmic Insider Tip

The coming months will require moderating your activities and balancing home and work obligations more carefully. Embracing them will make your efforts more efficient and enjoyable.

Rewarding Days 1, 4, 5, 13, 14, 17, 18, 21, 22, 23, 26, 27, 28

Challenging Days 2, 3, 9, 10, 15, 16, 29, 30

Affirmation of the Month I accept my new responsibilities.

Aries/July

In the Spotlight

Don't be surprised if this month you spend a lot of time at home and like it. The planets are drawing you inward to a quieter, more creative period. You may be remodeling or redecorating—even building—and this or other family affairs will divert your attention away from your more public pursuits.

Wellness and Keeping Fit

As Mars transits your solar Twelfth House—and goes retrograde there on July 29—you'll need to be extra vigilant in keeping your immune system balanced. Your body may react to the stresses of the past few months by needing more rest than usual, and it is wise to respond as soon as you notice a dip in energy.

Love and Life Connections

Your relationship interactions may be more frequent with those in your home than those you know outside it. You've got enough on your plate now, and even you are not so interested in people as usual. Romance and social activity do pick up after July 13, but by the end of the month you're ready for a quiet home barbecue and the TV again.

Finance and Success

Trust your instincts the first half of the month, as you will be able to follow through on some ideas and possibilities that came up last fall. You may feel depressed by all the work you have ahead of you. Although you'd really prefer someone else to do it for you, just take it in small chunks if you can't delegate.

Cosmic Insider Tip

The challenge of this month is to engage in sustained effort. Persistence and patience will make the next two years easier, so it will be good to incorporate these into your nature now.

Rewarding Days 1, 2, 3, 10, 11, 14, 15, 19, 20, 24, 25, 29, 30

Challenging Days 6, 7, 12, 13, 26, 27, 28

Affirmation of the Month Persistence furthers my goals.

Aries/August

In the Spotlight

You may find that you are not sure that you want what you've been chasing after; or others may back out due to uncertainty. Generally, it is best to maintain a holding pattern right now, as everything settles into new positions. You'll know what to do after the end of September, if not sooner.

Wellness and Keeping Fit

If there is any suggestion of unusual symptoms or illness, do not hesitate to head for the doctor. Your health may be vulnerable now, and new conditions may surface. By keeping yourself focused and paying attention to your body, you will avoid injury and serious illness.

Love and Life Connections

If you can take a vacation with your partner and/or family, this is a great time to do it. You need the break, and the planets will support you in such an effort. There may be trouble brewing somewhere, but it's likely to get better, not worse, through temporary inattention. Although it may be necessary to stay, take your vacation away from home if you can. You'll feel lighter and more energized.

Finance and Success

It's the end of the yearly Jupiter cycle, and you're likely to be tying up loose ends on enterprises started at the end of July last year. This has been a great year for you. The next one, starting August 22, will focus more on your work effort and the use of technical skill in establishing yourself in your field. It's a time to work in the background and prove yourself in some way.

Cosmic Insider Tip

You've had a great year of expansion and personal growth. Let it end gracefully and dig in for some work. It's okay to take a big break this month though—you'll be missed least now.

Rewarding Days 6, 7, 8, 11, 12, 15, 16, 17, 20, 21, 22, 25, 26

Challenging Days 2, 3, 9, 10, 23, 24, 29, 30, 31

Affirmation of the Month I can allow myself to rest and relax.

♈ Aries/September ♈

In the Spotlight

Several retrogrades daunt us this month as they interact: Mercury, Mars, and Uranus. This reaches a peak as Mercury, Venus, Uranus, Mars, the Sun, Pluto, Jupiter, and the Moon collide at the beginning of the month. While it may not affect you directly, it's a good time to tread water—and not try to swim through the big waves now crashing onshore.

Wellness and Keeping Fit

It's time to get a handle on your activities and re-establish your daily routines. This is a good time to change some of these if necessary, but you'll be better off making small changes rather than sweeping ones.

Love and Life Connections

Your best efforts in relationship right now should be to provide support for others in the middle of crisis, because there will be others who are affected more than you are by the planetary events early in the month. An awareness of how "it could be you next time" will help you keep events in perspective.

Finance and Success

The markets are probably not doing well right now, and this makes it a poor time to act. September 3 or thereabouts may produce volatility that touches you. This is a month to keep putting one foot in front of the other; do everything you can to foster stability. By month's end, as Mercury and Mars turn direct, you will be recovering well.

Cosmic Insider Tip

A time of confusion is not a time to act. In the turmoil of the first few days of the month it is worthwhile to take time to make decisions. In the long run, things will work out, no matter how far off track you are thrown in the moment.

Rewarding Days 3, 4, 7, 8, 12, 13, 16, 17, 18, 21, 22, 23, 30

Challenging Days 5, 6, 19, 20, 26, 27

Affirmation of the Month I am calm in the face of adversity.

Aries/October

In the Spotlight

Everyone has started to recover from the challenges of September as the planetary pressure cooker starts to cool off. You have internalized a high level of stress, and your work and daily life have certainly been affected. Re-establish contact with others, as these contacts will help you forge your own personal road to recovery.

Wellness and Keeping Fit

You may not feel up to par right now. Go easy on yourself. This is the time for gentle nurturing, not harsh self-discipline. You'll recover a lot faster this way than if you fight the way you really feel.

Love and Life Connections

Your relationships are top on the list right now, and rightly so, as the planets oppose your Sun. You may be getting feedback from others that offers encouragement in a particular direction on the one hand and suggests obstacles elsewhere on the other. Be receptive to the clues others give, because they are your guidance from beyond.

Finance and Success

Recovery reaches into business and finance as well, but it may take longer to manifest. Seek the advice of others in signing documents with anyone whom you don't know and trust well. Still, others are fairly well disposed toward you now, so all should go well, especially after October 9. You may feel especially busy and burdened around October 24 as Saturn turns retrograde; you'll find out what your major tasks will be for the coming five months then.

Cosmic Insider Tip

Allow yourself some time to rejuvenate after the recent shocks. Listening to your inner self will result in faster replenishment and a clearer head.

Rewarding Days 1, 4, 5, 9, 10, 14, 15, 19, 20, 27, 28

Challenging Days 5, 6, 19, 20, 26, 27

Affirmation of the Month My interaction with others strengthens everyone involved.

♈ Aries/November ♈

In the Spotlight
Your star begins to rise again this month as the Sun, Mercury, and Venus begin their ascent to the top of your chart. You'll still want to be on retreat, but the need for this is waning if you want to step out more. The eclipses bring a change in focus in those around you.

Wellness and Keeping Fit
You're feeling stronger—quite like yourself, in fact. An expedition to parts unknown may be in order. The excitement you feel in encountering something completely new is like a healing salve for the soul, as good as any medication. Such an adventure will do much to restore your usually resilient solar force.

Love and Life Connections
This is a great month for meeting friends and potential lovers from foreign lands or in places far from home. If you're already settled on that score, take your beloved with you on a journey, whether physical or spiritual. You may want to get away from it all in a secluded cabin, explore a foreign culture, or attend a unique cultural event.

Finance and Success
It's important to put some time in on your projects. Leaving them to the last minute creates inconvenience, high stress, bad feelings, and difficulties in maintaining your position in your field, especially if you're overdue on deadlines. You'll begin to see light at the end of the tunnel next month. Advisors, should you seek them, will be especially helpful this month.

Cosmic Insider Tip
This month presents a relatively stable planetary pattern which you can use to catch your breath and make some choices that are not forced by circumstances. The eclipses on November 8 and 23 will give you a sense of direction.

Rewarding Days 1, 2, 5, 6, 7, 10, 11, 12, 15, 16, 24, 25, 28, 29

Challenging Days 13, 14, 20, 21, 26, 27

Affirmation of the Month I make good choices when I listen.

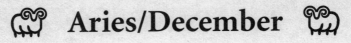 Aries/December

In the Spotlight
Once again, you're on top. You've found a new direction that promises success. You've resolved the issues that arose early in the year, and you've got a handle on what happened this summer and fall. No planets impede your progress until December 17, when Mercury turns retrograde.

Wellness and Keeping Fit
Overwork seems inevitable this month, but it is important to fill yourself energetically each day in order to have enough to give the next. Take time to get enough sleep, eat well, and take some exercise, even if you are riding an exercise bike while you study.

Love and Life Connections
There doesn't seem to be enough time to enjoy your family and friends right now, and you'd like to put the holidays on hold. If that's what you need, then do it. Tell them you'll be available after January 5 (Mercury is direct then), and then make sure you are. They'll understand because they love you. It's better than being not really present for the sake of the status quo.

Finance and Success
Everything seems to be hitting at once, and you'd be tearing your hair if you had the time for it. There's a lot to be accomplished, but admit it, you also enjoy the challenge of getting it all done. You like putting out fires, and if you focus on the challenge aspect of it, you'll have more energy and efficiency to get it done in time.

Cosmic Insider Tip
The current high level of work won't last. The cycles give way and you get more time to yourself after January 5. Pace yourself and know that all things must pass. In the meantime, make sure that you deal with life one day at a time without regrets.

Rewarding Days 2, 3, 4, 7, 8, 9, 12, 13, 14, 21, 22, 25, 26, 30, 31

Challenging Days 10, 11, 17, 18, 23, 24

Affirmation of the Month I can replenish myself each day.

ARIES ACTION TABLE

These dates reflect the best—but not the only—times for success and ease in these activities, according to your Sun sign.

	JAN	FEB	MAR	APR	MAY	JUN	JUL	AUG	SEPT	OCT	NOV	DEC
Move						29,30	1-13					
Start a class					31	14-29						
Join a club		1, 13-28	1-27									
Ask for a raise			2-27	1, 22-25								
Look for work	23-31	1-12					31	1-27	20-30	1-6		
Get pro advice	23, 24	19, 20	18, 19	15, 16	12, 13	9, 10	6, 7	2, 3, 29-31	26, 27	23, 24	20, 21	18, 19
Get a loan	25, 26	21, 22	20, 21	17, 18	14, 15	11, 12	8, 9	4, 5, 31	1, 2, 28, 29	25, 26	22, 23	19, 20
See a doctor			6-31	1-5			31	1-27	20-30	1-24		
Start a diet			18				31	1-27	20-30	1-6		
End relationship				16								
Buy clothes							14-31	1-21				
Get a makeover			22-31	1-5								
New romance							29-31	1-22				
Vacation	1, 27, 28	23, 24	22-24	19, 20	16, 17	13, 14	10, 11	6, 7	3, 4, 30	1, 27, 28	3-30	1, 2, 21, 22

TAURUS

The Bull.
April 20 to May 21

♉

Element:	Earth
Quality:	Fixed
Polarity:	Yin/Feminine
Planetary Ruler:	Venus
Meditation:	I trust myself and others.
Gemstone:	Emerald
Power Stones:	Diamond, blue lace agate, rose quartz
Key Phrase:	I have
Glyph:	Bull's head
Anatomy:	Throat, neck
Color:	Green
Animal:	Cattle
Myths/Legends:	Isis and Osiris, Cerridwen, Bull of Minos
House:	Second
Opposite Sign:	Scorpio
Flower:	Violet
Key Word:	Conservation

Positive Expression:	**Misuse of Energy:**
Prosperous	Avaricious
Loving	Jealous
Self-contained	Inflexible
Enduring	Uncompromising
Faithful	Possessive
Steady	Resistant

Taurus

Your Ego's Strengths and Shortcomings

Solid, dependable, stable—that's you, Taurus. Or could that be stodgy, stubborn, and impenetrable? It's partly in how you define it, but it's also in how you balance your energies with the universe.

It's true that you are here to make things last. However, durability is a relative concept; nothing is meant to last forever in a universe of change. How can life spring anew if it's buried under old stuff? The key is to know when to hold on and when to let go. ·

You are the master of matter, or at least working on your mastery. Learning to mold and shape the physical universe—whether it's in the form of a financial portfolio, a garden, or a piece of wood—is what makes you tick. If there's beauty in everything, you are the one to find it! Indeed, you have a natural eye for beauty, and you make the world a better place through your efforts.

You live very much in the now, and this makes you very practical, present, and grounded. People find it easy to rely on you, reassured by your constancy and loyalty. You seem to be an anchor to them, even if you are well aware of other, flightier aspects of your nature. This can also lead others to confide in you, which gives you an opportunity to express the warmth you carry inside. You are likely to share a fountain of ideas in response, because yours is a fertile awareness—you know how to make things grow.

However, just as a garden must be weeded to give the right plants the room they need, letting go of outworn ideas, objects, and relationships is essential to life as a healthy Taurus. What's more, holding on takes energy—energy that could be used in embracing the changes that inevitably are required.

Being so solid can also make you feel immovable at times, as if you are more rocklike than human. Keeping yourself active, pursuing interests that continually reawaken your curiosity or challenge you, and engaging in regular exercise will put wings on your feet!

Shining Your Love Light

Your sensual side really comes out in your love life. You want a partner who will literally be "in touch." Sometimes all it takes is a casual stroke to make you feel loved. You prefer long-term partnerships, since you like something you can build on. In addition, it often takes time for you to develop the trust you need to have a really rewarding relationship. Don't let your natural stability get you stuck in a rut—it will kill the relationship through lack of spontaneity.

You can find the stability you seek with the other earth signs—Virgo and Capricorn—but they may not give you the lift you need to keep your love lively. Aries brings life and joy, but may not stick around long enough to build a good relationship. With another Taurus, you will find the stability you cherish and feel an unparalleled resonance, but it may be too easy to become fixated in your habits. Gemini brings a lively quality that contrasts with your steadiness, but it may be hard to feel comfortable with it. Cancer ranks security needs and concerns at the top of the list just like you, so this can be a very easy relationship to maintain. Leo's sunny temperament may fill you with warmth, but Leo's need for attention can make you feel neglected. You admire the good sense and proficiency of Virgo and find shared sensuality as well. Libra's attraction to beauty and the arts puts you on common ground, but may be too impractical for you. Scorpio, your opposite sign, has just the thing to balance you—the ability to transform—if you dare to delve in. It may be difficult to find something in common with Sagittarius's wild ways until you talk about philosophy and values, which fascinate you both. Capricorn's skills and interests dovetail with yours in constructive and productive ways, but stodginess could get in the way. Aquarius's tendency to play devil's advocate may bring out your stubborn side, but there's no doubt it will be stimulating. Pisces's gentle spirituality brings out your innate warmth and strength, creating a relationship with great complementarity.

Making Your Place in the World

You prefer a steady paycheck to the perilous path of self-employment or business ownership. Still, you will consider anything that seems assured of financial success, even if it means taking a job that you don't particularly enjoy. You want what's steady, low-risk, and secure, even if it seems plodding. To bring out your own creative talents and really enjoy life, however, you need to be willing to take risks, starting with the risk of asking for what you want.

You are talented at working with and developing structures, so you may find yourself working in banking, finance and accounting (the structures of the business world), business management, or a building trade such as carpentry or masonry, or interior decoration and design, or even urban planning. If you are more comfortable with risk, you may feel drawn to the financial markets, construction contracting, or even architecture. Your sense of beauty could lead you to landscape architecture and design, horticulture, or professional gardening. Any other career where beauty and beautification are important may attract you as well: hairstylist, fashion designer, craftsperson, artist. With your gift for bringing the beauty out in anything or anyone, you're sure to bring joy wherever you serve.

Power Plays

Your focus tends toward whatever you can build or grow, and this is where you see power. The generative processes, whether of man or of nature, are fascinating to you, and you feel centered when you are involved in them. There's nothing like the power of nurturing growth, which we can also call the power of fertility.

Fertility in the general sense is about being able to foster development: knowing how to guide a vine onto a trellis, how to build cabinets in a kitchen, or how to lead children into thinking for themselves. It's about being productive in business, being a manifester of ideas into form. The key to this power is in holding the energy in containment until the time is right for its release. The seed is planted at just the right time, the tree is trimmed just so to encourage fruit, the child is curbed just enough to engender self-discipline. Creating and sustaining life is your specialty, and this leads you to appreciate and mimic the slow growth processes you see around you. The only danger in this is the possibility of getting stuck in a pattern, so that development ceases or you resist making changes when needed, which will deplete your power.

Famous Taureans

Jane Campion, George Clooney, Judy Davis, Daniel Day-Lewis, Roma Downey, Carmen Electra, Enya, Mary McDonough, Michael Palin, Thomas Pynchon, Ving Rhames, Leonardo da Vinci

The Year Ahead
for Taurus

The planets move into more harmonious zones in 2003 after being in awkward or strident places for many years. After all that has gone before, you may be somewhat gun-shy about what the cosmos will dream up for you next, but there is good news! The new planetary scene will combine to allow you to flow into your changes much more gracefully, often without inconvenience or difficulty.

If you've been much less a homebody than usual in recent months—or you've been remodeling and showcasing your home—there's a reason. Jupiter has been in Leo and your solar Fourth House. Near summer's end it moves into Virgo, when you'll be free to let the good times roll! We all need the time to replenish our battery stores by engaging in spontaneous activity. Although spontaneity is not normally your strong suit, you may feel driven to cut the rug with some fancy dance steps once Jupiter moves you. This fountain of energy may attract romance into your life as well.

Saturn in Gemini required you to tighten the belt a little in order to pay off some debts, accomplish some larger goals, or make some big expenditures. If you have made the right choices, the wisdom of your persistence and faith in the future will become evident as the products of your efforts endure the test of time. These measures have not been for the fainthearted, so you'll be happy to know that the pressure will shift starting in June, when Saturn moves into Cancer. This is both more harmonious for you and gives you relief from a challenging three years. For the next three years you may find it desirable to give up some of your cherished notions; this usually means admitting we've been wrong about something or learning something new. Chiron in your solar Ninth House may have you wondering about the subtle forces of the universe. You know you could see them if you could understand them. You've already been feeling them; perhaps a little study in healing and metaphysics will fill in the gaps.

Uranus has been a thorn in your side for nearly seven years, bringing the most surprising outcomes in your efforts to improve your life circumstances. You are probably nowhere near where you thought you'd be seven years ago. When it moves into Pisces in March, the surprises will take a much quieter tone. You may find yourself drawn to unique people and groups as a source of human sustenance. You may want to drink from a more spiritual well. There is a rhyme and reason to this which may be obscured now, but trust your instincts. Neptune remains in your solar Tenth House, continuing your direct contact with higher energies (which some call God). As a new vision of life imbues you with inspiration, rely on those you trust to advise you on how to bring it down to earth. Pluto has probably both wreaked havoc on your finances and empowered you to bring more money in. If not, this is part of the plan. Transitions are not easy, especially when there's so much to move (symbolically or otherwise). They are made easier if you can bring yourself to let go. Diversification and flexibility are the key elements to rising from the ashes stronger than before.

Since the middle of last year you've seen of a shift in the energies, making your actions count for more, especially in relationships. The good news is that the need to make distasteful financial decisions is behind you. Now you can focus on bringing the loved ones you cherish closer to you—or on the obstacles to creating that fulfillment in your life. It could be a matter of trust.

If you were born from April 20 to 23, Uranus entering Pisces on March 11 will sextile your Sun from your solar Eleventh House. Seven years ago you experienced some disruptive changes in career and business which you have since integrated into your life. Now Uranus's move signals a more pleasant period ahead, with life alterations coming in areas that are less threatening to your sense of security. Instead, you will be looking at your social milieu, thinking about ways you can benefit by your associations and interactions with others. You may be contemplating the value of your group associations—the people you spend time with voluntarily. Do you enjoy their company? Do they do things you like to do? Are your goals in alignment with theirs, or are you looking for something different, possibly deeper? You may also be thinking about group dynamics in a more political or philosophical way, such as how a society's needs are met by a government. No matter how deep or wide-ranging the extent of your musings, you are likely to feel inspired or imbued with a new creativity that can lead to more fulfilling group associations. Your insights may lead to greater leadership positions in the future and recognition of the skills and dedication you bring to the groups you serve.

If you were born from April 20 to May 3, Saturn entering Cancer on June 4 will sextile your Sun for the rest of the year from your solar Third House. This begins a period of harmonious restructuring of your understanding of the world and how it works. This can come in many ways, from casual contact with new ideas in the course of your daily activities to a conscious effort that comes through following a course of study. No matter how it occurs, the events in your life will naturally begin to reveal to you the ways in which your thoughts may be limiting your potential. In particular, concerns about safety and security may curtail your efforts to succeed, because we often have to take the risks of trying new things if we are going to progress. This time may lead you to question your past decisions about avoiding risks, and examine what holds you back from being more adventurous—what leads you to interpret an experience as risky when others may consider it safe. This type of consideration—and others like it—can be liberating if they lead you to free your mind of fears. You may also find that you are naturally drawn to focus more on communication, from style to content to meaning. You may decide that this is the right time to start writing your book or learning a new language. Perhaps it's time to start marketing yourself or your business in a new way. Because this aspect is a sextile, it's something we do not have to take advantage of and so can overlook its potential. However, if you take care to nurture this one, it will support your efforts later, when the events of life are not flowing so smoothly.

If you were born from April 30 to May 3, Neptune will challenge your Sun by squaring it from your solar Tenth House. Even though this is a powerful aspect, you may not notice it. Neptune's effect is subtle and changes things by dissolving them. You may feel many changes in inner awareness, such as idealism, inspiration, insight, confusion, and disillusionment. Neptune transits cause us to ask questions, especially about areas where we experience meaninglessness. Because it is in your solar Tenth House, these questions are likely to be about your career, calling, and standing in society. You may also feel out of step with authority figures, such as your father or boss. Your job may seem intolerable if you find it dull or purposeless. You may even find yourself searching for more relevance in religion—for a more meaningful relationship with your chosen form of deity. You are likely to feel that you need a closer, more personal relationship with spirit, without intervening authority. Under these pressures you can feel disillusioned and directionless, or you can dream the vision of your next direction. Although this transit does not usually prompt us to take action, other transits to your chart this year may do so and lead to satisfying solutions.

If you were born from May 7 to 11, Pluto will quincunx your Sun this year from your solar Eighth House. This will intensify issues related to money—especially those involving other people or institutions. Chances are you already know what landmines lie in the fields of finance for you, but you either couldn't deal with them or you avoided them. Now, however, you are likely to feel compelled to act in some way. The trouble is, there isn't likely to be a clear-cut, one-fell-swoop solution. Rather, the situation may be more like "robbing Peter to pay Paul" and sacrificing in one area to satisfy another. If you can do this by diverting discretionary funds into areas of necessity, it will only require a temporary belt-tightening. If you are already stretched to the limits of your budget, you may be forced to create a problem in one area to solve a problem in another. Other ways this may manifest is through your partner. If your partner's way of handling finances does not match yours, Pluto may bring things to a head. A struggle of wills can result unless a compassionate team approach is taken to the problem. Finally, this transit can bring out new interests in the mysterious inner workings of the universe. You may find yourself studying the occult or even the arcane recesses of an obscure science. On the whole, the issues that arise through Pluto this year are not insurmountable, but they will probably take time and patience to overcome. They provide you with a valuable adjustment period to head off other, larger problems, which could appear further down the road.

If you were born from May 13 to 22, Saturn will semisextile your Sun from your solar Second House until it leaves Gemini on June 4. This is an adjustment period that will hearken back to the spring of 2000. It will naturally lead you to ask yourself if you are on the way to fulfilling the dreams that inspired you at that time. Since then you have been adjusting your goals to match your dreams and gathering information about how to fulfill them. You have had the opportunity to push your plans forward, to blend past and future. And, since you are human, you have felt doubts—and this will be especially true over the first half of the year. All the obstacles you've encountered in the past will come up. However, this is not a test of your resolve but an experience in creative problem-solving. You have stored away the problems that you feel you haven't solved adequately, and since part of any successful strategy must be to overcome foreseeable obstacles it is natural for such thoughts to rise to the surface. The most important thing is to avoid thinking that your doubts and fears are telling you that your dreams cannot be fulfilled. Perhaps they need adjustment, but you gave birth to them in a moment of vision which perhaps should not easily be set aside.

If you were born from May 17 to 22, Uranus will be squaring your Sun from your solar Tenth House. This could be a milestone period in your life, when you find it necessary and possible to break free of old rules, systems, and constraints. You may be finding that your job is not giving you the freedom to fulfill your potential that you once thought it might. You may be feeling oppressed by the new boss who disregards your hard work and good efforts, or you may just need a chance to do something entirely different. If there ever were a time when you would be most likely to get out of a Taurean rut, it would be now. You may also be interested in a more anarchist approach to religion or spirituality, or at least something more focused on individual growth and potential. You may also be shocked by certain events into discovering some aspects of human nature that you had not understood before, either in yourself or in others. This may lead you to substantially change the way you interact with others and open new doorways to you in the long run. In some ways, the best outcome of this transit may be that you learn more about what kinds of risks you can take and still succeed.

Tools for Change

You've been through years of shaking and quaking, as Uranus has transited square to your Sun and broken up old, brittle attitudes, actions, and beliefs. Now, as the pieces of the past lie shattered around you, they're being dissolved away by Neptune. Although Uranus's clang and clatter has distracted you from the subtler process of Neptune, this year it is being highlighted as Uranus finally leaves Aquarius and Jupiter opposes Neptune. This aspect will challenge you to develop new ideals based on a deeper understanding of who you really are in the core of your being, as shown to you through your roots, your heritage, and your own biological nature.

It is most important for you to let go of fear and insecurity, for they choke your potential and retard fulfillment. Tools that may be especially useful in reaching for new heights include, first and foremost, education—because knowledge dispels fear. This may mean formal learning in a school-type setting, but it certainly must signify the learning that comes from encountering new situations in the world and investigating them. You may find that self-motivated and self-directed study is more meaningful to you because it allows you to work at your own pace and explore just those aspects which are relevant to you at the time. This "grounded" way of learning is more practical and often easier to apply in life immediately.

However, it is equally important to rise above the pragmatic world you usually inhabit to the level of philosophy. Philosophy requires an overview of mundane experiences and circumstances in order to see the cause-and-effect relationship between actions and entities that reveal motivating influences and aspects of nature. Discovering the hidden patterns leads to an understanding of human tendencies and universal laws that is a salve for the soul, inducing calm and peace because the course of events can usually be predicted. This is an often overlooked drive in Taurus, yet essential to rising above your tendency to avoid risk.

Astrology can be instrumental in reaching this level of understanding, since it teaches about the motivations and the usual manifestations of each sign and planetary archetype. Not only will you be able to understand yourself better, and thereby acquire more self-confidence, but you will understand those around you at a more profound level as well. Your level of risk is lower when you understand the world you live in, so you can shoot for the Moon.

♉

Affirmation for the Year

I trust the universe to bring changes that are right for me.

Taurus/January

In the Spotlight

This month is a blessing, but you'll have to wait until the end to experience it, as Mercury retrogrades for most of the month. For you, it's mostly a waiting game and a chance to build more opportunity into what's coming your way.

Wellness and Keeping Fit

You're not particularly stressed, and you may even get a chance to relax and enjoy life more than usual. If your diet or exercise program needs reformation, this is an excellent time to begin.

Love and Life Connections

Communications may suffer a little this month, especially if you find yourself dealing with a language barrier. Letters, electronic communications, and translations may be misdirected. However, this does not much inconvenience you, nor does it much affect your personal relationships.

Finance and Success

You may be passed over for promotion or in some other way be ignored in business or the workplace. This should point out the necessity of making sure your efforts are better appreciated. You may also need to take a look at your ideals and intentions. Are you really where you want to be? If not, start the changes now by thinking about where to go next.

Cosmic Insider Tip

The planets are relatively supportive of you now, so it's a good time to take care of some less-urgent tasks that will support long-term development of your goals. You understand their importance, but perhaps have difficulty getting them started. Taking the time now, while you have a little more repose, will give you one more tool in the toolkit when you need it.

Rewarding Days 2, 3, 6, 7, 8, 9, 12, 13, 16, 17, 21, 22, 30

Challenging Days 4, 5, 18, 19, 20, 25, 26, 31

Affirmation of the Month I can make great use of downtime.

Taurus/February

In the Spotlight

It's as if the dam has broken and the flood is upon you, but in a good way. Many of your desires are being fulfilled, many of your goals achieved. Yes, you're busier than ever, but it's a good kind of busy because it's productive.

Wellness and Keeping Fit

It's easier to stick to your routine until February 12, when your work activity level suddenly skyrockets. If you need to back-burner those healthy habits, don't let it be for long. You will gain great inner benefits from getting away when you can, because it seems that your spiritual consciousness is eager to flow.

Love and Life Connections

Your relationships flow smoothly now as Venus reaches the harmonious top of your solar chart. You may not feel as appreciated as you should be, but at least you're well treated by those at the top. Events occurring at home continue to keep you partially focused there.

Finance and Success

Prosperity may come from the home front this month, perhaps through real estate or inherited possessions. Get those heirlooms out of the attic and have them appraised, or enrich your home by investing in objets d'art. Projects begun two to four months ago may require action now, but they will not be completed until April.

Cosmic Insider Tip

You may feel maxed out now, but there's a purpose behind the high activity level, and you're making progress toward it. Keeping your eyes on the goal will give you impetus. By the end of February you'll be able to return to a relatively normal pace. In early April you'll start to see some results for your efforts.

Rewarding Days 3, 4, 8, 9, 13, 14, 17, 18, 26, 27

Challenging Days 1, 2, 15, 16, 21, 22, 28

Affirmation of the Month I can relax in the midst of an active life.

Taurus/March

In the Spotlight

As the fast-moving planets wing through your solar fourth quadrant, you are completing many initiatives begun at your birthday last year. Now, as Uranus enters Pisces on March 11, the world becomes a kinder place.

Wellness and Keeping Fit

A lot of energy is available to you this month as Mars trines your Sun from Capricorn. However, you have to want to use it—it won't force itself upon you through muscle tension or stress, so you could get a little lazy.

Love and Life Connections

For most of the month Venus is in your Tenth House, suggesting harmonious relations in work or business. Your attention is likely to be focused on those outside the home as much as possible, but you don't want to forget about the long-term enterprises that are going on in your private life. You won't want to drain your personal relationships by leaving those to others for long. Indeed, they will be a counterbalance to the external activities that now grab you.

Finance and Success

You're being pulled in two directions: into the feel-good expansion on the private or home front and into the make-money tasks that form your daily existence. Since what really inspires you are the things happening outside work, it will help if you remember that the outer-world activities are what give you the security to do the home activities you so enjoy.

Cosmic Insider Tip

You are energized and inspired to fulfill your ideals right now, so use the energy while you have it! No need to rush, but the thrust to reach your goals will gradually mellow out as we get into the fall.

Rewarding Days 2, 3, 7, 8, 12, 13, 16, 17, 18, 25, 26, 29, 30, 31

Challenging Days 1, 14, 15, 21, 22, 27, 28

Affirmation of the Month I can balance my activities.

Taurus/April

In the Spotlight
Results are starting to come in and your private world is blooming, especially after April 3. There are supports showing up from mysterious, perhaps unknown, sources. As we approach April 26 Mercury's slowdown reduces the pace. By month's end you will be making adjustments, perhaps in the way you see yourself.

Wellness and Keeping Fit
You are not likely to have time to give this area much focus this month, but, even as you are pulled in every direction, it's important to take a few sanity-inducing minutes for yourself every day.

Love and Life Connections
In your haste to complete all the tasks hitting you this month, words will be especially important. What you say after April 11 will be important and may come back to haunt you. Be wary of making promises between April 12 and 26. After that, you'll know why.

Finance and Success
You are so close to the goal post that you want to push ahead, but that's not the way it works. Later this month the Mercury retrograde will show you what needs adjusting, and will require some changes in the way you are handling the home/work balance of energy and time expenditure. You may feel as though you're coming unglued as the number of demands on your time crescendo. Just do what you can. If there are pieces to pick up when it's all over, so be it.

Cosmic Insider Tip
April is crunch time for you, the biggest since perhaps May 2000. After April 3 this month is likely to be a blur as it flies past. You can cope better with it if you line up support from others before everything hits. It may help to recall that this is a good development in your life, with only a few minor snafus occurring as you fulfill it.

Rewarding Days 3, 4, 5, 8, 9, 10, 13, 14, 21, 22, 25, 26, 27

Challenging Days 11, 12, 17, 18, 23, 24

Affirmation of the Month I can overcome all obstacles.

Taurus/May

In the Spotlight

With Mercury retrograde in your sign this month, two things happen: Your ability to move forward appears to hampered in some way; and you will be in training for something all year, learning something major, often delightful, that you didn't know before.

Wellness and Keeping Fit

You are looking at your life now and wondering what needs to be changed. You're probably detecting some areas where you need to make dramatic changes and assert new self-discipline. If you're typically Taurus, this is in the food department.

Love and Life Connections

Words once said are hard to retract. Speaking (or writing) carelessly will create difficulties this month in the midst of all that you have to do. Others can be relied on to help you, as both Venus and Mars are harmoniously placed. Any difficulties in relationships will greatly improve after May 16.

Finance and Success

You've been working since at least last summer to fulfill a goal that is very important to you. Right now there are problems, and it could even seem as though the whole project will crash and burn. Hang in there. After May 20 you'll be able to make progress again, and you will eventually find that the changes made before were essential to your ultimate success.

Cosmic Insider Tip

Every eight years we spend a year learning something new, doing something completely different, or treading unfamiliar ground. This month starts one such year. For contrast, think about what you were doing eight years ago, in 1995.

Rewarding Days 1, 2, 6, 7, 10, 11, 19, 23, 24, 28, 29

Challenging Days 8, 9, 14, 15, 20, 21, 22

Affirmation of the Month I enjoy exploring new worlds.

Taurus/June

In the Spotlight
Time marches on, and with it the dilemmas of May pass into oblivion. After June 3 you'll find the planets even more harmonious as Saturn enters Cancer. This transfers your focus from finance, possessions, resources, and budgets to attitudes, commerce, communication, and writing.

Wellness and Keeping Fit
Self-discipline is going to be easier for the next two years, now that Saturn is harmoniously aspecting your Sun. Make what you're planning to do fun, and take the time to really understand what pulls you off track.

Love and Life Connections
You may be distracted from your loved ones by concerns in other areas of your life right now. It would be good to let them know what's going on. Next month you'll be more on target to give them some extra time.

Finance and Success
This is a month of financial transition for you. Your portfolio may need tweaking, and you may actually have to take some money out of your savings account in order to follow up on some commitments or make necessary purchases. Some expenditures, both anticipated and unexpected, are likely to arise this month, but they will further your interests and goals.

Cosmic Insider Tip
Uranus and Pluto are both active this month, and your finances will be subjects for deeper consideration. Pay especial attention to problems lurking in groups that you belong to, as potentially difficult situations you notice now are likely to surface as problems in July, August, and September.

Rewarding Days 2, 3, 6, 7, 8, 15, 16, 19, 20, 24, 25, 26, 29, 30

Challenging Days 4, 5, 11, 12, 17, 18

Affirmation of the Month Transitions are essential to my goals.

Taurus/July

In the Spotlight

As the personal planets contact Saturn, the focus is on thinking and rethinking your life during July. More than just a month-long interest, the tasks you take on now may be the work of about two years. At the end of the month the Mars retrograde draws your attention to group dynamics and organizational politics.

Wellness and Keeping Fit

You may find it necessary to change the venue or circumstances you rely on for your fitness routine. Anger or aggression may play a role in your decision. You don't want conflict to interfere with your wellness goals, and there's no reason why it should.

Love and Life Connections

Your relationships with your familiars are especially nurturing this month. It's a great time for you to connect with your loved ones by taking them to events and sites you all will enjoy. Go to the museum, see an art exhibit, visit a favorite restaurant. Associations within your broader social network, however, may be troubling. You may be aware of power struggles there. You are probably not directly involved, but you may decide to get out of the way for a while.

Finance and Success

Finances are more stable in July, and the difficulties others are having, some financial, are not affecting you so directly that you cannot engage in your normal pursuits. Keep an eye on the markets, since a period of volatility is coming and you may want to move some assets in response to instability in evidence now.

Cosmic Insider Tip

There is a storm brewing in the heavens, and it will hit starting August 22. Watch for signals about what's coming, and respond now in careful, well considered ways.

Rewarding Days 4, 5, 6, 13, 14, 17, 18, 22, 23, 27, 28

Challenging Days 1, 2, 3, 9, 10, 15, 16, 29, 30, 31

Affirmation of the Month I can respond to the signs of the times.

Taurus/August

In the Spotlight
There is a gathering planetary storm thundering in the distance. The lightning could strike you—or anyone—this month, but in the meantime keep on with your planned activities.

Wellness and Keeping Fit
It is difficult to continue with the routine activities that keep you sane and healthy when the sky is falling, but this is what you must do to the best of your abilities. The rhythms of habit will keep you emotionally stable and therefore healthier.

Love and Life Connections
Home and family are going especially well right now. Vacations, better taken early in the month, may be in the offing, and the children are generally a delight. Engaging them in fun but useful pursuits now will calm them, stave off end-of-summer boredom, and reduce the buildup of tension as the planets gather for a brouhaha.

Finance and Success
Your finances aren't directly affected by the planetary events of this time, but those of others will be, and this will affect you. If you are relying on someone among your network of acquaintances to fund a project, you may find this delayed for a couple of months, or even prevented. Mars retrograde brings out what was already there anyway. There can be unpleasant truths which need to surface, but ultimately they bring protection to you by averting harm.

Cosmic Insider Tip
It will be helpful to take an attitude of increasing surrender to your circumstances and experiences as the month wears on. You can't control others' behaviors, and these could border on the irrational by month's end. Don't take it personally, because it has nothing to do with you.

Rewarding Days 1, 2, 9, 10, 14, 15, 18, 19, 20, 23, 24, 25, 28

Challenging Days 5, 11, 12, 13, 26, 27

Affirmation of the Month I can ride the waves without harm.

Taurus/September

In the Spotlight
Usually a fun, creative time for you, September this year adds more layers of complexity to your life. The time from August 22 to September 3 revealed all you need to know for your next actions.

Wellness and Keeping Fit
You should try to climb back in the saddle again as soon as you can. After September 3 your daily experiences will gradually assume a more routine expression, and you can get back to reassuringly habitual activities. Try especially to have some fun.

Love and Life Connections
With Mercury and Mars retrograde, communications can sometimes be difficult. Sometimes those around you don't want to accept the way things have to be. While this time your personal life is not especially affected, the lives of those you love may be, particularly your children's. If someone is nursing a broken heart you may not be able to do much, but a general mood of support without fostering self-pity is perhaps the best path.

Finance and Success
Your finances are likely to come through the crisis relatively unscathed. After September 20 you'll see any matters which have gone out of balance move back to their centerpoint of stability. September 27 brings welcome relief in your business associations as Mars turns direct.

Cosmic Insider Tip
Perhaps the most frustrating experience for you right now is how much you can't do to help or protect others. This month is a lesson in personal limitations and how others must be left to learn things on their own if they are really going to get it. Listen without advising, unless you are asked.

Rewarding Days 5, 6, 9, 10, 11, 14, 15, 16, 19, 20, 24, 25

Challenging Days 1, 2, 7, 8, 21, 22, 23, 28, 29

Affirmation of the Month I can empower others to grow.

Taurus/October

In the Spotlight

The planets continue to release energies bottled up in May and June. This is a welcome relief, as finally all of your enterprises can move toward resolution. Around October 24 you tie yourself to a responsibility that will take five months to fulfill.

Wellness and Keeping Fit

Your health assumes greater importance right now as your immune system dips. Get a checkup and take what health treatments are necessary. Back off the exercise in favor of milder pursuits.

Love and Life Connections

Your social index is going up and you'll find yourself invited to several more happenings than usual this month. The organizational issues seem to have abated for now, perhaps even solved themselves. After October 8 your chances of being with the right people at the right time increase, and the potential for business or long-term personal relationships increases. The situations that arise may seem to lose their momentum around October 24, but they just need time to germinate while Saturn retrogrades.

Finance and Success

Put in your best work effort now, because this is your best chance to prepare for "prime time," which will start next month. The need for more outreach or training will be ongoing, but you'll be gainfully employed while fulfilling those necessities. Starting October 24, you'll be working on something of five months' duration related to dissemination of information.

Cosmic Insider Tip

The events that unfold will contribute to the completion of old processes and projects, or they will advance current plans and future goals. These will generally fit into the realm of the expected.

Rewarding Days 2, 3, 6, 7, 8, 11, 12, 13, 16, 17, 18, 21, 22, 29, 30

Challenging Days 4, 5, 19, 20, 25, 26, 31

Affirmation of the Month I welcome opportunities.

Taurus/November

In the Spotlight

Contacts with others, agreements, and commitments are significant this month, as you reach the halfway point in your yearly birth cycle. You may experience a flurry of activity, especially around November 8—the date of the solar eclipse and Uranus's station.

Wellness and Keeping Fit

Your daily wellness routines are likely to be disturbed again this month, especially around November 8, when events may collide and sweep you away. You can combat this by getting enough sleep and not overeating.

Love and Life Connections

Others perceive you as a person to reckon with this month, so they may take opposing positions as if they are threatened by you. Remaining calm, consistent, and reluctant to change course will reveal the corrections you need to make. Yes, you will need to change, but it is more an evolutionary change than simply a response to someone else's bidding.

Finance and Success

The eclipse on November 8 can be miraculous, but it could also break up rigid and outworn patterns in your life—things you don't want to give up. You will probably shift direction in a significant way as a result of events on or around the eclipse, but you won't entirely know how until they occur.

Cosmic Insider Tip

Uranus and the eclipses shake us up by taking away something that we're accustomed to having. Both help us find out how we've become complacent or are not fulfilling our deepest inner needs. By flowing with their influences, you will come out a winner.

Rewarding Days 3, 4, 8, 9, 13, 14, 17, 18, 19, 26, 27, 30

Challenging Days 1, 2, 15, 16, 22, 23, 28, 29

Affirmation of the Month I can flow with change.

Taurus/December

In the Spotlight

You have been called upon to change course, and you're finally able to make some long-desired changes, although in unexpected ways. You'll have time to sort it all out and redirect your efforts this month as Mercury turns retrograde.

Wellness and Keeping Fit

It is possible to injure yourself this month if your physical activities tend toward the risky. You are also at risk when engaged in normal activities if you're not paying attention. A health-oriented vacation would go far this month toward clearing your head for the big decisions you have to make.

Love and Life Connections

You are being careful in maintaining good relations with others—and they are being generally supportive, even if they don't know what's going on in your life. Problems within the family that emerged in early September may return toward the end of the month; you may catch wind of them before then. It's good to pay attention the first time you suspect something is wrong.

Finance and Success

Your financial well-being may have been affected by the events of November, but it doesn't follow that it's in a bad way. If it is, you will be able to turn it around, but it will take time. Look forward to how to solve the problem, and not backward at mistakes you made.

Cosmic Insider Tip

It is important to identify our errors so that we don't make them again, but if you dwell on them or make them the sole basis for the changes then you are reacting, not rebounding. You are where you are, so look to the future and the possibilities that exist there.

Rewarding Days 1, 5, 6, 10, 11, 15, 16, 23, 24, 27, 28, 29

Challenging Days 12, 13, 14, 19, 20, 25, 26

Affirmation of the Month I can see new possibilities in the current circumstances.

Taurus Action Table

These dates reflect the best—but not the only—times for success and ease in these activities, according to your Sun sign.

	JAN	FEB	MAR	APR	MAY	JUN	JUL	AUG	SEPT	OCT	NOV	DEC
Move							14-30					
Start a class						29, 30	1-13					
Join a club			3-21, 28-31	1-21								
Ask for a raise					1, 17-31	1-10						
Look for work		14-28	1-4							7-31	1-12	
Get pro advice	25, 26	21, 22	20, 21	17, 18	14, 15	11, 12	8, 9	4, 5, 31	1, 2, 28-29	25, 26	22, 23	19, 20
Get a loan	1, 27, 28	23, 24	22-24	19, 20	16, 17	13, 14	10, 11	6, 7	3, 4, 30	1, 27-28	24, 25	21, 22
See a doctor			22-31	1-25	20-31	1-12				7-31	1-12	
Start a diet				16	16							
End relationship						31						
Buy clothes						31	1-31	1-30	1-6			
Get a makeover				6-25	1, 20-31	1-12						
New romance								23-31	1-15			
Vacation	1-31	1-28	1, 2, 25, 26	21, 22	19, 20	15, 16	12, 13	9, 10	5, 6	2, 3, 29, 30	26, 27	23, 24

GEMINI
The Twins
May 21 to June 21

Ⅱ

Element:	Air
Quality:	Mutable
Polarity:	Yang/Masculine
Planetary Ruler:	Mercury
Meditation:	I explore my inner worlds.
Gemstone:	Tourmaline
Power Stones:	Ametrine, citrine, emerald, spectrolite, agate
Key Phrase:	I think
Glyph:	Pillars of duality, the Twins
Anatomy:	Hands, arms, shoulders, lungs, nervous system
Color:	Bright colors, orange, yellow, magenta
Animal:	Monkeys, talking birds, flying insects
Myths/Legends:	Peter Pan, Castor and Pollux
House:	Third
Opposite Sign:	Sagittarius
Flower:	Lily of the valley
Key Word:	Versatility

Positive Expression:	**Misuse of Energy:**
Articulate	Talkative
Curious	Distracted
Rational	Fickle
Quick-witted	Mischievous
Resilient	Inconsistent
Thoughtful	Flighty

Gemini

Your Ego's Strengths and Shortcomings

Talk, talk, talk—is that all you do, Gemini? Well, some people might think so, but you know better. There is depth in your nature, and sensitivity too. In fact, you are sensitive to all the twists and nuances of reality, the influences of new information, and the flow of energies from one person to the next.

You are the Great Experimenter. That is, you have to try just about everything at some time in your life. You won't do anything that is truly against your nature, but you will try things that are dangerous, illegal, and inconvenient if you think you'll learn something useful. At times your curiosity will get the best of you, and you may find yourself, like the kitten stuck in the tree, needing the help of others to free you.

Your mind is ticking along all the time, adding in this factor, subtracting that. By trying out new ways of experiencing a situation with others you are constantly re-mythologizing, reinventing your life. The danger is that others could see this process as fickleness or inconsistency in your character. As you flit from one person to another your story may change, and your personality with it. If you add to this your natural desire to avoid conflict you may find, when faced with the prospect of telling your story to the authorities, that it is easier to "embellish the truth" than run the risk of punishment.

Bouncing all these ideas off others is your way of learning to figure out just what the truth is. As you get feedback from your world you learn to evaluate your experiences in ways that are consistent with the society around you; this is your work as a Gemini. But, while you are learning, your bubbly creativity and endless desire to know more is enriching others' lives, awakening their own youthfulness, and rejuvenating their interest in learning what make the world tick.

Shining Your Love Light

Variety is the spice of life, and only you can decide whether you'll express this by enjoying lots of different partners over your life or by exploring the world's endless diversity of experiences with just one person. You thrive so much on human contact and the joy of making connections that you need a partner who is tolerant of your wide range of social activities and tastes—preferably one who shares them. Since your relationship with life is so mental, you especially appreciate a partner who partakes in experiences mentally as well.

Your easiest matches will be with Libra and Aquarius, the other air signs. Their intellectual perceptions match your approach. Aries can keep up with you and lend focus to your scattered ways. Taurus slows and steadies you, but this may make you feel like a fish out of water unless you try to blend these qualities with your own. With another Gemini you'll be like the twins of legend, chattering about your experiences with each other, but you may lack focus together. Cancer's strong emotional nature may be difficult for you to identify with, but it can bring out your ability to nurture if you are so inclined. Leo is more easily your match, igniting to your ideas and carrying them out with you. Virgo is a mental mate with a focus on logic and practicality to complement your capacity for storing and sharing knowledge, but your different styles could grate at times. Libra's desire for companionship matches yours, and your desire to explore new things gives Libra a chance to find harmony. Scorpio's depths may be unfathomable for you, the dabbler, but Sagittarius, your opposite sign, may balance your tendency to scatter experiences far and wide by helping you set goals and fulfill them. Capricorn's dutiful attitude does not make a natural match, but you may find this sign's breadth of vision and political savvy a fascinating view of life. Aquarius is more comfortable, with the ability to stand outside the process and mentally survey ideals and principles. You can understand the flighty nature of Pisces, as it is akin to your own, but it may bring out the giddy frivolousness in both of you, unless you use other parts of your nature to tone it down.

Making Your Place in the World

With your eclectic approach to life, you are always inventing new ways of seeing and doing things that can be invaluable to others. The trouble is, what you are thinking of doing may be so new that it doesn't have a name. You are especially good at making connections for others. This makes you gifted at any job where the arts of communication are involved: public relations, marketing, translation, journalism, technical writing, freelance fiction or nonfiction authorship, editing, and publishing. Your skills with people are eternally in demand; you can use them in any public service or customer relations position. You are also talented at planning—if you can develop a way to stay organized. Wedding planning, personal assistance, secretarial work, and administrative positions will use this strength. You can also work in fields where physical connections are important: computer construction, programming, and repair; electronics; and technical work in sound, to name a few.

The one weakness that could limit your success is a tendency to be scattered and disorganized. This will prevent you from completing work, meeting deadlines, and fulfilling your highest potential. When you've added organization to your natural ability to make the right things connect, you'll be a winner.

Power Plays

With your multifaceted nature, you are constantly encountering new experiences and incorporating the lessons you learn into your psyche. You like to experiment with different ways of doing things, and you may try several approaches to the same activity or experience in order to see all sides of it. If curiosity killed the cat, it gave you life and a reason for living.

Your power lies in your ability to see both sides of an issue. You are so used to trying on different perceptions of reality that it is second nature. This allows you to disengage from the drama of the process, often giving you the ability to arbitrate between factions in a power struggle. You do this by helping each side to understand what they have in common: the motivation that created the conflict to begin with. Then you support them in seeing the other's point of view. The danger for you lies in internal conflict, because you can get caught in the drama of the moment and lose the power of detachment that makes it possible to resolve problems quickly.

Famous Geminis

Ice Cube, Paul Gauguin, Steffi Graff, Neil Patrick Harris, Greg Kinnear, Tara Lipinski, Julianna Margulies, Malcolm McDowell, Ian McKellen, Natalie Portman, Ally Sheedy, Brooke Shields, Elisabeth Shue, Wallis Simpson, Dr. Ruth Westheimer

The Year Ahead for Gemini

This is a year of transition for you, Gemini. Jupiter and Uranus will bring changes to your career and home environments as you strive to break free from the confines of old structures.

With Jupiter in Leo and your solar Third House since mid-2002, you have undoubtedly been busier than ants at a picnic. It may seem as if every opportunity of your life has come all at once, and now you're trying to cover all the bases. Although you thrive on activity, there is a limit; over the next few months you'll gain greater benefit if you can be more selective in which enterprises you support. When Jupiter enters Virgo in August the emphasis will shift. You'll be able to spend more than fifteen minutes in your home at one time, and you might even consider entertaining once in a while again. It can also be a time for home improvement or expansion. There could even be a reunion or a substantial growth in the family over the coming year.

Saturn in Gemini has required you to work double-duty—unless you've figured out how to delegate or use the word "no." It has been unrelenting in its demands, but if you've played your cards right you've gained a substantial reward (possible promotion, etc.) during this time. It may also have been a time of endings and beginnings in your relationships. You know now that it's really about setting boundaries, both professionally and personally. Saturn enters Cancer in June, putting the emphasis on managing your resources. This suggests more discipline in your financial affairs and possibly a re-evaluation of what you value and what you're willing to spend time and money on. Whether it's paying off consumer credit debt or saving for your future, you are likely to benefit greatly from looking ahead and matching your financial goals with your inner ideals. Chiron in Capricorn and your solar Eighth House reiterates the focus on finances. You may find that your income is not what you would like it to be, and you want to change that somehow. You may also have discovered occult or metaphysical studies, especially those relating to inner dimensions of reality.

Uranus's move into Pisces in March ends seven years of relatively graceful change. Now get ready for the big stuff. Uranus is about to revolutionize your whole outlook on life: your career, social standing, view of God(dess) and the cosmos, and way of life. This will take place over the next seven years, and it is meant to be a "cosmic direction finder," ensuring that we fulfill the purpose we are meant to fulfill. Over the coming years you will give a great deal of thought to your purpose and the meaning life has for you. You will want to deepen your experience and do what feels right—not just what pays the bills. Neptune continues to give you visions of what the future can be. However, it's not going to do this forever—so it's important to put some of those dreams into action if you haven't already begun. You may think that they're foolish and unattainable, but how do you know until you try? Pluto has presented the greatest challenges you've faced in the past ten years. It has dug up every possible power issue in every relationship you have (or have had). It has brought some tragic endings and some promising new beginnings. You will continue to notice that others see themselves in you more than they see you for who you really are. This is possibly because you are more inclined to own your power than you were before this transit began in 1995. In looking back, the lessons have been tough but indispensable to the happiness you now enjoy. If you can see these experiences as triumphs of the human spirit and defeats of the ego rather than wounds of the personality, you will have gained the highest reward of your journey through Hades. Keep your head up; just because you can see your flaws doesn't mean you have more of them than others. In fact, you probably have fewer because you've been able to work on them.

The eclipses of late 2002 signaled a decreased intensity after a year of heightened emotion and activity that brought many of the inner changes of the last eight years into manifestation in your external affairs. 2003's eclipses will be a time to stabilize, to find the inner value of the external experiences. It can also be a time to attend to health matters.

If you were born from May 21 to 25, once Uranus enters Pisces on March 11 it will square your Sun from your solar Tenth House. This signals a time when you may find it difficult to stay in one place, especially where your career is concerned. For someone who finds it easy to adapt to new circumstances, the issue is not about how to change, but what. It may seem easy to just change everything and be done with it, but this can destabilize your life in unnecessary and undermining ways. It may be more helpful to discern just what needs changing and approach it one step at a time. This way, you won't be overwhelmed by circumstances during the transition. The transition process is likely to last a year, but if part of it is spent in planning well then it can proceed in an orderly fashion. Inspiration is likely to come easily to you as well during this time. Don't be surprised if some of your thinking defies convention, and, as action follows thought, ruffles a few feathers. People are often threatened by change because it represents an uncontrolled element in their lives. Once they see the good in what you are creating (providing you have planned well), they will get on board.

If you were born from May 21 to June 4, Saturn will semisextile your Sun once it enters Cancer on June 4. This aspect brings on a helpful adjustment period, when the plans you began to hatch in 2000 and 2001 need some refinement. Although still in the formative stage, your ideas hold great potential, but making alterations to the original impulse may be part of what ultimately makes them work. This is part of a thirty-year cycle related to the fulfillment of your personal potential, so don't be afraid to proceed with your most ambitious plans. Often, the first challenge we face is self-doubt: Did I dream the right thing? Do I deserve this? Do I have the courage and power to create it? This is part of the refinement process, for our doubts are useful in exploring the obstacles that lie in our path. As long as you don't allow them to dissuade you from following through on a really good idea, sorting through all your concerns will be worthwhile. With your wide-ranging interests you may also be trying to decide between various ideas. While this is important at this stage of the cycle, don't be in a rush to limit your options. It may be possible to develop more than one thing at a time.

If you were born from May 30 to June 4, Neptune will be trining your Sun this year. This is good news, since it clears the way for you to fulfill your dreams. This transit is not enough to make your life perfect, but at least you know that Neptune won't be in your way, and it will be providing strong background support by lending its insight and flexibility to the ways you fulfill your goals this year. Sometimes the important thing is the way we feel about what happens to us, not what actually happens. Success and happiness are in the eye of the beholder. With Neptune in this position, you can expect to feel more at peace about what happens in your life, even if things don't change that much.

If you were born from June 8 to 11, you will face the tests of Pluto as it opposes your Sun this year. You've watched as it has hit others you know, and perhaps you have an inkling of what it may change in your life. Get ready for some big changes, because Pluto can change everything, especially when your Sun is involved. Because it is in your solar Seventh House, you can expect that your relationships with others will be especially affected. This may include those in the workplace, business partnerships, and anyone who serves in a counseling or advisory capacity. You may feel that the people around you are changing or that their needs are placing more demands on you. This may bring you to adjust your relationships with others, possibly by setting firmer boundaries or even eliminating some unhealthy relationships. Existing relationships may be tested by profound changes that either you or the other person is going through. These changes may include therapy—an excellent way to channel Pluto's drive to plunge into the depths. This is also a good time to be cautious about forming new relationships, especially those with an obvious obsessive quality about them. Actually, Pluto will just bring to the surface the ways in which we have not been keeping ourselves safe in relationships. If we get burned it is probably because we proceed too quickly to truly learn about the other person before we get involved. Not all relationships formed under a Pluto contact will turn out poorly, but you may not be sure about them until after the transit has passed. By then you'll have a good foundation that has been tested by the fires of transformation.

If you were born from June 13 to 21, Saturn will be conjoining your Sun for the first half of the year. Until Saturn enters Cancer on June 4 you'll be engaged in creating the structure for a new thirty-year cycle, deciding where you want to go and what you want to accomplish. You may feel the burden of overlapping responsibilities as you phase out one part of your life and bring in a new one. You may be working extra hard as new doorways open and new potentials develop. Or you could be using Saturn's energy to develop greater efficiency or to limit your responsibilities by delegating tasks so that you can make room in your life for other interests. No matter what adjustments you feel drawn to make your restructuring will be the foundation for the next thirty years. Accordingly, the new initiatives that are spawned now can be substantial. They should also be geared to meet needs and correct weaknesses in your current life as much as to fulfill your inner desires. Saturn conjoining the Sun often leads us to firmer resolve and greater self-discipline, so this is a good time to attempt changing old habits or giving up addictive behaviors. In the end you may look, act, and think differently than you did before this year, and reap the benefits of the greater wisdom that results when we work with Saturn instead of against it.

If you were born from June 17 to 21, Uranus will be lending strength to your Sun by trine in 2003. This is generally an exciting and pleasant aspect which will liven up your life and bring about some desired changes in a harmonious way. We all have goals that we hope to achieve, but we usually don't have a downhill slide on the path to realizing them. This year, you may encounter this easy ride to the finish line. You may also find yourself drawn into intriguing and surprising journeys or quests, whether physical, mental, or spiritual. These experiences could provide the input that will launch your next crop of creative efforts, perhaps germinating into the seedlings of a new career in a few years' time. The only pitfall of this transit is that you may find yourself feeling cavalier about all these opportunities or undervaluing them because they came so easily. Don't forget that a lot of background work went into getting yourself to the place where it looks so effortless.

Tools for Change

As a mutable sign, you've been revitalizing yourself under the imperious eye of Pluto since 1995, and Saturn since 2001. This year Uranus and Mars in Pisces also participate in your makeover—the kick-off of a seven-year refresher course in being you. This can leave you one very confused Gemini. Out of the multiplicity of who you are, you will be challenged to find what's more important and burn away the rest.

To make the best of this process your top priority should be to stay as centered as you can. This means taking on the task of reconciling the opposite energies within you—the prime directive of Gemini. Out of the two (or more) parts of yourself you are meant to find the unifying core of your being. If you are experiencing inner conflict and turmoil between the various parts of your personality, it will be much more difficult to take on the challenges that lie ahead. While you are thus agitated your nervous system takes a beating, and you may become anxious, distracted, and on edge. When you are centered serenity radiates from you, and it's easier to see your way through the obstacle course of events.

Key to reconciling opposites is finding the place of peace and clarity within. The easiest way is to find a physical or mental place where the amount of stimulation you receive from your environment is reduced. This can be a garden, park, meditation group, a quiet corner of your home, or a place you visualize in your mind to instantly relax you. When you go there, set boundaries on your experience. Turn off the phone, close the door, and remove your mind from the cares of your day, even if this takes persistent effort. Even if it is difficult at first, it will get easier with practice. Activities can also induce this type of inner harmony, such as yoga, tai chi, walking, hiking, or exploring the local museum or park. Given your natural penchant for mental activity, you may find writing to be of value to you. Embark on the journey of writing your great novel, or turn your own career experience into a self-help or career guidance book. Keeping a journal can be a profoundly satisfying experiences of personal growth, as it provides you with a chronicle of your progress and helps you develop an awareness of your core. Of course, there is eternally the value of education to be considered—one of your favorite pastimes, since it quenches your curiosity. Learning about subjects you've always wanted to explore is an excellent way to develop self-knowledge. Lastly, to get closer to your core self, commit yourself to a series of energetic healing sessions where you focus on core energies. With so many options available you'll be prepared for the demands of this year's planetary events in no time and make the most of them.

Ⅱ

Affirmation for the Year

Everything I touch helps me to know my true self.

Gemini/January

In the Spotlight

Your attention is drawn to finances this month as the Mercury retrograde highlights this area of your solar chart. Your relationships with others are also a source of activity, which is likely to be more pleasant and rewarding.

Wellness and Keeping Fit

You may be prone to infections, inflammations, and injuries until January 17, when Mars leaves Scorpio. This is a good time to be careful, pay attention to your energy levels, and seek health treatments to shore up your fluctuating immune system. Activities that calm the nerves will also help, such as meditation and yoga.

Love and Life Connections

You may experience strong responses, even angry outbursts, from those around you after January 16. You may just be in the wrong place at the wrong time, but if these responses are coming from those who know you well, look for an element of truth in what they say.

Finance and Success

If you've been mismanaging your finances, it will come back to bite you this month. The bill collectors will catch up with you and all of them will want appeasing at once. If you've been doing well, you may find that the bottom line takes a dip as some sources of income shift or even dry up. Enterprise on your part may be necessary to create new sources.

Cosmic Insider Tip

The challenges of this month are signs of deeper problems if they are very big or long term. You can expect them to catch up with you in June and nearly force you to deal with them once Saturn enters Cancer then.

Rewarding Days 4, 5, 9, 10, 14, 15, 18, 19, 20, 23, 24, 31

Challenging Days 1, 6, 7, 8, 21, 22, 27, 28

Affirmation of the Month I can use my experiences this month to prevent future problems.

Gemini/February

In the Spotlight
Travel, higher education, teaching, and foreign cultures are emphasized now. If you have been engaged in commerce, trade, or educational endeavors, your involvement in them will reach a peak this month. Because Jupiter and Neptune are in the houses ruling these areas, you could be on the way to fulfilling some cherished ideals.

Wellness and Keeping Fit
With Mars in your solar Seventh House, you will enjoy taking exercise with a partner or friend. You find that you don't even notice the challenge of exertion when you are conversing. You are likely to be more interested in being outdoors after February 12.

Love and Life Connections
Although you make it a point to be sociable with everyone, your energies are being directed more toward personal relationships right now than toward impersonal ones. Others' interest in you may also be higher than usual, but at times this could be negative, as aggression could also come your way. Skirting such situations will go far toward resolving them.

Finance and Success
Your best bet this month is to keep your commitments. This will free you to pursue new opportunities over the coming year. After February 22 an obligation is fulfilled after years of hard work. You'll find your step springier as the associated responsibilities shift away from your shoulders.

Cosmic Insider Tip
You've been reaching for your current goals for about seven years, and hopefully they are nearly fulfilled. As Uranus leaves Aquarius you'll find that the preparation is over; it's time now for some high-profile action.

Rewarding Days 1, 2, 5, 6, 7, 10, 11, 12, 14, 15, 19, 20, 28

Challenging Days 3, 4, 17, 18, 23, 24

Affirmation of the Month I am alert to new opportunities.

Gemini/March

In the Spotlight

Both newness and intensity are in the air as Uranus enters Pisces on March 11 and Pluto turns retrograde. Your activity level will intensify accordingly over the coming months. Right now, go with the flow. Finances could be difficult again after March 4.

Wellness and Keeping Fit

You may choose to work out at the company gym after March 4 as your workload increases. You could also suffer from nervous tension as your stress levels rise, so preventive measures are in order. Do your breathing practices, take periodic breaks from your focused activities, eat well, and get enough sleep.

Love and Life Connections

Between March 2 and 27, your personal partnership could benefit greatly if you get away from it all. Go someplace that you both enjoy, so the pleasure is not one-sided. The time away promises to be especially harmonious, and it will benefit you both in other ways as well.

Finance and Success

Your best bet this month is consistency. If you've had difficulties, they may reappear after March 4. Keep making your payments; you'll recover, even though the end is not yet in sight. If you're in fine financial fettle, be careful about how you obligate yourself this month. No matter what, be cautious about accepting the advice, especially the sales pitch, of others this month.

Cosmic Insider Tip

If you broaden your perspective of time to look at the past few years, you can see the benefits that have come from your consistent efforts. This is what will be required of you in a new way in a few months' time.

Rewarding Days 1, 4, 5, 6, 9, 10, 11, 14, 15, 18, 19, 27, 28

Challenging Days 2, 3, 16, 17, 23, 24, 29, 30, 31

Affirmation of the Month I appreciate the fruits of my efforts.

Gemini/April

In the Spotlight

You're in your element this month as the planets emphasize social activities and events. Your circumstances and contacts are generally supportive of your career and overall goals in life until April 26. An enterprise which focuses on communication or education takes a turn for the better around April 4.

Wellness and Keeping Fit

The fever pitch of activities may have you at your wits' end. If you combat this by engaging in physical exercise, sleeping well, and staying away from junk foods, you'll fare much better.

Love and Life Connections

You'll be looking mostly to make contact with people outside the home this month as career pursuits and contacts fill your time. This is a good time to build business associations for future success, since your star is rising. After April 12 your typical tact may occasionally desert you. Relationships may suffer as a result. You'll have a chance to correct them after April 26.

Finance and Success

Your financial prospects improve this month with the opportunities that emerge. Work is mostly focused on teamwork and administrative tasks. Difficulties could seemingly come out of nowhere after April 25, as the Mercury retrograde brings out the weaknesses in your communicative and organizational skills, but the things you manage will be on firmer footing as a result.

Cosmic Insider Tip

Using your considerable people skills this month will bring out the best in others and help in the development of future opportunities. These prospects may not appear right away, but they will come back to you in their own time.

Rewarding Days 1, 2, 6, 7, 11, 12, 15, 16, 23, 24, 28, 29

Challenging Days 13, 14, 19, 20, 25, 26, 27

Affirmation of the Month I open myself to new opportunities.

Gemini/May

In the Spotlight

You're overstimulated and need a break—a time of silence. Without interruptions, you can get your work done and feel better doing it. This feeling dissipates after May 20. Once the eclipse on May 30 occurs events will take you in a new direction, out of your reverie.

Wellness and Keeping Fit

You need silence, stillness, and peace in order to recharge your batteries. This is the one month each year when the planets conspire to give you a break. Taking advantage of it will enable you to greet the challenges that arise after May 20.

Love and Life Connections

If you have the chance to be alone, take it. You might even want to get away by yourself for a few days. We all need a break from each other and time to get re-acquainted with ourselves. Take some time to write, read, and contemplate now, because when your new birth cycle begins you'll want to return to normal levels of externalized activity, clear about your direction. Communicating clearly about your intentions to your loved ones will avert difficulties.

Finance and Success

It's okay to put this part of your life on hold for a while, outside of handling your bare minimum obligations. A time of rest will refuel you for future successes and higher levels of productivity with less downtime for illness, lack of focus, and low energy levels. Delegate what you can while you're "on leave," and then let go of it mentally. You won't miss anything.

Cosmic Insider Tip

The eclipse on May 30 will energize you and spark your interest in new ventures. Choose carefully what needs to be changed: Some things are good enough to hang on to.

Rewarding Days 3, 4, 8, 9, 12, 13, 20, 21, 22, 25, 26, 27, 30, 31

Challenging Days 10, 11, 16, 17, 23, 24

Affirmation of the Month I can take time off without penalty.

Gemini/June

In the Spotlight
This is your month, Gemini—the time when you begin your new yearly cycle. As Saturn enters Cancer on June 4 new challenges await you in handling finances and other resources, including time.

Wellness and Keeping Fit
After June 13 your energy levels are better. Focus on the inner you and make a plan for maintaining your calm stability and high level of vitality. This will need to include activities that induce peace, such as meditation or a walk in the woods, as well as nutritious food.

Love and Life Connections
You'll be especially attractive to others this month, especially after June 10, as Venus transits your solar First House. Relationships will intensify around June 9. It may seem as though those around you are testing your strength and resolve regarding changes you've recently made. When we change, it makes others insecure about their roles in our lives, so it is helpful to be firm in our purpose and reassuring in our response.

Finance and Success
Saturn has entered your money zone, and that means that in all likelihood a new level of discipline is in order. Perhaps your portfolio needs reorganizing, or you want to change some of your investments to match your social and political conscience. Or perhaps you need to try to get out of debt, develop a budget, and establish a 401(k) plan.

Cosmic Insider Tip
Your career and business activities assume greater importance after June 17, when Mars enters Pisces. Observing what happens now will assist you in August and September, especially if you can anticipate potential problems and deflect them.

Rewarding Days 1, 4, 5, 9, 10, 17, 18, 21, 22, 23, 26, 27, 28

Challenging Days 6, 7, 8, 13, 14, 19, 20

Affirmation of the Month I can improve my material conditions.

Gemini/July

In the Spotlight

Career and business events and experiences fill your mind in July as Mars slows down to retrograde on July 29. You have several financial dilemmas for which you have not yet worked out a plan. This month the planets will help you develop a strategy.

Wellness and Keeping Fit

Make sure you are focused on one thing at a time as much as possible: Remove distractions like background noise or talking (radio, TV, etc.) when you are trying to think. Give yourself time to relax, even if you can think of a million things to do.

Love and Life Connections

The pressures that plague you are not in the home or family, but they could spread there if you don't "tend the garden." This could even mean that, by bringing a virus home from work, you create more stress at home. Clearly, a strong immune system and open communications are your best defenses.

Finance and Success

You're on the road to success, but you may not be able to see it right now. Not only do you have lots of new things on your plate but it's too early to see results. In six months you'll be for the most part over a big obstacle; in a year it will be a distant memory. Let go of a need for instant or constant reassurance. Perhaps you've never experienced this before, but you'll have to give it more time to germinate before the sprout will show visible growth.

Cosmic Insider Tip

This may seem like a dark and confusing time if you are confronting deep and frightening issues. However, the best way to dispel fear is to face it. You have to be bigger and more stubborn about getting what you want than the conditions you face.

Rewarding Days 1, 2, 3, 6, 7, 14, 15, 19, 20, 24, 25, 29, 30

Challenging Days 4, 5, 10, 11, 16, 17, 18, 31

Affirmation of the Month I face my fears with strength.

Gemini/August

In the Spotlight

More than the weather is hot this month as six planets pile up in Virgo and Pisces. With Pluto and sometimes the Moon involved, you face the greatest challenges. Although you will receive signals from this all month (as you have in July), the planetary alignment is strongest from August 22 through September 3.

Wellness and Keeping Fit

Concentrate on keeping your stress level down. Do what you can to support your health by eating and sleeping well, exercising (mildly when you feel tired), and meditating. One of the greatest healing salves for you right now is conversation. Talk to those who care about you, or, if you can't talk about it, write it out.

Love and Life Connections

Your loved ones can be a great help right now, and you need them. Use your greatest gift—communication. Let them know what's wrong, what's worrying you. Choose the friends who listen sympathetically but do not get caught up in drama. There may be someone on whom you can't rely, but you have plenty of other support.

Finance and Success

Finances may be threatened, but they are not a direct problem right now, so don't worry about them. The business or career that you engage in is having to shift to handle larger economic or political factors, and this is trickling down to you. Even though the forms in your world are changing, you will find new structures to support you.

Cosmic Insider Tip

A calm demeanor, flexibility, and robust optimism are the best tools you can bring to the situation that arises this month. Look at your situation from a broad perspective. Seek assistance if necessary. You are meant to have it if you need it.

Rewarding Days 2, 3, 11, 12, 15, 16, 21, 21, 26, 27, 30, 31

Challenging Days 1, 6, 7, 8, 13, 14, 28, 29

Affirmation of the Month I can face challenges that come my way.

Gemini/September

In the Spotlight
The planets continue to focus their energies on your home and career, but their grip will loosen as the month wears on. Substantial improvement will occur on September 15, 20, and 27. Your attentions are focused mostly in the home until September 24.

Wellness and Keeping Fit
Managing your stress and anxiety level is the most important factor in your well-being now. It may help to realize that, if you can clear your mind of fear, this time has great potential for positive change.

Love and Life Connections
It may seem as though, when you and your loved ones should be hanging together, you feel a separation. Words spoken in haste can be taken the wrong way when we feel fragile. If you are the one feeling hurt, try to see what has happened in a more forgiving light. If someone else is feeling hurt, try to overlook their pained reaction and find something to apologize for.

Finance and Success
Your cash flow may be affected by all the events that have occurred, but direct problems may not yet exist. If this is the case, let go of your fears for the future. They will impede your ability to get back on the income-producing track. If you need to liquidate some assets in order to make the right change there's never been a better investment than your future happiness and well-being.

Cosmic Insider Tip
Letting go of old expectations, timelines, and mindsets is essential to solving the problems that arise when life takes an unexpected turn. It will take a few weeks, even months, to recover from the events of the past two months, so give yourself the time and space to do it. You don't have to be perfect.

Rewarding Days 7, 8, 11, 12, 13, 17, 18, 21, 22, 23, 26, 27

Challenging Days 3, 4, 9, 10, 24, 25, 30

Affirmation of the Month I take time to make the right changes.

Gemini/October

In the Spotlight

It's as if the clouds have lifted and dissipated, and now blue sky appears. You've taken steps inspired by your new reality and the world is starting to respond positively. In fact, matters could move along at a relatively fast pace. Improvements are in the works!

Wellness and Keeping Fit

Stresses are reduced and your health and vitality are on the upswing. This is an excellent time to get back on your regimen. Eat plenty of proteins and greens and do a variety of workouts: some gentle to reduce stress, and some vigorous to develop stamina.

Love and Life Connections

After last month, you're especially appreciating good relationships and the support they provide. If there is still difficulty in an important one, give it longer to heal. It may take time to rebuild trust. Support through counseling services may be desirable if the person is someone important to you.

Finance and Success

It looks like you'll be getting back to your usual work routine in some way after October 9. The normal, comforting rhythms of life are thoroughly re-established after October 24, when you will be able to focus more single-mindedly on the tasks before you. The security of habit is soothing for the nerves. Financial planning may be highlighted toward the end of the month.

Cosmic Insider Tip

The physical realities that we face are based on the metaphysical realities that we create. This is the interaction of Saturn and Uranus. As they harmonize with each other over the coming months you will be able to tap their flow to create a life that is in better alignment with who you really are.

Rewarding Days 4, 5, 9, 10, 14, 15, 19, 20, 23, 24, 31

Challenging Days 1, 6, 7, 8, 21, 22, 27, 28

Affirmation of the Month I accept the good that comes my way.

Gemini/November

In the Spotlight
Work is the key word for this month. You will find plenty to keep you occupied. After November 12 the tasks are reduced, and relationship contacts are emphasized. November 8 is a turning point, as an eclipse and Uranus station bring an unexpected release. Just as significant is the eclipse on November 23, which will affect your sense of self and direction one last time.

Wellness and Keeping Fit
Your health may be under assault as you strive to keep up with all the demands on your time. Mild exercise, at the very least, will maintain your balance and relax your mind and musculature.

Love and Life Connections
There is a special bond developing between yourself and those from whom you may have been estranged—or there is an opportunity to foster one. This is an excellent time to make amends by being consistent. You don't have to make a big splash of the truth, nor do you have to succumb to steely resistance if someone drops an emotional bomb in your lap.

Finance and Success
You're able to build goodwill by putting in extra time and effort this month. After November 12 you'll get some feedback which may not be positive. Don't give up; eventually you'll get the answer you want, especially if you can adjust to what you learn. Somehow, through your work, you're able to keep your nose above water.

Cosmic Insider Tip
"Don't give up" is good advice this month, as events unfold in ways you may not want them to. If each obstacle you encounter spurs you on with greater determination, it's not an impediment. Systematic effort will bring the results you want in every area of life.

Rewarding Days 1, 2, 5, 6, 10, 11, 12, 15, 16, 19, 20, 28, 29

Challenging Days 3, 4, 17, 18, 24, 25, 30

Affirmation of the Month My determination will see me through.

Gemini/December

In the Spotlight

Doorways begin to open for you starting December 16, and even more after December 21. The Mercury retrograde on December 17 slows down the cash flow from external sources, but this will improve after January 6.

Wellness and Keeping Fit

Your physical energy will continue to rise as the fast-moving planets transit to friendlier positions. Don't relax your regimen once you feel better or you will make yourself unnecessarily vulnerable to the virus of the moment after December 16.

Love and Life Connections

Finances can drive a wedge in the best relationships, and yours may be no exception. However, your interactions improve after December 21, even though nothing on the outside has changed. It could be that your beloved has realized you're doing the best you can, or perhaps she or he is just getting used to conditions.

Finance and Success

There's no doubt about it, your finances are not as strong as they could be. It could be poor spending patterns, running up debt, a string of bad luck with the extra expenditures to match, or loss of a needed source of income. A shot in the arm may be in order: a loan, cashing in some stock, or digging into savings.

Cosmic Insider Tip

Your secret ally this month is your relationship with those in the world at large. Reconnect with those in your broader network of associates. Go to meetings and social events; let people know what you need, what your plans and capabilities are. This will be especially helpful and effective after December 16. Results will come after the holidays are over.

Rewarding Days 2, 3, 4, 7, 8, 9, 12, 13, 14, 17, 18, 25, 26, 30, 31

Challenging Days 1, 15, 16, 21, 22, 27, 28, 29

Affirmation of the Month I can reach out to others.

GEMINI ACTION TABLE

These dates reflect the best—but not the only—times for success and ease in these activities, according to your Sun sign.

	JAN	FEB	MAR	APR	MAY	JUN	JUL	AUG	SEPT	OCT	NOV	DEC
Move							31	1-27	20-30	1-6		
Start a class							14-30					
Join a club			22-31	1-5								
Ask for a raise					31	11-30	1-4					
Look for work										25-31	1-30	1, 2
Get pro advice	1, 27, 28	23, 24	22-24	19, 20		13, 14	10, 11	6, 7	3, 4, 30	1, 27-28	24, 25	21, 22
Get a loan	29, 30	26, 27	1, 2, 25, 26	21, 22	19, 20	15, 16	12, 13	9, 10	5, 6	2, 3, 29, 30	26, 27	
See a doctor				6-25	20-31	1-29				25-31	1-12	
Start a diet					16					25-31	1-12	
End relationship						14						
Buy clothes									20-30	1-24		
Get a makeover					31	14-29						
New romance									16-30	19		
Vacation	4, 5, 31	1, 2, 14-28	1-28	23, 24	21, 22	17, 18	14, 15	11, 12	7, 8	4, 5, 31	1, 2, 28, 29	22-31

CANCER

The Crab
June 21 to July 23

Element:	Water
Quality:	Cardinal
Polarity:	Yin/Feminine
Planetary Ruler:	The Moon
Meditation:	I have faith in the promptings of my heart.
Gemstone:	Pearl
Power Stones:	Moonstone, chrysocolla
Key Phrase:	I feel
Glyph:	Crab's claws
Anatomy:	Stomach, breasts
Color:	Silver, pearl white
Animal:	Crustaceans, cows, chickens
Myths/Legends:	Hercules and the Crab, Asherah, Hecate
House:	Fourth
Opposite Sign:	Capricorn
Flower:	Larkspur
Key Word:	Receptivity

Positive Expression:	Misuse of Energy:
Nurturing	Possessive
Resourceful	Controlling
Empathetic	Insular
Sensitive	Evasive
Sympathetic	Distrustful
Compassionate	Manipulative

Cancer

Your Ego's Strengths and Shortcomings

Although you would prefer that most people don't know it, you're a soft touch, Cancer. Like your symbol, the crab, you arm yourself with a thick shell to protect that soft interior. The people around you are either "inside" or "outside." The outsiders are acquaintances, colleagues—sometimes even friends. The insiders are family—or you consider them to be family, and you share your deepest secrets with them.

For this reason, not many people get to know you as you know yourself. Often, others don't realize how sensitive you are until your emotions overflow in tears or joy. Once someone has earned your trust they experience you as warm, sometimes moody, and protective of yourself and those you love.

In fact, that is your prime directive: to protect the group with which you identify, and to create your identity in terms of that group. Whatever group that is, you probably think of and act as if that group is your family. This is the attraction that many Cancer signs have for the military: It is both a family that creates a sense of belonging and a group whose purpose is to protect.

Underneath it all, a sense of belonging is what makes you tick. When you have that, you can step out of your shell and be who you are. Otherwise you are on guard, and not quite yourself. When you feel like you belong you are emotionally secure, and this unleashes all the powers of your intuitive nature. You have incredibly strong instincts, which can lead you to act in just the right way even before you've had a chance to think about it. These instincts are a combination of survival urges and psychic ability, and they lend a magic to your nature that leaves other people in awe of this talent.

On the other side of the coin, your attunement to feelings can make you moody. This is a sign that you are not paying enough attention to what your feelings are telling you. In a culture that values the mind over the heart it can be difficult to be aware of and responsible to the parts of yourself that others seem quite capable of suppressing forever. However, it is a gift, and it is best to see it that way, because it is an intrinsic part of who you are.

Shining Your Love Light

For you, loving is as much about caring for and protecting each other as it is about sex or shared experiences. You feel loved when your partner fixes you a gourmet meal or cleans the house. Part of your idea of relationship also revolves around family, both sharing your families of origin and having one of your own. Creating a sense of unity is easier when it is based on blood ties, because there's something inside that binds you no matter where you go or what you do. It gives you a sense of fulfillment and deep inner security to know you'll be loved and have a place to belong, no matter what.

It is easiest to develop bonds with those of the same watery approach to life: Scorpio, Pisces, or another Cancer. They navigate the same emotional seas as you do and innately feel the same types of communication that words cannot express. Aries is as passionate as you are, but your interests may differ widely and be hard to reconcile. This could become a tug of war unless you agree to cooperate on a single project or take turns on different ones. Taurus has a stabilizing effect and places a high value on physical security, and your emotional interests are compatible. Gemini's flood of information may wear you out, but the objectivity can lift you out of a funk. Life with another Cancer can be your best bet, as another Cancer is likely to be as loyal and nurturing as you, with a deeply shared set of values. Leo, too, is loyal, but also needs more interaction with those beyond the home. This can work if you can let go, and just join in with the audience.

Virgo is a natural for you, and this sign's groundedness, efficiency, and devotion provide you with just the supports you need to create your family nest. Libra's cooperative spirit dovetails with your urge to nurture and create a loving home, but Libra may want more exclusivity than you do. Scorpio understands the world of emotion you live in and can help you explore it, but too much drama could result. Sagittarius's need for independence may be hard to reconcile with your clannishness, but this sign can help you learn to lighten up and let go when the time is right. Capricorn, your opposite sign, provides a structure to support the needs of the family or tribe, but you have to learn that occasional remoteness allows this sign to function in the outer world with fewer bruises. Aquarius signs are sheer novelty to you because of their urge to be different, but they are as interested in group membership as you are. You share a sympathy with Pisces that is hard to match, as your instinctual side and this sign's visionary side need no explanation but exist in simple harmony and understanding.

Making Your Place in the World

Your drive to nurture and protect draws you toward a broad range of much-needed roles in society today. As a nurturer you may find rewarding work in the healing and helping professions, such as social worker, psychologist, nurse, cook/chef, restaurateur, nutritionist, physical therapist, healer, physician, acupuncturist, and the all-important role of parent. In a protector role you may find yourself fulfilled in the military (particularly the Navy or Marine Corps), law enforcement, the Coast Guard, or as a lifeguard, nanny/au-pair, teacher, guardian, trust executor, or guidance counselor, and again as a parent.

Your interest in caring for others can endanger you if you forget to care for yourself. It is the wise nurturer who remembers to first nurture him- or herself. You can't give to others from emptiness or you will be exhausted and unable to carry on. With practice and careful vigilance you will be able to balance your needs with those of others and lead a highly rewarding life.

Power Plays

You are aware of all the energies that flow around you, especially that of emotion. Since most human power has emotion driving it, you are acutely aware when the forces of flow and dominance are in play. In your special role of fostering the growth and health of those you love you have felt the power of protectiveness surge through your veins.

Your strength is the power of family and the force of identity that you draw from it. You know that when you have a feeling of belonging, a sense of membership in an intimate group, that you are stronger. You feel more self-assured, confident, and powerful. So the way to strengthen yourself, so long as you do not give beyond your means, is to strengthen your "tribe."

Where this can go wrong is when you give to the point of exhaustion, or you don't nurture the exchange of power so that it flows equally to all members of the family. By nurturing them wisely you contribute to a healthy group whose members support each other. There is no greater strength than that which derives from a firm group identity.

Famous Cancers

Giorgio Armani, Kathy Bates, Lisa Nicole Carson, Shelley Duvall, Mary Baker Eddy, Bob Fosse, Robert Heinlein, Henry VIII, Anjelica Huston, Helen Keller, Camilla Parker-Bowles, Ralph Reed, Geoffrey Rush, J. Michael Straczynski, Nikola Tesla

The Year Ahead for Cancer

With several planets entering new signs this year you'll have the opportunity to make some changes. They will certainly involve hard work, facing up to reality, and making difficult choices. However, the need is there, and it's far better to know and understand what's going on than to be oblivious. What's more, the universe is helping you out by putting a couple of pivotal planets in just the right places to support your efforts. A willingness to grow will make the world your oyster!

At the end of August, Jupiter moves into Virgo and your solar Third House. Until then you'll be putting your purchasing power into practice, maybe tweaking your portfolio just a little bit more after the overhaul you gave it during the last half of 2002. Watch your spending. Large purchases may be required now as a part of the natural cycle and that's okay, but beware of thinking that you can pay back any amount no matter what. High risk is not your strong suit, and once Jupiter changes sign you may feel dismayed at your material gluttony. Once the change is made you'll shift to adventures in commerce and communication. You may open your vistas by studying something new, or you may find that life by itself brings you a fresh outlook.

You've been dealing with secret worries and hidden issues over the past two years, perhaps feeling trapped. However, once Saturn enters Cancer in June you'll begin to make progress again toward the things you want the most. It's time to cut the meat from the bone and keep just what's valuable. The next three years can be incredibly empowering and rewarding because you are willing to go it alone if necessary, and you have the self-discipline to take on tasks you might otherwise shun. Saturn battles are won by small, consistent efforts, even in the face of no apparent progress. If you are willing to work hard and think long-term, this can be a decisive time for you, and you can make changes that you felt helpless to effect for several years. Chiron in your solar Seventh House has been bringing out every relationship issue in the book since late 2001. You may realize that your partner is wounded in some critical way, psychologically or spiritually, or she or he may actually be ill.

This is the time to bring healing into your life, and the first step may be finding the answer to the question: What wound am I hiding from myself?

Uranus's move into Pisces in March may introduce an unfamiliar sense of abandon to your nature. You may want to jump ship, travel the world, and forget about your obligations. You may yearn to broaden your mind, read Aristotle, or just head for the wilderness. Whatever path you choose for your quest, to do so is to keep yourself young. Eventually you'll be able to sort out what's worth pursuing. The fact is, you do need to make some changes in your direction—maybe big changes. Feel them through now, listen to your instincts, and make some course adjustments in the next few years. You'll be much better off when the heavens light up and require you to change in that direction anyway seven years from now. Neptune is still creating uncertainty in your finances; if you can surrender your fears over what you can't control anyway, you'll gain profound treasures (which may or may not be financial). Pluto has made you really conscious of how important health is to happiness and a sense of security, and you've probably revolutionized your lifestyle as a result. Continue your efforts (including making more changes), even if you're not getting all the results you want. You know you have to do it, even if sometimes it's hard to break those old, self-destructive habits.

The eclipses of mid-2002 brought issues out of the woodwork that you knew were important–you just didn't know they were *that* important. This year will bring you an awareness of what the deeper spiritual lessons are and give you time to change, with more stabilizing influences to support your efforts in the form of groups, friendships, and your own creativity.

If you were born from June 21 to 24, Uranus will trine your Sun once it enters Pisces on March 11. This is usually a helpful aspect, because it will ease your way in making changes in your life. Although you often find it difficult to let go of the familiar even if it's time to change, this aspect will make change pleasant, even exhilarating. The changes you will welcome at this time are probably related to goals you've long sought. They may be more inwardly satisfying than outwardly significant, like the peace that comes from finding an resolution to a philosophical issue that has nagged at you for years. Uranus could also stimulate your interest in foreign cultures and languages, travel, and the pursuit of higher learning. It may inspire you to take on new, daring goals and shake up your sense of direction in life in a good way. Most of all, this aspect will lend you optimism—hope for the future. This in itself can be life-changing, since our attitudes ultimately rule our experiences. Overall, this year will be enjoyable under the influence of this aspect.

If you were born from June 21 to July 5, Saturn will be conjoining your Sun starting June 4. This aspect may bring a sweeping restructuring of your life because it changes your relationship to yourself. You may find it necessary to examine certain parts of your nature—your personality, behavior, beliefs, and attitudes—and decide if they need improvement. Negativity, self-doubt, self-pity, and narrow-mindedness limit us all, and Saturn to the Sun will bring these up so you can make decisions about whether you want to change. This may leave the impression that you are facing greater limitations when actually you are just becoming aware of the limitations you have operated under all along. If you can take the opportunity to face yourself and your fears, this will be a time of marvelous growth—a freeing experience. All too often, however, we feel mired in the moment, as if time has slowed down and life become stagnant. The process of looking inside can be laborious. In addition, you may feel burdened by additional work or be obliged to take an extra job or additional tasks in the workplace or at home. What is perhaps worst of all, you may feel like you are not making progress toward your goals. However, these are just the illusions that arise when Saturn is a strong influence. Great things are accomplished during these times, and it is better to be aware of the pitfalls and possibilities so that you can make the most of this time. When Saturn leaves your Sun next year you will start to see the benefits, and when it leaves your sign you will see these benefits grow. These benefits will build over the next fifteen years, creating a robust platform for all your future successes.

If you were born from July 1 to 6, Neptune will be connecting to your Sun by quincunx from your solar Eighth House. This may have a challenging effect on your finances or income in ways that are hard to identify. You may have a drain on your income; if you received part of your income through commissions you may find that you lose some accounts or activity is diminished. There may be a gradual shift in your source of income—a migration from one source to another. While this is occurring it can be confusing or worrying. You may also wish to change your sources of income to contexts that are more spiritual. Since Neptune challenges us to search for meaning, you will want to be sure that your livelihood and investments are meaningful. You also will want to make sure that there are no hidden costs undermining your efforts.

If you were born from July 9 to 13, Pluto will require adjustments by quincunxing your Sun from your solar Sixth House. This can bring up deep-seated issues related to health, work, and daily routines. This year you may find a compelling reason to change patterns in these areas quite dramatically. There could be a health issue that requires immediate lifestyle changes if you are to avoid great problems further down the road. You may want or need to adjust other daily routines as well to incorporate more rejuvenatory habits into your life such as meditation, exercise, or a more nutritious diet. There may also be some upheaval in the workplace among employees or colleagues. There could be a need for layoffs, or there could be a sudden turnover in personnel due to overwork, too little pay, or negative influences from one or more staff members. The most common change that people experience under this transit is that they work harder at their jobs, and overwork can be the source of poor health discovered at this time. While this transit is often no more than a wake-up call to help you avoid calamity in the future, the effects can be noticeable and your life can change for the better as a result.

If you were born from July 14 to 23, Saturn will semisextile your Sun until June 4. This heralds a preparatory period for a time of renewal and restructuring which will begin in about two years. During this time you will be completing projects, lessons, and relationships that have been with you for as long as twenty-seven years. You may also tend to look backward this year to ponder your experiences and what you've learned from them. There is still time for some corrective measures if they are needed, but they are more important for future rather than current circumstances. If what you get out of this time is a sense of greater satisfaction and closure related to the past, then you have done well to prepare yourself for the cycle that is about to begin.

If you were born from July 19 to 23, your Sun will receive a quincunx from Uranus this year. This is likely to shake your foundation and make you focus on how you're doing with changes you made seven years ago. While not nearly as dramatic as that time was for you, this time offers the opportunity to adjust your course. The bottom line may be the gains you are receiving as a result of those changes. This refers not just to money but also to inner satisfaction and fulfillment. Chances are you will want to make some minor changes now, but it may be daunting to figure out the best way to do it. It may seem as though there's no clear path to your goals, that everywhere you look, there are encumbrances. We are usually more successful with quincunxes if we take a slow and gentle approach. Although this flies in the face of Uranus's innate nature, if you can manage it you'll probably be happier with the result.

Tools for Change

Unparalleled opportunities come your way this year, Cancer, as Uranus begins to trine your Sun from Pisces, Saturn enters your sign, and Chiron continues to oppose it. While the Chiron and Saturn contacts are not normally thought of as immediately beneficial, if you use them to open doorways of personal growth they cannot be equaled. Both planets will lead you to address weaknesses that you have not seen clear to tackle in the past. If you accept their challenge you will be released from bonds that have hindered your forward momentum.

The key to surmounting the blockages they present is to adopt a realistic view of your experiences. As a Cancer, you sense the ocean of feeling that we all inhabit. You feel the ebb and flow of its tides, its floods, rainshowers, storms, and droughts. You respond instinctually, and it is a survival skill to have your finger on this pulse. However, if you do not have mental filters between what you sense and how you act you will not be completely free to fulfill your greatest potential, because you will not truly be choosing your actions. Mental filters screen what you experience and give you insight into your full range of options. They lend an objectivity to your inner processes that allows you to act with more pragmatism and reciprocity toward others.

Our mental filters develop through two primary means: undoing mis-education from the past, and replacing it with new knowledge. Looking in your family's history can be one of the most profound and effective ways of undoing the past. You may gain clues from learning family stories, doing genealogical research, going to family or individual therapy, or studying your astrological chart from a familial perspective. A more general study of psychology will also bring detachment from your own emotional responses and help you to become more aware of your choices.

Acting from a core of peace in your center is also important. Time spent alone or in your own comfortable environment is also highly effective in calming the reactions you generate in response to your experiences. Since your home is so important to you, set off a corner of it for yourself. This could be part of your study, bedroom, or a workshop area in the house or garage. Making your home a more satisfying nest by remodeling or redecorating may also provide a needed support for inner peace. In addition, you may benefit by engaging in water sports, which will help burn off extra emotional energy. Whatever you choose, you have a golden opportunity for growth before you.

Affirmation for the Year

I forgive myself for past mistakes
and allow myself to correct them.

Cancer/January

In the Spotlight
Your relationships are highlighted this month as the planetary energy collects in your opposite sign, Capricorn. The Mercury retrograde there suggests that communications may not be as clear enough to avoid backtracking. Problems clear up after January 23.

Wellness and Keeping Fit
It's important that you take care of yourself during this time so that you don't break down physically and require downtime yourself. Leaving work at a reasonable hour is your greatest support for wellness now. You are especially vulnerable to fevers and inflammations from January 17 to 23.

Love and Life Connections
You may have to cover the needs of those around you, as your family members may become ill or otherwise not be available. Temporary rifts could arise due to careless communication, and it will be up to you to clear the air at the right time. Patience and forbearance will go far this month. Difficulties will clear up after January 23.

Finance and Success
You may find that extra responsibilities fall to you because others are not able to keep up with their usual duties. As long as the need for you to pick up the slack is only temporary, there is no harm in it. However, if downsizing means that you are given permanent new tasks, it may be in your best interest to find ways to deflect or delegate the workload.

Cosmic Insider Tip
Don't be so distracted this month that you ignore larger issues. There may be something undermining your ability to handle your finances with complete success. It is likely to be something subtle, and awareness now can avert problems later this year.

Rewarding Days 6, 7, 8, 11, 12, 13, 16, 17, 21, 22, 25, 26

Challenging Days 2, 3, 9, 10, 23, 24, 29, 30

Affirmation of the Month I can manage tasks that come my way.

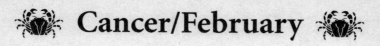 Cancer/February

In the Spotlight

Resources may be stretched thin this month as income and expenditures are emphasized. There may be a planned purchase that finally must be made, but extra costs are likely to be attached to it.

Wellness and Keeping Fit

Your fitness level is threatened by the need to put in extra time at work. You may also be tempted to slack off on your diet, to eat what's quick and easy. If you do, go easy on yourself, but resolve to do better next time. Stress could suppress your immune responses, so make sure you get extra sleep if necessary to compensate.

Love and Life Connections

You are making relationship connections more smoothly and clearly, both at work and at home. You may need to communicate about some unpleasant financial realities that affect others. It may be important to cut back on some expenditures or to work within a budget. Your family pattern with respect to borrowing money may need to change. A compassionate approach will bring better results.

Finance and Success

The benefits of making a big purchase is that you get the product or experience you've bought in the exchange. However, it does mean that you have to part with some of your hard-earned cash. If you can think of it as an investment, either in yourself, your loved ones, or in appreciable assets, you will be more willing to move forward. There is an emphasis on the work product right now rather than on relationships, which seem to be going fine.

Cosmic Insider Tip

The benefits of several months' hard work start to show up after February 22. You've been working behind the scenes and perhaps wondering if you'll ever get acknowledgment. Your time will come.

Rewarding Days 3, 4, 5, 8, 9, 10, 13, 14, 18, 19, 22, 23

Challenging Days 6, 7, 20, 21, 25, 26, 27

Affirmation of the Month I make wise investments.

Cancer/March

In the Spotlight

Events flow virtually without a hitch this month. You get a surprising boost in the right direction as Uranus enters Pisces, where it will remain for seven years. You can look forward to less interference and more support from the unexpected events in your life now.

Wellness and Keeping Fit

It's time to get out of town and express your physical nature in the great outdoors. You'll have a broader perspective and a calmer approach as the endorphins do their work.

Love and Life Connections

Relationships soar and you feel supported. You feel more secure, and you're starting to adjust to the new structures created as a result of last month's added expenses. This is a good month to discuss your long-term goals and ideals with your partner, especially between March 4 and 21. Taking a vacation together to an unaccustomed spot might bring you closer together after March 27.

Finance and Success

Your mind turns to fulfilling your goals and assessing your progress toward your highest ideals this month, especially between March 4 and 21. This is especially significant since, starting March 11, this emerges gradually as more important to you. There may be dreams that you've all but given up on that suddenly gain momentum. It is important to listen to the voice of change because the best is yet to come, and you want to be ready when it does.

Cosmic Insider Tip

You've become more receptive to change, and now it will pay off as a quiet revolution takes place in your life. You can focus its energy by re-establishing the direction you want your life to take, because as you think, so shall you create.

Rewarding Days 3, 4, 7, 8, 9, 12, 13, 14, 17, 18, 21, 22, 30, 31

Challenging Days 5, 6, 19, 20, 25, 26

Affirmation of the Month I am ready to fulfill my goals.

Cancer/April

In the Spotlight

You reach your yearly pinnacle of fulfillment and career activity as the fast-moving planets wing their way across the top of your solar chart. You experience financial release around April 3.

Wellness and Keeping Fit

You may find it enjoyable to engage in your fitness routine with a friend. This could even result in romance. Foreign foods and restaurants may claim your attention, since you feel adventurous enough to try new things.

Love and Life Connections

Relationships are very smooth now and provide support for your career and long-term goals. Communications are good, and you'd like to spend more time with loved ones, but the demands at the office are high at this time and keep you from fulfilling your personal goals with complete satisfaction. After April 26, group politics become uncomfortable.

Finance and Success

Finances are fine this month, and you may even have unusually high income levels as others go out of their way to seek your services. Your bank account promises to swell especially after April 21, but the Mercury retrograde may delay some payments until next month. Not to worry: It will all balance in the end, although you may suffer some inconvenience. Your trajectory to success continues unimpeded.

Cosmic Insider Tip

There is a deep, perhaps hidden, issue in your relationship life that no one wants to talk about. You don't have to talk for healing to take place. Support and acceptance can be provided in other ways, and this will do quite nicely until the doors of communication open.

Rewarding Days 4, 5, 9, 10, 13, 14, 17, 18, 26, 27

Challenging Days 1, 2, 3, 15, 16, 21, 22, 23, 28, 29, 30

Affirmation of the Month I accept success that comes my way.

Cancer/May

In the Spotlight
The background focus of your efforts shifts slightly in May from health and work matters to romance, children, and groups. You may find yourself receiving attention for work you've done without anyone's notice. After May 20 it may be a good time to ask for a raise.

Wellness and Keeping Fit
Your health will be on an even keel this month, so just maintain a balanced routine. Take care not to congest your system by overeating during all those social gatherings, especially through May 20.

Love and Life Connections
Distractions and miscommunications may plague your efforts to get along with others as Mercury retrogrades until May 20. You may find that politics cloud the air in the groups and organizations you belong to, even though the issues don't affect you directly. The benefits of your interactions with others increase after May 16.

Finance and Success
Group membership is your power source this month, and it's wise to take advantage of it. Go to those meetings, because you'll meet someone especially significant to your future success, even if nothing seems promising in the moment. After May 20 potential opportunities become more explicit. The more energy you focus on bringing in the receipts, the more you'll succeed. This is a very fruitful time to call upon those with overdue accounts.

Cosmic Insider Tip
In the confusion that reigns around you, remain calm and wait for the dust to settle. A situation is emerging that will demand your attention; it may indirectly have long-term effects on your income stream. This ties into the issues that arose at the end of January.

Rewarding Days 1, 2, 5, 6, 7, 10, 11, 14, 15, 23, 24, 28, 29

Challenging Days 12, 13, 19, 20, 25, 26, 27

Affirmation of the Month I am patient in bringing my dreams and hopes to fruition.

Cancer/June

In the Spotlight

The projects you've been working on for the past two years call your attention one more time. As Saturn enters your Sun sign on June 4 you'll be challenged to take on new responsibility.

Wellness and Keeping Fit

With renewed interest and focus you can give more time to fitness and health than you have been recently. You may decide that it's time to get some restorative health treatments—massage, acupuncture, a mud bath, or perhaps a crystal healing.

Love and Life Connections

You may need some alone time this month, as you need to recharge your batteries and reassess your options. It has little to do with your loved ones, because no real changes are due there, but it's important to reassure them as you change your routine that you just need some time in your cave. June 9, 12, and 17 each take you deeper into yourself. A trip to a remote seaside retreat might be especially valuable after June 17.

Finance and Success

You will no doubt need to work this month, but if you can do so in quiet, without interruption, you'll be able to extend your sorely needed retreat into your work environment at least a little bit. Working at home, early or late hours, or pushing the do-not-disturb button on the phone will accomplish the desired effects. The dreaminess of this month will feed your productivity level later.

Cosmic Insider Tip

Give yourself some time to reach for what you really want. It will take care and planning, because your decisions affect not just you, but your family and partner as well. Then be brave enough to go for your highest ideal.

Rewarding Days 2, 3, 6, 7, 11, 12, 19, 20, 24, 25, 26, 29, 30

Challenging Days 9, 10, 15, 16, 21, 22, 23

Affirmation of the Month I can take the time I need to grow.

Cancer/July

In the Spotlight

Your energy level is high now and you're feeling refreshed after having time to yourself last month. It's a good thing, because there are difficulties brewing on the foreign, educational, or far-away scene that, if you can anticipate them this month, you may be able to head off in August and September.

Wellness and Keeping Fit

You may have a tendency to be too ambitious where your health and fitness are concerned and to overreach safe limits. Injury or illness could result. By being alert and heeding the signals your body sends you, you'll avoid such trauma.

Love and Life Connections

This is a good month to make travel a part of connecting with your loved ones, especially after July 4. You may find it difficult to do so by the end of the month because other events and experiences intervene. Others also look dotingly upon you and will grant unexpected favors.

Finance and Success

The initiatives that seem to be moving along now may start to lose steam as the month wears on. This is because Mars is slowing down and going retrograde on July 29. It's important to make your contacts and move ahead as planned, even though results may be delayed as unanticipated problems arise in August and September.

Cosmic Insider Tip

There will be signs this month that something is going to go amiss, but you may not be able to do much about it. Sometimes people have to go through it the hard way; you can't control every circumstance you encounter. However, you will ride the waves of events by remain calm and alert; go with the flow until you see an exit.

Rewarding Days 4, 5, 8, 9, 16, 17, 18, 21, 22, 23, 26, 27, 28, 31

Challenging Days 6, 7, 12, 13, 19, 20

Affirmation of the Month I keep my focus during challenges.

Cancer/August

In the Spotlight

With Mars retrograde for the next two months you are sure to experience some changes in plans. After August 21 the planets pile up in your solar Third and Ninth Houses. These bring changes in perspective at the same time that they open you to new possibilities.

Wellness and Keeping Fit

The most difficult thing about this month will be finding the time to take care of your health. It's time to be careful about how you use your body, since inflammations and injuries are an increased possibility when Mars is retrograde.

Love and Life Connections

Travel may disrupt your relationship plans this month. If a vacation is in the offing it may be difficult to get to or from your destination. If you travel for business you may find that you are away from home more than is comfortable or convenient. You are not likely to have much time or energy left to focus on your personal ties, so being honest and open about that early on will avert misunderstanding.

Finance and Success

Foreign conflicts or unrest may disrupt your business dealings if you are involved in international interactions. Travel could be a source of difficulty as well, either by being required more than usual or by being impossible to conduct without major obstacles. Weather could be a factor in business difficulties, especially toward the end of the month.

Cosmic Insider Tip

The biggest planetary collision occurs between August 22 and September 3. Be cautious in making plans that will be fulfilled during that time, since they are likely to be disrupted or postponed. If it is necessary to do so, make arrangements for when things go wrong.

Rewarding Days 1, 4, 5, 13, 14, 18, 19, 23, 24, 27, 28, 29

Challenging Days 2, 3, 9, 10, 15, 16, 17, 30, 31

Affirmation of the Month I am alert to potential difficulties.

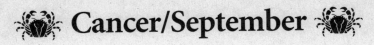 Cancer/September

In the Spotlight
Mercury, Mars, and Uranus have collided in retrograde motion with the Sun, Jupiter, and Venus—and Pluto has raised the stakes. The knots of difficulty begin to unravel on September 15, with more improvements on September 20 and 27.

Wellness and Keeping Fit
The need to refresh your mind can be fulfilled very well by getting out of the house, away from work, and out of the range of your cell phone long enough to relax your mind.

Love and Life Connections
Our siblings and neighbor relations may be a focal point at which both good and bad come from the same area of our lives. For instance, one sibling could be presenting a problem, while another provides support. Your neighborhood could be threatened in some way before September 27. Look to those who can support you, and offer what help you can.

Finance and Success
Finances recede into the background in favor of intensive mental work. This could be the analysis required to produce a report, the research involved in a school paper, or the memorization related to examinations. There may be a mountain of paperwork you must organize or integrate, or the burden of communicating with others in a foreign language. The workload lets up as the month ends.

Cosmic Insider Tip
It seems as though you've buried your long-term goals and ideals under mounds of activities. But just because you haven't consciously tended to them doesn't mean you aren't working with them. When the dust settles you'll have a better perspective.

Rewarding Days 1, 2, 9, 10, 11, 14, 15, 19, 20, 24, 25, 28, 29

Challenging Days 5, 6, 12, 13, 26, 27

Affirmation of the Month I can engage in mental activity without being overwhelmed.

Cancer/October

In the Spotlight

Finally you get some time to take care of private matters, to stay at home and decompress. You are likely to be drawn deep into yourself and your family, where love will nurture your spirit back to health.

Wellness and Keeping Fit

The most important practice for your health this month should be to recover your emotional balance. A time of collapse and warm nurturing is just the thing. Soups, teas, and gentle activity or exercise such as yoga and walking will bring you back to yourself. You'll feel substantially better, ready for action, after October 24.

Love and Life Connections

You finally get to focus your attention on matters at home, and you welcome this time with relish. You more than most are by nature a homebody, and it's like starving for you to be away from home and family for long periods of time. Share with those you find within your four walls, just as they will share with you; it's the interchange that supports you. October 9, 22, and 24 bring improvement.

Finance and Success

Work, finances, and studies are all taking care of themselves after October 6. It's not that they don't need some attention, but that your home and yourself need the most. It is a natural part of the cycle, and, blessedly, there's no conflict in ignoring the outer world for a while. You'll feel like resuming normal activities after October 24.

Cosmic Insider Tip

Tinkering around the house is your healing formula until October 24. You are aware that new episodes of challenge and drama await you, but they aren't here yet. Living in the moment is a fine art—and it is one that will serve you well as you recharge your batteries in a secure and familiar environment with those you love and trust.

Rewarding Days 6, 7, 8, 11, 12, 13, 16, 17, 18, 21, 22, 25, 26

Challenging Days 2, 3, 9, 10, 23, 24, 29, 30

Affirmation of the Month I can take time to recharge my batteries.

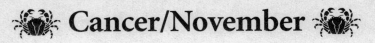 Cancer/November

In the Spotlight
Play—having fun—will draw your focus, and you will feel better if you indulge your whims in a healthy way. Adjustments to your health routines and daily activities are also featured as Mercury, Venus, and the Sun enter your solar Sixth House during the month.

Wellness and Keeping Fit
Health practices and fitness routines take center stage as the month wears on, and you'll want to adjust your habits to get back in line with what you know is best for you. Wholesome, healthy living will do much to get rid of the aches and pains.

Love and Life Connections
The eclipse on November 8 may highlight changes in your family if you have children. They may be growing in ways that draw your attention and need more care than previously. They could be expanding their horizons to explore new social or educational realms. It is most important to be alert to what may be needed from you as a parent, since this will likely be the first time action has been desirable.

Finance and Success
Your work life once again becomes more important, and your productivity level is good. Relations with coworkers are harmonious—the work may even be enjoyable. Not long from now you will be putting more effort into fulfilling your ambitions, but for right now it is enough to get back on track and place your projects on a routine footing again. Finances are stable.

Cosmic Insider Tip
As Mars completes its transit of Pisces you're feeling the stirring of your ideals and goals again. If you can squeeze in a vacation now, go for it, because you'll be too busy after this month to fit one in.

Rewarding Days 3, 4, 8, 9, 13, 14, 18, 19, 22, 23, 30

Challenging Days 5, 6, 7, 20, 21, 26, 27

Affirmation of the Month I can influence my children's lives.

 Cancer/December

In the Spotlight

Agreements, commitments, and career advancement issues assume prominence in December. A project or prospect you pursued in the spring and early summer has reappeared or has been replaced by a similar opportunity. This one will work out.

Wellness and Keeping Fit

After rebuilding over the past two months you've got the resistance to stay healthy. There is some danger, however, from December 31 through January 6, if you ignore fatigue or signs of stress.

Love and Life Connections

A few hot nights on the town are just what you need to revive the romance in a comfortable relationship. A fancy 'do, an orchid corsage, and a little black dress will fan the flames of love. Don't push for more than is willingly offered, even though you want more. There is likely to be some backpedaling after December 16. Give your paramour some time to get used to an idea that is undoubtedly on both your minds.

Finance and Success

Your star is ascending and the possibilities are endless, or so it feels. There are many career doors which could be opening now, but just as they seem poised to unlock, the Mercury retrograde creates a pause in the action starting December 17. This is what you would expect with the holidays anyway; the trouble is, you were hoping for something that defies the cultural norms, and that's not going to happen. January comes soon enough.

Cosmic Insider Tip

Setbacks and hard work seem to be your lot right now, but your patience will be rewarded in the new year. Events soon after December 31 will reveal the potential of what is to come.

Rewarding Days 1, 6, 7, 10, 11, 15, 16, 19, 20, 27, 28, 29

Challenging Days 2, 3, 4, 17, 18, 23, 24, 30, 31

Affirmation of the Month I am confident of my path.

Cancer Action Table

These dates reflect the best—but not the only—times for success and ease in these activities, according to your Sun sign.

	JAN	FEB	MAR	APR	MAY	JUN	JUL	AUG	SEPT	OCT	NOV	DEC
Move									26	8-24		
Start a class							31	1-27	20-30	1-6		
Join a club				6-25	20-31	1-12						
Ask for a raise				1-5		29	5-28					
Look for work	29, 30	26, 27	22-31									
Get pro advice			1, 2, 25, 26	21, 22	19, 20	15, 16	12, 13	9, 10		2, 3	29, 30	26, 27
Get a loan	31	1, 2, 28	1, 27, 28	23, 24	21, 22	17, 18	14, 15	11, 12		4, 5, 31	1, 2, 28, 29	
See a doctor	23-31	1-12				14-30	1-13				13-30	1-16
Start a diet						14					13-30	1, 2
End relationship							13					
Buy clothes										10-31	1-11	
Get a makeover						29, 30	1-13					
New romance										10-31	1, 2	
Vacation	6-8	3, 4	2, 3, 6-21, 25-27		23, 24	19, 20	16-18	13, 14	9-11	6-8	3, 4, 30	1, 27-29

LEO

The Lion
July 23 to August 23

♌

Element:	Fire
Quality:	Fixed
Polarity:	Yang/Masculine
Planetary Ruler:	The Sun
Meditation:	I trust in the strength of my soul.
Gemstone:	Ruby
Power Stones:	Topaz, sardonyx
Key Phrase:	I will
Glyph:	Lion's tail
Anatomy:	Heart, upper back
Color:	Gold, scarlet
Animal:	Lions, large cats
Myths/Legends:	Apollo, Isis, Helios
House:	Fifth
Opposite Sign:	Aquarius
Flower:	Marigold, sunflower
Key Word:	Magnetic

Positive Expression:	Misuse of Energy:
Confident	Self-involved
Faithful	Stubborn
Powerful	Aggressive
Regal	Pompous
Assertive	Dictatorial
Generous	Ostentatious

Leo

Your Ego's Strengths and Shortcomings

If there's anyone who enjoys being on stage, it's you, Leo. You're just like your ruling planet, the Sun: You want to shine, to radiate, to bask in the warm glow of others' admiration and affection.

This is because your source of energy, your great well of strength, is your heart—and love is its language. Through your heart you connect to others and enrich their lives, and so they naturally want to return love with love. This is your lifeblood, and that's why you're the grease in the gears of human connectedness. Your willingness to reach out to others, your generosity of spirit and enthusiasm, are all it takes to make the world go round.

This leads you into all kinds of socially oriented pursuits, from stage or film acting to sales to teaching to competitive sports. You are the life of the party, and social events are always more successful with you there. In any group, if there is a need for someone to take a leadership role, you'll be happy to volunteer, as long as it doesn't require the shouldering of too much responsibility.

As long as your heart is open and flowing, all the best parts of your Leo energy are easy to express. However, it is often difficult to maintain an open heart in a bruising world. You can be hurt and want to withdraw in shock and pain. You may think about whether you can take the risk of loving openly.

Or worse, you may hold yourself distant from others, which, with your natural regal bearing, looks like pride and arrogance. You may feel as though you are stuck in this role, not knowing how to break out of it. Or you may focus on trying to get the people who disdain you to love you, seeking their approval.

The key to breaking through any of these patterns is first to love yourself. When we love ourselves we are less affected by others' slings and arrows, because we know that the issue is usually mostly about them, not us. When we learn not to take things personally or become upset we are free to love openly, since we are firm in our esteem of ourselves. In this way you can maintain your balance and stay centered in your warm, loving, generous self.

Shining Your Love Light

You have so much heart, Leo, that it is unimaginable to you that others will not be as generous as you or take kindly to your generosity. So you give freely of yourself, and the miracle is, you usually find your love returned. You are happiest in a relationship where love is shared without reservation or barrier, where there is no fear of manipulation or withholding, rare though that is. But once you find it you are undyingly loyal and sincere in your own love offering.

You're most likely to encounter that sincere, unabashed love from the signs of your element, fire: Aries, Leo, or Sagittarius. Aries is alight with ideas that spark your interest and ignite your enthusiasm, as well as romance. Taurus is ordinarily a little too slow for you, but if you are patient enough a fine and lofty product can result. Gemini fills your head with information that fertilizes your drive to create and express your creation, while Cancer's caring nurturance can be endearing but often cloying enough to dampen your fires. Sharing yourself with another Leo can spawn a wonderful heart-to-heart communion—as long as you keep that fiery competitive spirit from separating you. Virgo may not be able to cut loose and engage in unreserved self-expression, and you may feel unnerved by the constant self-examination. Libra has the relaxed attitude and social interests you do, but may prefer less-public interactions. Scorpio's intensity is intriguing, and you appreciate the insights into human nature, but it can get too heavy for you at times. Sagittarius, although less steadfast in loyalty, flies with you on wings of hope and inspiration. Capricorn has less panache than you do, but this sign's leadership style is the perfect complement to yours. Aquarius, your opposite sign, provides an intellectual objectivity that you could find enlightening or annoying. Pisces's sensitivity may keep you at a loss at times, but this sign shares your love of the arts as well as the creative process.

Making Your Place in the World

You were born to shine, Leo, and you'll certainly want to choose a career that allows you to do so. Many Leos go into an entertainment field for this reason; you could find yourself dancing, acting, doing stand-up comedy, singing—anything to place you in the limelight. You may be drawn to leadership positions as well, since you usually have the panache to step up to the plate and take charge. People are naturally inspired by you, and they easily do what you ask after contact with your infectious enthusiasm. Your comfort in front of an audience could lead you to become a motivational speaker, or, if you are a quieter type, sales may be for you.

Perhaps above all else, you like your efforts to be admired and approved. So you may also be attracted to work in a creative art—painting, illustration, music, writing. Your sense of play and joy could bring you to work with children, since they open easily to your ways. Teaching is natural for you, especially when it involves young people, because it combines all the Leo gifts into one package.

One pitfall to avoid is a tendency to want the glamour and recognition without being willing to do the work. Leo leaders must be willing to take responsibility and dig in when needed.

Power Plays

Being a fire sign, you feel the power flow through you, granting you the drive to be a whirlwind of energy, creativity, and dynamism. All that you do originates in this raw force that flows through you. You are fortunate in that, more than the other fire signs, your energy is sustainable and gives you more endurance. The only drawback to the fire-sign style is that you may lose perspective when you are in the midst of the experience; your fervor could be misdirected—a reality that may not hit you until after the fact.

The greatest source of power for you is love. Love can come in many forms: enthusiasm for a project or cause, joy in creating, the excitement of winning, the fire of passion, the spiritual glow of enlightenment, or the open-hearted tenderness you feel for a loved one. Anywhere you go, when you feel love you spread this energy in your wake, and like fairy dust it settles on all who are in contact with you. This adds new meaning to doing what you love, because the more that you do, the more you will provide true inner benefits to others as well as yourself.

Famous Leos

Ben Affleck, Gillian Anderson, Lucille Ball, Antonio Banderas, Kathleen Battle, Sandra Bullock, Confucius, David Duchovny, The Edge, Aldous Huxley, Lisa Kudrow, Matthew Perry, Mae West

The Year Ahead for Leo

What a year you have in store, Leo! New opportunities are arriving, and some of the pressure comes off your relationships. You may find joy in unexpected places, but don't bet the farm on a long shot.

Jupiter starts off the year in your sign. Since last August you've had the Midas touch more than usual. You still have time to look through the window on your future that Jupiter opens and set some plans in motion, but chances are you're already doing that. Don't worry about which opportunities to energize—go with the flow. You'll have time after Jupiter changes signs in late August to begin to sort all that out. When Jupiter makes that move into Virgo it's time to look at which of the projects excites you the most. It's not what's easiest or what might make the most money, but what fills your heart enough to engage you for the next twelve years in some fashion. That's the right path.

Saturn in Gemini has forced you to accept some discipline and discernment in choosing your social milieu. Some people can just get you into trouble, and it's better to choose the right people than to have to resist their negative influences. By now you should be settling into a new social environment that is more supportive of you. Great timing, because Saturn is about to enter your closet when it goes into Cancer in April. It will route out all those unconscious issues that keep you stuck, rattle a few skeletons, and, best of all, declare open season on self-deception. This is perhaps your greatest pitfall, Leo. It is good to imagine the world the way we want it to be, but we still need to stay in touch with the way it really is. Since the end of 2001 Chiron has been pointing out to you the ways in which your lifestyle may not support your health. You may find yourself more sensitive, and your number of visits to the chiropractor may have doubled. Healing is good; over the next two years, you'll have the chance to get to the bottom of your bad habits and uproot them. Maybe you'll even feel good enough to help others.

Uranus has been in Aquarius and your solar Seventh House since 1995, bringing excitement—perhaps chaos—into your relationships. Changes in your partnerships, changes in what you want in a partnership, have all been part of the tableau for seven years. Now, with Uranus's move into Pisces in March, the landscape will shift to finance and other things beyond your direct control. From windfall profits to winning contests to losing your shirt, all are possible. The message is to rely on your inner self to guide you. You may also find that things occult and spiritual are suddenly relevant in your life. Whether because of a psychic experience or a normal event which takes on deeper meaning, the unknown and unseen may fascinate you now. Neptune in Aquarius is still adding the mystical and mysterious to your close bonds. From business and personal partnerships to more adversarial interactions, you may find yourself mystified by the responses you get from others. Don't let it shatter your usual self-confidence, Leo. Learn from it and move on. With Pluto in your solar Fifth House your frivolous and fun activities have taken on a more serious tone in recent years. You've found power in your creativity, whether released through a meaningful hobby or a more serious pastime. You may find these pursuits increasingly fulfilling, and even though you do them because they make your heart sing, you may find that others respond to them, too. You could make money just by doing what you love.

The eclipses this year are leading you to think about your life path more seriously. Are you headed in the right direction? Are your fulfilling your purpose in life? Are you happy with your chosen career path? Is parenthood in the picture? You may also be discontented with where you are living or want to take on that dream remodeling project. Look deep inside to make your decisions rather than worrying about what others will think.

If you were born from July 23 to 26, Uranus will quincunx your Sun from March 11. After the changes you went through about seven years ago, you've tried to settle into a new version of normal. The changes have been exciting and in some ways disruptive, but you've slowly gotten used to this new routine and the new creative outlets for your energies. Now, however, it's time for musical chairs again, time to make another shift. The ability is there this year to soften or even eradicate the problems that you have had since then. This will not occur without discomfort, however. You will have to face the tough issues and answer the questions that arise without flinching. You may have to take some difficult actions. Some of these may concern finances. You may need to change the positioning of some of your investments or change jobs in order to further your overall career. These should be changes that are in alignment with the general direction you want to head, however—not just anything that's different from what you were doing before.

If you were born from July 23 to August 6, Saturn will semisextile your Sun once it enters Cancer on June 4. This signals a shift from a socially oriented period to a time when you will be more inwardly directed. That is because you are preparing for a new long-term cycle which will begin in about two years. Before then it's a good time to tie up loose ends from the past twenty-seven years and begin to turn your attention to what you may want to accomplish in the next thirty years. This first necessitates deciding what you feel is left undone at this point in your life. These things are likely to be part of the focus of the new cycle. There will be some initiatives that you want to carry forward, of course. The inward direction of this period may also lead you to retreat. Perhaps this will manifest as just wanting to stay home more; however, you may wish to engage in more spiritually oriented activities such as meditation. As with all Saturn transits, it may seem as though time is standing still. The activity that you do engage in may place you in the background. No matter what, it is important to listen to your heart during this time in order to get the most out of this year.

If you were born from August 1 to 6, Neptune will oppose your Sun this year. This aspect will affect your relationships as well as your sense of who you are. It will bring to the surface any difficulties that currently exist in your relationships, but in a subtle way. One of the ways it will do this is by helping you see yourself in those around you. You may feel as if the universe is holding up a mirror for you so you can see yourself more clearly. This can be uncomfortable when we discover that the traits we dislike in someone else are also in ourselves. You may also discover that you have idealized some of those around you. Since all people have feet of clay in some way, it is inevitable that they will fall from their pedestals. Neptune often removes this cloud of fantasy from our relationships, stripping away the veils of illusion so we can see others in their true light. However, if you are not alert others may take advantage of you—even con you—or find a way to control you. This is because during this Neptune transit your natural defenses and filters may be down because you are focusing on other parts of reality. It is common for us to see the best in another person, their soul potential, under a Neptune transit. This is all well and good, but if you don't pay attention to what's in the personality here and now you may be rudely awakened when this transit is over. This does not mean you should refrain from partnership activities during this time, whether business or personal, but rather you should give yourself time to develop trust and clarity in forming commitments.

If you were born from August 10 to 13, Pluto will be trining your Sun this year from your solar Fifth House. This is an empowering aspect, one which should allow you to grow in whatever way you choose. Some say with Pluto, "Be careful of what you wish for, because you will get it," and this is the only pitfall of this aspect. This is a time when you can put rocket fuel behind your flights of fancy, so it's important to make sure that what you are igniting is what you really want. This is a great time for a romance with fireworks, but sometimes we can get burned by this type of relationship. It's best to proceed slowly with such situations. It may not be as exciting, but if you want it to last you have a better chance. This can also be a time of high creativity for you. If you are involved in the creative arts as a career, setting aside some time for these efforts will be fruitful. Even if you are a hobbyist, or want to pick up a new hobby, you will reap great rewards in personal fulfillment from your endeavors this year.

If you were born from August 15 to 23, Saturn will sextile your Sun during the first five months of the year. This is actually the final few months of this transit, most of which took place last year. During this time you may have focused more thought and energy into groups and organizations. You may have had the opportunity to take on a position of responsibility or received some sort of recognition for past efforts. You are finding it easy to shine your light amongst those in your social world, as others are attuned to your message and naturally see your potential as a leader now. This is a great time to consciously decide amongst which groups you want to spend your time, and then to build relationships there. You may make these decisions based on business and career goals rather than a desire for enjoyment or entertainment. Although it may not seem like the most important thing to focus on as you survey your life at this time, it is a "higher order" concern that, if you give it juice now, will reap far-reaching rewards in the future, even if no progress is visible immediately.

If you were born from August 19 to 23, Uranus will oppose your Sun this year. This is a big, once-in-a-lifetime milestone when you can break away from situations that are holding you back and rejuvenate your life by replacing them with contexts that are more meaningful and fulfilling. This may come by shaking up your relationships, but this isn't the only way that you may change, or the only area in which change may come to you. Under this transit you may find yourself jittery, excitable, and eager to burst from the cage of security you've made for yourself. The changes that you feel inside cannot go unnoticed, and as you express them you see them reflected in the reactions of those around you. This could make it seem as though others are the source of our challenges, and this may be true to a certain extent. However, if you want to be more of a directive force in working with this energy, try being more conscious of your own need for freedom and change, your own drive to manifest your sense of purpose in life. Ultimately, this transit should help you to feel younger, more alive, and excited about your life. Although Uranus has a tendency to wreak havoc in the lives of those who resist change, for those who embrace it as a part of daily life it will flow more smoothly, taking you to a new level of awareness as well as reality.

Tools for Change

With Jupiter in your Sun sign and Neptune opposing it, your greatest challenge this year will be to discern the best ways to expand your options and set a course for the next twelve years. This is a turning point in your life, because your future growth and happiness depend on the plans you set for yourself now. Neptune will naturally open you to heights of imagination, idealism, and spiritual connectedness, but your task will be to bring your new ideas down to earth so that you can do something real with them.

One of the best ways to do this is to develop your creativity. Creative insight is needed in every area of life, not just the arts, so no matter what your career, the flow of innovation will assist you. To get your ingenuity going it helps to engage in activities that light the spark. The bottom line is that these activities must be fun for you and engage you in a certain amount of spontaneity. It helps if there is a spiritual component to your pastime. It doesn't have to be a hobby or involve any skill. Some forms of amusement that come to mind are Sufi dancing, which integrates music, dance and spiritual practice, as well as drama, stage, or film projects. You may also be drawn to the traditional creative arts: music, painting and drawing, or crafts. You may also be drawn to stand-up comedy, art therapy, or spiritual practices to open the heart, which can include yoga and meditation. You can focus your efforts by learning to read the messages from your unconscious mind, most easily tapped through dreams. Learning about dream symbolism and keeping a dream journal can bring significant breakthroughs.

You may also find that sports indirectly open your creative channels because they clear blockages and open the body's energy centers. You may especially be drawn to games where competitiveness and elements of the unexpected reign supreme. Soccer, basketball or baseball, volleyball, equestrian sports, frisbee, or even playing tag with the kids can delight you. It is even more fun when you change the rules of the game to suit yourself and your fellow players.

Health treatments and regimens that will support your well-being include Sun or heat treatments, chiropractic, aromatherapy, and hair analysis to find and correct nutritional deficiencies. Once you feel the inspiration flowing, ideas will become plans, and plans opportunities. You will be able to do what is so deeply meaningful to you—to give and receive from the heart.

♌

Affirmation for the Year

By listening to my heart, I am inspired.

Leo/January

In the Spotlight

Even before the new year started you found plenty of work to do, and by January 2, when everybody else is waking up bleary-eyed, you're hard at it. Other events draw your attention to home and pleasurable pursuits, so it will be easier to keep your balance.

Wellness and Keeping Fit

Your heavy workload creates the potential for illness if you overdo and miss vital nutrition, exercise, or sleep. This is especially true January 2 through 23. If you find ways to make your routines more convenient you will be more successful at fitting it all in.

Love and Life Connections

You feel like sticking close to home, enjoying some special leisure activities, and being with loved ones—and it makes good sense to do so. Don't deny your inner needs and urges, even though your mind may be telling you to work more. You'll have more interest and need to socialize, to do creative and spontaneous things, after January 17. After January 23 it will even feel less like stolen time.

Finance and Success

The necessary ingredient for success for you right now is work. People are expecting you to complete certain tasks, and you have to put your nose to the grindstone a little more than usual to do it. This may help to stave off cash flow problems later in the year, when Mars retrogrades in your house of other people's money (the source of our income). If your work involves creativity, inspiration may come to you after January 8.

Cosmic Insider Tip

Don't be afraid to take extra time and energy for your health this month, as it may help to avert future problems. Preventive therapies can be especially useful now.

Rewarding Days 1, 9, 10, 14, 15, 18, 19, 20, 23, 24, 27, 28

Challenging Days 4, 5, 11, 12, 13, 25, 26, 31

Affirmation of the Month I can take care of myself.

Leo/February

In the Spotlight

Interactions with others, both at home and in business, are key to your progress this month. You've conquered the heavy workload after February 12, and you're even having fun at the office now.

Wellness and Keeping Fit

Keep the emphasis on fun in your fitness routine. You're almost feeling rambunctious, and this is a good way to burn off energy and appeal to your natural sense of play. You may want to do some endurance running or horseback riding.

Love and Life Connections

Romance can play a key role in your life this month as Mars transits your solar Fifth House. Your attraction for exotic, intellectual, or foreign types may be active again. If you have children, they will be vigorous and healthy, perhaps focused on sports or other athletic activities right now. Exercising your own independence is in alignment with everyone else's needs.

Finance and Success

Connections with others are essential now, so a few working lunches may be in order. Agreements are especially important, and the way is clear to sign contracts anytime this month. You might find it helpful to plan casual events with colleagues, such as a day of golf or a run in the park. You may be able to clinch a big deal at the beginning of the month, but don't push anything. Some new enterprises may come out of it, too, but not right now.

Cosmic Insider Tip

Jupiter reaches a culmination point in your sign on February 2, so some breakthroughs are possible. However, since Neptune is involved the effect may be muted or delayed. The effect will be complete by the end of October.

Rewarding Days 5, 6, 7, 10, 11, 12, 15, 16, 19, 20, 23, 24

Challenging Days 1, 2, 8, 9, 21, 22, 28

Affirmation of the Month I balance my needs and desires.

Leo/March

In the Spotlight

Finances, including taxes, are on your mind this month, and there could be some surprises in store for you there as Uranus enters Pisces. A new phase of spiritual growth could be in the offing as well, as you become fascinated by what makes the world turn.

Wellness and Keeping Fit

You may want to fine-tune your routines a little to meet your current needs, but they don't need complete revamping. Inflammations and injuries are more possible after March 4, so take extra care to stay focused and grounded after that time.

Love and Life Connections

Your partner is especially amicable this month, and you'll want to spend time with just the two of you together. Don't worry if you have some sticky subjects unresolved between you. You may get the chance to discuss them, or you may decide it's better not to bring them up, building rapport instead. Be receptive to your partner and you'll find yourselves in balance.

Finance and Success

The emphasis is on your link to other people's money. This could mean loans, insurance, legacies, credit-card debt, your financial portfolio, or taxes. If you are preparing taxes now, you should know that for this and the next six years it's important to be especially truthful on your tax return. There could be some surprises coming from this area of your life, and an audit or two could be one of them.

Cosmic Insider Tip

Uranus in your Eighth House for seven years suggests that you could be especially curious about spiritual and occult matters. You may want to understand what's hidden below the surface, and you are fascinated by those who can make sense of it all.

Rewarding Days 4, 5, 6, 9, 10, 14, 15, 18, 19, 20, 23, 24

Challenging Days 1, 7, 8, 21, 22, 27, 28

Affirmation of the Month I feel free to explore new realms.

Leo/April

In the Spotlight
Everything flows this month, and even though you may feel like the sky's the limit, it is better to moderate your Leonine vigor somewhat, as not every planet is behind you now. Still, this is a good time to reach for your goals, especially before April 26.

Wellness and Keeping Fit
You may find your desire to break free quite consistently pulling you outdoors for your exercise. Work may intervene around April 26 as Mercury slows down in your Tenth House of career and focuses your energy there.

Love and Life Connections
You may receive gifts or other signs of generosity from those around you, and this can feel very good, but you may be wondering what strings are attached. If you are unclear, you will be wise to clarify the intentions behind it. You may experience some assertive or even aggressive responses from the people around you after April 21.

Finance and Success
Those around you are likely to be rather more generous toward you this month, especially before April 21. As you approach April 26, Mercury retrograding in your solar Tenth House will bring more challenges in your career, possibly through an increase in paperwork or logistical matters that require extra input from you. Keep organized and make sure you return every phone call to ensure success.

Cosmic Insider Tip
Something big that you started last summer could show signs of development, even fruition, around April 3. If it doesn't fulfill itself by April 26 you could be in for a delay. Don't fret; the really strong initiatives will outlast setbacks, which will be largely over with by May 20.

Rewarding Days 1, 2, 6, 7, 11, 12, 15, 16, 19, 20, 28, 29

Challenging Days 3, 4, 5, 17, 18, 23, 24, 30

Affirmation of the Month I listen to the truth my heart tells me.

Leo/May

In the Spotlight

The pressure is on in your career, and the potential for success is great if you can stay the course. Everything converges after May 16 to focus on expansion, and the forces acting upon you may be hard to withstand. By keeping your attitude balanced and calm you will be able to deflect tensions headed your way.

Wellness and Keeping Fit

Your body may take a beating from stress this month as several planets converge around May 20 to demand fast action from you. You will want to engage in stress-reducing activities, and this is a good time to be gentle with yourself.

Love and Life Connections

As you focus more energy into work it is natural that you engage in more interaction with people in that arena. Your home life may be on the back burner, relatively speaking, but that doesn't mean you should ignore your loved ones. Give them loving attention early in the month before you are swept away by events outside the home.

Finance and Success

Your finances will need consistent vigilance to keep them from changing in unexpected ways. If, for instance, your partner needs to curb his or her expenditures, it is a good time to get in touch with that before the situation worsens. Take a team approach to any problem areas if you want those you are working with on your side.

Cosmic Insider Tip

Tensions abound this month, and the days from May 15 through 22 are the most volatile. Don't try to accomplish too much during that time, but stay focused on what comes to the surface. Letting go of your schedule will reduce your blood pressure, heart rate, and breath rate tremendously.

Rewarding Days 3, 4, 8, 9, 12, 13, 16, 17, 25, 26, 27, 30, 31

Challenging Days 1, 2, 14, 15, 21, 22, 28, 29

Affirmation of the Month Success comes as I go with the flow.

Leo/June

In the Spotlight
Your life is a social whirl in June as the Sun, Mercury, and Venus enter your house of groups and organizational affiliations. You have done much to cultivate the growth of your life and career through social contacts over the past two years, and over the coming years you will begin to reap real rewards.

Wellness and Keeping Fit
Team sports may be just the way to satisfy both your physical and social needs this month. Baseball, golf, and tennis are just a few of the ways to combine fitness, business or romance, and pleasure.

Love and Life Connections
Your opportunities for love, romance, or just plain social interaction are great this month, but they increase dramatically after June 10. If you have a partner, taking him or her with you to these events increases your cachet. You'll enjoy the attention and the aftereffects of being the most stylish couple at the ball.

Finance and Success
This is a great month for you as you naturally gain positive attention from others. You've garnered as much success as is possible in this round, and reward time is here. You may receive some recognition for your past efforts. This is also a great time to ask for a raise. You may need to focus on financial matters after June 16.

Cosmic Insider Tip
Your spiritual and occult studies receive a boost after June 17 as your interests turn to things deep and mysterious. Think about how you want to structure your spiritual studies now, as Saturn enters your Twelfth House, because you may want to spend more time on this part of your life.

Rewarding Days 1, 4, 5, 9, 10, 13, 14, 21, 22, 23, 26, 27, 28

Challenging Days 11, 12, 17, 18, 24, 25

Affirmation of the Month I cultivate social contacts that are a source of wealth, pleasure, and well-being.

Leo/July

In the Spotlight
Your focus this month should be on health and well-being. You need some time to decompress. To this end, you will probably feel like staying home more frequently than usual, or at least avoiding the usual haunts.

Wellness and Keeping Fit
Time away from the office is just what you need. You may not feel like you want to drop out of the exciting world you live in, but without a break your input will become stale. Get plenty of sleep, knowing that in another month you'll bounce back with more vigor than ever.

Love and Life Connections
You may be alone this month or only in contact with a few loved ones. This may be because you are confined in some way, due perhaps to illness or a vacation in a remote location. This is probably in harmony with what you feel like doing anyway. It does not fit your usual personality, but it may be standard procedure for your typical July. Give yourself the time away, and you'll be back by your birthday, ready to catch up on everyone's stories and tell your own.

Finance and Success
Trouble could be brewing in the financial world, and it could affect you in unpleasant ways. This is a good time to carefully re-examine your portfolio and long-range plans to make sure that you have your assets in safe places. There is a storm coming which will be felt around July 29 when Mars turns retrograde. You may be able to avert difficulties now if you are alert and intuitive.

Cosmic Insider Tip
Your intuition will be close to the surface this month if you give yourself some time to look inside. This could save you from many difficulties during August and September.

Rewarding Days 1, 2, 3, 6, 7, 10, 11, 19, 20, 24, 25, 29, 30

Challenging Days 8, 9, 14, 15, 21, 22, 23

Affirmation of the Month I can take the time off I need.

Leo/August

In the Spotlight

This is your month, Leo! You're completing a great year that is set to put you on a new level of success. There are challenges as the planets align for a showdown in your financial houses, and this could be reflected in conflict in that area of your life. Everything comes to a head between August 22 and September 3.

Wellness and Keeping Fit

If you can avoid the urge to give in to unhealthy desires this month, you'll be that much more ahead. Sometimes routines can be soothing, even if it is hard to break away from the prevailing drama.

Love and Life Connections

Relationships may be touchy as financial difficulties peak. There could be issues of control, as you may feel that your partner isn't exercising enough self-discipline in managing money. Or you could be the one primarily at fault. If so, admit your mistake, apologize, and make amends as best you can. Taking a "we're in this together" approach will be more helpful to finding a permanent solution.

Finance and Success

Finances aren't the only measure of success, and this month you may have to look to other values to feel good about yourself. It seems as if everything is forcing your attention upon finances, but this is still a good month for you to get some new initiatives under way. Even if all you do is to plan your activities for when everything dies down, that is an essential effort in this seed-planting phase.

Cosmic Insider Tip

Your best bet this month is to ride the waves. There will be a lot of activity. Some of it will not affect you, and some of it will, but you won't be able to control it. Relax and negotiate your way through what you can't control until the time comes when you can.

Rewarding Days 2, 3, 6, 7, 8, 15, 16, 17, 20, 21, 22, 25, 26

Challenging Days 4, 5, 11, 12, 18, 19, 29, 30, 31

Affirmation of the Month I handle all circumstances successfully.

Leo/September

In the Spotlight

By now you know what the planetary crunch is all about. It's over early this month, and then you can recover. The planets will begin to disentangle themselves after September 3, with noticeable improvements after September 15, 20, and 27.

Wellness and Keeping Fit

If you are emotionally depleted it may take a physical toll, and no amount of mental cajoling will make your body ready for a rigorous workout. By the end of the month you'll be back in the saddle again.

Love and Life Connections

Your relationship life could be difficult if you and your partner have had to face some tough truths. Gradually, as each of you gets over the shock of change, lets go of pride, and begins to reconcile yourselves to the new reality, you will come together again. However, if your relationship is on shaky ground for other reasons, those reasons are likely to come to the surface and prolong your feelings of separateness. Seek help if you need it.

Finance and Success

It won't get any worse once this month is over unless you decide to dig a hole for yourself. Assuming you don't, you will resume increasing control over your material life as we approach the end of the month. If you are invested in an area of the markets that is dropping, you won't be able to stop the slide, but at least the bleeding will stop around September 27.

Cosmic Insider Tip

It's okay to be in discord with others if gaining their approval requires you to compromise your values and principles. Many times we have to let others discover truth on their own and wait patiently for their return.

Rewarding Days 3, 4, 12, 13, 16, 17, 18, 21, 22, 23, 26, 27, 30

Challenging Days 1, 2, 7, 8, 14, 15, 28, 29

Affirmation of the Month It is important to honor my inner truth.

Leo/October

In the Spotlight

Mercury and Mars are back on their normal path and the other planets are giving us a break as well. You're free and clear to make the adjustments you have wanted to make. Communications are important this month, and you may be thinking a lot about what you really believe—even changing your mind.

Wellness & Keeping Fit

Walking or running in your neighborhood will economize on time. If you invite a friend or family member to come along you add the benefit of social interaction and relationship building to create an added relaxation benefit—and fun!

Love and Life Connections

Focusing your attentions close to home is essential this month, even though you have other activities to manage. Think very carefully about what your values and principles are after last month's events. You may find that you have new insights as the dust settles. If you make changes, it's important for you to let others know about them. Admitting our mistakes is the key to being a good partner. When someone else admits theirs, be ready to forgive.

Finance and Success

Finally, you can put concerns about money on the back burner. Now it's time to think about outreach, public relations, and even training. Toward the end of the month something you've been working with since June takes on more prominence and defines a major focus for the next five months.

Cosmic Insider Tip

You're looking for deeper meaning, for something to change, but you may not know what yet. This knowledge will be evolutionary, but you will get clues about it in the days surrounding October 24.

Rewarding Days 1, 9, 10, 14, 15, 19, 20, 23, 24, 27, 28

Challenging Days 4, 5, 11, 12, 13, 25, 26, 31

Affirmation of the Month I resolve issues in their own time.

Leo/November

In the Spotlight

There's more emphasis on the home front this month—perhaps some deep cleaning, repairs, or modifications. Your family may claim your attention and you may plan some special amusements with them. Eclipses on November 8 and 23 affect your romantic life and children, as well as your career.

Wellness and Keeping Fit

This is a great month for fun-oriented fitness activities. Make sure it's lighthearted—a sport, running on the beach—with no performance standards, no worries. Give yourself some time for romance, too—it's one of the best healing cures.

Love and Life Connections

You're almost acting like a crab, not wanting to come out of your shell. You do need a break. Your relationships at home may still be a little stilted, but they are improving, especially after November 12. The eclipse on November 23 could bring your thoughts to romance (not a bad idea!) or happenings with the kids. Plan some special social event that means something to your loved ones.

Finance and Success

Finances are still in flux, but there is improvement. You're even able to see when you can safely put them on the back burner. This is not a time when business, career, or the things we normally associate with success are prominent for you, unless you are involved in the creative arts. If so, this can be a highly creative time, and you can develop new works in your chosen field.

Cosmic Insider Tip

Situations that you've been dealing with for the past seven years come to the surface again. This month is your last chance to resolve issues that have arisen—at least in the way that you see them now.

Rewarding Days 5, 6, 7, 10, 11, 12, 15, 16, 20, 21, 24, 25

Challenging Days 1, 2, 8, 9, 22, 23, 28, 29

Affirmation of the Month My future is bright.

Leo/December

In the Spotlight

You're dividing your time between work and pleasure this month. The responsibilities mount, but after December 16 you can take a break. Your workload may increase around December 17 but if your vacation is scheduled already, just take your cell phone.

Wellness and Keeping Fit

Health routines and treatments receive more emphasis this month as your immune system may take a natural, cyclic dip. You may be more sensitive than usual, and you may want to strengthen your system by adopting a cleansing diet with herbs and supplements.

Love and Life Connections

Your love connections are greatly improved, and just in time for holiday celebrations. As you shift your emphasis to work, and perhaps health, you receive the support and sympathy of those close to your heart. This will be a special time for you and your partner—even more so if you can get away from civilization for a while.

Finance and Success

After December 16 the financial concerns built over the past few months are on maintenance. It often takes time to rectify such matters, but you don't have to think about it constantly anymore. There are new business prospects in the works for you, but the holidays being what they are, you can safely take time away. Your opportunities will pick up where they left off in January.

Cosmic Insider Tip

Don't worry about the Mercury retrograde when it comes to travel. It doesn't have to be difficult if you're flexible—it can be part of the adventure. Take extra precautions to make sure that your logistics are secured, have a back-up plan, and stay on the ground during the Mercury station—mostly because of weather.

Rewarding Days 2, 3, 4, 7, 8, 9, 17, 18, 21, 22, 30, 31

Challenging Days 5, 6, 12, 13, 14, 19, 20, 25, 26

Affirmation of the Month I can take time to get away from it all.

Leo Action Table

These dates reflect the best—but not the only—times for success and ease in these activities, according to your Sun sign.

	JAN	FEB	MAR	APR	MAY	JUN	JUL	AUG	SEPT	OCT	NOV	DEC
Move										25-31	1-11	
Start a class									16-30	1-9		
Join a club					11-31	1-4						
Ask for a raise							29-31	1-22				
Look for work	1, 23-31	1-28	1-4	6-25	20-31	1-12						3-16
Get pro advice	4, 5, 31	1, 2, 28	1, 27, 28	23, 24	21, 22	17, 18	14, 15	11, 12	7, 8	4, 5, 31	1, 2, 28, 29	25, 26
Get a loan	6-8	3, 4	2, 3, 29, 31		23, 24	19, 20	16-18	13, 14		6-8	3, 4, 30	1, 27-29
See a doctor	1, 23-31	1-28	1-4			30	1-30					3-16
Start a diet	1, 23-31	1-11					13					3-16
End relationship								11				
Buy clothes							14-31	1-22			3-26	1, 2
Get a makeover												
New romance											3-26	
Vacation	9, 10	6, 7	4-6, 22-31	1-5, 22-29	1-16, 26, 27	22, 23	19, 20	15-17	12, 13	9, 10	5-7	2-4

VIRGO

The Virgin
August 23 to September 23

♍

Element:	Earth
Quality:	Mutable
Polarity:	Yin/Feminine
Planetary Ruler:	Mercury
Meditation:	I can allow time for myself.
Gemstone:	Sapphire
Power Stones:	Peridot, amazonite, rhodochrosite
Key Phrase:	I analyze
Glyph:	Greek symbol for containment
Anatomy:	Abdomen, intestines, gall bladder
Color:	Taupe, gray, navy blue
Animal:	Domesticated animals
Myths/Legends:	Demeter, Astraea, Hygeia
House:	Sixth
Opposite Sign:	Pisces
Flower:	Pansy
Key Word:	Discriminating

Positive Expression:	**Misuse of Energy:**
Analytical	Critical
Practical	Tedious
Skillful	Petulant
Thorough	Intolerant
Precise	Particular
Thoughtful	Skeptical

Virgo

Your Ego's Strengths and Shortcomings

You are the harvester, reaping the efforts of others and putting them to use for the good of all. It's a big task, and you make it your business to be competent because there's so much to be done. A person who's capable is always in demand.

Others see you as logical, intelligent, and perceptive. You are admired for your loyalty and dedication. However, you seldom reveal your earthy, sensual side or the passions that propel you. Your passion is for the purpose you feel within, to which you are completely devoted.

Just as you are precise in executing your duties, you are rigorous in maintaining your health. Whether it is because of your body's value as the vehicle of the soul or because stress gets to you at times, you are conscious of nutrition and fitness. You are more comfortable with activities where you work alone and measure progress against yourself than you are with competitive sports. You may be drawn to routines that include relaxation, such as yoga or the martial arts.

Taken to extremes, these qualities can be hard on you. Your perceptiveness can become criticism; your practical efficiency can become unfeeling logic. Your concern for quality can become perfectionism and engender anxiety. You may also unconsciously stifle your gifts because you feel unprepared to live up to others' imagined standards. What's more, you may shy away from the limelight because it could reveal what you fear the most—not being good enough. An objective comparison of your own efforts to those of others will show you how extraordinarily talented you are.

Shining Your Love Light

No matter what your age, there is something of the purest maiden in your nature, and a part of you which belongs to no one but yourself, no matter how close you become to another. In your modesty, you may fail to see what you have to offer another in a relationship. This could lead you to be shy, to repress the expression of your true nature when you are around others whom you admire. Others may fail to see the real you.

Those who understand the low-key nature of your way of loving are likely to have the other signs of the earth element in their make-up—Taurus and Capricorn—or Virgo itself. Like you, they will share your appreciation of work as an expression of love and will honor your loyalty and stability.

With Aries, you will find yourself stimulated to act instead of just analyze, but you may find the lack of persistence annoying. Taurus will inspire you to build castles in the sky, and they may actually become a reality with your mutual gifts of manifestation. You'll have loads of fun matching wits with Gemini, but it will be a challenge keeping up with the changeling aspects of this sign's personality. Cancer is your match in loyalty and caring, and can make friendship take on a new meaning. You can share secret delights with Leo, who brings out the light in you, but you may find the need for social interaction tiring at times. Another Virgo will be naturally appreciative of your quest for excellence, but you'll have to find ways to spice up your life together to keep routine from overwhelming you.

You'll enjoy the airy heights of intimacy with Libra, but you may having difficulty bringing this sign's head-trip down to earth. Scorpio knows how to unlock your secret passions, hidden away only for those who deserve your love. Sagittarius will find a warm place by your hearth but may not want to stay long enough to satisfy you. Capricorn knows the meaning of duty, honor, and responsibility—words that shine a light in your heart. Aquarius shares your delight in the mysteries of technology, but you may find the need for the love of humanity unsettling. Pisces, your opposite, draws you with utter fascination and shares your quest for spiritual truth, but this sign's visionary nature may leave no room for the manifestation of those dreams and ideals that you crave.

Making Your Place in the World

No matter what you do in life, it needs to be "quality," whatever that word means to you. It's not enough to do a mediocre job or to fulfill a role where only mediocrity is possible. You have to do something that allows you to rise to the heights of excellence. When you are given the freedom to really do your best you'll perform to a much higher standard than others usually expect of you. You may not notice this, though, since you are intent on the perfection you seek.

The natural warmth of your generous heart lends itself to fulfilling the needs of others. It's as if things are most worth doing when you are serving others. You could find this satisfaction in a number of careers: nursing, government service, nonprofit organizations, counseling, administration, or raising a family. You could choose something less conventional, such as holistic health or even astrology. The logical side of your nature could lead you into positions that emphasize mental precision, such as accounting, computer science, writing, or publishing. Wherever you wind up, you'll be the one quietly doing your job with quality and dependability.

Power Plays

You prefer to look at life in other terms than the power structures and struggles that exist around you. However, you may have found that ignoring power issues doesn't allow you to avoid them. What's more, you recognize that power is often a necessary side effect of accomplishing the goals you dream about. To accomplish great things, from rectifying a social injustice to caring for your family, you must often take on the trappings of power.

To you, power comes through competency: If you're skilled at what you do, you will be rewarded. This would be enough in a world full of Virgos, but in a realm where flash and noise override quiet strength your competency will be overlooked unless you can attract more attention. Underneath it all you are sometimes uneasy with power and the perks that accrue as a result. At these times you fear that you are not deserving enough, not good enough for these rewards. Since others are often more than willing to step into the breach, you may be passed over, even though you are more capable.

Once you accept power, however, you are likely to interpret its meaning in the best of ways—as responsibility. You have no delusions about the fact that power means work. In addition, your native ability to analyze difficulties and find solutions will make you an excellent person to have in the driver's seat in any enterprise.

Famous Virgos

Agatha Christie, Sean Connery, Colin Firth, Greta Garbo, Hugh Grant, Lenny Henry, Sophia Loren, John McCain, Jada Pinkett Smith, Lily Tomlin, Damon Wayans, Trisha Yearwood

The Year Ahead for Virgo

This is a year of endings and beginnings for you, Virgo. While we're all experiencing many new feelings and ideas, yours will be a wonderful new adventure. While the first half of the year will find you finalizing the efforts of the past eleven years, you'll discover that you have the Midas touch by summer's end. All this newness may test your delicate nerves, but this year will give you the keys to open doorways to fulfillment if you can stay on the path.

Jupiter will move on August 27 from Leo into your own sign. Until then you will experience the sweet swan song of an ending cycle, tying up the loose ends of the past eleven years. During this completion and integration time you may enjoy being alone so you can more deeply understand the past and dream the future. Your spirituality will assume a greater significance for you, and you will rededicate yourself to the inner purpose you feel even as you refine your perspective on it. A new, exciting area of study may consume you, and you may spend long hours poring over your latest library find. Most important, you will get in touch with your secret self, which you may find is happiest when you dare to express the true you. Once Jupiter enters Virgo (and the Mars retrograde damper goes away in late September), your life will light up like Times Square on New Year's Eve! People will notice you, see your potential. You're likely to have more opportunities than you can handle. Remembering that not every opportunity is right for you, with time you'll find that, like cream, the best new endeavors will rise to the top.

Saturn in Gemini over the past two-and-a-half years has led you to focus on your goals and has required hard work. It has brought its share of rewards, but it was a volatile place for you, so you've had your share of ups and downs. As it moves into Cancer in June, Saturn is more harmonious, and you will have access to the people you need to succeed. You'll finally be recognized for your diligence and quiet competency; you may be called upon to fulfill a more public function or given the opportunity to shine by popular demand. Chiron in your solar Fifth House suggests healing benefits can come from creative pursuits. It's okay to make mistakes—that's the source of some of the world's greatest creative works and inventions.

Uranus brings new excitement this year when it moves into Pisces on March 10. This will spice up your relationships and challenge you to find ways to kindle the flame with your partner to keep your connectedness evolving. Neptune is still creating physical sensitivity for you; take advantage of this by learning to read the signals your body is sending. If you can see this as the doorway to your spiritual side that it is, you'll gain the most profound treasures from the experience. By now you're used to Pluto's power plays—the ways that you seem to find yourself dealing with the most difficult aspects of the people closest to you. You're even learning to accept it with grace and wisdom when you end up on the "hot spot." Even though you anticipated the need for change, you are learning the most unexpected things—for instance, that you know what you're talking about and that it's not necessary to back down at the first sign of resistance from others.

The eclipses of 2003 will be a mixed bag for you. The ones in midyear 2002 brought up survival issues that you've not yet fully recovered from and capitalized on. The good news is that you have this entire year to work things out, and there are some stabilizing influences on the horizon.

If you were born from August 23 to 25, Uranus opposing your Sun could bring just the shake-up you need to accomplish your most hoped-for goals. It's a new energy, and a new life awaits you if you can dare to embrace it. Even if you've been thinking out of the box in recent months, the events of this year are likely to take you by surprise, especially from March 11 to September 27, because the way you expect things to go is no match for what actually happens.

This transit will bring many good changes to you in the long term, but dealing with its short-term effects can be challenging. The hardest for you, Virgo, is the effect it has on your nervous system, which will be more fragile during this time. Counteract those effects by building in some time for fun, relaxation, physical activity, and meditation. It helps to remember that worry doesn't make things turn out better; it only blinds us to options.

This transit could involve separations, sometimes from those we love. Uranus challenges us to think on a higher plane, and to love there, too. It helps to remember that love is not limited by distance;

just because someone we love isn't with us now doesn't mean we can't love them or feel their love for us. Whatever emerges during this time will not be complete until the first half of 2004, so practice those virtues for which you are so well-known: patience and forbearance. Add to the mix a faith that things will work out in your favor, and you'll have the recipe for success!

If you were born from August 26 to September 6, Neptune is quincunxing your Sun this year. This influence will have a subtle effect, one that may be hard to pin down, not just because it's Neptune, the planet that dissolves boundaries, but also because the aspect is a quincunx. This means that you may experience a weakening of your normally steadfast resolve in accomplishing your goals as well as a slowing down of the time frame for those accomplishments. However, this is not as bad as it seems. When we become firmly affixed on a goal we can become hardened and resistant to adjustments that needs to be made. If we recall that all difficulties arise out of our own inability to go with the flow of life, we can see that Neptune will bring us the chance to adjust by giving us the time to pause and reconsider. Chances are good that you will gain great advantage from this necessary hiatus in your path to accomplishment. During this time you may feel your vitality level fluctuate. You may be sensitive to foods, sounds, scents, or psychic energies. Spiritually, it is a good time to become better acquainted with your inner reality, although the perception of "busy-ness" due to the adjustments you feel you must make in your everyday life could have you making excuses. Finding the time for inner work will be well worth it.

If you were born from September 7 to 15, Pluto squaring your Sun signals that the transformations you've anticipated are finally upon you. You have been waiting, perhaps without knowing it, half hoping that the situations that need to change will somehow magically disappear or transform overnight. This is because the areas that need changing will require colossal upheaval in our lives, and we are usually unwilling to take it on until it is thrust upon us. This is the role of Pluto. So chances are you know what it is and you've seen it coming, but the courage to take it on has eluded you until now. With Pluto, the changes may come from the outer world, or you may just decide that living with things as they are is more painful than the transformation would be. Either way, your experiences will be mesmerizing. Whatever happens, you will find your life renewed, and your outlook invigorated. Although you are not normally one to love the new and exciting, it's high time to accept some of it in your life. Pluto doesn't bring its effects quickly; generally, you can expect its shift to take two years to complete, and even then you'll be adjusting for years to come—but in a good way. Even if some of the challenges you face are unpleasant in the short run, in the long run, you will be stronger, more resilient, and have a life more in balance with the truth of who you really are.

If you were born from September 16 to 22, Saturn is in the picture for you during 2003. Whatever else it is, Saturn means work, and this is something you're very good at. The trouble is, though, that you may already be maxed out, since work is often Virgo's solution to everything. In that case, you have to find ways to curtail your less-meaningful efforts. Find what is not working for you and eliminate it; set boundaries on what you will and won't do for others; increase the efficiency of what you decide to take on. Saturn shows us that when we do the work we get the rewards—maybe not right away, but over time. Slow development, Saturn's domain, is robust and stays with us once gained. This is also a time to reconsider things we began about twenty-one years ago. They reached a culmination seven years ago, and for the past seven years we've been reaping rewards. Now it is time to see the deeper significance of those accomplishments, to find in them someday the seed for the future. For now, these accomplishments will continue to reward you, and you will be focused on sustaining the reward period for as long as possible.

If you were born from September 20 to 22, you will be experiencing the quincunx of Uranus to your Sun. This could find you feeling off balance and out of step with the "real you." It can be a wake-up call, one that reminds you to pay attention to what can go wrong, to create a "Plan B." Chances are you'll be wanting to make some adjustments in your plans for the future, to shore up your preparations or perhaps develop a few new skills. No matter what you do, even your Plan B may need to be adapted slightly as circumstances emerge. Above all else, don't give in to impatience. Think long-term with this transit—it will be seven years until you experience a culmination in relation to your efforts. Don't be disheartened in the meantime. Some things are meant to come to fruition sooner than that, but the things that are on the seven-year arc will benefit by patient and persistent development. This can also be a time when health matters arise, or you may decide proactively to head off potential difficulties with your gift for understanding your physical body and its tendencies. This is excellent timing; such efforts can head off many future health issues that could come at a time that would otherwise bring unfettered joy and reward.

Tools for Change

Your body is a temple, and you know that the more you treat it that way, the better you are at being yourself. You are aware that all your roads to success begin with your own health. Because of this, you are likely to expend considerable thought and effort on finding the best way to approach your wellness through nutrition, exercise, and lifestyle patterns. You try to find the right balance between fun, work, and health routines.

One of the overlooked aspects of health in our culture can have devastating consequences for you, Virgo, and that's the need to relax, have fun, and find peace within. It is the thing you need the most, and, ironically, it may be the thing you think of the least. Science and culture are beginning to acknowledge the role that stress plays in our lives and our health. Recent research has shown that high cortisol levels, arising from stress, play a major role in all degenerative diseases, as well as in weight gain and resistance to weight loss. Our cortisol won't be high if we are at peace with ourselves.

This is especially important to you, Virgo, because of your tendency to live in a constant state of low-level anxiety (stress) that eats away at your health, no matter how many good foods and exercise programs you engage in. For this reason you benefit as much, if not more, from relaxation programs and practices: meditation, breathing practices, aromatherapy, yoga, tai chi, and chi gung, to name a few. You will also benefit from therapies and substances that heal the emotions or reduce fear and anxiety, such as Bach flower remedies, psychotherapy, and relaxing massage treatments.

Just as important are the therapies we can provide ourselves through everyday activities, such as doing one thing at a time. When we "multitask" we take on more stress. This can be exciting and challenging, but it is important to be aware of the point when challenge becomes stress. Then it's time to back off or take a break. Sometimes simple daily rituals are the best therapies and the easiest to maintain: eating lunch in a quiet place as a moment of contemplation; drinking tea with a trusted friend; taking a deep breath before plunging in; a daily walk, meditation, or yoga routine. Other times, you will need others' help, but a daily relaxing routine can do a great deal to set you on your path eagerly and energetically—your path to success and fulfillment!

♍

Affirmation for the Year

I find time for myself every day.

Virgo/January

In the Spotlight

You worked just as hard last month as ever for those you love most, and you deserve a break. Your larger tasks may lurk in the background, but that shouldn't prevent you from taking time to play.

Wellness and Keeping Fit

Make your activities a foray into the unexpected and you'll find just the spice you need to sustain your interest. Give your digestion a break from holiday sweets and fats, or you may find yourself slowed down by the virus of the month.

Love and Life Connections

If it seems like last month's bubble has burst, it's just the inevitable ups and downs of love. The "rough spot" that comes up on or after January 1 will show you how true this is and hint at a deeper issue hidden in impetuous words. If you've misunderstood or misspoken, apologize, forgive yourself, and let it go. What's underneath will surface around January 26 and again during February. Accept it in the short run. True love will overcome all in the long run.

Finance and Success

It's not the right time to stop all actions and negotiations, but it is definitely the time for caution. From January 1 to 23 watch for hidden agendas and unconscious factors in any agreements you're inclined to make. Make sure that you read every contract in all its fine print during this time. The way is much clearer for all business and financial transactions after January 23, but best after January 26.

Cosmic Insider Tip

Practicality has its limits and whimsy its wisdom. Let humor lighten your feelings of being flawed. This will allow you to continue with the big and noble tasks that you value so much. Next month will find you naturally industrious.

Rewarding Days 2, 3, 12, 13, 17, 18, 21, 22, 25, 30, 31

Challenging Days 1, 6, 7, 8, 14, 15, 27, 28

Affirmation of the Month I am patient with myself and others.

Virgo/February

In the Spotlight

In February you will find your mind returning gradually to your projects, although you are not whole-heartedly into it until February 12. Intense events through February 20 may distract you from your preferred activities. Attending to what's happening on the home front but still taking time to smell the flowers will keep you in balance.

Wellness and Keeping Fit

This is a good time to firm up your resolve regarding your approach to health and fitness. Don't forget to create a "Plan B" to use when your day doesn't go the way you expect it to. Remember to accentuate the positive in your approach: Focus on what you can do, not what you don't want to do.

Love and Life Connections

The time for redecorating (yourself or your home) is over. Now it's time for some fun and romance! Don't fall into that "I'm not good enough" routine to excuse yourself from engaging in life. You won't benefit from it, and neither will anyone else. It's okay to bring him or her home.

Finance and Success

Resist the urge to hit the panic button the first part of the month. You may feel as though you are in a tight spot, especially February 1 through 5. After February 22 you'll be on firmer ground and better prepared to take the contemplated big steps. Let them arise from your rational side, not your fears.

Cosmic Insider Tip

You're working hard, you're deserving, but it's not the right time yet. Let the rhythms of life bring rewards to you in their own time. Trust that it will come and don't try to rush things. You'll start to see results in a few weeks.

Rewarding Days 8, 9, 13, 14, 17, 18, 21, 22, 25, 26, 27

Challenging Days 3, 4, 10, 11, 23, 24

Affirmation of the Month I accept the flow of life.

Virgo/March

In the Spotlight

This is the time for action, when the things you started around your birthday will begin to take on a life of their own. Your power runs high around March 10, but you will miss it in the stress of the moment unless you can stand back from yourself and see the responsibility that the situation implies.

Wellness and Keeping Fit

Your resolve is good, and the effects of changes you've made begin to take effect. Progress begins to show after March 4, so don't let your social calendar pull you away from the plans you've been following. Engage in social sports to blend the best of both worlds.

Love and Life Connections

By March 2, after having fun last month, you think you're ready to go back to the familiar grind refreshed and renewed. However, your feet are still finding the door every time you have an excuse. Go ahead—explore, climb a few rocks! Friends, family, and lovers all give you energy this month. Build on love bonds (re-)energized in the last days of 2002. Time enough to work another day.

Finance and Success

You've been wanting to take the plunge on something, but you're right to be cautious. Your urge is to throw caution to the wind—to do something. Wait: Opportunities will be better by June. In the meantime, lay your foundation and build toward the time when you encounter just the right thing.

Cosmic Insider Tip

Moments of intensity are like waves. They come and they go. When one gets to us, we ride it the best we can. When it's over, we need to take a breather before the next wave reaches us. This month has a few waves for you, Virgo. Take each one as it comes.

Rewarding Days 7, 8, 12, 13, 17, 18, 21, 22, 25, 26

Challenging Days 2, 3, 9, 10, 11, 23, 24, 29, 30, 31

Affirmation of the Month I am the water, not the wave.

Virgo/April

In the Spotlight
Money is in the spotlight this month for you, Virgo, whether it's yours or someone else's. Multiple planetary forces come together on your behalf, bringing opportunities—if you can allow yourself to accept them. This is also a good time for re-establishing contact with your spiritual side or picking up your studies of life's mysteries.

Wellness and Keeping Fit
Use gentle approaches to balance your emotional side, which will be surfacing this month: Yoga, hiking in remote locales, and meditation will keep you going strong. This is especially important near and after April 26.

Love and Life Connections
Relationships continue to be important to you this month, though in a more businesslike, results-oriented way. Your natural loyalty needs loyalty from others, and so you crave commitment, even if it's of the mildest form. You like to know where you stand. Money issues could arise as well and need clarification.

Finance and Success
Some ideas and opportunities come together for you this month, perhaps "out of the blue." This illustrates the universal law that our efforts produce results indirectly, not tit for tat. Finances should especially improve if you can meet your benefactors halfway. So go ahead, let providence open the door.

Cosmic Insider Tip
Your success comes in realizing that there's more to it than skill and hard work. Success also involves "people skills." This means communicating about who you are (public relations) and smiling once in a while.

Rewarding Days 3, 4, 5, 8, 9, 10, 13, 14, 17, 18, 21, 22

Challenging Days 6, 7, 19, 20, 26, 27

Affirmation of the Month I accept the avenues of success and financial gain that open up to me.

Virgo/May

In the Spotlight

You're reaching toward your goals, searching for just the right places to put your energies, and the planets are cooperating. The time is right to put your plans into action during the first two weeks. The way is likely to get foggy around midmonth, however. If you find your motivation flagging and your efforts stymied then, it's all part of the plan. Action will resume after May 20.

Wellness and Keeping Fit

Even if you're not into long-distance running, you'll find yourself wanting to get away from it all this month. Combining this need for retreat with your fitness routine creates the kind of dovetail of purpose that you're famous for. Get thee to the woods, smell the pine, and see the flowers.

Love and Life Connections

The way others are behaving around you may create a crisis for them, but that doesn't mean it has to be that way for you. What use is it if everyone is out of sorts? Sympathizing doesn't mean that you are obligated to go there, too. Keep your chin up and discern the part you've played in their scenario.

Finance and Success

The business and financial hurdles of the past are gone. The new prospects are still in the womb of time. Let things be, for now. It's okay to coast on follow-through. Your new mantra: Work is not always the most important thing in my life.

Cosmic Insider Tip

A time of confusion is not a time to act. Although our culture thinks we should be productive all the time, that's not the way it works. Allowing yourself peaks and valleys of creativity and production allows you to act in clarity and get more bang for the buck.

Rewarding Days 1, 2, 5, 6, 7, 10, 11, 15, 18, 19, 20, 28, 29

Challenging Days 3, 4, 16, 17, 23, 24

Affirmation of the Month Let it flow.

Virgo/June

In the Spotlight
Great energy contains great potential, so, if you can experience events as exciting rather than stressful, you'll make great strides toward your most cherished goals. Learn to set priorities and let go of finished products before they're your brand of perfect.

Wellness and Keeping Fit
Discretion is the better part of valor in exercise and fitness this month. Carelessness or overextending yourself may end up in injury around June 7, 14, or 21. High stress levels may require a little more focus on health routines and finding ways to relax.

Love and Life Connections
A sea change has been brewing from inside you, erupting into your awareness with increasing frequency since March 10. It's about the need for growth in the way you relate to those around you. It will awaken in you more strongly this month, especially from June 1 through 21, but you may not as yet know where to take it. Be patient with yourself and let your awareness evolve. The hurdles you face didn't develop overnight, and it will take time to unravel them.

Finance and Success
The challenges of relationships extend into business and work as well. Don't be drawn into deals for the sake of expediency or the promise of unearned reward. Others sense your vulnerability now and want to take advantage of it, particularly around June 7, 14, and 21. Pacts formed June 22 to 26 are more constructive and supportive of your efforts, those on June 24 to 26 especially so.

Cosmic Insider Tip
A time of confusion is not a time to act. When we feel clear, the way clears for us. Clarity and focus will begin to resurface June 22, but it will be a "work in progress" until after November 8.

Rewarding Days 2, 3, 7, 8, 11, 12, 15, 16, 24, 25, 26, 29, 30

Challenging Days 1, 13, 14, 19, 20, 21, 27, 28

Affirmation of the Month I benefit from what life brings to me.

Virgo/July

In the Spotlight

You know how valuable your circle of friends and acquaintances is to you, and you'll have some chances to increase its range this month. The greatest benefits come early. As Mars slows in the last half of July your frustrations with others may mount. Choose to look at what you have, not what you don't have.

Wellness and Keeping Fit

Whether it's cycling or going to the gym, things go better with a friend—just don't get carried away by your friend's pace or the social whirlwind you could find yourself in this month. Set your own pace and keep your energy high by getting sleep and eating for nutrition.

Love and Life Connections

You may wonder what you did to deserve the responses you're getting lately. Sometimes we are just in the wrong place at the wrong time, but if there's a history you've contributed to, your natural humility will help you through. Be mindful of your tendency to accept responsibility for what is not yours. It does no one any good if you do, but you don't have to feel obligated to broadcast it either.

Finance and Success

Finally, the gates of heaven open! Or have they? Remember, this is the physical world, the one with the obstacles and challenges. Your new ideas are basically good, but they have to be refined. You'll get to do that in August and September. In the meantime, put out those feelers. There'll be some "no" answers, but the "yes" answers will show you where to go next.

Cosmic Insider Tip

You don't have to rush to rectify a problem situation. Wait and see how it works itself out. Sometimes we find it isn't even ours to fix. In this way, we have a chance to develop clarity.

Rewarding Days 4, 5, 8, 9, 12, 13, 21, 22, 23, 26, 27, 28, 31

Challenging Days 10, 11, 17, 18, 24, 25

Affirmation of the Month I can let things develop their own way.

Virgo/August

In the Spotlight

As your yearly cycle ends, you can enter the new cycle with a clean slate and renewed clarity if you give yourself a chance to clean it all up. The feeling of organization is invigorating, and the work will distract you from the obstacles everyone is experiencing at this time. When the bar is set higher at the end of the month you'll be ready.

Wellness and Keeping Fit

Stay aware of your body—particularly your feet. Just as important is keeping your stress level in balance. You can choose to let go of stress by allowing yourself to admit to and make mistakes.

Love and Life Connections

It's nearly time to let go. You know it's coming, that it has to happen. It's a natural part of life, a healthy step for everyone, and you can't imagine doing anything different. Put it aside for now; enjoy the swan song while it lasts. Don't make the wound bigger by dwelling on it. And you wouldn't dream of trading this time for not having had the experience at all.

Finance and Success

You're in the clear until August 9, so make changes in your portfolio before then. Business ventures, stock picks, and contracts are likely to be sources of reconsideration, even regret, if they are initiated after that time (until September 27). Resist the urge to make sudden changes from August 9, even if you have to sit on your hands.

Cosmic Insider Tip

By keeping your eyes on the prize, you'll make it over the inevitable bumps in the road. You'll find it easier to be at your best, and you very much want to be there now. You will adjust, and when it's all over you'll have the satisfaction of having done well.

Rewarding Days 1, 4, 5, 9, 10, 18, 19, 23, 24, 27, 28

Challenging Days 6, 7, 8, 13, 14, 20, 21, 22

Affirmation of the Month A bright future is unfolding from my present experiences.

Virgo/September

In the Spotlight

Life springs eternal, and it's the nectar of the gods for you now. Hang in there, it's getting better! Your new "normal" will be better than before.

Wellness and Keeping Fit

Go easy on yourself. Gentle movement and just the right high-quality foods are the ticket for you now. When you can't do more, meditate. (And when you *can* do more, meditate.) Spending time with people you love is a healing all by itself. Do what you need.

Love and Life Connections

The time for letting go is here. You've put on your brave face to get through it, but others need more from you. They need to know your pain so that they can express theirs as well. Remember, this is only a new beginning, life in a new form. You'll all adjust. Allow yourself and other loved ones your small comforts. Don't lie about what's real, and it will pass sooner.

Finance and Success

With all the distractions, finances may seem unimportant, yet in spite of it all you will notice the stirrings of new ideas around you. Against all probability people are showing an interest in you. It's okay to press the "Pause" button. New enterprises will develop from some of these seed thoughts, but you can wait until you're feeling better. In fact, it's probably best to back-burner any large efforts until after September 27.

Cosmic Insider Tip

A big transformation promises a big new beginning, and renewal builds upon renewal. Although it started August 28, you'll really feel it as we put distance between ourselves and September 27.

Rewarding Days 1, 2, 5, 6, 14, 15, 19, 20, 24, 25, 28, 29

Challenging Days 3, 4, 9, 10, 11, 16, 17, 18, 30

Affirmation of the Month There is no arrival without departure, no departure without return.

Virgo/October

In the Spotlight

Your new year is off with a bang, Virgo! Now it's time to ground your new ideas into action. This is still the investigative stage, so do what you love. Find facts! Analyze! Those around you will love it, and you'll feel the full force of their appreciation. Don't forget to ask for a fair exchange if you're doing work for someone else.

Wellness and Keeping Fit

It's time to reaffirm your commitment to your "Plan A" fitness regimen. You'll probably need to tweak it a little, because you have new freedoms and a different time schedule.

Love and Life Connections

Surrounding yourself with beauty is one way to bring the balance you crave into your life right now. Buying fresh flowers, filling that empty wall with photos, or seeing the latest art exhibit with a friend will help you to tap into your creativity. Deep discussions over latte are more appealing after October 9. The sweet joy of companionship can deepen to love now.

Finance and Success

Don't bite off more than you can chew this month. You are feeling extra optimistic now, but don't let that override your natural common sense. Let that confidence out just enough to take small risks in new areas. After the new enterprises have proven themselves, you can reach for the fruit on the skinny branches.

Cosmic Insider Tip

Whew! That was a close one! You made it through. Life goes on, and there's lots to look forward to. Your new, unburdened feeling gives you the energy to take advantage of opportunities this month. Let go of your guilty feelings—this is not about atonement, it's about getting what you deserve.

Rewarding Days 2, 3, 11, 12, 13, 16, 17, 18, 21, 22, 25, 26, 29, 30

Challenging Days 1, 7, 8, 14, 15, 27, 28

Affirmation of the Month Wonderful opportunities surround me.

Virgo/November

In the Spotlight

If you're reaching out, wanting to learn, you're right in tune. The eclipses on November 8 and 23 emphasize the theme of reaching for what you want. You'll still want to stick close to home sometimes, even though life begins to call you further afield.

Wellness and Keeping Fit

In your excitement over the new prospects in your life, don't ignore your body. Jupiter transits sometimes bring weight gain, but you can turn that into physical activity and greater health. Even if weather or out-of-routine plans prohibit outdoor activities, turn your current four walls into a gymnasium for a few minutes every day.

Love and Life Connections

After the summer of discontent, love is slow to get on its feet. However, it is gaining momentum. You're in a new playing field now, and the rules are different. Enjoy the company of long-time, trusted friends and family until you feel like coming out of your cocoon in a couple of months.

Finance and Success

Here's something you can talk about with excitement! Projects are blossoming like so many flowers. Eventually, you'll have to prune and thin them, for you can't cultivate them all. For now, they're all of equal strength and possibility, so enjoy the excitement of pure potential while it lasts. This is a great month for making solid investments if you're in the market.

Cosmic Insider Tip

Lots of activity this month energizes instead of exhausts you because you're working on exciting projects. Could it be that, when something tires you out, it's time to phase it out? If this isn't practical, change its form or your approach to it.

Rewarding Days 8, 9, 13, 14, 18, 19, 22, 23, 26, 27

Challenging Days 3, 4, 10, 11, 12, 24, 25, 30

Affirmation of the Month It's time to reach for the stars.

Virgo/December

In the Spotlight
A cozy chair, a warm fire, a steaming cup of tea, and a good book—these will fill your heart and replenish you for the year ahead. You could almost enjoy being bored, but fortunately life and the planets won't let you rest. It's another exciting month, but you thrive on it.

Wellness and Keeping Fit
In spite of holiday events, you may find that it's relatively easy to live a healthy lifestyle. You'll want to change some of your old patterns after December 17, but it's just your eternal efforts at self-improvement at work. Some new insights assist you.

Love and Life Connections
Yes, there's lots to keep you home, but once you set foot outside the door you'll be glad you went. There's a lot of life happening out there, and you won't know what you're missing unless you go. The potential for romance runs high around December 11.

Finance and Success
Your prospects are looking extremely good this month, and it's tempting to act as if nothing can go wrong. The dangers of over-commitment and overconfidence may reveal themselves around December 10 and 12. The key is, if something sounds too good to be true, it usually is. There are, however, more reasonable propositions that, although less exciting, are likely to be efforts you can sustain over the bumps in the road.

Cosmic Insider Tip
Allow yourself to stay home when it suits you. We all need "downtime." It will give you the chance to get in touch with the inner you, and you'll be rejuvenated when you feel like stepping outside your door again. In the meantime, enjoy that long, steamy bath and evening behind a facial mask.

Rewarding Days 5, 6, 10, 11, 15, 16, 19, 20, 23, 24

Challenging Days 1, 7, 8, 9, 21, 22, 27, 28, 29

Affirmation of the Month It's okay for me to pamper myself.

VIRGO ACTION TABLE

These dates reflect the best—but not the only—times for success and ease in these activities, according to your Sun sign.

	JAN	FEB	MAR	APR	MAY	JUN	JUL	AUG	SEPT	OCT	NOV	DEC
Move											13-30	1, 2
Start a class										16-31	1-4	
Join a club						29, 30	1-29					
Ask for a raise								23-31	1-15			
Look for work		12-28	1-21			13-28						
Get pro advice	6-8	3, 4	2, 3, 29-31		23, 24	19, 20	16-18	13, 14		6-8	3, 4, 30	1, 27-29
Get a loan	9, 10	6, 7	4-6		26, 27	22, 23	19, 20	15-17		9, 10	5-7	2-4
See a doctor		13-28	1-21				14-31	1-27	20-30	1-6		
Start a diet		13-28	1-4					12				
End relationship									10			
Buy clothes	23-31	1-28	1, 2	23, 24								
Get a makeover							30, 31	1-27	21-30	1-7		
New romance		5-28	1, 2									
Vacation	11-13	8, 9	7, 8	3-25, 30	1, 2, 17-31	1-12, 24, 25	21-23	18, 19	14, 15	11-13	7-9	5, 6

LIBRA

The Balance
September 23 to October 23

Element:	Air
Quality:	Cardinal
Polarity:	Yang/Masculine
Planetary Ruler:	Venus
Meditation:	I balance conflicting desires.
Gemstone:	Opal
Power Stones:	Tourmaline, kunzite, blue lace agate
Key Phrase:	I balance
Glyph:	Scales of justice, setting sun
Anatomy:	Kidneys, lower back, appendix
Color:	Blue, pink
Animal:	Brightly plumed birds
Myths/Legends:	Venus, Cinderella, Hera
House:	Seventh
Opposite Sign:	Aries
Flower:	Rose
Key Word:	Harmony

Positive Expression:	Misuse of Energy:
Impartial	Self-absorbed
Artistic	Remote
Poised	Indecisive
Logical	Critical
Objective	Thoughtless
Cultured	Argumentative

Libra

Your Ego's Strengths and Shortcomings

Yours is the energy of grace and civility, Libra. All that we call the highest forms of civilization are your domain. You are the glue that holds society together. Your inspiration formed the fine arts, music, literature, and the pure sciences, for it is only in a sophisticated and peaceful society that these things can be practiced, that creativity can be given its wings.

While this may not be a fashionable approach to life in the current "nice guys finish last" culture, you are the ones to hold the vision of less-violent times until others understand the value of what they've lost (or perhaps never had). You are likely to be strongly anticrime and antiwar, just as you are anticonflict in your personal life. Peace and harmony are what make you tick, and you create them as much as possible wherever you go. When they are nowhere in evidence, you suffer intellectually as well as personally for their lack.

Personal relationships are often very important to Libra. The sunset is more magnificent when there's someone there to watch it with you. This can make you an expert negotiator, but it can also make you want to submit to others rather than assert yourself and risk losing their love. Being too tied to companionship can also limit you if you feel a need to wait to do things until there's someone else to do them with.

Just as Libra seeks harmony and balance in relationships and art, you may also seek these qualities in a more abstract form. Many Libras are as pleased by the symmetry of a chemical compound or the laws of physics as they are by the sweep and balance of a great painting or a beautiful ballet. From the flow of freeway traffic to the polyphony of a Bach fugue, you can find the harmony in all things.

Shining Your Love Light

The greatest mystery in the world for you is the mystery of another person. You love nothing better than to explore another person's psyche and find out what makes him or her tick, to share intimately in his or her experiences. You want to see the world not just with your own eyes but with the eyes of your beloved. It takes practice and discipline to maintain your sense of self when you love to get lost in another's personality so much.

Your easiest matches are with the other signs of the air element, Gemini and Aquarius, since they approach the world with the mind, just as you do. Aries, your opposite sign, has a strong sense of self—a model for you in developing the balance of self and other in your own personality. Taurus has a similar regard for beauty and grace, but the earthier approach is not your style. You can really understand Gemini's sociable way of sharing information, and feel very comfortable. Cancer shares your interest in intimacy, but they may be more interested in extending it through a family group, and not just with a partner, as you do. Leo's focus on creativity and social interaction is very much like your own, and feels supportive. Virgo's logical approach appeals, but you don't share this sign's concern for efficiency and technique. Another Libra will share your interest in finding the divine in each other, but it may be hard to decide who's leading whom. Scorpio's emotional intensity clashes with your intellectual approach—you just don't have the taste for so much Sturm and Drang. Sagittarius can lift your spirits and ideals to new heights, but may not stay long enough to satisfy you. Capricorn may erect barriers to the intimacy you crave, but if you're willing to be patient it will be worth the wait. Aquarius loves to relate, but may not want to get as close as you do, as busy as these signs are with their groups and organizations. Pisces's creative vision of the world may entice you but be too far into the ethers for your mental approach.

Making Your Place in the World
Your life is ruled by balance, and you will unconsciously seek a career that will allow you to create balance through your efforts— even if it is just as a background factor. You could balance people through counseling or therapy, especially with couples or families. You could balance sounds by being a musician or sound technician. You may balance elements by being a chemist, or you may create harmony in numbers via mathematics.

The arts are also a place of significant expression for you. Librans often manifest their sense of color and harmony through such media as painting, drawing, illustration, sculpture, textiles, or clay.

You can create through graphic design, interior decoration and design, architecture, CGI, or feng shui. Other pursuits could be beauty or fashion makeovers, hair styling and manicures, or fashion consulting. Whatever you do, remember to take care of yourself. It may be too easy to think only of the other person and ignore your own needs.

Power Plays

Although you shy away from conflict and prefer not to think about power, the use of it is nonetheless a vital part of your nature. You would just as soon avoid power struggles, and so you like power issues to be in the background. The trouble is, power is still there, and if it is not out in the open, others may perceive you as manipulative—even though nothing could be further from the truth.

Your true power lies in the ability to see the divine in the things around you. Whether it is a book, a painting, a building, or a person, when you see the pure spirit within them you bring it out in the open. When you see the beauty in an object, you begin to respond to it by harmonizing with the colors and shapes, and so create positive energy around you. This process, called harmonic induction, is the way that all healing takes place. You bring out the positive energy in people when you recognize it, because that reinforces the energy in them. What's more, it uplifts both you and them by the same phenomenon of harmonic induction.

Famous Librans

Michael Andretti, Sylvia Browne, Neve Campbell, Truman Capote, Elizabeth Dennehy, Dwight D. Eisenhower, Janeane Garofalo, Walter Matthau, Melina Mercouri, Kevin Sorbo, Sting, Stevie Ray Vaughan, Christine Todd Whitman, Oscar Wilde, Kate Winslet

The Year Ahead for Libra

The year 2003 will bring just enough change to keep you interested in life, Libra. This will be a time of both intellectual and social expansion, creativity, and personal achievement.

Jupiter moves through Leo and Virgo this year, your solar Eleventh and Twelfth houses. The first half of the year will continue your efforts at increasing the size of your network. You may see some rewards and recognition come your way for your hard work and generosity over the past eleven years. Once Jupiter enters Virgo in August you may find yourself more inwardly directed. This is a good time for reflection, a sabbatical, or just a time to study the things you've had to put off during the past few active years. Whether you know it or not, you're preparing for a new phase, a new initiative which will last twelve years. However, now it's time to integrate the last twelve-year cycle into your consciousness and consolidate your base. It will be the springboard from which you launch your new plans next year, so don't rush into the future. Taking time now to look back and to know yourself may seem out of character, but we all need "downtime" to rejuvenate.

Saturn in Gemini has been very good to you. Even when others were struggling, you've been able to see the big picture, to use its structure to make progress in fulfilling your goals. Saturn has also helped you to see yourself as equal to others whom you might have revered in the past. This is not iconoclasm, it's just seeing your own strengths and talents. When Saturn enters Cancer in June you will experience more challenge, but that doesn't mean you will be worse off. Far from it: You will find that your efforts are bringing you to a pinnacle in your career. While there are certain challenges ahead—due primarily to the unfamiliarity of the heady realms you now inhabit—you are likely to enjoy the ride if you can set aside your fears of the unfamiliar. This may also mean striking out on your own—disagreeing, even breaking, with others. Sometimes it is lonely at the top. Still, this is a time to stand on your own feet, not rely on others. If you insist on depending on others, you will find the next three years more difficult, because there will be someone who is happy to run your life. With Chiron in Capricorn, you may be noticing all the flaws and weaknesses of your family and wishing you could bury them in your past. If you can overcome your fears of confrontation and talk to them, you may be able to bury the hatchet instead.

In March, Uranus contributes to the sea change in your life by moving into Pisces. This means that the ripple of awakening shifts from the realms of creativity and play to the arena of health and lifestyle. Don't be surprised if you find that it's not enough to live a life of fun and games anymore. There are most serious matters, and it will dawn on you, perhaps unpleasantly, that your body is worth being treated more like a temple than a trash heap. The initial wake-up call can be startling, but that doesn't mean you are powerless to effect changes. Think of it as the beginning of the new you! Neptune is still safely helping you build a world of fantasy, and you may find that your imagination continues to fuel you in helpful—even spiritual—ways. Pluto continues to transform your mind and your understanding of the world, so you may find yourself being less willing to speak without forethought. Sometimes silence is the most eloquent message we can give. You know that words and thoughts are power, so you are less likely to squander them.

We have been in much the same eclipse pattern since mid-2002. The eclipses this year are more purely about building stability, or making sure we don't throw the baby out with the bath water when we do make a change. Typically these eclipses create resistance to change, but that can sometimes make us want it all the more. Your values and finances will change during the coming year, or at least you will want them to.

If you were born from September 23 to 27, Uranus will quincunx your Sun this year from your solar Sixth House. This suggests that mischief is afoot in your workplace, health, and daily routines. You may get some unexpected and possibly unpleasant surprises in these areas. However, it is far worse to bury your head in the sand, because whatever you're hiding from won't disappear. You'll just be unprepared for what comes up, and you will have fewer opportunities to direct the energy in ways you want it to manifest. What's worse, delaying the effects will only make them more intense. You can balance the negative effects of this transit by being responsible in the areas affected. Make sure that you stick to the routine of your job and do your work well. Get a thorough health checkup and adjust your lifestyle according to what you find. This may involve changing your diet, exercise routine, and ways of responding to the stresses of life (meditation, recreation, taking time off, etc.). You may find that you feel especially restless now and want some changes. You may feel as though it's time to leave your job, even though there are many good things about it. No matter what, there are two basic factors to be aware of under this aspect. First, anything that you consider to be a problem has both good and bad aspects to it, so it will be more difficult to make decisions. Second, waiting until you're clear about what you want to do often brings a better result, since we often act too quickly under a quincunx.

If you were born from September 23 to October 7, Saturn will square your Sun from your solar Tenth House starting June 4. This heralds a time when you will be challenged, but the potential for accomplishment and success is very good. You may be called upon to take greater responsibility in your business or career, possibly without an increase in pay. You may be given more authority, or, depending on your circumstances, have to deal with a different authority in your own life. This may mean that you have a new boss or you have to deal in some way with institutions of government or religion that require you to submit to someone else's control. You may feel stifled under this aspect, and you may have to work very hard. However, if you do the work you will get the reward—not right away, but over the next five years. This actually begins the last quarter of a thirty-year cycle. It may help you to think back to what you've accomplished since 1982, when this cycle began. How you fare under this Saturn aspect depends a lot on how well you handle responsibility, especially for yourself, as a general rule. If you are good at it, and put good, solid effort into your endeavors, then by facing whatever arises honestly and proactively you will find this transit is very pleasant and carries some perks with it, since others will now recognize your abilities and adjust your status accordingly. If, however, you have made a habit of hiding from your obligations and haven't been too good at applying the elbow grease, you may find that the door is open this year for you to correct some past mistakes. Either way, focus and eager effort will go a long way toward making the most of this transit.

If you were born from October 2 to 7, Neptune will be trining your Sun from your solar Fifth House. If you are at all a creative type, this is the year to really indulge in your creative side. Even if you aren't, you may find some hidden talent by exploring this aspect of your nature. Music may be especially alluring because of the places it takes you. You may want to pursue leisure activities that have an element of the spiritual to them, such as hiking in the mountains, sailing, or photography. You may be drawn to the visual arts—anything from drawing and painting to photography and film. You may simply want to do things that bring more peace into your experiences. You may find yourself alone in these pursuits, but you will not be lonely, because your life will be filled with your inner experience in these moments. Of course, being Libra, you may find someone with whom you can engage in these activities, so the moments become shared experiences. This may also be a time when you find yourself inspired to create your life in a new way, since our life's path is our most important creative product. We could also find fulfillment through experiences we share with our children, which may be artistic, spiritual, or just plain fun.

If you were born from October 10 to 14, Pluto will be sextiling your Sun from your solar Third House this year. This gives you the opportunity to transform the things with which you come into close, daily contact. This can include the information you feed yourself (TV, radio, mail, magazines), the places you frequent on a regular basis (retail stores, your workplace, movie theaters, roadways), your neighborhood (neighbors, scenery, animals), and your extended family (especially siblings). Another constant companion comes to us in the form of the thoughts we have. While we have many original and creative thoughts relevant to the moment in which we have them, much of the time we engage in habitual thoughts—tapes that we run in our heads based on past experiences, whether or not they are helpful now. Habitual thoughts hold us back by preventing us from seeing a situation as it really is so that we can find an original solution to it. If you were to experience a change in any one of these areas, the transformation would be profound and far-reaching. Pluto can affect all of these areas and may do so by the time its transit is over. However, that does not mean that you will find this unpleasant. It may be exciting, even exhilarating. Often, we encounter changes in these areas by encountering something new that draws us away from our old pursuits and ways of thinking. We may decide to pick up a subject to study, whether taking a class or just reading a book. We may be drawn into a new circle of friends, discover a new place to shop, or find a new movie theater with more comfortable seats. If you are curious, you are likely to find this a highly satisfying time in your life, especially if you enjoy freeing your mind and making improvements in your daily activities.

If you were born from October 14 to 23, Saturn will trine your Sun from your solar Ninth House. This is a time when progress will be visible and easy for you to accomplish. You will have the satisfaction of seeing some of your aims fulfilled and the opportunity to move on to your next set of goals. This is likely to be a time of reaching out, exploring new realms, perhaps even traveling to unknown places. Or you could decide to learn something completely new—a new language, a unique skill that will set you apart in the workplace, or something that takes your mind into new levels of abstraction. This will be a relatively easy time for you, when your extra efforts bring visible benefits. However, sometimes when things are easy we tend to rest on our laurels rather than using them to take us to the next pinnacle. Since you have a peak coming in about two years, this is a good time to engage in meaningful enterprise—something that will bring new recognition and status when that pinnacle arrives. Of course, if you need the rest, take it, because you have had your struggles over the last five years. No matter what, you'll feel lighter and more carefree this year.

If you were born from October 19 to 23, Uranus will be trining your Sun from your solar Fifth House. This will put the spring in your step and the twinkle in your eye! This year could be just plain fun if you don't take unusually high risks in your efforts to find thrills. You may want to do something adventurous, even out-landish—bungee jumping, extreme sports, snowboarding, skydiving. That adrenaline rush will be especially enthralling to you now. If you are by nature into tamer pursuits (as most Libras are), you can channel this energy into anything else creative or active and different from what you usually do. Go to a museum or dance club you've never been to before. Attend the slug races in northern California. Go mountain hiking or do an AIDS walkathon. The sky's the limit at this time when, instead of thinking "why," you're thinking "why not?" The pitfalls of this aspect are generally mild if you are good at keeping your Libran balance: The risks you take could be just a little too high—an indiscrete relationship, gambling more than you can afford to lose, spending money you don't have on the cosmetic surgery you've always wanted or that expensive hand-embroidered silk dress. Just a modicum of caution will keep you in balance and make this one of the most fun years of your life!

Tools for Change

With Saturn and Uranus moving into less-harmonious signs for you this year, it's time to tackle some of the bigger issues that have become more noticeable in your life of late. You may find that you are discontented with your career—perhaps something about it is distinctly unhealthy for you. It may be the moment for a change, one that will take some time to achieve and require that you work harder for a while.

Since your inner drive is all about creating balance, you may find that balancing and harmonizing activities and therapies is just what you need. Polarity therapy helps to equalize both sides of the body and also strengthens the role of the nondominant (creative) side of the brain. Chinese medicine is especially appropriate for you, with its focus on balance. Ageless techniques applied through acupuncture, acupressure, and herbs bring equilibrium to your system and fortify the organs and functions associated with them.

You will also not want to neglect the need for physical fitness, since exercising the body brings it into better balance each day. You may find fitness tapes or classes, dance, yoga, and Pilates to be enjoyable enough for you to do them regularly. It is also important for you to get enough sleep and drink plenty of water to keep your chi strong. Your immune system may be supported via echinacea, schizandra, vitamins A and C, and B complex vitamins.

On a mental and spiritual level, practice in or experience of the arts can be uniquely uplifting. Music, whether listening or performing, brings vibrational resonance from the high, spiritual energies contained in good music. Drama, especially involving rich character development, will also have a healing quality for you.

You're also constantly aware of the need to center your attitude in order to maintain an optimistic outlook. You may find your ability to do so enhanced by studying the principles of Taoism, the science of balancing yin and yang. The I Ching is a way to stay in touch with the influences to which we are constantly subjected, and a way to help you remain neutral in the midst of their flow.

When you are in your center, you are stronger and more resilient. By supporting your own balance, you can bring harmony to others as well as accomplish your long-range goals.

≏

Affirmation for the Year

By staying centered, I accomplish my goals.

Libra/January

In the Spotlight

Your home environment, family, and private life need more attention this month. This may have an impact on finances or your ability to carry on as usual at work, especially between January 2 and 23. After January 20, your creative energies soar.

Wellness and Keeping Fit

Illness could be a factor in what you decide to do, as you will certainly be exposed to a virus when Mercury retrogrades from January 2 to 23. If you're caring for an ill family member, it's hard to stay clear of the bug, but try to get enough sleep and eat well to support your immune system.

Love and Life Connections

Your loved ones pull you home this month, perhaps through illness, or just because you've got a project going. There may be communication problems or necessary repairs that reduce the quality of the time you spend there, so try to reward yourself and those nearest you by going to a local diner or a community event. If the weather's foul, watching a movie or sharing a good read may be just the thing.

Finance and Success

Budgets—the balance of income versus expenses—may be on your mind early this month as you look over the holiday bills. These concerns dissipate after January 17, however, as you pay things off. After January 8, you may want to plan an outreach program, but don't embark upon it until after January 23, when Mercury goes direct. Others will hear you better. Commerce will pick up then as well.

Cosmic Insider Tip

As the Sun catches Neptune on January 30, dream your new visions for the year. This is the time to make resolutions that, even if you don't keep them, will shape your future and help your life to flow.

Rewarding Days 1, 4, 5, 14, 15, 18, 19, 20, 23, 24, 27, 28, 31

Challenging Days 2, 3, 9, 10, 16, 17, 29, 30

Affirmation of the Month I am healthy and fit.

Libra/February

In the Spotlight

The planets are much friendlier this month as they trine your Sun from your creative Fifth House. A culmination point for enterprises that were started last summer occurs on February 2, perhaps leading to the fulfillment of some dreams in the next three months.

Wellness and Keeping Fit

This is the right time to reorganize your health routines: Adjust the time and frequency of exercise, reaffirm your dietary plans, and develop new health and fitness options to hold your interest.

Love and Life Connections

Your social life revolves around your friends and family this month. You may have visiting relatives, or you might just want to hang around the house more than normal. Perhaps you'll travel short distances to visit your relations yourself. You may decide to entertain at home and invite family or friends over for dinner or throw a party. Communication difficulties clear up by February 12, unless deeper problems exist.

Finance and Success

February is especially good for outreach and marketing efforts. Send out those mailers, get on the phone, revamp your website. Your mind is working especially creatively after February 12. Give your imagination free rein to envision the way you'll develop your initiatives over the next six months. Work and fun are easy to combine, as your artistic side helps pave your path to success.

Cosmic Insider Tip

A new cycle of innovation and revelation begins on February 17. Listening to your intuition around this date will reveal what needs to change over the coming year, but the ways of getting there may be hard to fathom, because miraculous forces will be at work.

Rewarding Days 1, 2, 5, 6, 7, 10, 11, 12, 15, 16, 19, 20, 23, 24, 28

Challenging Days 8, 9, 13, 14, 25, 26, 27

Affirmation of the Month My imagination supports my success.

Libra/March

In the Spotlight

March's planets will draw you to concentrate your energy in work, health practices, and daily routines, perhaps with some unexpected results starting March 11. Your efforts produce more fruits from now until June, based on projects begun last June.

Wellness and Keeping Fit

With Uranus's ingress into Pisces on March 11, we begin a seven-year period when you'll be challenged to clear out ineffective work and lifestyle patterns. If you are unhappy with anything in your life, you will get the wake-up call from your body.

Love and Life Connections

Love is in the air this month, as you open your heart to the world. You are feeling especially drawn to share yourself with others, and this brings warm responses from the world at large. Let yourself go and enjoy a night or two on the town, as this is an excellent time to meet new people. If you have a partner, use this time to rebuild the romance in your relationship.

Finance and Success

Your hard work this month will be the foundation of future success. There may be some sudden changes in the workplace, presaging what is to come. It may be that the disruption that arises could continue for the foreseeable future. If so, don't hide your head in the sand. It will get much worse in the summer and fall before it gets better. Plan accordingly.

Cosmic Insider Tip

You will be sensitive to others' energies for the next seven years. You may want to get training from qualified professionals to help you understand and deal with others' emotional, mental, and psychic energies. You may even develop a career from it.

Rewarding Days 1, 9, 10, 11, 14, 15, 18, 19, 20, 23, 24, 27, 28

Challenging Days 4, 5, 6, 12, 13, 25, 26

Affirmation of the Month I tap the unseen forces of the universe.

Libra/April

In the Spotlight

Your sense of progress peaks around April 3, until it may seem like you're spinning your wheels by April 26. By taking a broad view of events, you'll weather the storm with little difficulty.

Wellness and Keeping Fit

Even though you'll have stressors this month, you'll have so much pent-up energy you feel like exploding by the end of the day. You can release it by engaging in a little competitive action with a friend—just enough to introduce a sense of play, release, and relaxation.

Love and Life Connections

Your social intelligence is high this month, and others are attracted to you. Romance is in the air, whether you're partnered or not. Your popularity is even greater than usual. You may feel like entertaining and making the social rounds, but don't overbook yourself at the end of the month, because you'll have other obligations then.

Finance and Success

Your links with others are important to your business success now, and there are ample opportunities in April as the planets populate your solar Seventh House. New agreements and partnerships are possible as creative ideas and optimism abound. Thinking long-term and acting with caution will avert midyear obstacles and permanent contract issues. It's best to sign contracts before April 26, but if you must sign after that, be very sure that every aspect of the agreement is clearly understood.

Cosmic Insider Tip

Things you began last summer will come to fruition over the next few months. However, there will be a delay for some initiatives, while others will still change substantially in their result. Look for progress in May, June, and October.

Rewarding Days 6, 7, 11, 12, 15, 16, 19, 20, 23, 24

Challenging Days 1, 2, 8, 9, 10, 21, 22, 28, 29

Affirmation of the Month I can flow with events.

Libra/May

In the Spotlight
With Mercury retrograde until May 20, events do not transpire exactly as planned. There may be delays or changes in course that occur. There may be changes in cash flow, or your links with others' money, including income, may need some attention.

Wellness and Keeping Fit
As is often the case, the activities that are not routine hold extra fascination for you, because of the extra bit of fun they add. Double your fun by bringing along a friend. Watch for digestive upsets through May 20, most likely from overindulging.

Love and Life Connections
Misunderstandings that arose last month will take some work to resolve, but a resolution will evolve out of new realizations that come before May 20. This is an excellent time to clear the air, since the problem existed long before now. As the two of you grapple with your financial realities and come to an agreement, your interest in life beyond your partnership improves. After May 20 the way is clear for some romance.

Finance and Success
It's time to get a handle on your expenses and balance them against your income. If you spend more than you earn, it will hamper your freedom and your future success. You get another big push to reach for new goals, which may involve school—even a degree program— or you could be teaching or publishing. You probably already have been thinking about an initiative in this area.

Cosmic Insider Tip
The eclipses on May 15 and 30 will be felt in your Third and Ninth houses. You may be shifting your values in response to ideas that spark different ways of thinking about your world.

Rewarding Days 3, 4, 8, 9, 12, 13, 16, 17, 21, 22, 30, 31

Challenging Days 5, 6, 7, 18, 19, 20, 25, 26, 27

Affirmation of the Month I am receptive to positive changes.

Libra/June

In the Spotlight

Lots of planetary activity promises a busy month. Once Saturn enters Cancer and your Tenth House, career advancement becomes more important, and possible, as you reach for a pinnacle in a thirty-year cycle.

Wellness and Keeping Fit

Your wellness plan receives a boost if you incorporate fitness exercises into your vacation or outing plans. The joys of travel and unknown places are especially sweet if you have company.

Love and Life Connections

You and your partner are primed to get away together. Find someplace you both enjoy, somewhere that has a combination of city and rural experiences. You'll want to get away from it all for a while, but you like showers and fresh linens too much to rough it for long. The important thing is to find solace for the soul and build your connection with each other. There will be unexpected occurrences, but they will be what you remember and tell stories about.

Finance and Success

Some long-overdue sources of revenue will come in this month, perhaps with a well-timed communique—especially before June 10. Once you've collected yourself, focus on fun and freedom. When you return there'll be plenty of work, as well as startling occurrences to grapple with, and you may sacrifice leisure time. Extra volatility exists around June 6 and 23, and there'll be an increase in inner tension after June 17.

Cosmic Insider Tip

What happens now is a portent of experiences to come in July, August, and September. Listen to the signals you receive around June 6, 17, and 23 for clues to larger issues that will arise later.

Rewarding Days 1, 4, 5, 9, 10, 13, 14, 18, 19, 26, 27, 28

Challenging Days 2, 3, 15, 16, 21, 22, 23, 29, 30

Affirmation of the Month I can enjoy myself in the moment.

Libra/July

In the Spotlight

There is a wrench in the works this month, as Mars turns retrograde on July 29, so prepare for unscheduled events and unplanned plot twists. June's vacation spirit ends on July 4.

Wellness and Keeping Fit

Your energy level is so high that some of it is being channeled into your nervous system and coming out as anxiety. Meditation, a quiet walk in the middle of a hectic day, or tai chi may provide the correct antidote. All other things being equal, it would be better not to schedule elective surgeries between July 29 and September 27.

Love and Life Connections

Your life is so focused on work, your social interactions are concentrated there as well. It's important to let those closer to you know what's happening so they feel included. Don't worry about accepting support without getting any in return. You provide plenty at other times.

Finance and Success

It is critical this month that you put your ear to the ground and listen for ominous rumblings in the workplace. Do what you can to reduce stress by staying organized, calling upon others for support, and prioritizing duties. Since the market may be wobbly by the end of the month, it won't hurt to make sure your investments are where you want them.

Cosmic Insider Tip

As Mars slows down, we get signals about what it will bring during its two-month retrograde. As your daily routines, health practices and imbalances, and work activities are affected, look for potential problems in those areas now. Any that materialize may end up affecting your finances and partnerships by the end of September.

Rewarding Days 1, 2, 3, 6, 7, 10, 11, 14, 15, 24, 25, 29, 30

Challenging Days 12, 13, 19, 20, 26, 27, 28

Affirmation of the Month I can detect signals of what's to come.

Libra/August

In the Spotlight
Inflammatory situations may arise in health and work as Mars backs up through your Sixth House. It seems as if all the energies bottle up starting August 22, so be patient and accept the events that come after as a part of the plan, even if you don't understand yet.

Wellness and Keeping Fit
You have to change your fitness plan, perhaps because of an injury or because you have not been exercising enough. Even though you're reluctant, you are likely to find that you benefit in the long run.

Love and Life Connections
When you're focused on just living, it's hard to think about someone else's needs. You are under stress, you have a lot on your plate, and you're doing the best you can. There are, however, others who will be much more greatly affected than you. If some of these happen to be your loved ones, their survival needs must come before produc- tivity needs at work. If you need help, ask for their support as well.

Finance and Success
The crunch is on as seven planets move into a single, dynamic con- figuration. It will build all month until it peaks between August 22 and September 3. With your vulnerability to others' approval, you could become overwrought about not fulfilling your obligations; however, these things happen—we can't expect everything to flow smoothly all the time.

Cosmic Insider Tip
When the planets have so much talking to do, it's important to lis- ten. If you get caught up in the drama of the moment, you won't be able to see what's really going on and direct the forces the way you want them to go. If you lose perspective, you'll become confused and won't know how to act. Maintaining clarity is essential.

Rewarding Days 2, 3, 6, 7, 8, 11, 12, 20, 21, 22, 25, 26, 29, 30, 31

Challenging Days 9, 10, 15, 16, 17, 23, 24

Affirmation of the Month I can act with wisdom and courage.

♎ Libra/September ♎

In the Spotlight

Your world has endured its darkest moment, and you have come through. Now it's time to climb up into the light again, or to assist others in doing so. The way out for you is through service and inner growth. Relief comes in stages on September 15, 20, and 27.

Wellness and Keeping Fit

You may be focused more on wellness than keeping fit as the planets transit your health houses. Take your pills on time, eat well, sleep as much as you need, and get all the help you require.

Love and Life Connections

You are likely to be called upon to support others this month more than to be supported yourself. If you are well enough to do so, you may welcome this as a way to express your caring for those close to you. However, it's important to take care of yourself as well by gently setting boundaries on what you can and can't do. The challenges are gradually reduced after September 15, with a substantial improvement after September 27.

Finance and Success

Your success secret this month is selfless service. If you bury yourself in whatever you can do to improve the situation, this will prove itself the best course in the long run. Don't try to take on too much; your capabilities are limited now. Leave the big push to someone else who finds themselves favored by the prevailing forces. Your time will come.

Cosmic Insider Tip

You want to be out front, doing something more visible, because that seems more important to the cause. However, your prayers and meditations may have just as powerful an influence, although unsung. You can be a nexus of peace and calm that serves the whole.

Rewarding Days 3, 4, 7, 8, 16, 17, 18, 21, 22, 23, 26, 27, 30

Challenging Days 5, 6, 11, 12, 13, 19, 20

Affirmation of the Month I maintain inward calm.

Libra/October

In the Spotlight
The planets are moving on, and so are you. Although we're all still in recovery mode, your robust strength is showing. You get to choose what you want to do, but choose carefully, because you're creating the blueprint for your activities for the coming year.

Wellness and Keeping Fit
If you've suffered a health setback over the past two months, don't overdo it. It can be tempting on days when you feel really good to try to skip steps. However, you may end up weakening yourself and delaying your progress if you do so.

Love and Life Connections
You will receive more attention from others in October. Your interest in social interaction is up, and you'll enjoy some fun and romance. Don't wait for others to ask you—create the opportunities yourself. This is a good time for a shopping spree, a novel hair style, or a fashion makeover to create a new self-image.

Finance and Success
New business and career opportunities are possible if you keep your eyes and ears open. Your charisma, naturally high, is even stronger now. You'll attract opportunities that will light up your life and lead to success in the coming year. The challenge will be to select among those that come your way. You could end up with more work than you bargained for. After October 9 you'll attract more money.

Cosmic Insider Tip
In choosing among the opportunities that come your way this month, let practical considerations dominate. Allow your own objectivity and experience to enter into the process and negotiate for your needs to be met.

Rewarding Days 1, 4, 5, 14, 15, 19, 20, 23, 24, 27, 28, 31

Challenging Days 2, 3, 9, 10, 16, 17, 18, 29, 30

Affirmation of the Month I choose the opportunities that are for my highest good.

♎ Libra/November ♎

In the Spotlight

November brings your attention to resources, as your bank balance goes up a little more than usual. This may induce you to higher spending levels as well, since the eclipses are highlighting this area and bringing out unexpected needs.

Wellness and Keeping Fit

You are entering a new way of life when it comes to your health—seeing it in new ways and giving it more importance. You will refine the process over the next seven years, as Uranus transits your health house, but the critical issues have been discovered.

Love and Life Connections

Your love life is focused on money matters and resources, so go ahead—go shopping! Take your partner or favorite shopping companion along and have fun with it. Delight yourself with a lunch at the mall or a "cuppa" at your favorite coffee shop. Even if you're on an austerity budget, it's okay to look. The experience is about the companion and the bond you share, not about what you buy.

Finance and Success

The eclipses highlight your financial power and the ways in which you can increase it. You may discover that a little more training can increase your employability or qualify you for a salary increase. If so, this is a great time to go for it. Even if it takes a few months to complete, you'll have some benefit at the end. Publicity or extra effort in commerce may be essential to what you're building right now.

Cosmic Insider Tip

November 7 and 8 are a planetary focal point, when the direction and momentum of our lives can change. If you are alert to the need for such detours, and flexible in executing them, you'll be responding to events positively and correctly.

Rewarding Days 1, 2, 10, 11, 15, 16, 20, 21, 24, 25, 28, 29

Challenging Days 5, 6, 7, 13, 14, 26, 27

Affirmation of the Month I respond to life's challenges positively.

 Libra/December

In the Spotlight
Your attention is drawn to education and your home life during December. Mercury retrogrades once again, this time in your solar Fourth House, suggesting a need to focus on your private life.

Wellness and Keeping Fit
You're on an even keel now, and you've never felt better, or at least you know fantastic health is on its way. Emotional issues could be unbalancing, however, as December 17 approaches. Rolling with the flow of events is a wise move.

Love and Life Connections
Your family relationships assume more importance this month— perhaps relatives visit from out of town, or you plan a special outing or vacation with them. Entertaining in the home may be featured, which could mean a decorating facelift or a deep cleaning. You may decide to get rid of some possessions that clutter your home environment, which is an excellent way to make use of Mercury's retrograde energy.

Finance and Success
Commerce and marketing continue to be important this month, and if you are in a learning environment this will be especially emphasized as well. Information gathering and dispersal will feed your goals and lead to fulfillment in six to seven months' time. You are naturally drawn toward home this month, so it may be time to de-emphasize public activities.

Cosmic Insider Tip
It's okay to look inward, to nurture your home and those in it, and to take time to relax there. It's what makes it all worthwhile and recharges your batteries for the increasingly externalized activities you'll be engaging in when January arrives.

Rewarding Days 7, 8, 9, 12, 13, 14, 17, 18, 21, 22, 25, 26

Challenging Days 2, 3, 4, 10, 11, 23, 24, 30, 31

Affirmation of the Month I enjoy my home and family.

Libra Action Table

These dates reflect the best—but not the only—times for success and ease in these activities, according to your Sun sign.

	JAN	FEB	MAR	APR	MAY	JUN	JUL	AUG	SEPT	OCT	NOV	DEC
Move	1, 23-31	1-12										3-16, 23
Start a class											13-30	1, 2
Join a club							14-31	1-22				
Ask for a raise									16-30	1-9		
Look for work	23-31	1-12	6-31	1-5								3-16
Get pro advice	9,10	6,7	4-6	1,2	26,27	22,23	19,20	15-17	14,15	9,10	5-7	2-4
Get a loan	11-13	8,9	7,8	3-5,30	1,2,28,29	24,25	21-23	18,19	14,15	11-13	7-9	5,6
See a doctor			6-31	1-5			31	1-27	21-30	1-24		
Start a diet			6-21						10			
End relationship										10		
Buy clothes		14-28	1-27									
Get a makeover									26	8-24		
New romance		1	3-27									
Vacation	14,15	10-12	10,11	6,7	3, 4, 30, 31	1, 11-30	1-4, 24, 25	21-23	17,18	14,15	10-12	7-9

SCORPIO

The Scorpion
October 23 to November 22

♏

Element:	Water
Quality:	Fixed
Polarity:	Yin/Feminine
Planetary Ruler:	Pluto (Mars)
Meditation:	I can surrender my feelings.
Gemstone:	Topaz
Power Stones:	Obsidian, amber, citrine, garnet, pearl
Key Phrase:	I create
Glyph:	Scorpion's tail
Anatomy:	Reproductive system
Color:	Burgundy, black
Animal:	Reptiles, scorpions, birds of prey
Myths/Legends:	The Phoenix, Hades and Persephone, Shiva
House:	Eighth
Opposite Sign:	Taurus
Flower:	Chrysanthemum
Key Word:	Intensity

Positive Expression:	Misuse of Energy:
Strengthening	Destructive
Sensual	Obsessive
Stimulating	Caustic
Rejuvenating	Excessuve
Passionate	Jealous
Creative	Spiteful

Scorpio

Your Ego's Strengths and Shortcomings

Strength of will is your calling card, Scorpio. Perhaps the least understood sign of the zodiac, your watery depths are hard for others to fathom at times. However, for those willing to stick around long enough to know you and gain your trust, the rewards are great. You are the most dependable, loyal, and faithful friend anyone could want. Although often shy, your warmth and affection for those you can rely on is an immense pleasure to experience.

Like the other water signs, Cancer and Pisces, you give way when others push, but neither you nor they should mistake this watery bending with the tides for giving in. You need to be aware when people push you too far, and you need to let them know. The alternative is that they will keep pushing because you haven't set a boundary, until you are pushed too far and you overreact. By the time that happens, you may feel like cutting away and burning your bridges. No one can decide but you whether this is necessary or not, but there are times when you might regret that this happens. Being more sensitive to your own needs and voicing them can help you to avoid such splits.

You have a deep intensity, a need to know. It can be like a bottomless pit that you want to fill with your passion for life and the knowledge of the way it all works. You want to know what drives us, what makes us who we are, and you may not always have a rosy picture of what that is. However, once you sort out realism from both cynicism and optimism, you will find your self at rest. Once you have learned to love and accept yourself, you will find a natural acceptance of and compassion for others, and this will fill the empty place as no substance or experience can.

Shining Your Love Light

No matter what your persona, you still find it hard to let others know the real you, which is deep, caring, and emotionally intense. This is why you need a partner who is willing to be patient and work with you to bring out those inner recesses. Once you have found a partner, you want to stay with him or her because you know how long it takes to build the real trust that the best relationships are based on. Once you open up, your relationships are a revelry in emotion and intimacy.

The other water signs, Cancer and Pisces, are the ones who will understand you most easily. They live in that same environment of emotional sensitivity that defies words, yet is felt and communicated so easily in other ways. You share with Aries the drive to take action, especially in defense of a cause, but Aries's impulsiveness may seem foolish to you. Taurus, your opposite sign, matches sensuousness to your emotional intensity, but you may each be too stubborn to settle disagreements. Gemini can match wits with you any day and you enjoy the challenge, but this sign may not be willing to plumb the depths of consciousness with you. Cancer is your emotional complement, expressing what you internalize and understanding what you can't convey. Leo offers the sunny warmth of love, but you can get burned out with all that brightness. You appreciate Virgo's candid logic and quick intelligence, and this sign can be a great companion in your investigations of life. Libra's interest in the "inner you" is refreshing, but may be just a little too nice for you. Another Scorpio will understand you—perhaps too well—while a Sagittarius may be too "on the move" for you to feel like you can really build a relationship together. Capricorn is safe and reliable, and you appreciate this sign's ability to take responsibility when it is due. Aquarius can keep up with your contrarian attitudes step by step, but this may not be the foundation of a comfortable relationship. Pisces touches your heart, and you know you need never fear lack of sensitivity.

Making Your Place in the World

You've got a lot to offer the world, Scorpio, but you may have a hard time opening up to give it. The key is to find your own quiet, background way of sharing your light with others, because you have many remarkable gifts.

Because you feel so deeply, you are naturally creative. You may wish to write, sculpt, or work at a craft. You could, counter to your natural shyness, decide to act. There's something about getting down into those deep gut feelings and expressing them that is transformative for yourself and others as well. Or you may want to work behind the scenes in orchestrating an emotionally moving piece, whether musical, theatrical, or cinematic. You can work in many capacities, from directing and producing to handling the technical details behind the scene.

Your desire to transform may also lead you into the healing arts in some way. You love helping people who can't help themselves, especially when you can help them regain control of their own world through the healing process. This could come through a conventional medical career or something alternative, such as massage therapy or energetic healing. Your gift with three-dimensional perception could also lead you into mechanical work. This could lead you to train as an automotive tech, computer analyst or technician, or other high-tech troubleshooter.

Power Plays

Although every sign has its own unique relationship with power, your connection to the universal forces is more explicit, for you are an understudy to them. Your drive to understand what really, at the core, makes everything tick is about harnessing these forces for your own use and protection. The forces of the universe are described in many ways and exist on many levels. The force that you find easiest to tap is the power of will.

Willpower in its common usage has lost much of its meaning, for we don't give often give much thought to what "will" is. For you, willpower is the emotional drive that propels you forward and guides your actions in any situation. However, you won't play well with others if your use of this power is too self-serving. So, your will must be refined by learning more about its impact on the world as well as the results in your own life. As you see more cause-and-effect actions take place around you, you understand more about how the world works, and you use your will power with beneficial effects for all involved.

Famous Scorpios

Abigail Adams, Bryan Adams, John Candy, Calista Flockhart, Dick Francis, Dennis Franz, Daisy Fuentes, King Hussein, Hedy Lamarr, Yasmin LeBon, Nia Long, Matthew McConaughey, Meg Ryan, Fernando Valenzuela, Buckwheat Zydeco

The Year Ahead for Scorpio

You've labored long under planetary patterns that have been rather inhospitable for seven years, and the past three years have been especially challenging. Well, your time to glow and go is coming in 2003, Scorpio! Saturn in Cancer and Uranus in Pisces in the latter half of the year will create a grand trine with your Sun, launching a new, more supportive time for you. The other planets will prove to be helpmates as well, making this year a real turning point.

You're always relished being able to stretch your abilities, and Jupiter in Leo, your solar Tenth House, has afforded you the opportunity. Since last July, Jupiter has brought challenge into your life as you have striven to gain long-desired goals. You've found yourself in unfamiliar territory, possibly socially and at work. As you've traveled this new territory, you have created a list of "Things You Never Knew Before." If you have been open to accepting these new ideas, you will find yourself experiencing the joys of accomplishment in the coming eighteen months. In August, Jupiter moves into Virgo and your Eleventh House. This will continue the period of recognition begun three years ago, but without so much hard work. It is also a good time to extend your social network, since the people around us are our greatest strength. Although this may be contrary to what you're comfortable with, if you look at it as a career move you'll find it easier to overcome your natural reticence.

Saturn in Gemini has brought certain financial constraints into your world. Perhaps the caprices of the stock market over the past few years have required budgetary cutbacks. You may have found yourself in too much debt. If nothing else, Saturn is good for "course adjustments," perhaps forcing you to take austerity measures that by now are having a positive effect. If you have responded responsibly to Saturn's energies, you will emerge this year with a stronger, healthier financial portfolio. Starting in June, Saturn enters Cancer—a more harmonious placement for you. You may find the way suddenly clear, and be able to move more freely toward your goals. As the way opens, you may be asking yourself, "What can I do to enhance my coming success?" Perhaps you'll decide to get some additional training, or even higher education. You could take on a training position or internship—something which allows you to earn while you learn. You've got about three years to pad your foundation for success, so don't be afraid to take on a big goal if that's what you have in mind. Chiron in your solar Third House could bring to your awareness all the bitterness and cynicism that has been holding you back. If you want to free yourself to be happier and more successful, start by healing these old mental wounds.

Uranus's move into Pisces in March will create unprecedented opportunity for you. You will have to be ready for change and willing to step into the breach when new ideas and energies are required. Your "ever-ready," survival-wise approach to life will predispose you to making the right decisions. This is what you've trained for. Give it time to develop if your instincts tell you to; you've got seven years for the pattern to play out. Neptune is still making your home life a drain on your energies and resources. Have patience: Time will heal this wound, too. You can diffuse some of the undermining influences by engaging in spiritual activities in your home—meditation, hosting classes, or reading a good metaphysical book. Pluto continues to transform your capabilities and sense of self. It has been remodeling your resources, everything from your toolbox of skills and talents to your money to your feelings about what you have to offer the world.

Since mid-2002, the eclipses have been partially in your sign. The eclipses this year move wholly into Taurus-Scorpio, ensuring that the changes you seek will be possible. The eclipses will create a break in the energy pattern of the past, which will bring relief from old situations and enable you to build better ones.

If you were born from October 23 to 27, Uranus will trine your Sun from your solar Fifth House. This is a time when you will naturally become more socially active. This may not be through any efforts on your own part, but rather because others are noticing you more and reaching out to you. This may come as a surprise, but it will be a pleasant one, because you've been feeling like you wanted to reach out more anyway. What's even better is that you feel comfortable with these new situations, perhaps because they come through people you know, or maybe just because you're more relaxed. This could also be a time when you engage in new games or sports, or some other novel leisure activity. Or it could just be that you find your niche with a pastime that you already enjoy. This also affects children and your relationship with them. You may find yourself in the same groove as your kids (or those of other adults), unexpectedly enjoying the same activities. You could also experience the pleasure of watching your children mature in some way that brings you great joy or satisfaction. Finally, this can influence your creative pursuits, leading you to change your style or interests in those areas. Overall, this is a stimulating, enjoyable time for you.

If you were born from October 23 to November 6, Saturn will be trining your Sun from your solar Ninth House after June 4. This presents a wonderful opportunity, when you will be able to reap rewards for the past twenty years of effort. This is a time when substantial progress toward your most important, long-term personal goals can be made. You may even reach the end of the rainbow. This is also an excellent time to gain perspective on past experiences—especially the struggles of the last five years—and make slight alterations in your path. You're likely to see life as a journey right now, enough so that you decide to make this year a personal quest of some sort. You may pursue the answer to a question that has puzzled you, visit a culture that has always intrigued you, or delight in the stimulation you receive from studying a foreign language. You may return to college, brush up some career-related skills, or otherwise lay the groundwork for future successes. No matter what, this year is likely to flow more smoothly for you and make you feel like you want to stretch your legs and see whether the grass really is greener on the other side of the fence.

If you were born from November 1 to 6, Neptune will square your Sun this year. This is likely to bring gradual, subtle changes in your identity from the depths of your inner being. You may find that you are absorbed by family matters. Whether you are caring for a sick parent, trying to find your biological mother, or exploring your family roots, you are likely to be involved with those you are closest to for the coming year. You may decide to move, or you may have problems with your home in structural ways, especially with water or plumbing. You may find it difficult to feel peace and solitude in your home environment because of what is happening there, or you may decide that the prevalent atmosphere must be changed to one where you can experience more tranquility. Putting in elements of water—a feng shui fountain, watery works of art, or decorating with blues and greens—may help assuage feelings of imbalance. You may feel confused and directionless during this time as well, but this will help to point out areas of meaninglessness in your life. If you do find yourself providing long-term care for someone, it will help to reaffirm the value of your role in the family. Just make sure that you ask others to support you as you provide extra support yourself. Many people feel as if they have to sacrifice themselves in some way during this transit, and they often feel overwhelmed. In such circumstances it is important to have faith in the process and try to see the spiritual value in the tasks that lies before you.

If you were born from November 9 to 13, Pluto will semisextile your Sun this year. This is a mild influence that permits you to revisit the changes made when Pluto conjoined your Sun in 1991–92. You will have the opportunity, from this new perspective, to make adjustments to your endeavors to better assure your path to success. Pluto brings profound transformation that can take years to understand completely. By now you're at an excellent vantage point to be able to get that deeper comprehension and apply it in your life. More than anything, it will affect your values, and you may decide that you want to redirect some of your efforts to achieve different goals. You may want to look for deeper happiness than that provided by money, and explore other, intangible resources like love, self-respect, and the joy that comes from mastering and applying a craft or skill well. One good thing about Pluto: Whatever lesson you learn will stick with you—you won't forget it. The challenge is in finding all the corollaries to that lesson, as well as the right way to apply it. This year, you get that chance.

If you were born from November 14 to 22, Saturn will quincunx your Sun for the first five months of the year. This is the end of a focus which began in 2002, a time of balancing conflicting needs and impulses. You may find yourself in the middle of a financial dilemma, or have incurred a substantial debt that may or may not be monetary. You may find that you have to adjust your way of handling money because of changes in your income requiring new (but not necessarily stricter) limits. When Saturn makes this relationship to our Sun we often feel as though our obligations to others are keeping us from fulfilling our true path or purpose. Only self-examination will determine if this is true. It is important to consider carefully every act that obliges us to another person. If we take on too much of such a burden, we can be waylaid from our path by the strings attached to those obligations. Consumer credit (credit card) debt often falls into this category. When we overspend on things that really are not a support for the furtherance of our goals, we tie ourselves down and make it more difficult to reach those goals. The Saturn quincunx will make you more aware of these encumbrances and motivate you to try to overcome them.

If you were born from November 18 to 22, Uranus is squaring your Sun from your solar Fourth House. Hold on to your hat, because you're in for a wild ride! Uranus is going to shake things up this year, get you out of your doldrums, and propel you up out of your rut. Everyone needs a push once in a while, and it's time for yours. This will be a period of active change, when you can begin to realize some of the initiatives that you started twenty-one years ago. Since then, you've been cruising along more or less comfortably (the other planets notwithstanding), but now it's time to reshape the direction you took at that time and reinvigorate it with a greater sense of purpose. You may feel like you're molting, to reveal a new personality which has been growing undetected under the one you're shedding. This can have an unsettling effect on your relationships with others, particularly those who are closest to you and rely on you. Because you tend to hold things inside, any changes you make, though you consider them to be long overdue, may shock others. Or possibly, you may not be aware of your own need to change until others shock you by altering their ways of being with you, requiring you to adjust as well. You will experience the worst of this aspect if you hold on to the past, to old forms that need to die. You will experience the best if you accept what comes with a sense of adventure, looking forward to the possibilities to come, and not backward at what you've lost.

Tools for Change

The influences of Saturn, Uranus, and Neptune have created an uncertain world for you over the past few years. This year, however, Saturn and Uranus move into more harmonious positions in Cancer and Pisces, giving you the support you need to expand in significant ways. At the same time, Neptune assists the process by dissolving old structures and patterns as Jupiter taps you to take more responsibility and a leadership role.

To fulfill the potential of these energies you must be willing and able to think outside the box. You will be better able to do so if you are confident in your own abilities as you face challenges and dilemmas you have never faced before. There are many ways to "know thyself" in this deeper way. One way which may fascinate you is through the I Ching, which is sometimes translated as the *Book of Changes*. You would love to be able to predict change, another way of keeping the energies and passions of your life under control. The I Ching provides a way to tap the forces of life that have been set in motion by you and those around you, as well as those prevailing through the planets. Astrology, of course, gives insight into the nature of the planetary forces in an archetypal way, bringing the symbols that you see in the world around you to life. Study in the mystery schools or occult practices can be beneficial, as long as you connect them to a meaningful philosophy and system of ethics.

You can also keep your inner self alive and well by engaging in creative endeavors. Artwork—computer graphics, airbrush, textile art, sculpture, or traditional fine arts—may be just the thing. Or perhaps you prefer writing that mystery novel or script to keep your juices flowing.

In your efforts to treat the inner self, don't forget the foundation of your physical body. Beef up your fitness routine through both aerobic and anaerobic activities, like running and weightlifting. Water sports can also help keep you in your element. Make sure you eat three squares a day, and stay away from savory snacks like chips or crisps. Treatments that may be of exceptional benefit include deep muscle massage and facial release as well as colonics and herbal detox programs.

♏

Affirmation for the Year

I have faith in myself and others.

Scorpio/January

In the Spotlight
You have something you need to communicate, or perhaps learn, during January, but it may not go as planned. It will take you into channels of thought that you never anticipated traveling. The outcome will be quite different from what you anticipated.

Wellness and Keeping Fit
Although you are usually steady, you may find yourself too much in a rush to stick strictly to your plan. Remember that, when you are trying to do a lot of mental work, your brain is fed by protein, complex carbohydrates (not sugars), and regular exercise.

Love and Life Connections
You may hear from brothers and sisters or other members of your extended family, and the news may not be good. Help in whatever way you feel comfortable without getting caught in the middle of a dispute. Relations at work and home should be harmonious, but beware of careless words between January 2 and 23 in any sphere.

Finance and Success
The emphasis is on learning, commerce, and communication this month, and you may make some mistakes in the execution due to disorganization, overwork, or unfamiliarity with the task. An attitude of openness, especially to the idea of receiving support from others, will help tremendously. They may not be trying to interfere or criticize. You may discover ways in which your approach or attitude needs adjustment.

Cosmic Insider Tip
Although you tend not to let your idealism show, you have flights of fancy like the rest of us. It's important this month to let those visions come through, especially at the end of the month. They may be the fuel of future plans, projects, and realizations.

Rewarding Days 2, 3, 6, 7, 8, 16, 17, 21, 22, 25, 26, 29, 30

Challenging Days 4, 5, 11, 12, 13, 18, 19, 20, 31

Affirmation of the Month I can open to new ways of perceiving.

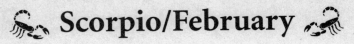 Scorpio/February

In the Spotlight
There'll be a dynamic interplay this month between work and home, and you may feel pulled in both directions. An initiative you've been working on since last summer moves forward another step, and you're sure of what you'll get out of it.

Wellness and Keeping Fit
It may be necessary for you to engage in lower-key activities to reduce your stress response, such as chi gung, tai chi, meditation, or a walk in the park. Companionship may help you release your anxieties and relax the mental tension that comes from so many changes.

Love and Life Connections
Relationship wrinkles from last month are ironed out and put behind you by February 12. Your family ties assume greater importance then, because you either want to spend more time at home or you need to stay due to others' needs—travel, illness, visiting relatives, or the like. Repairs, especially to your water or sewage system, may be needed.

Finance and Success
Money is emphasized this month on both sides of the balance sheet, and there may be a deferred expenditure that will require careful financial planning to manage. You've overcome the difficulties of last month, learned what you needed to know, and are paving your road to success with communication and new insights.

Cosmic Insider Tip
February's planets ask you to strike a balance between structure and change. In each case, new perspectives and dilemmas will begin to present themselves this spring and will persist for several years. Use your deep mind and keen intuition to sniff out what's coming so you can be prepared.

Rewarding Days 3, 4, 13, 14, 17, 18, 21, 22, 25, 26, 27

Challenging Days 1, 2, 8, 9, 15, 16, 28

Affirmation of the Month I can relax in the midst of change.

Scorpio/March

In the Spotlight

March is smoother and more routine territory as the planets give you a break. Uranus moves into Pisces this month, ending a seven-year stretch when you've been under pressure to change from the core of your being. Now it begins to get easier.

Wellness and Keeping Fit

The key word is "fun." Make it fun, and it will contribute to your well-being. Anything dull, routine, or boring to you will not induce the necessary physiological response that will migrate to your emotional, mental, and spiritual bodies.

Love and Life Connections

You're drawn to spend your time at home with those who are closest to you until March 22, but that doesn't mean you don't feel like going out on the town once in a while. Romantic interludes, or any social contact, will give you the inspiration to fulfill the creative yearnings you feel, especially after March 5. A play, an art exhibit, or a special cultural event will feed your soul.

Finance and Success

The emphasis on financial matters ends on March 4 as communication and education once again resume significance. By now your experience allows you to work more efficiently, which is good since the maze of activities you have in this area is considerable. Your creative energies are strong all month to aid the process.

Cosmic Insider Tip

Uranus begins making its energies of innovation and invention available to you on March 11, beginning a seven-year cycle of fun, romance, and creative expression. Taking the time to explore your inner reaches and adding unique life experiences will make the expression of this energy easier.

Rewarding Days 2, 3, 12, 13, 17, 18, 21, 22, 25, 26, 30, 31

Challenging Days 1, 7, 8, 14, 15, 27, 28, 29

Affirmation of the Month I listen to my inner creative voice.

Scorpio/April

In the Spotlight

You've been working for six years toward a career objective, and you're almost there. If the planetary picture were simpler you could look forward to unbridled success in the near future, but unfortunately Mercury slows progress after April 26 by going retrograde.

Wellness and Keeping Fit

You may want to add a new option to your fitness routine options, improve your nutritional program, or schedule checkups. Health matters can be headed off now, before sensations become symptoms.

Love and Life Connections

Communication and connection with those who mean the most to you become more significant after April 5. You're feeling generally very good about your current partner, and you may be thinking of increasing the level of commitment. However, your need to be sure you're not rejected may prevent you from fulfilling this impulse. You'll be more sure of what you want by the end of May.

Finance and Success

Your career success hinges on your ability to be productive right now. This is one of those times when you have to do extra work without thought of reward or compensation. Your willingness will accomplish just as much as the quality of your product, with both leading to rewards in the long run. Don't be convinced by a promise. Wait for that signature on the bottom line.

Cosmic Insider Tip

Although the month starts off with a rush of activity, there will be a gradual slow down to a virtual standstill on April 26, when Mercury retrogrades. Don't let your anticipation of this prevent you from taking action, but don't attempt to push anything through when you encounter resistance.

Rewarding Days 8, 9, 10, 13, 14, 17, 18, 21, 22, 25, 26, 27

Challenging Days 3, 4, 5, 11, 12, 23, 24, 30

Affirmation of the Month I am patient in dealing with delays.

Scorpio/May

In the Spotlight

You're not sure what the problem is, but you know somehow you have to clear the air. After May 20, the confusion begins to dissipate, but with the eclipse on May 15 you may find you're suddenly in a whole new ball game.

Wellness and Keeping Fit

You need some time alone to sort out your thoughts, and your exercise time may be just the thing. As your body releases endorphins, you'll relax and enter a meditative state. This will heal you in profound ways and quiet your mind so insights bubble to the surface.

Love and Life Connections

The pressure is on, and you're wondering what you've contributed to the conflicts you're now experiencing. It's important for you to look objectively at your own role and seek help from someone you trust rather than dwelling on fears and suspicions. Give yourself the time you need to figure it out, then try to resolve matters where conflicts have not been resolved. You can't make it all better—you can only do your best. Conditions improve after May 20, but may not be completely cleared until after June 11.

Finance and Success

Business partnerships and contacts are volatile this month, as those you work with may hesitate about a plan or arrangement. This is not as serious as it seems, but if you ignore their misgivings and push for follow-through, they'll back out altogether. Let it ride until after May 20, when a change in perspective will occur.

Cosmic Insider Tip

A more compassionate and understanding response comes from others after May 16, in spite of all the other events. It may be subtle, but if you let it seep into your consciousness you'll feel better.

Rewarding Days 5, 6, 7, 10, 11, 14, 15, 18, 19, 23, 24

Challenging Days 1, 2, 8, 9, 20, 21, 22, 28, 29

Affirmation of the Month I can face and resolve conflict.

Scorpio/June

In the Spotlight

Finances take center stage, whether they're yours, your partner's, or that of the larger financial world. You may have extra sources of income this month through gainful employment, getting an insurance or tax reimbursement, or taking out a loan.

Wellness and Keeping Fit

Sports—the kind you play, not watch—may balance your moods and stop you from brooding. Spending this time with friends can be reassuring and draw you out of yourself.

Love and Life Connections

Your relationships are normalizing, and your trust is beginning to rebuild. Give yourself time to recover. That doesn't mean that you can stay in your den with a chip on your shoulder; try to smile and carry on everyday activities, even if your heart isn't quite in it. Look for signs of love and support, but don't blind yourself to insincerity if you detect it. Finances may require collaboration this month, and this could be a point of reconciliation.

Finance and Success

Your finances require a little more focus this month. Perhaps you've decided to strengthen your portfolio, change your insurance coverages, or take a loan to accomplish a major goal. It's okay to go ahead with business partnerships this month, especially if they look clear before June 17. If you've made sure that the contract is fair and offers you the protection you need, it's all right finally to move forward.

Cosmic Insider Tip

Actions taken after June 17 are likely to be challenged and may become a lead weight. While you can't avoid taking actions completely after this time, there is likely to be some delay or obstacle that will enter into the process of its fulfillment.

Rewarding Days 2, 3, 6, 7, 8, 11, 12, 15, 16, 19, 20, 29, 30

Challenging Days 4, 5, 17, 18, 24, 25, 26

Affirmation of the Month I am alert to potential challenges.

Scorpio/July

In the Spotlight
Even though it's time to reach for your goals and accomplish them over the next three months, Mars will delay the process as it connects with six other planets at the end of August. July is clear of such time bombs, but you can't rush your projects. If there's a change of course or delay as July 29 approaches, take it in stride.

Wellness and Keeping Fit
You may be torn between taking time off for your usual fitness vacation or staying home to further your current aspirations. Take a day trip into the woods and hike off the desire to test your physical strength this time.

Love and Life Connections
Your personal life has settled down and romance is in the air again. However, there may be something stale about it as you search for what's missing. Maybe you can't be content with a shallow relationship right now, or maybe you need to adjust your ideals to fit what's available to you. Right now, it may just be a vague feeling that will have to grow for you to understand it.

Finance and Success
It's important to realize that, even if we don't understand it, setbacks are part of the overall design. They bring out the flaws in our circumstances that could have been much more harmful had we encountered them later. Between July 13 and 28 you will be able to complete some aspects of what you're working on.

Cosmic Insider Tip
Take advantage of the harmonious planetary energies that flow with you to take care of your personal needs. This may include taking a break from work, spending more time working on your creative products, or going to your favorite nightclub.

Rewarding Days 4, 5, 8, 9, 12, 13, 16, 17, 18, 26, 27, 28, 31

Challenging Days 1, 2, 3, 14, 15, 21, 22, 23, 29, 30

Affirmation of the Month Everything I do is relaxing.

Scorpio/August

In the Spotlight

You'll find that some risks you've taken, or some life and creative decisions, are affecting the outer world arena from which you gain your livelihood. Starting August 22, planetary clashes may prevent progress at the usual rate, but they will bring pre-existing issues to the surface and improve your chances of success.

Wellness and Keeping Fit

This is not the best time to be engaging in high-risk or extreme sports, if that is your penchant. Injuries and inflammations can result that may be long-lasting, if not permanently damaging.

Love and Life Connections

Romance may not go as planned this month—your dream date is a poor conversationalist; the restaurant served late and the food was overrated; the concert was canceled. Perhaps simpler pleasures and lower expectations will do the trick. If you are involved in a new romance, problems may develop due to as-yet-undetected personality flaws in your chosen partner. Keep your eyes open.

Finance and Success

You could feel cheated if you think it is your right to attain your goals right now. The planets are not going to cooperate. It is possible for the whole thing to blow up, and you are probably not to blame. However, patience will serve you in good stead, since by mid-November you'll be better off than you at first thought was possible.

Cosmic Insider Tip

When up to seven planets are interacting in a discordant way, it's better for us humans to stay off the firing range. Let yourself flow with the course of events during the "flood," then look for ways to redirect and focus the energies to the greatest benefit of all, and you'll be serving your own needs as well.

Rewarding Days 1, 4, 5, 9, 10, 13, 14, 23, 24, 27, 28

Challenging Days 11, 12, 18, 19, 25, 26

Affirmation of the Month I am acting for the good of all.

Scorpio/September

In the Spotlight
The planetary pile-up begins to disperse after September 3. After that it releases in steps on September 15, 20, and 27. With each release you have more room to move, and you'll probably have more freedom of movement than many around you.

Wellness and Keeping Fit
Your health formula contains a heavy dose of helping others throughout the month, but don't ignore your own needs. At least eat well and get plenty of rest. You are strong enough to withstand the cessation of normal activities until the challenges have been met.

Love and Life Connections
The support you give to others right now endears you to those in your personal life, as if your giving comes from them, too—and make no mistake, it does. Make sure that, wherever you are applying your energies, your support is wanted in the way you are giving it. It may be hard to see what others want right now, and there could be misunderstanding, especially where young people are concerned.

Finance and Success
Although accolades may not come now, you will be recognized for your strength and wisdom at some point. There may be political issues that are difficult to get through, and they could affect you, although indirectly. Don't try to extricate yourself—just let them wash over you without acknowledging them, and you'll emerge relatively unscathed.

Cosmic Insider Tip
Through September 20, you've been watching people "dig their own graves." It's difficult to let others make mistakes that you know could be easily avoided. If you can accept that this is part of a larger learning process, it may help you to stay out of the way.

Rewarding Days 1, 2, 5, 6, 9, 10, 19, 20, 24, 25, 28, 29

Challenging Days 7, 8, 14, 15, 21, 22, 23

Affirmation of the Month I can perceive when and how to help.

Scorpio/October

In the Spotlight

The planets provide assistance in making connections with the people you need to meet. There should be more breakthroughs than obstacles until around October 24, when Saturn's change of direction will bring out new issues suggesting a modification in goals.

Wellness and Keeping Fit

Allow yourself to be nurtured in some way, either by taking a supportive friend or your partner along, or enjoying a week at the local health retreat spa. Taking time to meditate will help you recharge your batteries, which is necessary between October 6 and 24.

Love and Life Connections

A romantic getaway may be just the thing to re-establish lost intimacy and signal your continuing appreciation of your partner. As October 24 approaches, outer-world concerns take precedence, and it may be hard to get out of town. Children continue to be in the spotlight as well, but don't forget to balance their needs with your own as they assume greater self-sufficiency.

Finance and Success

Now, finally, you can pursue the creative projects you put on the shelf in August. Life provides grist for the mill of creativity, and you've got new ideas. Follow your enthusiasm by putting your inspirations into form, and you'll be reaping rewards for the next two years. This is important to your future success, and it may be a way for you to do more of what you love in the future.

Cosmic Insider Tip

With the Sun in your solar Twelfth House, it's important to take care of yourself more than anything or anyone else. This is not selfish, it's necessary; it allows you to fill yourself and engage in selfless activities during other parts of the yearly cycle.

Rewarding Days 2, 3, 6, 7, 8, 16, 17, 18, 21, 22, 25, 26, 29, 30

Challenging Days 4, 5, 11, 12, 13, 19, 20, 31

Affirmation of the Month I can take time for myself.

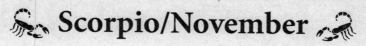 # Scorpio/November

In the Spotlight

The Sun fills your energy field in November as the eclipses high-light areas that need change. Income and expenditures assume more importance as the month ages, perhaps related to the upcoming holidays or a large purchase you want or need to make.

Wellness and Keeping Fit

You're likely to feel like putting extra time into physical activities, with a leap forward in fitness as the result. Your health is good, and you've never felt better.

Love and Life Connections

It's gratifying the see the results of your extra efforts with your children this month. They've made it through a difficult passage. Romance may also be in the air, although not necessarily with the same person who accompanied you a few months ago. Attending local events with friends—a game, a concert, or a drink at the local bar—can also be very satisfying if a minimum of planning if required. You may be positively surprised by the response you get from others, especially around November 8, as your magnetism is up.

Finance and Success

You may have been thinking about a large purchase or expenditure, perhaps for fun instead of the usual repair or renovation. Everyone deserves to splurge once in a while, and, well planned, there will be little financial indigestion as a result. It may also be a good time to get your financial affairs in order. A person with an organized life is at peace with themselves and can reach for new successes.

Cosmic Insider Tip

Give yourself some time to enjoy life this month, even though some events may surprise you. If being realistic requires some modifications in plans, at least persist with your general goals and objectives.

Rewarding Days 3, 4, 13, 14, 17, 18, 19, 22, 23, 26, 27, 30

Challenging Days 1, 2, 7, 8, 15, 16, 28, 29

Affirmation of the Month I can accomplish my goals.

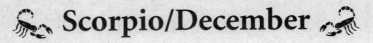 Scorpio/December

In the Spotlight

Increased activity in mental pursuits will highlight learning, organization, and paperwork this month. Work and mundane tasks
absorb your time and energy after December 15 as a new cycle of
financial empowerment begins on December 11.

Wellness and Keeping Fit

An herbal cleansing, immune system support, plenty of sleep, and a
reduction in sugar consumption may be just what the doctor
ordered to prevent illness during a stressful period.

Love and Life Connections

It's tempting to expect that those at home won't need your expressions of love while you're working so hard, but this is not a good
habit to get into. Find little ways to reassure people of your love for
them. Illness may strike those at home and require extra nurturing.
Even if you are not called upon to provide direct care, your offer to
do the shopping would be greatly appreciated.

Finance and Success

Commerce, perhaps related to the holidays, is keeping you going
after hours. While this can be good for business, it presents other
challenges, and one that can arise as December 17 approaches is an
unexpected run on supplies or purchasable items that leaves you
unable to meet patrons' needs. The shortfall will be over in early
January, so if their needs are seasonal there may be nothing you can
do in time for the appropriate holiday.

Cosmic Insider Tip

Your workload peaks on December 31, as Saturn opposes the Sun,
and your work on a long-term project reaches a culmination point.
It will be good to allow yourself time for relaxation and celebration,
since the deadline is not here yet.

Rewarding Days 1, 2, 11, 12, 15, 16, 17, 20, 21, 24, 25, 27, 28, 29

Challenging Days 5, 6, 7, 13, 14, 26, 27

Affirmation of the Month I can balance work and leisure.

Scorpio Action Table

These dates reflect the best—but not the only—times for success and ease in these activities, according to your Sun sign.

	JAN	FEB	MAR	APR	MAY	JUN	JUL	AUG	SEPT	OCT	NOV	DEC
Move		1, 14-28	1-4									
Start a class	1, 2, 23-31	1-12										
Join a club							31	1-31	1-15, 20-30	1-7		
Ask for a raise										10-31	1, 2	
Look for work			22-31	1-25	20-31	1-12	14-30					
Get pro advice	11-13	8, 9	7, 8	3-5	28, 29	24, 25	21-23	18, 19	14, 15	11-13	7-9	5, 6
Get a loan	14, 15	10-12	10, 11	6, 7	30, 31	1, 27, 28	24, 25	21-23	17, 18	14, 15	10-12	7-9
See a doctor			22-31	1-25	20-31	1-12				8-31	1-12	
Start a diet			22-31	1-5						10		
End relationship											9	
Buy clothes			6-21, 28-31	1-21								
Get a makeover										25-31	1-12	
New romance			3, 28-31	1-21								
Vacation	16-18	13, 14	12, 13	8-10	6, 7	2, 3, 29, 30	1-28	23, 24	19-21	16-18	13, 14	10, 11

SAGITTARIUS

The Archer
November 22 to December 22

Element:	Fire
Quality:	Mutable
Polarity:	Yang/Masculine
Planetary Ruler:	Jupiter
Meditation:	I can take time to explore my soul.
Gemstone:	Turquoise
Power Stones:	Lapis lazuli, azurite, sodalite
Key Phrase:	I understand
Glyph:	Archer's arrow
Anatomy:	Hips, thighs, sciatic nerve
Color:	Royal blue, purple
Animal:	Fleet-footed animals
Myths/Legends:	Athena, Chiron
House:	Ninth
Opposite Sign:	Gemini
Flower:	Narcissus
Key Word:	Optimism

Positive Expression:	Misuse of Energy:
Intellectual	Condescending
Exhilarating	Excessive
Thoughtful	Opinionated
Tolerant	Self-righteous
Expressive	Extravagant
Wise	Rash

Sagittarius

Your Ego's Strengths and Shortcomings

Straight as an arrow to the truth—that's your path, Sagittarius. And "path" is the right word, because you are likely to envision your life as a path or quest for a goal. Just like the hunter-Centaur, the symbol of your sign, you search for what's inwardly correct as if it were the most prized game animal.

As the hunter faces danger in his quest for sustenance, there are perils on the path to truth, and you are learning all of those in your travels. You are learning that sometimes truth is personal, not always universal; you are learning that sometimes different but equally valid versions of the truth clash. You are learning how to use the truth—as a guiding light for your own philosophy and code of behavior, not as a sword to brandish at others. Your are also learning when to reveal what you know and when to let people find their own way—not an easy thing for a fire sign who wants to share joy and enthusiasm with everyone.

Once you learn the fine art of understanding and speaking the truth (at least one lifetime's task), one of your natural talents emerges: the ability to teach. This talent comes from a natural receptivity to others, based on an awareness that each person must follow his or her own path to the truth. This gives you the freedom you crave, the source of all your wanderings. Once you know this, you can share your knowledge with others without feeling a need to impose it upon them.

Freedom is another word that makes your eyes light up, for you love wide open spaces, whether of the heart, the mind, or the physical landscape. You may enjoy athletics (usually individual sports and/or those covering long distances), or you could be the perpetual student, nose buried in a book. You may find foreign cultures fascinating, studying their languages and social patterns. This could culminate in travel to far-flung places, as you follow your quest. Ultimately, you are searching for what makes us human, for what ennobles us. Your quest is fulfilled when you make that discovery.

Shining Your Love Light

You need a fellow adventurer, someone who will explore the realms that fascinate you, be they foreign lands, thoughts, or experiences. Boredom is a problem for you in relationships, so you're best off with someone who keeps you guessing—someone who spices up your life with new ideas and activities to make sure the next thrill is always just around the corner.

The candle will burn more brightly, and perhaps at both ends, with your fellow fire signs, Aries and Leo. Aries will incite you with ideas and challenge you with prompt action, but don't expect follow-through. Taurus can balance your need for speed and give you a sense of stability, if you can stand still long enough. Gemini is your opposite sign, capable of manifesting your philosophies and dreams into the world of knowledge, but you have to be willing to bear the trappings of civilization. Cancer will care for and create a nest for you, but you must soften your energy to bring out lower-key passions. Leo gives you energy and enthusiasm—or is it you giving it to Leo? Although skilled at taking on any task, Virgo may tire of the adventure before you do. Libra will love relating to you and sharing your explorations, but may insist on plumbing and clean sheets every night. Scorpio will enjoy the challenges you face and have the strength to keep up, but the serious demeanor may tire you. Another Sagittarius will understand you in style and approach, but if you want to explore different things you'll be ships passing in the night. Capricorn is good at comprehending your wise pronouncements, but won't follow you on to your next conquest because of a busy work schedule. Aquarius shares your humanitarianism and zest for the unusual—a fantastic companion, if a little dry at times. Pisces is just a little too vulnerable for you, but shares your idealism and can help you dream the future.

Making Your Place in the World

Your ambitions are as high and wide as your vision is far-reaching, and truly, the sky's the limit for you. You know you can accomplish anything you set out to do if you stick with it long enough.

You are a broadcaster and conceptualizer, and this makes you a natural at communicating. When others are searching for the truths of life, you can speak those truths in one simple phrase that captures the heart. You could be drawn to be an academic, trainer, teacher, or motivational speaker. You may also find yourself attracted to a career in the legal profession. Your inquisitive mind could also lead you into highly intellectual work, such as philosophy, ethics, or political analysis.

If you are more the physical type, you may have a gift in athletics or sports. You are more a solo competitor than a team player, and you may prefer endurance or long-distance sports. Or you may decide to travel, making the exploration of other cultures your specialty. You could go into travel photography, cross-cultural sociology, or international trade relations. Independence and mental challenge is the key where you're concerned!

Power Plays

Power is not something you seek or pay much attention to, but you need to be aware of it, because it forms part of the world you're spending so much time trying to understand. If your power is unconscious for you, you will be unaware of the ways you use it, the effects it has, and whether it is being taken from you by others. Your "take-it-or-leave-it" attitude could also bite you if you use your power carelessly or do not take responsibility for your actions and their consequences.

Your strength lies in the power of truth. As a Sagittarius, you have an innate awareness of truth and honesty. The key, however, is in how you handle this knowledge. The secret is that deep inside everyone knows the truth, although they may not be aware of it. What's more, unless it is revealed at the right time, it may be harder for others to accept, and it will delay their doing so. This means that you usually don't have to say anything about it—you just have to adhere to the truth and become a living demonstration of it. So, silence is your optimum tool, allowing others to uncover what they already know.

Famous Sagittarians

Louisa May Alcott, Benjamin Bratt, Andrew Carnegie, Shirley Chisholm, Crazy Horse, General George Custer, Daryl Hannah, Mariel Hemingway, Lisa Howard, Milla Jovovich, Sam Keen, Christina Onassis, Branch Rickey, Ridley Scott, Monica Seles

The Year Ahead for Sagittarius

This year brings lots of growth and progress for you, Sagittarius! As three of the major planets change signs, you will find yourself in those new surroundings you so relish, with new realities to discover and explore.

In August, Jupiter moves into Virgo and your Tenth House. Until then its placement in Leo carries forth the harmonious period you entered last summer. You will be especially inclined to engage in your favorite activities with little hindrance: travel, study, or exploring the realms of your latest interest in your own way. By now you've established your goals for the cycle, and if you execute your plans wisely (or change course if necessary), you will be adding knowledge in order to build the future of your dreams. Once Jupiter enters Virgo the dynamic energy around you will build, and others will begin to recognize you and your abilities in substantial ways. From August of this year to August 2004 you'll be in the spotlight, so do what you're so good at: Spread the word!

Saturn in Gemini has been especially challenging for your relationships, and humbling as you have realized your own role in creating them as they exist now. You may have learned about your own potential for callousness (which is really you avoiding conflict out of fear of confrontation), or what it means to avoid commitment (sometimes, being alone). If you've used this energy positively, you've focused on your relationships and gained deep insights into yourself as well. You've had the chance to revisit experiences from the past seven years, put them in perspective, and get a little more healing. Starting in June, Saturn goes into Cancer and your solar Eighth House. While this relieves the pressure, it doesn't leave you with a clear mandate for change and a strong sense of direction like you had before. It can leave you feeling in-between. Saturn in Cancer brings our focus to our feelings, perhaps showing us where we're not managing them very well. You may find that this new directive leads you to untraveled territory in your psyche—or at least unexplored since 1976. However, renewed focus on emotional discipline and responsibility will benefit us all—even you, my wandering friend. Chiron's position in your solar Second House may bring out your feelings of inadequacy about yourself and your skills. You may question what you have to offer. You may also feel the pinch of past overspending and really have to do something about it now.

Uranus's move into Pisces in March will bring it into your solar Fourth House, emphasizing emotional growth in another way. This could have an unsettling influence on you, but one which may be more satisfying and allow more latitude for personal choice than the Pluto transit you've been experiencing since 1995. The key to using Uranus's energy well is to be as closely aligned to your deep inner sense of purpose as possible. Likely you will find yourself wanting to make fundamental changes in your private life over the next seven years, but there's no need to rush into things until you're clear on what will work best for you. Neptune is still fogging your mental windshield, dulling your usual rapier wit and keen memory. You're not losing your memory, you're just learning to access it in a different way, and with it will come a greater ability to detect the real truth in a situation. Pluto's absolute hand has been felt across your cheek for so long now, you've developed a callus. Without realizing it, you've grown in strength and learned to value yourself more in spite of the ravages of external opinion. Only years from now will you fully realize what you've gained from your impossible experiences.

For years you've been thinking about making changes without the wherewithal to do so. From the middle of 2002, suddenly, the circumstances have presented themselves for action. The ones this year will find you under less pressure to act, so you can let the dust settle and see where you stand before undertaking the next big initiative.

If you were born from November 22 to 26, Uranus will square your Sun after March 10. This will create a new energy in your life. Although the past few years have brought many changes, you will encounter even more this year. After the drawn-out process and sustained energy the past required, this year's energies will be refreshingly different. The impulses you feel now will be clean and distinct, if not startling. Uranus does bring in the unexpected—accidents and miracles—and it depends on the things you've cultivated in your life up to this moment to decide which way you'll describe your story. Uranus can seem capricious, as if the universe has unfathomable whims to which we are prey, but it is actually quite orderly in its effects. It makes sure that we are aligned with our life purpose, that we are fulfilling the needs of the soul, at least as much as possible. Seen from this perspective, Uranus opens doorways for us and is truly miraculous. If we need to be shocked, Uranus does the job. If we are on our purpose, Uranus is more like a gentle breeze nudging the doors of opportunity open for us, showing us the way. Your Uranian experiences will seem to stem from your home, family, and private life. You may be emotionally unsettled by the actions of those closest to you. Someone in your family may decide to break free of an old role that doesn't fit (it could be you). You may discover that old hurts that you thought you had buried are springing back to life to be truly healed. Anything that holds you back emotionally is likely to be exposed now, so that you can understand it in the light of the soul and truly release it. Although difficult in the moment, it is hard to imagine a greater blessing.

If you were born from November 22 to December 6, Saturn will quincunx your Sun starting June 4. This can create a feeling of being in two worlds, in an "in-between" state, not quite out of the old and not yet completely in the new. After the changes of the past two years there is still much to be accomplished; yet, if you can continue in your efforts without flagging, you can reap great rewards in another three years. Your concerns at this time will probably involve your relationships with others. Money is also often involved. Perhaps you have debts that you want to pay off (which could be emotional or financial). For this reason we often are impelled to follow a strict budget and then to feel burdened by it until we develop other ways of handling the crisis, such as expanding our income base. There's no doubt Saturn often means hard work, but it promises good things for our efforts (and it keeps its promises). This also can be a time of questioning yourself and your motives from a deeper level, because some of our most difficult unconscious motivations can emerge as weaknesses during this transit. This is good if you can come to understand and forgive yourself as a result. You can live with the ambiguity of this time and keep your spirits up in spite of the feeling of no progress by setting boundaries on your efforts. Take time to have fun and just forget about it all on a regular basis.

If you were born from December 1 to 6, Neptune will sextile your Sun from your solar Third House in 2003. During this time you are likely to experience subtle changes in your ways of thinking about and perceiving the world. You may start to see things in a more spiritual way, or you may become confused because some of your old ways of thinking just don't seem to fit any more. You may become more idealistic or become more imaginative; you may even be inspired to write a novel or engage in other artistic expression of your thoughts. You could also decide to take classes or some other form of training, especially those focused on spirituality, the arts, photography or film, or the ocean. If you have brothers and sisters, you may find that they seem to be more expressive of Neptunian dynamics—spirituality, artistic expression, or pursuits associated with water. This is generally a mild aspect that indicates opportunity, not crisis. It is one of those times when, if we can invest some time and focus in its direction, we will emerge strengthened in our efforts to deal with other dilemmas in life.

If you were born from December 9 to 13, Pluto will be conjoining your Sun this year, signaling a period that you will likely remember as a milestone in your life. This aspect often brings a revolution—here to your personality, sense of purpose, and basic identity. Naturally, this will touch every area of your existence, and it could result in a radical shift in direction, new style or appearance, and a new way of expressing yourself. The motivation at the core of all these possible changes is to make life more real, more authentic for you. You are likely to feel driven—compelled to do some things that in the past you only thought out. Now it is not enough just to dream of being who you really are—becoming the real you is an imperative. Accordingly, all falsehoods and foibles are in peril of being dismissed from your reality. You will want to make changes in every area where you have masked the real you. There is the danger, however, that you will continue to resist these transformations. Sometimes it can feel overwhelming to think of changing everything that needs to be transformed. Sometimes we feel unprepared, or as if the changes will be impossible to enact, because they will be so global. It takes courage to step into something just because it feels right, since the mind may be screaming that it is not possible. It often seems easier to remain in the familiar, stagnant place we inhabit now than to unleash the tiger that could ravage your life. Yet this death and rebirth process is essential to living, and something that everyone experiences at least once in their lives. Like a cold shower that leaves you breathing from the core of your being and tingling all over, this transit will give you the same feeling, but on a sustained basis. It will take several years to "get" all of what happened when it is over, but you will find your life enriched in ways you can't imagine now. As time elapses, you'll find that this transformation was not just worth it, it was essential.

If you were born from December 14 to 22, Saturn will be opposing your Sun until June 4. This transit actually began last year, and it is a watershed period for you, because it will show you how well you've been applying yourself to the things you have really wanted to accomplish for the past fifteen years. If you have been cultivating your garden of achievement with determined vigilance, pulling the weeds of distraction and fertilizing the flowers of self-fulfillment, you will find that this time is a pinnacle in some way. You may be able to achieve some long-desired goals and eliminate some elements in your life that you no longer need. If you have lacked direction or been pulled away from your goals, you may find this period to be less satisfying. No matter what, you are likely to find that there are many demands on your time. Partnerships and other relationships could move into the forefront. They may be restructured or curtailed due to demands in other areas, either yours or your partners' lives. You may also receive feedback from those around you about behavior patterns that limit your ability to interact smoothly with others and get what you want. You could form business partnerships or make a commitment in a personal relationship. Above all else, you will be able to accomplish a great deal, since your solar energies are activated while this transit takes place.

If you were born from December 18 to 22, Uranus will sextile your Sun this year from your solar Third House. The gates of learning and verbal creativity are opening for you this year, and this is welcome news for a Sagittarius! You love the sense of a wide-open consciousness with limitless possibilities, and this is the feeling you'll get if you focus your attention this way during 2003. The halls of learning may beckon you again—to get that extra certificate that earns you a little more, but most importantly makes your job more intriguing. You are also naturally likely to encounter new ideas that especially pique your interest. Since mind expansion is one of your favorite pastimes, you are sure to find this period quite enjoyable. You may experience an opening or awakening in other areas as well. Your relationships with siblings could change for the better. Your neighborhood may get a facelift, the roads may be reconditioned, or the neighbors might remodel and re-landscape their property. You may acquire a new shopping center, library, or other convenience to make life easier. There is no pressure from this transit to solve problems or perform in a particular way, but if you take advantage of it you will be laying the foundation for later successes.

Tools for Change

Although you have been through many changes over the past few years, this year brings new perspectives to consider, since Uranus and Mars square your sign. Although you are excellent at maintaining perspective, you may have difficulty with it, as the forces of excess stress threaten you in midyear. A great many opportunities are likely to arise, but you won't be able to take utmost advantage of them if you get caught in the details.

The best way to maintain your detachment is to put some distance between yourself and the objects of your focus from time to time. This can be accomplished by engaging in the activities that you love so well, such as adventure sports and excursions. Take a trip to a wild place or somewhere you've never been before, even if it's not that exotic or far away. When you can, of course, take yourself to that exotic locale—it's a balm for the Sagittarian soul. Hiking and backpacking or mountain biking is especially beneficial for you, since it allows you to cover long distances in the peace and solitude of the wilderness. You may also respond to extreme sports or thrilling activities like white-water rafting or downhill skiing. Activities that allow you to cover extensive areas, such as long-distance running, horseback riding, and cross-country skiing, give you a sense of triumph and challenge your abilities to the max.

To keep your mind active, you may want to pick up a new study. If you work on it in your own time without deadline, you will find that it can be quite relaxing. There are plenty of educational materials on CD-ROM now: Study that foreign language you've always fancied knowing, or get in a little deeper by picking up a book on linguistics to learn more about what happens inside languages. You may also find the study of philosophies and religions to be quite intriguing, as they help you to discover what the human species longs for.

If you're athletic, you don't have to be convinced to eat well, but you may find that your body needs extra nutrients during high-stress times. Get a nutritional evaluation through hair analysis or kinesiology to determine your unique needs. Don't hesitate to schedule extra health treatments to keep your body in good working order. Psychostructural rebalancing does more than realign your musculature; it also allows the psychic energy to move freely through your energy field.

♐

Affirmation for the Year

I am always uncovering new, delightful parts of myself.

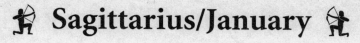 Sagittarius/January

In the Spotlight
Your reluctance to join civilization wanes after January 17, as you are inspired by new ideas and initiatives. Money is also in focus between January 2 and 23 as you reconsider purchases recently made or encounter unforeseen expenses.

Wellness and Keeping Fit
Before January 17 you are completing a natural and necessary period of downtime. You may even be ill if you overextended yourself toward the end of last year. Don't let your eagerness to experience life lead you to ignore your inner needs.

Love and Life Connections
Someone in your household may have been overspending, and it could be you. If this is the case, it's time to 'fess up and do what you can to make amends. It may take a few weeks or months to work yourself out of the hole, and the rest of your household will be affected. If you have needed to take care of an unexpected repair or health matter, this brings the point home even more powerfully.

Finance and Success
There is never a better time to work on balancing your own budget than when you are clearly in financial difficulty. The problems may not be large, but if they are you will need to apply your inventive mind to finding a creative solution. It is just as important that you learn from this experience so that you can avoid making the same mistake again.

Cosmic Insider Tip
Your inner balance is disrupted each time you go to extremes. It takes its toll in other areas of your life in subtle but certain ways. By diverting energy and attention away from them you prevent yourself from focusing on and achieving your highest goals.

Rewarding Days 1, 4, 5, 9, 10, 18, 19, 20, 23, 24, 27, 28, 31

Challenging Days 6, 7, 8, 14, 15, 21, 22

Affirmation of the Month I can see myself clearly.

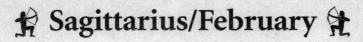 Sagittarius/February

In the Spotlight
You've never felt more enthusiastic or hopeful about life and its prospects. Now you can pursue opportunities that have come to you in the past two months and create a few of your own.

Wellness and Keeping Fit
This is a great time to increase the amount of exercise you engage in, but it must be done slowly, or injury and overall loss of fitness could result. Err on the side of caution and make your routine less rigorous by inviting a friend to join you.

Love and Life Connections
Your finances begin to recover, and with them your family ties. You may even be tempted to take your loved ones shopping as some extra money comes in, but it's important to remember the lessons of last month. Share something more meaningful with your family: your time.

Finance and Success
You have some extra cash coming in this month, and you're tempted to spend it, but this will undermine the resolution you made last month to save. Resolve your dilemma by saving a percentage of this extra cash. Then figure out how much you can save of everything that comes your way. Write down some of those innovative ideas that keep popping into your head this month. They're the seeds of the new projects you'll launch yourself into over the coming year.

Cosmic Insider Tip
As your inspiration flows, write down your thoughts. Sort through them a little, and the right ones to place at the top of the list will emerge in the coming weeks.

Rewarding Days 1, 2, 5, 6, 7, 15, 16, 19, 20, 23, 24, 28

Challenging Days 3, 4, 10, 11, 12, 17, 18

Affirmation of the Month I can balance the exciting new developments in my life.

Sagittarius/March

In the Spotlight
Your focus turns inward to your home environment in March. This is reinforced by Uranus, which enters Pisces and your solar Fourth House of the home and family. Its ingress will bring many changes in the way you view your home, family, and private life during the coming seven years.

Wellness and Keeping Fit
Your high level of energy mellows out a little after March 3, and you move into a slightly more relaxed but steadier fitness routine. You will want to focus on activities that build your endurance. Resist the urge to engage in emotional eating after March 27.

Love and Life Connections
Your love connections are strong right now, and you feel like staying close to home and nurturing them. There's nothing like settling in for a good meal and a movie with those you love, or going to your favorite fun spot together. Even though your attention will soon turn to other pursuits, the simple pleasures with those you love most are the ones you'll remember.

Finance and Success
Your bank account seems to be on the mend, and your attention is on to other things after March 2, like fixing up your home. We all need to spend time there periodically, both to refuel ourselves and to take care of needed repairs and upkeep. This is the perfect time, as the demands on your time from outside the home are at a low.

Cosmic Insider Tip
You started a new yearly Pluto cycle of self-empowerment at the beginning of December last year. Challenges related to this arise around March 23. Being aware of what's going on will help you understand and bend gracefully in the winds of events.

Rewarding Days 1, 4, 5, 6, 14, 15, 18, 19, 23, 24, 27, 28

Challenging Days 2, 3, 9, 10, 11, 16, 17, 29, 30, 31

Affirmation of the Month I accept challenges that come my way.

Sagittarius/April

In the Spotlight
Everything flows this month as the planets harmonize with your Sun. Games, sports, and cultural events may attract you, and there's so much to do you can hardly choose. A goal you've been working toward since last summer is coming to fruition.

Wellness and Keeping Fit
Activities that have an element of fun or adventure to them will pique your interest now. After April 5 you'll want to monitor your energy levels. You could experience a dip in your reserves that brings on the latest virus, especially as April 26 approaches.

Love and Life Connections
Engaging your family in the activities you enjoy is especially fulfilling this month, and you'll find plenty to do. Pressures from work or tiredness could make you lose your communicative clarity as April 26 draws near, so be alert for gaffes and apologize as soon as you are aware of them. Tensions may rise in the workplace and place an extra burden on you emotionally as well as organizationally.

Finance and Success
Jupiter's return to direct motion allows projects you began last summer to move forward. This in addition to work you've generated since then intensifies pressure. While this should be a temporary condition, it is worsened around April 26 by overlapping workloads, dual deadlines, lack of planning, or equipment breakdown. If you can perform beyond the call of duty, it will further your career.

Cosmic Insider Tip
April is so full of opportunity that, if you are not careful, you can overdo, no matter how excited you are about the possibilities. Prioritize your tasks each day and stop work when you feel yourself beginning to be tired or ineffective, no matter what remains to be done.

Rewarding Days 1, 2, 11, 12, 15, 16, 19, 20, 23, 24, 28, 29

Challenging Days 6, 7, 13, 14, 25, 26, 27

Affirmation of the Month I nurture myself so I can care for others.

Sagittarius/May

In the Spotlight

Your workload continues to be a burden in May, as you struggle with what may be called "too much success." The pressure shifts after May 15, although the eclipses may throw you a curve ball on May 15 and 30. Mercury's return to direct motion on May 20 sets you back on the straight track.

Wellness and Keeping Fit

You'll need to take extra time to relax and recover when the work is safely dispatched. If your chi is depleted, acupuncture will boost your recovery. Of course, extra sleep and good food are a must.

Love and Life Connections

You're needing support from those around you now, so don't forget to express your gratitude. You may feel frustrated with circumstances, though, and you could find it difficult not to manifest that verbally. Searching carefully for ways to release that energy, such as screaming into a pillow or going for a walk, will keep your relationships on an even keel.

Finance and Success

Your long-term success depends on your accomplishments this month, although you won't be acknowledged for it right away. Planetary crisis points on May 15, 20, and 30 are likely to coincide with inconvenient events, so plan ahead for them. Giving yourself more time than you think you need will help you maintain your aplomb.

Cosmic Insider Tip

Taking one day at a time will help you reduce stress and remain productive during May. Multiple planetary events between May 15 and 30 will precipitate crises waiting to happen. Accept this as par for the course. This is just the universe reminding us that we are not infallible. It's okay if you're not perfect.

Rewarding Days 8, 9, 12, 13, 16, 17, 21, 22, 25, 26, 27

Challenging Days 3, 4, 10, 11, 23, 24, 30, 31

Affirmation of the Month I manage my time effectively.

Sagittarius/June

In the Spotlight
Now you are visible, and others listen to you more carefully. You're freer and more mobile. Finally Saturn has stopped holding you down through your relationships as it enters Cancer, and now it will help you develop discipline in the financial realms.

Wellness and Keeping Fit
Your health has been revitalized, and you're ready to start a new regimen. Since you find it hard to stick to a schedule or routine, you may be better off finding ways to get exercise and good food in the course of other activities.

Love and Life Connections
A situation in the home may erupt into disagreement on June 6 and catch you off guard. It may be that a need to change has been suppressed, and now there's no denying it. Although the person who initiates the action may vacillate, eventually the need must be fulfilled in some way. Being willing to work it out will smooth the way.

Finance and Success
Perhaps you have a stock portfolio that you've been meaning to restructure, and this is the time to do it, before the planets create market volatility, which is likely to come in mid to late summer. Or, you may suddenly find that your debt obligation is too high, and you need relief. If so, seek help. Long-term discipline may be in order.

Cosmic Insider Tip
A transformational process involving you and those with whom you share commitments culminates on June 9. This is part of a redefinition of who you are that has been taking place since 1995, but this year's task began to unfold in early December 2002. Attuning yourself to this cycle will make the outcome more fruitful.

Rewarding Days 4, 5, 9, 10 13, 14, 17, 18, 21, 22, 23

Challenging Days 1, 6, 7, 8, 19, 20, 27, 28

Affirmation of the Month I can become more responsible without giving up my freedom.

Sagittarius/July

In the Spotlight
You may hear ominous rumblings, especially from within your home, family, and private inner self. Ordinarily you could ignore them, but not now, because Mars is turning retrograde on July 29, creating quite a stir by the end of August.

Wellness and Keeping Fit
Even though you hear the thunder—you even may know what's coming—you need to carry on as usual. It is the rhythmic quality of our health routines that create physical health and the sense of normalcy that soothes the emotional and mental bodies.

Love and Life Connections
Your relationships at home might be ready for a good clearing out, and if so it's best to accept it responsibly rather than trying to avoid the issue. There may already have been unrest or dissatisfaction, and you may expect the discontented parties to follow through on their threats. However, they could have second thoughts as they think about what would really result if they did.

Finance and Success
Chances are that you're in a bit of a fix. It could relate to taxes, insurance, loans, and other forms of indebtedness; it could even relate to the liabilities related to a legacy or death, such as an insolvent estate or a family feud over who gets what. This month is the time to get in touch with what's in that Pandora's box and begin the road to overcoming the problem.

Cosmic Insider Tip
The big event this month happens on July 29, and all other happenings point to that. However, if you act now, you could push someone to do something that they don't really want to do. Instead, focus on situations that grabbed your attention in early June.

Rewarding Days 1, 2, 3, 7, 8, 10, 11, 15, 16, 19, 20, 29

Challenging Days 4, 5, 17, 18, 24, 25, 31

Affirmation of the Month I can act wisely when it is time to act.

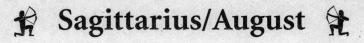

Sagittarius/August

In the Spotlight

The planets are thick as thieves, and they become more challenging to deal with as the months wears on. The peak conflicts will occur between August 22 and September 3. Lucky for you the Sun and Venus are on your side most of the month.

Wellness and Keeping Fit

Do what you can to keep your balance in the midst of turmoil. You may not be able to keep up your normal fitness routines, but you can do things that replenish: walking, yoga, tai chi, and meditation.

Love and Life Connections

For the most part, the less said the better, once your wants and wishes are known. Repeating them will only make it harder for the other party to choose a path that you favor; you could drive him or her away. The temptation will be especially strong after August 27, but if you give in, you will most likely wish you hadn't. Open up when you are asked or if your opinion truly is not known, and then only if the person shows signs of receptivity.

Finance and Success

Your workload increases and others are relying on you. The efforts you've put out over the past year are now coming to fruition, and yet problems loom on the horizon. Sometimes when there's a problem it's a sign that the project is fatally flawed. This could be the case here, and you'll have to decide whether it's true or not. The outcome could depend on you. If it is fatally flawed, pulling out now is better than digging yourself into a deeper hole.

Cosmic Insider Tip

Sagittarius is associated with right (compassionate and well-timed) speech. Knowing when to be silent is one of the three golden rules of right speech. You will find silence a valuable tool this month.

Rewarding Days 2, 3, 6, 7, 8, 11, 12, 15, 16, 17, 25, 26, 29, 30, 31

Challenging Days 1, 13, 14, 20, 21, 22, 27, 28

Affirmation of the Month I can be silent until I find openness.

🏹 Sagittarius/September 🏹

In the Spotlight
The changes are upon you. However, it isn't that bad. At least you know what the problem is, and this is prerequisite for solving it. Now you can act, and you prefer action over waiting. The planets' vise-like grip will begin to relax on September 3, with subsequent releases on September 15, 20, and 27.

Wellness and Keeping Fit
Find little corners of time to do relaxation techniques: deep breathing, seated stretches, using the stairs. Carve out a corner where you won't be found so you can periodically decompress.

Love and Life Connections
Doing nothing except listening is still the best strategy, and it's a good thing, because you're under so much pressure from work that you may feel like you're going to implode. You may see some results of your discretion as early as September 3. There will be further releases on September 8, 10, 15, 20, and 27, especially if you've kept your own counsel.

Finance and Success
Good, perhaps great, things are going to come out of the efforts you are putting forth right now in your career zone. Not only are you completing delayed projects that started last summer, but you're starting new ones that promise to be bigger than ever. The unprecedented level of activity may have caught you off guard, but if you can go the extra mile you may pull it off.

Cosmic Insider Tip
If you feel as if your survival is threatened, it is because you are attached to those things which are in a state of change. If you focus on yourself as the center of energy you'll feel more protected, plus, it will be easier to let go of what you are holding on so tightly to.

Rewarding Days 3, 4, 7, 8, 12, 13, 21, 22, 23, 26, 27, 30

Challenging Days 9, 10, 11, 16, 17, 18, 24, 25

Affirmation of the Month I am flexible in dealing with change.

🏹 Sagittarius/October 🏹

In the Spotlight
On October 6 and 21 you may note a shift in the tenor of events. The home front is more relaxed, the business environment is stabilizing, and you may even get some compensation or recognition this month for all your efforts.

Wellness and Keeping Fit
It takes time to build true strength, and you will end up weakening yourself if you push too hard. You like to go for the goal, but it's better to live in the process and observe your interaction with it. This will keep your ego in check.

Love and Life Connections
You're still getting used to the new realizations and realities that came over the past two months where your home and family are concerned. Give yourself time to heal and don't be afraid to seek the support of others around you if you feel drawn to them. Your network of acquaintances and colleagues may provide solace.

Finance and Success
You're doing well enough now to contemplate getting to those networking events you've been missing for a few months. This in fact is a power move for you, since the planets support this area of your chart now, and others will be naturally drawn to you. Since so much of success relies on the goodwill and kind regard of others, you need to keep your hand in.

Cosmic Insider Tip
After October 15 you may feel like retreating. This is natural—a part of what you feel around now every year. Allowing yourself to do it, at least a little, will energize you for the next yearly cycle which starts on your birthday. A few weeks of working quietly in the background will make up for a world of overexposure.

Rewarding Days 1, 4, 5, 9, 10, 20, 23, 24, 27, 28, 31

Challenging Days 6, 7, 8, 14, 15, 21, 22

Affirmation of the Month I embrace the future and all it holds.

⚹ Sagittarius/November ⚹

In the Spotlight

This is a retreat month, at least until November 22. Taking time to go inside allows you to recharge your batteries for another year of high flying. Without it, you'll be less creative, innovative, and healthy.

Wellness and Keeping Fit

Health becomes a focus as the eclipse casts its shadow in your health houses on November 8. Make sure that you get the support you need, whether standard care, advice, or alternative treatments. This is not necessarily something serious, but it's important to know.

Love and Life Connections

You need a break—some time to be with yourself—and you can do it when you get in your "explorer" mode. There's a part of you that craves independence, and this is the part you need to feed right now, especially before November 12—but it could be beneficial up until your birthday, if you wish to continue longer. This will refresh you and allow you to truly appreciate others when you're ready to return, good for another year.

Finance and Success

Success this month is more about not doing anything than any activity you may pursue. It's time to find the right seeds to plant in your field of success, to be tilled, fertilized, and seeded next month. If there are loose ends to tie up, if there are lessons to learn or reports to write, this is in harmony with the energies, too.

Cosmic Insider Tip

You've had two years of turn-on-a-dime action as the eclipses have traversed your sign. Now, as they migrate to your Sixth and Twelfth House solar axis, you've made the necessary external changes; it's time to take care of the inner you.

Rewarding Days 1, 2, 5, 6, 7, 15, 16, 20, 21, 24, 25, 28, 29

Challenging Days 3, 4, 10, 11, 12, 17, 18, 19, 30

Affirmation of the Month I can take the time I need to heal.

🏹 Sagittarius/December 🏹

In the Spotlight

Your own personal New Year is here, Sagittarius! Already you're feeling like getting back into circulation, contacting your friends, and attending all the social events to be found. Don't miss out on the cues that exist for new business opportunities.

Wellness and Keeping Fit

You may be discovering that a substantially new and healthier lifestyle is very important right now, and you're having to change some habits of a lifetime. Make yourself notes and take the time to set up a structure that will help you.

Love and Life Connections

As you go through changes in routines, as you develop new initiatives, those whom you love are there for you. After December 17 extra expenses could require that the purse strings be tightened. However, all is going well for the most part, as the strife which upset your household is mostly a thing of the past after December 15. So enjoy this holiday season without reservation!

Finance and Success

Your latest health needs or personal initiatives may require more cash outlay than usual, but that is part of the natural cycle of life. You have to be willing to give something to get something back. Even though Mercury retrograde puts a damper on your spending after December 17, if you are disciplined you'll be able to maintain your rate of progress on your long-range financial goals.

Cosmic Insider Tip

A new Pluto cycle beginning on December 7 signals the start of a new yearly cycle of self-empowerment and personal transformation for you. By paying attention to the events and experiences of that and the surrounding days, you'll be a step ahead.

Rewarding Days 2, 3, 4, 12, 13, 14, 17, 18, 21, 22, 25, 26, 30, 31

Challenging Days 1, 7, 8, 9, 15, 16, 27, 28, 29

Affirmation of the Month I plant the seeds of a wonderful year.

SAGITTARIUS ACTION TABLE

These dates reflect the best—but not the only—times for success and ease in these activities, according to your Sun sign.

	JAN	FEB	MAR	APR	MAY	JUN	JUL	AUG	SEPT	OCT	NOV	DEC
Move			3, 5-21									
Start a class	1, 13-28		1-4									
Join a club									16-30	1-24		
Ask for a raise											3-26	
Look for work			3-21	5-25	20-31	1-29						
Get pro advice	14, 15	10-12	10, 11	6, 7	3, 4, 30, 31	1, 27, 28	24, 25	21-23	17, 18	14, 15	10-12	7-9
Get a loan		13, 14	12, 13	8-10	6, 7	2, 3, 29, 30	26-28	23, 24	20, 21	16-18	13, 14	10, 11
See a doctor				5-25	20-31					24-31	1-29	
Start a diet				6-25	20-31	1-13						
End relationship											9	8
Buy clothes			22-31	1-5, 21-30	1-16							
Get a makeover											12-30	1, 2
New romance												
Vacation	19, 20	15, 16	14, 15	11, 12	8, 9	4, 5	1-3, 13-31	1-22, 25, 26	21-23	19, 20	15-17	12-14

CAPRICORN

The Goat
December 22 to January 20

Element:	Earth
Quality:	Cardinal
Polarity:	Yin/Feminine
Planetary Ruler:	Saturn
Meditation:	I know the strength of my soul.
Gemstone:	Garnet
Power Stones:	Peridot, diamond, quartz, black obsidian, onyx
Key Phrase:	I use
Glyph:	Head of goat
Anatomy:	Skeleton, knees, skin
Color:	Black, forest green
Animal:	Goats, thick-shelled animals
Myths/Legends:	Chronos, Vesta, Pan
House:	Tenth
Opposite Sign:	Cancer
Flower:	Carnation
Key Word:	Ambitious

Positive Expression:	Misuse of Energy:
Thorough	Apprehensive
Dependable	Controlling
Patient	Solitary
Responsible	Inflexible
Careful	Dictatorial
Disciplined	Overbearing

Capricorn

Your Ego's Strengths and Shortcomings

Some say that Merlin, the great magician of the Welsh tradition, grew younger as time passed by. This is a great archetype for you, Capricorn, because you follow the same pattern.

You are born wise, and over your life you learn to use that wisdom. When you are young, all that understanding can lead to fear of the consequences of your actions. This fear can at times be immobilizing, but as you learn to reach out you find the "zone of manageable risk" in everything you do. It's only then that you learn to play, a skill that many people take for granted. As a result, life gets better and you get younger with each passing day.

You above all others know the value in putting your responsibilities first. You know that to shirk them is to invite problems that will take more time to resolve than if they are dealt with quickly and cleanly. The challenge is to limit the responsibilities you take on. Others can easily see how good you are at shouldering a burden, so they are happy to give theirs to you. You may take on a group presidency here, a volunteer position there, that "extra credit" task in class or at work, or worse, the work someone else leaves undone because they know you will do it. Then, before you know it, you've got an endless ocean of "musts"—yours as well as those of others. There's no time for play, for healthy alternatives to work, or for the moderation in all things that you aspire to.

Generally, however, setting boundaries is one thing you're good at (or becoming good at). By being aware of what is naturally your own domain of self-interest and self-determination, you will be able to discern what is fairly your work to do. This realization will unblock the doorway to spontaneous activities—otherwise known as fun!

Shining Your Love Light

You're looking for someone strong and stable who will share your life in its totality. Because it takes a while for you to open up, you need a partner who is willing to develop your relationship slowly. You value level-headedness, stability, and wisdom, but you also hope to find a person who sees through your defenses and will reach into your isolation, to help you bring out the feelings few others know are there. You want to share the warmth you harbor inside with that someone, the stuff you can't share in your outer life.

The signs that will understand you best are the other earth signs, Taurus and Virgo. Aries is a challenge for you, but you can move mountains together. Taurus provides ideal support in your efforts to create structures by lending stability and a sense of beauty. Gemini can be a fountain of knowledge to feed your inquiring mind, but you prefer action to talk and may grow weary of the chatter. Cancer is your mirroring, opposite sign and gives you the warm nurturing you crave, but you may find the clinginess inconvenient sometimes. Leo's pride may get in the way at times, but you admire this sign's courage and ability to motivate others.

Virgo has the common sense and skills you need to build your life together. Libra may not care about the big picture the way you do, but will provide companionship for your greatest tasks. Scorpio thinks big and sees deeply—two qualities you hold in high esteem—and has the will to stick by you through thick and thin. Sagittarius can articulate the principles upon which your life is based, but lacks the steadiness of effort you enjoy in a partner. A fellow Capricorn has the same inner needs, so you can tear down each other's walls to intimacy together. Aquarius's irreverence may annoy you at times, but this sign's sense of the political world and how to reform it opens your mind to new possibilities. Pisces's dreamy visions of the future inspire you to lofty manifestations of your own dreams.

Making Your Place in the World

Your natural gift for manifesting ideas into form can take many expressions that civilization finds valuable. A profoundly effective way to do this is through government, and you may find yourself in politics, law, or public service so that you can perfect the way the system works. You're a natural manager and leader, because you recognize that leadership means taking responsibility. You may find yourself a leader in a corporation, organization, or the military, or you may become a business owner in your own right, especially with the proper training.

You could also find yourself applying your gift in physical form and work in a trade, manage construction projects, or handle design and drafting. Monies—the financial, stock, and commodities markets—could appeal, and you may be very successful in this edgy environment because of your level-headed approach.

No matter what, it's important for you to temper your ambition. It's not that you shouldn't reach so high, but that you need to be patient and ethical in getting to the top.

Power Plays

You've never kidded yourself about the allure of power and the benefits it can bring, both to you and others in your sphere of influence. Although you may be a reluctant leader at times, since you see the responsibilities involved, the reason you accept positions of leadership is because of the power it brings. You wouldn't be interested in power if you didn't think you were good at wielding it. You may feel that you know what's best for others, so accepting power is the way to ensure that they get it. There are two potential dangers in this thinking: First, you could be fooling yourself into thinking you're acting on behalf of others when you really have unconscious self-serving motives; second, you may think you're doing what's best for others, but you haven't checked with them to get their input. In either case, the expression of power can run amuck.

Your power lies in the political acumen you have acquired in your daily life, commonly called "savvy." From the moment you were born, you've been absorbing information like a sponge and generalizing it into "rules of thumb" to guide your path. This makes the world of what at first seems like human whimsy become quite predictable. When you've gotten to the core of what makes people tick as a group, you know how to work with them, redirect their thoughts and actions, and lay the foundation for their happiness.

Famous Capricorns

Debbie Allen, Isaac Asimov, Shirley Bassey, Nicolas Cage, Tia Carrere, Clarence Clemons, Robert Duvall, Cuba Gooding, Jr., Caroline Kennedy, Butterfly McQueen, Tex Ritter, Soupy Sales, Sporty Spice, Bart Starr, Mao Zedong

The Year Ahead for Capricorn

You've been waiting and working to get to a higher place, and some things have begun to work for you. To continue the trend, you'll need to sustain your efforts and build on what you've got now. If finances have been unpredictable, don't give up. It takes time to build something really good.

Once Jupiter entered Leo in the middle of last year you began getting better financial compensation for your efforts. You've had to work for it, and you can't stop yet. Make sure your energy output is sustainable, since burnout is a possibility. Unaccustomed sources of income may have been surfacing since then as well—everything from insurance benefits to bequests and inheritances could come your way if they haven't already. After August 27, Jupiter in Virgo makes the flow easier. You may feel adventurous, high-minded, and full of wisdom. You and your work are hooked to a rising star that will reach its peak in 2004–05. It's a good time to engage in a project with broad or even global reach to further your overall goals. This is feeder energy for the next seven years, so don't think too small or curtail reasonable expenditures in time and money.

Saturn has been in Gemini since April 2001, requiring you to put in a lot of time for comparatively little reward, at least in one area of your life. You may have been working harder than your body can handle, resulting in some stress-related symptoms if you haven't taken the time to vary your activities. Or it may have brought to the surface some overlooked health issues that needed attention. As Saturn leaves Gemini you may find the pressure is off in terms of the need to act, but that doesn't mean the problem has gone away. Once Saturn enters Cancer in June the energy will shift in a positive direction for you. You will find your work receiving more attention as people begin to notice you more for no apparent reason. It's as if your words inexplicably carry more weight than they did a few months ago, even though they may have been quite similar.

With Chiron in your own sign since late 2001, the emphasis on health and healing continues for another two years. Although it's a time of perhaps painful self-examination and self-discovery, it is nonetheless the doorway to self-improvement and greater well-being. Uranus is finally moving out of your Second House of resources and into your Third House of communication and commerce. For the past seven years you've been discovering resources you never thought you had—and figuring out what you really want to do with your life. Starting in March, you may feel inspired to study something deeply meaningful to you, or to launch yourself into a new, wacky niche with your products or services. Chances are you'll be on the cutting edge of the new wave of fashion or social need. Neptune is Uranus's "clean-up crew," making sure the vision matches the inner need in your recently adjusted path to success. Pluto continues to keep you on your best behavior by bringing all your past transgressions out of the woodwork. Not to worry—it's just the universe's way of helping you build a better future.

The eclipses have been submarining you for about a year, sending up messages from the depths of your unconscious, perhaps isolating you or drawing you into spiritual pursuits. In 2003 they will shift your focus gradually to friendlier pastimes, like networking and building your stock portfolio. You might find the time to engage in creative pursuits, or even the odd team sport, once in a while.

If you were born from December 22 to 26, Uranus will sextile your Sun starting March 11 from your solar Third House. This is a time when your ability to open your mind will be greatly increased, as new information, contacts, and opportunities naturally flow your way. You are likely to find yourself greatly stimulated by your environment in a pleasing way. This could involve study—anything from a book you pick up to a formal training event or course. You may find that your relationships with your siblings improve—that they make sudden changes which benefit you in some way. This may also be true with neighbors and your extended family. Perhaps a family reunion or family e-mail list will bring together those who are estranged or have lost touch. An investment in electronics for personal growth, entertainment, and learning could also benefit you at this time. Any expenditures or activities that increase your "information power" are going provide the long-lasting benefits that you as a Capricorn thrive on.

If you were born from December 22 to January 4, Saturn will oppose your Sun from June 4. This aspect will challenge you to look at yourself from others' perspectives and see how you measure up to their standards. The answer will depend on how well and wisely you have been using Saturn's energy in the past, especially during the last fourteen years. If you have been persistent in pursuing your goals, consistent with your work effort, and forthright in fulfilling your responsibilities, you will find this to be a very satisfying time. If, on the other hand, you have not felt up to that effort, not been able to focus on what's important to you or shirked obligations, you will fare less fortuitously during this time. To be sure, you will be looking at your long-term goals and achievements and judging your growth toward them, no matter how well you've done. You will also have cause to examine your life outside your goals for success, such as in the area of personal relationship. If you've overemphasized the work effort, this could become painfully clear, since people close to you may ask more of you as a partner during this time. Or, they could decide that you are not capable of giving what you need, and move on. Emotional deficits are likely come to the surface under these circumstances, as Saturn helps us balance our lives from this position.

If you were born from December 31 to January 4, Neptune will semisextile your Sun this year from your solar Second House. Neptune produces a dissolving influence, and, in the area of values and resources, you may find that your finances go through a slow change, possibly a deterioration. You may find that skills that you have relied upon for years are eroding due to age or lack of interest. You may find that what you have done in the past simply isn't enough—that you feel empty inside. Perhaps your values are changing, becoming more spiritual—or you feel disillusioned with the career path you have chosen and your prospects for the future with your current skill set. Generally, this aspect will take you back to the time, fourteen or so years ago (1989–90), when Neptune conjoined your Sun. Then, you were asked to surrender to the deepest spiritual influences, to seek spiritual meaning in your life, and perhaps you set off on a new idealistic path. Now you may discover that, although you have tried to follow this path, you need to make some adjustments to fulfill it more completely. Any signals that you receive from the universe, such as deteriorating finances or interests, are only giving you feedback that you can empower yourself to change. Although you may not know what to do at first, since Neptune's truths emerge slowly, have faith that there is a way out and continue to seek it until it is found.

If you were born from January 7 to 11, Pluto will semisextile your Sun from your solar Twelfth House. Pluto here can open the doorway to some deeply transforming experiences as it leads us to explore the hidden factors that move mountains in our lives. When we repeat or recycle experiences—say, attracting the same type of partner again and again in spite of our best efforts—this is a sign of unconscious influences from previous conditioning, things we have mislearned either in this or previous lives. There may be ways in which you feel trapped by circumstances you have dealt with for many years—they just aren't tolerable anymore, but you don't see a way to change. Or, you may see a change coming that you don't want or feel you can't cope with. Generally, you may feel inner conflict during this time as such awareness comes to light. You may struggle against your circumstances, not willing to let go of what you feel is right. You may become more tenacious under Pluto's influence. While this is a quality you will need in order to deal with Pluto, it is best put to use in directing the changes it is thrusting upon you rather than in resisting them.

If you were born from January 12 to 20, Saturn will quincunx your Sun this year until June 4. This is the last half of a period of influence which began in June of last year, so you are already in the midst of the experiences it is bringing to you. This aspect requires adjustments, especially in your lifestyle choices and daily routines. These are likely to be prompted by health considerations or conditions in your workplace. This is an excellent time to get a complete health examination, if you have not done so already. Our ability to deal with a quincunx is greatly enhanced by gathering information. It is the unknown factor which can catch us off-guard. What you do know is preparation for a very important, active, and potentially successful period coming in about two years. The efforts you make now will finish the foundation you've been laying for twelve years.

Although you may feel as though you have to sacrifice one thing to satisfy another, you can meet the challenge by becoming more efficient—working smarter, not harder. Keeping the elements of your life in balance will be a challenge, but it's a challenge you can meet and overcome.

If you were born from January 16 to 20, Uranus will semisextile your Sun from your Second House this year. This may suggest that some adjustments in your handling of finances and other resources are in order. For the last seven years you've been on a new path that you expect to bring you greater rewards and self-fulfillment, perhaps quite different from what came before. You may even have changed career or life direction in order to be more deeply yourself. Now it may be time for some slight alterations in your course. You may find, as you continue to evolve after that shot in the arm, that your values have changed or you are thinking about life differently. If so, you owe it to yourself to respond to this new understanding. This may involve taking risks for things you really believe in, or letting go of more activities and possessions from the past that no longer suit you. No matter what, self-examination should reveal with little prodding what the possibilities are. After that, it is for you to choose which way to go.

Tools for Change

This second year of Chiron in Capricorn makes health and healing an especial emphasis for you again. In addition, as Saturn enters Cancer, a new dynamic enters which may make your need to act with discipline more urgent. Your health issues may be the result of some long-term habits that stress certain areas of the body. For instance, your penchant for classic good foods may result in high dietary fats, which stress the liver and gall bladder. This may be remedied by adopting a low-fat diet, which may mean learning to cook some of these wonderful foods your own low-fat way.

You may find dietary supplements a solid way to enhance your well-being. Capricorns often benefit by adding minerals such as calcium, magnesium, and trace elements to their diet. Zinc supports the immune system and clears the skin, as do vitamins A and C.

Another pattern which may have been a part of your past is a lack of exercise. You've been too busy, but now you can't afford to ignore your body any longer. Taking time for fitness not only helps you build muscle mass and a strong heart and lungs, it relieves stress because of the endorphins released during physical exertion. Besides, when you're exercising, you're not working. It gives your left brain a break so that the right brain can generate new creative ideas. Mountain climbing or rock scrambling, or just hiking, may be the way to make your heart sing when you can get away. The rest of the time, a stationary bike or other home equipment may be your best bet.

Another key to your health is taking time off. It is absolutely essential that you find ways to take vacations, weekend retreats, and mini-breaks on a regular basis. This may be the only way you'll be able to let go of the work mentality for any time at all, but ideally you want to be able to make a clean break every day and have some time left to yourself when you're done. Then, discipline your mind to let go of the worries and concerns associated with your tasks and responsibilities. Anything you call "fun" gives you the respite you need. You may be drawn to project-oriented hobbies that give you a sense of accomplishment: building a ship in a bottle, sewing a shirt, assembling a jigsaw puzzle or a piece of fine furniture.

Be sure to take time to laugh; hook into a great comedy show on TV and make a habit of watching it. Treat yourself and your partner to comedic movies as they are released.

♑

Affirmation for the Year

I can heal my wounds by being in touch with myself.

⚸ Capricorn/January ⚸

In the Spotlight

Although normally you start the year with lots of energy and constructive ideas, this year there is uncertainty. The feeling is temporary, lasting no later than January 23. After that, you'll be able to pick up on delayed or derailed activities with new insights.

Wellness and Keeping Fit

You may be fighting off illness as the month begins, and the feeling of that vague sore throat may be with you until January 23. Rethinking your daily routines and making lasting adjustments will help you avoid future health problems, even if this one gets you.

Love and Life Connections

The words may not come out of your mouth right in spite of your best efforts this month, especially between January 2 and 23. You're probably feeling cranky and wanting to stay away from everyone so you can sort things out. This is a far better course of action than trying to relate congenially with your loved ones when you don't feel like it. You'll know it and they will, too.

Finance and Success

You are not likely to be terribly effective in communicating or executing actions, as your mind is fuddled. Anything you can do on background, if you must do it, is the best use of your time and energy. Even though the yearly rhythm tells you it's launch time, your heart and mind are telling you to retreat. This is what you should do, and your body will force the issue if you don't take the hint.

Cosmic Insider Tip

The setbacks you experience now will produce their benefits in time. You've got time to rethink the status quo, the regular way of doing business, and this is the fountain of creativity that can lift you above your current circumstances if you embrace it.

Rewarding Days 2, 3, 6, 7, 8, 11, 12, 13, 21, 22, 25, 26, 29, 30

Challenging Days 9, 10, 16, 17, 23, 24

Affirmation of the Month I accept my need for downtime.

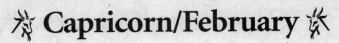 Capricorn/February

In the Spotlight
You're coming out of it now—in fact, you're almost visionary. You've got grand ideas and great schemes for what the year will hold. Still, something keeps pulling you back into your cave, as if you need more inner time to create your dreams.

Wellness and Keeping Fit
This is generally a good time to go forward with medical procedures (excluding February 16) if needed. If you are otherwise well, it is good to focus on establishing those new habits you vowed to form: more exercise, more sleep, better food, and more time to relax.

Love and Life Connections
You're feeling more sociable this month, but you will still benefit from some time alone on a regular basis. The creative energy within you is wanting expression, and alone-time fosters this. You should, however, be able to resume normal relations with those around you, although this is directed more toward those in your personal rather than public life. Your charisma increases after February 3.

Finance and Success
The financial situation looks good—very good—as a big project begins to produce more than dreams around February 2 and a long-term initiative, possibly involving government, shifts gears in your favor after February 22. You'll meet, even exceed, your productivity goals this month with little effort, after months of putting extra effort into the success of these enterprises.

Cosmic Insider Tip
February 16 could bring unexpected events out of the blue that will jolt everyone, but don't let it distract you from your usual broad perspective on life. A new yearly cycle of innovation and financial opportunity begins for you on February 17, so be alert.

Rewarding Days 3, 4, 8, 9, 17, 18, 21, 22, 25, 26, 27

Challenging Days 5, 6, 7, 13, 14, 19, 20

Affirmation of the Month I can be open to new successes.

Capricorn/March

In the Spotlight

The emphasis is on communication and outreach as the planets pick up speed and move into your Third House. After March 11 activities in this area will take on the glow of the unexpected. After March 4 that feeling of being pulled back into yourself vanishes.

Wellness and Keeping Fit

As Mars travels through your Sun sign you feel stronger and more vigorous—just what you need to put some enthusiasm behind your resolution to work out more. You're good with discipline, but you just haven't felt like it until now. It's important to build slowly.

Love and Life Connections

You're much more companionable this month—in fact, you feel like getting out with friends and family. A little shopping, a museum, a fine little French restaurant—all with friends, family, or your partner—are just the things to make you feel alive right now. Scintillating conversation is enough to bring any relationship out of the doldrums.

Finance and Success

Money continues to come in, and it appears as though the source will last a while longer. In the meantime, your power activity this month is outreach. Get some new publicity out there, because it will have more impact, especially between March 5 and 21. Your message is still strong through April 21, so keep up the campaign.

Cosmic Insider Tip

Although it will dip back into Aquarius in the fall for a few weeks, Uranus enters Pisces on March 11. This is the beginning of a seven-year period emphasizing preparedness for the tasks you or others wish to perform. This suggests a revolution in your understanding of the world and how it works.

Rewarding Days 2, 3, 7, 8, 16, 17, 20, 21, 25, 26, 29, 30, 31

Challenging Days 5, 6, 12, 13, 18, 19

Affirmation of the Month I can communicate clearly for success.

Capricorn/April

In the Spotlight
April gives a release of energy in your Eighth House of finances, giving your income a boost in response to projects begun last summer. This burst of activity is bottled up toward the end of the month, however, as Mercury slows down to retrograde on April 26.

Wellness and Keeping Fit
You've been living within your new health regimen for several months. If you've exerted enough self-discipline, you'll find yourself with new, healthier habits. If you've slacked off, you have a chance at the end of the month to regroup and get back in the saddle.

Love and Life Connections
Your love interests are focused close to home—perhaps on family, siblings, and others close to you. You may choose to entertain privately, putter around the house, complete repairs and upgrades, or just stay at home and feed your Moon. There could be illness in the family, so that someone requires extra care and attention—especially toward the end of the month.

Finance and Success
You may find it helpful to work some at home, especially after April 21, since this is where you are drawn right now. It's not that you can't accomplish things, it's just that you want or need to be around, and yet you are capable of working productively. This will be an excellent time to work quietly. You may decide to spend money on a large purchase after April 21.

Cosmic Insider Tip
You're feeling confident now, but try to keep your balance. Flying high could bring a precipitous crash later, and the planetary patterns are not as friendly during the late summer. Pay attention to how you feel around April 25.

Rewarding Days 3, 4, 5, 13, 14, 17, 18, 21, 22, 25, 26, 27

Challenging Days 8, 9, 10, 15, 16, 28, 29, 30

Affirmation of the Month I listen to my body's signals.

Capricorn/May

In the Spotlight

Even though Mercury is retrograde until May 20, this is a month of ease for you. Your creative juices flow, romance is on your mind, and finances continue to be good. It's time to have fun. Enjoy it now, because a period of harder work is just around the corner.

Wellness and Keeping Fit

If you don't want to catch the prevailing illness, you must take basic care of your body. Breathe deeply, drink plenty of water, sleep until rested, and do at least some light exercise. You can resist the virus if your system is strong.

Love and Life Connections

Even though you want to connect socially with others this month, it may not be possible as often as you'd like, since circumstances are pulling you away from the fun stuff. This is not permanent, however, nor is it unrelenting. Even if events make it difficult, you can and should squeeze in some time for play. This will work better after May 20, but don't think waiting until then will be enough.

Finance and Success

You continue to gain benefits from the projects you started last year, but you're not one to rest on your laurels. You can sense that a new cycle will begin soon—at the end of August, in fact. You're already thinking about what you may want to create for the new cycle. The eclipses on May 15 and 30 will give you clues. The former may be especially helpful, since it may lead you to meet the right people, so don't be a stay-at-home.

Cosmic Insider Tip

You'll be very busy and less able to focus on relaxation over the next few months, so give yourself permission to blow off steam now. The best time for it is after May 16, but take your chance when you can.

Rewarding Days 1, 2, 10, 11, 14, 15, 18, 19, 23, 24, 28, 29

Challenging Days 6, 7, 12, 13, 25, 26, 27

Affirmation of the Month I enjoy life and live in the present.

Capricorn/June

In the Spotlight
It's time to put your nose to the grindstone as the planets enter your solar Sixth House of work. You may begin an educational process, whether learning or teaching, after June 17. Shifts in long-term cycles tend to make you think more deeply about the future.

Wellness and Keeping Fit
You've made many changes in your lifestyle, but just because the pressure is shifting elsewhere now doesn't mean you can give up your new wholesome habits. You must remain vigilant.

Love and Life Connections
When Saturn enters Cancer you begin a two-year period of restructuring. This may mean changes in the commitment level in your partnerships. This feels like a burden, until you discover how you're contributing to your own experiences by feeling isolated. Your partner could pull away due to external circumstances such as work or travel, or because of a rift in your relationship.

Finance and Success
Saturn opposite your Sun can also bring a pinnacle of success, especially if you've done your work and held up your responsibilities over the past fourteen years. It also boils down to how well you treat others, since our social contacts form part of the web upon which our good fortune depends. You may get an inkling of what lies ahead during June, but much more will be revealed in October.

Cosmic Insider Tip
Education, communication, and knowledge in general are going to assume more importance in your life over the next seven years, while Uranus is in your solar Third House. The choices you make now will cast your lot for the coming few months and augur your choices, needs, and experiences for the longer cycle.

Rewarding Days 6, 7, 8, 11, 12, 15, 16, 19, 20, 24, 25, 26

Challenging Days 2, 3, 4, 9, 10, 21, 22, 23, 29, 30

Affirmation of the Month I make wise choices.

Capricorn/July

In the Spotlight
You reach a culmination in your yearly cycle in July, but don't let that blind you to more subtle energies—the planetary hints of things to come. You may come into contact with new ways of thinking that prove you wrong about something.

Wellness and Keeping Fit
Issues in health could climax this month as you gain new information, perhaps through examinations, treatments, or tests. Part of taking care of yourself is keeping yourself safe, so exercise a little extra caution on or after July 29.

Love and Life Connections
Others are drawn to you, whether at work, at home, or on social occasions. Take advantage of this to improve business prospects, but also use the time to create more closeness in your intimate relationships. You may not have time for a romantic getaway, but spend an evening out doing something that's special for both of you.

Finance and Success
You may be especially focused on information processes and services this month, as Mars slows down to retrograde on July 29. Perhaps the computer network is down, or it's being upgraded. Possibly you're taking classes or training in a field adjunct to your career, and it's consuming your time and energy. Do what you can, but don't let these distract you from successes in other areas.

Cosmic Insider Tip
Listen to what's happening and do what you can to head off problems. You may not be able to do anything, but if you are able to figure something out, it will relieve the pressure on you in August and September, the time of Mars's retrograde.

Rewarding Days 4, 5, 8, 9, 12, 13, 16, 17, 18, 21, 22, 23, 31

Challenging Days 6, 7, 19, 20, 26, 27, 28

Affirmation of the Month I can balance my present circumstances with what I sense about the future.

☡ Capricorn/August ☡

In the Spotlight
Challenges will only become stronger by the end of the month, as six planets powerfully interact with each other between August 22 and September 3. You will feel the influence in your solar Third and Ninth Houses—the information gathering and dispersing areas. Don't be surprised if your energy is increasingly consumed by activity in these areas as the month wears on.

Wellness and Keeping Fit
A vacation is just what you need, and perhaps it's a part of your yearly rhythm of activities, but something may be holding you up. Perhaps something closer to home or more practical will work better.

Love and Life Connections
Communications could be painful, as words said in haste reveal thinking that you are usually at pains to mask. This is especially possible after August 22. If apologies are in order, the sooner said, the better; then the healing can begin. Silence may be wiser than honesty, as it allows others to find the truth themselves and save face.

Finance and Success
Difficulties over information services come to a head at the end of the month. Since so much of business is information oriented, this could cover a broad spectrum of possibilities: marketing, electronics, training, education, distribution, as well as the tone and quality of messages. This is a good time to tell the truth if you are asked directly, as prevarications could result in legal action.

Cosmic Insider Tip
This month's planetary square dance promises many events, and obstacles may result. Your lessons may be mostly symbolic. If so, count yourself lucky and accept them graciously. Then help others who need it.

Rewarding Days 1, 4, 5, 9, 10, 13, 14, 18, 19, 27, 28

Challenging Days 2, 3, 15, 16, 17, 23, 24, 29, 30, 31

Affirmation of the Month I live in the truth.

🜨 Capricorn/September 🜨

In the Spotlight
The worst is over, and you can slowly start climbing out of the depths. Conditions improve by degrees on September 3, 12, 15, 20, and 27. By the end of the month, wounds are healing and recuperation is coming to pass. Now perhaps you can get away for a few days.

Wellness and Keeping Fit
A health issue you've been dealing with since at least April gets resolved around September 18, so now you can rest easier. The need for vigilance continues, but you know what's happening now. Work with whatever healing methods seem appropriate for the symptoms you have and the people who are attuned to your unique situation.

Love and Life Connections
Travel may be in the picture this month, after a delay. While this could be for business, why not try to fit a pleasure jaunt in? The planets suggest it, and you and your loved ones certainly can benefit. There may be a pause in events before September 15 that permits it.

Finance and Success
Delays and pressures are slowly relieved as deadlines are met and reports are completed. Don't expect the rigor to end entirely until the very last of the month, however, when Mars turns direct. After September 15 you begin to arc toward a pinnacle of power, which requires you to make wise decisions in a leadership capacity.

Cosmic Insider Tip
It's still important to go with the flow, and the flow is going your way as the planets in Virgo trine your Sun. This means that you will probably be in a position to help others who were not so favored by the planetary events.

Rewarding Days 1, 2, 5, 6, 9, 10, 14, 15, 24, 25, 28, 29

Challenging Days 11, 12, 13, 19, 20, 26, 27

Affirmation of the Month I can heal myself and others.

⚹ Capricorn/October ⚹

In the Spotlight
You've reached the top of your form, and the efforts of many months are coming to fruition. The planets are back on the straight track, and a vision you have held since January begins to fall into place. There are still concerns with the matters overwhelming you for the past three months, but they are fast coming to a close.

Wellness and Keeping Fit
As life resumes some sort of normalcy, your excuses for a disrupted health program are waning. By October 24, you can begin getting back into a rhythmic pattern of fitness, good nutrition, and your regular healing treatments.

Love and Life Connections
People in your public world fill your awareness now, and that's okay as long as you save a little for those closest to you, who have stuck by you for so long. It's slow, accomplishing the goals you've set, but you'll be clear of the extra tasks by mid-December. If you are realistic about when you'll be more available, others will be more patient.

Finance and Success
You're working on two fronts now: the educational process you've had going since July, and the efforts you started in January based on your current career path. Both are important to your future, so you'll just have to throw all the balls in the air and juggle for awhile. Prioritization will get you through. Another project, perhaps partnership related, begins around October 24.

Cosmic Insider Tip
Let the forces of the times carry you; you will find your position more compelling to others when you get there naturally rather than by your own efforts. Once in a position of power, deferring to those whom you serve is the tried-and-true path of leadership.

Rewarding Days 2, 3, 6, 7, 8, 11, 12, 13, 21, 22, 25, 26, 29, 30

Challenging Days 9, 10, 16, 17, 18, 23, 24

Affirmation of the Month I make wise choices on behalf of others.

⚶ Capricorn/November ⚶

In the Spotlight

The emphasis is on social interaction this month, as your areas of focus dovetail more easily. The work is familiar, and completion is near. A new plot twist arises around November 8, as an old situation dies and a new opportunity presents itself.

Wellness and Keeping Fit

On November 12 you enter a natural cleansing period that comes before your birthday every year. This is an excellent time to give your body a healthful and rejuvenating break from the usual lifestyle patterns you follow.

Love and Life Connections

Be sure to include your family or partner whenever possible on those work-related social events. Even a few quiet moments together can be quality time. You are needing some time alone now to assimilate everything that's happened lately. Be sure to honor that need, but also to balance it with the need others have for you to interact with them.

Finance and Success

Reward and recognition may be yours this month as you complete several initiatives and reconnect with others in preparation for new ones. Groups and organizations will be especially receptive to you this month, so try to build in some bookings and networking events, or maybe a conference. This is a good month to ask for a raise, all other things being equal.

Cosmic Insider Tip

If you've diversified your skills, you are ready to take on a new, more creative emphasis in your activities. This is an excellent step, as it adds versatility—and also makes you more secure, because you have more skills with which to make it in the world.

Rewarding Days 3, 4, 7, 8, 9, 17, 18, 19, 22, 23, 26, 27, 30

Challenging Days 5, 6, 13, 14, 20 21

Affirmation of the Month I accept the good that comes my way.

✳ Capricorn/December ✳

In the Spotlight
You may feel like getting started on some of those new initiatives you've been dreaming up. However, Mercury retrograde in your sign starting December 17 suggests that you'd be better off just enjoying the holidays.

Wellness and Keeping Fit
Your wellness efforts should revolve around creating inner health, as the Sun transits your solar Twelfth House. Meditate, write in a journal, and spend time by yourself so that you can be alone with your thoughts and allow your soul's wishes to emerge.

Love and Life Connections
You'll be wanting to focus more on home and family as the month passes, and after December 16 you'll get to do so. If you've taken care of yourself you won't become ill during the Mercury retrograde, so you can really enjoy your loved ones without that barrier to bonding with them. The usual holiday social events and activities are fine, but make sure you do something special for your partner— a wonderful gift or experience you know she or he will enjoy.

Finance and Success
Although you like to be productive, internalizing now will increase the power and reach of your productivity later. It's time to let go of all the work and worry and let your mind rest. This will probably be more possible after December 16. Resist the urge to keep moving.

Cosmic Insider Tip
Creativity relies on a free and spontaneous spirit, and that means you have to play once in a while. Let your whims take hold. Don't fear losing control by listening to your heart. You'll still be your grounded, practical self, no matter what.

Rewarding Days 1, 5, 6, 15, 16, 19, 20, 23, 24, 27, 28, 29

Challenging Days 2, 3, 4, 10, 11, 17, 18, 30, 31

Affirmation of the Month I can take time off and know I will be welcomed back when I return.

CAPRICORN ACTION TABLE

These dates reflect the best—but not the only—times for success and ease in these activities, according to your Sun sign.

	JAN	FEB	MAR	APR	MAY	JUN	JUL	AUG	SEPT	OCT	NOV	DEC
Move			22-31	1-5								
Start a class			3, 6-21									
Join a club										10-31	1-12	
Ask for a raise		5-28	1, 2								28-30	1-16
Look for work						14-30	1-13			8-24		
Get pro advice	16-18	13, 14	12, 13	8-10	6, 7	2, 3, 28, 30	26-28	23, 24	20, 21	16-18	13, 14	10, 11
Get a loan		15, 16	14-16	11, 12	8, 9	4, 5	1-3, 29, 30	25, 26	21-23	19, 20	15-17	13, 14
See a doctor						14-30	1-13				13-30	1-16
Start a diet						14-29						8
End relationship	18											
Buy clothes				6-25	20-31	1-13						
Get a makeover	23-31	1-12										
New romance					20-31	1-9						
Vacation	21, 22	17, 18	16, 16	13, 14	10, 11	6-8	4, 5, 31	1-31	1-30	1-6, 21, 22	17-19	15, 16

AQUARIUS
The Water Bearer
January 20 to February 18

≈

Element:	Air
Quality:	Fixed
Polarity:	Yang/Masculine
Planetary Ruler:	Uranus
Meditation:	I am a wellspring of creativity.
Gemstone:	Amethyst
Power Stones:	Aquamarine, black pearl, chrysocolla
Key Phrase:	I know
Glyph:	Currents of energy
Anatomy:	Circulatory system, ankles
Color:	Iridescent blues, violet
Animal:	Exotic birds
Myths/Legends:	Ninhursag, John the Baptist, Deucalion
House:	Eleventh
Opposite Sign:	Leo
Flower:	Orchid
Key Word:	Unconventional

Positive Expression:	Misuse of Energy:
Open-minded	Flighty
Friendly	Foolhardy
Compassionate	Detached
Independent	Undirected
Reserved	Aloof
Altruistic	Defiant

Aquarius

Your Ego's Strengths and Shortcomings

There's nothing you love more, Aquarius, than to be called a trend-setter! You love thinking of yourself as cutting edge, a member of the avant garde. Whether it's fashion, philosophy, love, or career, you want to be hip and progressive. You may be a slave to "weird" because it just suits the part of you that likes to tweak people and remind them that it's okay to be unique.

This is because you like to think you have your finger on the pulse of the "group" (whether it's society, an organization, a corporation, or family) and know where it's headed. You may not want to be considered a full member of the group—that may violate your need for independence of thought. Still, you know what the group wants, what its hidden agenda is, and what its ideals are. You have an innate sense of the political landscape and how to manage it. For this reason, you're a very good advisor to others who must deal with politics, even though you may shudder to think of participating in them yourself. You like to consider yourself above the fray, aloof and indifferent to the worries that ravage those who take on more central roles.

Being Aquarian is really about balancing your own self-hood with the identity placed on you by the group(s) with which you align yourself. Well balanced, your own identity neither dominates, nor is it dominated by, the group. This is not as easy to maintain as others may think. For instance, in a corporation there often seems to be an implicit expectation that your personality will be submerged in favor of the corporate personality. For this reason, many Aquarians find it difficult, if not impossible, to work in a corporate environment unless there is an acceptance of individual expression and freedom of thought.

While other groups may afford its members more freedom, even those may be difficult for you to declare actual allegiance to. The fact is, you are energetically sensitive to the consciousness of the various groups you contact. This often makes you cautious about making commitments to a group. But when the energy feels right, it's okay to give it your stamp of approval and join in!

Shining Your Love Light

You're a mover and a shaker, and you want your partner to be savvy in the socio-political realms as well. You want a partner who can carry the torch of reform alongside you and share in your political triumphs. However, you also need a partner who won't begrudge you your independence and your need to circulate among many friends. In fact, you will do best with someone who has a lively existence outside your relationship, just as you have.

You will find the most natural harmony in the other air signs: Gemini and Libra. Aries is a good companion for you, with the focus and initiative to supplement your will to do good. Taurus's earthbound pursuits may not thrill you, but you appreciate this sign's persistence and gift at creating beauty. Gemini is socially adept, putting everyone at ease—and won't tire before the party's over. Cancer may be too inwardly focused and emotional for your liking, but this sign shares your concerns for the welfare of the group. A partner with the sign opposite yours, Leo, brings enthusiasm to your high ideals and noble-minded goals, but may create more drama than you care for. Virgo's mastery of technology can make you want to solve the problems of the world together, but the attention to detail can be daunting. Libra's intellectual approach is a breath of fresh air that allows you to relax in a bath of mental stimulation, without the emotional drama. Scorpio's in-depth understanding of the human condition can lead you to new insights, but this sign may lack your social stamina. Sagittarius shares your idealism and commitment to improving the human condition. Capricorn may seem too earthy and pragmatic at times, but this sign's knowledge of the way systems work is a superb aid to your activist efforts. The joy of commonality can be discovered with another Aquarius, but the emotional atmosphere could become so dry as to crackle with electricity unless you make a point to nourish your relationship. You may share Pisces's commitment to spiritual pursuits, but this sign's need for peace and solitude runs against your need for a high level of social interaction.

Making Your Place in the World

You can find many ways to translate your mental electricity into a prosperous career in our modern electronic society. You may be drawn to anything in the broad field of computer science, from computer repair, analysis, and training to web design.

Your inventive side can be satisfied by a career in research and development, engineering, or entrepreneurial invention. You may also be led by your intellectual nature to a calling in any science—but you may be especially attracted to astronomy, chemistry, or the biological sciences. Your free-thinking side could draw you into astrology, healing, or some far-out energetic work focused through the latest New Age tools and techniques. You are also talented in working with groups of people, which could draw you to organizational management or psychology. You are especially good in a team environment where everyone works on the same level.

It's a fine line between uniqueness and eccentricity, and your success could be hampered by a need to rebel or be different. If you can be a joiner, but hold on to the individual and special core of your being, you will find the balance for accomplishing all your goals.

Power Plays

Working with the forces of group consciousness can seem a daunting task, what with the sheer contrast in size between the individual and the community. It helps to have an ace up your sleeve and to know how to use it. One of your special powers is the power of objectivity. Objectivity emanates from your airy intellectualism and allows you to stand back and see the big picture.

Your secret is the knowledge that, even though the group is made up of individual members, the community that is formed has a single, evolving consciousness of its own, and its direction can be shifted by just the right words and intention if that community is understood at its deepest levels. Objectivity permits you to tap that deep level and find the right message to guide the group to its highest good. It brings you closer to your innate Aquarian sense of justice and gives you insight into how to express it.

Famous Aquarians

Marisa Berenson, Mikhail Baryshnikov, Edward Burns, Stockard Channing, Sheryl Crow, Minnie Driver, Benny Hill, Jack Nicklaus, Rene Russo, Gene Siskel, Jerry Springer, Gertrude Stein, Eddie Van Halen, Laura Ingalls Wilder

The Year Ahead for Aquarius

This year promises change, Aquarius, but not the upheaval you've been dealing with over the past seven years. It won't solve all your problems—in fact, a couple of new ones will surface—but nothing will compare to the wild ride you've had since 1996.

Are you ready for a relationship adventure? Jupiter spends most of the year in your opposing sign of Leo, and that's what may be in store. Jupiter here can bring partnership opportunities, lots of partners, a partner who travels (wanna go along?), or even a partner who goes astray. Generally Jupiter bodes well, and it can bring lots of response to your efforts from the world around you. If you are involved in any business that uses personal effort to create success, you will find this to be a "peak" period. If you do counseling or one-on-one work with others, you will find this to be a very profitable time. Once Jupiter enters Virgo in August the emphasis goes to money—as in getting more of it. There could be a temptation to spend extravagantly as well. Keep in mind that this is a peak in a twelve-year cycle, and that there may be a leaner time in a few years to correspond to this time now. Jupiter periods are good for building a reserve.

Saturn in Gemini has been one of its lovelier placements for you. Of course, it's not great to have Saturn anywhere in the short run, but in the long run Saturn brings us our greatest, most robust rewards—if we do our work and live an honorable life. Though Saturn's placement in Gemini put a damper on your "fun," it also meant that you were serious enough to want to create things of lasting value. By now, you should be seeing some manifestations of that. However, it will be ten years before the full fruits of your labors will show, so be patient. Starting in June, Saturn will be in Cancer, putting the spotlight on your solar Sixth House of health and lifestyle. There will be no better time to adopt a new health regimen or dietary plan because you'll have the discipline to go with it, even if it's just the fear of cholesterol as a result of your latest checkup. Relax—you've got three years to work it out. Allow yourself to travel the road of slow, steady progress, because that's what lasts. Chiron is in your solar Twelfth House, and there's a whole lot of healing going on. You may have been uncovering wounds, both physical and emotional, since early last year. An active role in healing—finding support or doing it yourself—is on the menu this year. You could also find yourself working, paid or volunteer, in a hospital or hospice.

The big news for you this year is that Uranus finally, *finally* is leaving your sign. It moves into Pisces in March, then makes its last-gasp return to Aquarius in September to finish out the year and make sure you've really gotten that final course correction. It will feel better in your solar Second House of finance and resources, but it is still in the heavens, and so it is still affecting our lives. Remember that it is more active when we move away from our center to an extreme position. If you like to take big risks, or become attached to your material possessions, Uranus will have fun with you in the coming seven years. You'll have fun with Uranus only if you can let go and live in the calm, moderate center. Neptune is still affecting your sense of self, and it means to dissolve away what is not spiritual and deeply meaningful in your life. It creates vision in order to see the big picture. If your schemes seem grandiose (not likely for an Aquarius), try learning more about whether they're possible. You can allow the outer world to temper your ideas of what to create, but you shouldn't let it kill your dreams. Pluto has been a sideshow for you compared to the other outer planets. Still, it's like the thief lurking in the brush. He may be after your neighbor's fortune, not yours, but you still could fall prey if you are careless. An open and fluid attitude is your best friend.

The eclipses are moving from your solar Fifth–Eleventh House axis to your Fourth–Tenth House axis. This shifts your focus from your social milieu to home and business. You may experience more challenges this year, but that means that there's something happening to challenge you, and that brings growth, which leads to success.

If you were born from January 20 to 24, Uranus will semisextile your Sun starting March 11. This will spice up your life by opening new possibilities to you in terms of using your existing resources or developing some new ones. In some ways, it may be as if you are looking at the world with new eyes, since this semisextile could indicate that you have changed your way of seeing things. You may be seeing the same things in new ways and finding opportunities where only obstacles or the same old boring drudgery existed for you before. Now, as you ponder the prospects, it may be helpful to look back to seven years ago, when you went through some radical personal changes. You may have felt at that time as if you were emerging from a cocoon, coming into your full flight and beauty. This time the changes are not so intense, but you may find that you alter your trajectory slightly in response to this transit.

If you were born from January 20 to February 3, your Sun is being quincunxed by Saturn starting June 4. After the last three years of relative calm in the material world, the road may be a little bumpier now. You've made lots of progress in the accomplishment of your goals, though, and now it's time to look at things from a different perspective and maybe work a little harder to ensure that you're on track. This may involve working additional hours at the office, starting a training program, or shoring up areas of your life that you've been neglecting. You may be tempted to ignore your physical health during this time, but that is not a wise plan—in fact, it is possible for health issues to emerge during this transit, so more focus there will bring the best results. Get a checkup, improve on your diet and exercise plan, and fit in some yoga or meditation to make sure you stay in balance. This is an important preparatory period for a burst of progress that will come in about two years—if you focus and sustain your efforts now. You may also be tempted to jump the gun and rush to the pinnacle you can feel coming. However, this is not the time. Allow events to come to you, and, although it will take longer, you will experience more robust results.

If you were born from January 29 to February 3, Neptune will conjoin your Sun this year. This is a significant process that will stand out in your memory for years to come, and will have far-reaching influences for the rest of your life. Neptune's influence is so intangible, unmarked by distinct events, that it may easily slip your notice. However, upon being identified, you will see how very pervasive it is. One of its effects is to dissolve boundaries. This could be anything from being absorbed by someone else's personality (caused by the loss of boundaries between yourself and the other person) to a leak in your car's water system. The loss of boundaries between yourself and others is the most common difficulty with this conjunction. You may feel drawn into another person's emotional or physical difficulties and feel compelled to make sacrifices for them. This is difficult because it may take you away from what would be your "normal" path. You may not be a good judge of others' character during this time either, for the best of reasons: You are able to see into the soul of the other person. Unfortunately, since not everyone's personality matches the purity of their soul, this can be dangerous, and you could be conned or manipulated by those around you. On the other hand, you may become aware of such manipulation during this transit, especially as you acclimate to its influence. Neptune does not obscure our perceptions; it merely takes us to another level of insight, where we have to learn to navigate based on other types of information offered from the inner, spiritual levels. As you become accustomed to it, you begin to see your world much more clearly, from a deeper, less obvious level. That is, it won't be obvious to others, but it will be quite clear to you. Herein lies the danger: In this new world, the physical/material and emotional worlds don't matter. This is why it's important to rely on the advice of people you have known and trusted for a long time. Ultimately, you must discern what makes life meaningful for you during this transit, and then seek to align yourself with this path in the coming years. This is what will provide the basis for the quest you follow for the rest of your life, and do much to determine your sense of inner fulfillment along the way.

If you were born from February 7 to 11, Pluto will sextile your Sun from your solar Eleventh House. This will bring a relatively quiet revolution into your life where group affiliations and identities are concerned. You may find that the people with which you have associated in the past no longer suit you—that you are looking for something deeper, more attuned to who you really are. You may find that group politics are too vicious for you, or that you have developed a distaste for some of the hidden dynamics you've seen. You may also find, however, that with this new knowledge you are empowered to do something. You may be selected to fill a leadership role, or you may find that there is some other way you can have a powerful (and positive) effect on the situation. You may also enjoy a boost in status because of your position in one or more associations—perhaps receiving an award or other special recognition. This may benefit you personally as well as professionally. After the hard work you've put in over the past decade, this could also be a good time to ask for a raise, since chances are very good that the business you work for is doing well, and the boss thinks well of your efforts.

If you were born from February 11 to 18, you'll feel the support of Saturn trining your Sun until June 4. This aspect began its influence last June, so by now you're familiar with its effects and are actively working with them. This influence will be felt primarily in your creative efforts, children, romances, and leisure activities. You may find yourself taking these things more seriously; for instance, a hobby may turn out to be profitable, or you may decide it's time to have children. You may get more serious about a romantic relationship and decide to make a commitment. You could decide that it's time to buckle down and work harder to accomplish your goals, instead of spending so much time partying. Generally, whatever projects you undertake now will go smoothly and open to your initiative. While it may take longer to gain ultimate success, and the road will not always be this smooth, when this transit is completed you will be able to see visible progress that will feed into a pinnacle of success in about three years.

If you were born from February 15 to 18, you will experience the awakening influence of Uranus conjoining your Sun this year. This is a momentous and exciting time for you, since you tend to like it when you encounter the unexpected, and life will never be the same again. Your world will be shaken up, but for the most part in a good way, as long as you embrace the changes instead of resisting them. Uranus brings us into alignment with our soul purpose, and if you are in alignment you will notice little impact in your life. However, if you have lost your way, if you've run aground in the density of everyday life and forgotten your goals, Uranus will lift you out of the quagmire and set you down closer to where you need to be in order to proceed more meaningfully. This means that any obstacles that lie in your path may be removed, and you may be surprised at what the obstacles are. Uranus usually teaches us to look at our circumstances differently—with less attachment—so that we can see what our true priorities are and then pursue them. You will be completely rejuvenated, invigorated, and refreshed by the clarity that comes when the ego has been set aside in favor of the higher part of yourself. You are likely to need more freedom in all aspects of your life while you explore your options. You may feel stifled by your job or the constraints of your relationship commitments. You may want to change the terms of a business partnership or get out of it altogether. You may decide that your career doesn't feed the real you and begin the processes of change, or perhaps a move will tickle your fancy. All in all, anything is game during this transit. As long as you add a strong dose of compassion to your actions, you will be setting the stage for successes in the years to come.

Tools for Change

Neptune in your sign and Jupiter opposite can make this a year of idealistic new beginnings, as well as the culmination of efforts begun six years ago. You'll experience bursts of power as well as extreme high and low tides in your energy level. Staying toward the midline with your output will help to balance these swings, and there are many tools that can assist you in the process.

One of the most important things is to vary your activities. Your tendency is to stay with something for long periods, and this increases stress reactions and puts more wear and tear on you. Diversifying your activities will stimulate your interest and reduce stress by giving the different parts of your nature intermittent rest periods. By changing gears every couple of hours, you'll be strengthening your body and mind as well as increasing your efficiency.

Physical exercise is vital in keeping your mind-body balance. Your mind is so strong that it can exhaust the body, resulting in chemical imbalance that changes brain function. Athletic activities like team sports can keep you engaged because they are combined with group social events as well. It's also important to include a fitness program in your daily routine; walking, running, working out at a gym, or aerobics classes may suit your style. You can improve your circulation—a potential weakness in an Aquarius—by getting plenty of the rejuvenatory vitamins A, C, and E. Herbs such as collinsonia also support good circulation. Eating regular meals also has a grounding effect and keeps you from experiencing blood sugar highs and lows. Be sure to avoid refined sugars and flours—and to keep complex, high-fiber carbohydrates in your diet to ensure good digestive function.

It is also vital that you be engaged in whatever activities you take on. While you won't enjoy every task you encounter at work, it will help you to endure routine tasks if you have something going on the outside that fires you up. Joining an organization centered around a hobby or political cause can keep you going, and may turn out later to be a source of income.

Get help from others when you need it. If you need your energy balanced, polarity therapy or energetic healing can be highly beneficial. Psychology, whether in the form of psychotherapy or your own study of human nature, can make a significant contribution to your overall well-being.

≈

Affirmation for the Year

I dream my future from the highest parts of my being.

Aquarius/January

In the Spotlight

With a couple of solar Twelfth House influences, you may feel mostly like hiding out this month. There are still things going on in the world out there, however, and they can benefit you. People will be patient as you recover your public self.

Wellness and Keeping Fit

This is more a time of improving the health of the inner you, so don't feel like you have to rush right out and join a health club. Meditation, yoga, or mild exercise will recharge your batteries.

Love and Life Connections

Others are receptive to you now, even eager to connect with you. The contacts are likely to come through your work and your broad network of friends and colleagues, so don't neglect those parts of your life right now. They will provide the foundation for the next three months, as Mercury starts a new cycle midmonth. If you're looking for new romance, these will be the potential sources, but don't expect much of new acquaintances during this month.

Finance and Success

While this is not a good time for making new investments, signing contracts, or making even verbal agreements, you can use this time well by cleaning up your desk, making necessary equipment repairs, and staying in touch with your business contacts. They may not have work for you now, but they will by February. Some new prospects could appear, but some will turn out to be fly-by-night or inappropriate, so weed those out.

Cosmic Insider Tip

Downtime helps you to have more direction and momentum when the cycle begins again, once the Sun enters Aquarius on January 20. Even if you're under the weather, you can watch a good movie.

Rewarding Days 1, 4, 5, 9, 10, 14, 15, 23, 24, 27, 28, 31

Challenging Days 11, 12, 13, 18, 19, 20, 25, 26

Affirmation of the Month I can take time to relax and enjoy life.

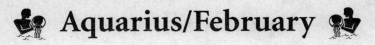 Aquarius/February

In the Spotlight

As the Sun enters your sign a new yearly cycle begins, and your energy level rebounds with it. You will feel renewed, ready to move forward, and the way is clear for you to do so. Uranus in your sign is a big influence as it turns direct, releasing you to new freedoms.

Wellness and Keeping Fit

Now is the time to get going on that new exercise program, at least after February 12. This is also a good time not to overeat, since your body will be naturally detoxing until your birthday.

Love and Life Connections

Mars in your Eleventh House will help your business connections really click this month. Since schmoozing is your specialty, you should be in your element. Taking business-related training isn't a bad idea either. You can combine business and pleasure by taking your partner with you, then going dancing after the business event—something special just for him or her.

Finance and Success

Partners may be skittish this month, and agreement further away than ever, but this is a temporary condition. If something comes to the surface, that means it can be addressed. If it isn't going to work, it's better to know now; if it is, it's time to get on with it. This is not a bad time to make investments; collaborate with paid advisers, not partners. The way clears for something big begun last year.

Cosmic Insider Tip

This is a seed-planting time, so don't expect fruits now. Instead, you'll need to rely on the fruits from previous cycles. In a couple of months your relationships will improve if you accept responsibility for your role and actively participate in solving the problem. Patience and humility are your power attributes right now.

Rewarding Days 1, 2, 5, 6, 7, 10, 11, 12, 19, 20, 23, 24, 28

Challenging Days 8, 9, 15, 16, 21, 22

Affirmation of the Month I patiently develop new opportunities.

Aquarius/March

In the Spotlight

This month is good for building skills, accruing cash, and buying equipment. Give the new initiative a dry run, but watch your budget. Things will be moving quickly now, so take advantage of the planets' natural momentum.

Wellness and Keeping Fit

Blend work and fitness if you must. Walk to work, park far away from the health-food restaurant, and use the stairs. Better yet, set aside your busy-ness for an hour a day and gain the inner peace (and lower blood pressure) that comes with getting away for a while.

Love and Life Connections

You're looking good to others this month as Venus enters your Sun sign. They will come to you as if magnetized by your wit and charm. Follow it up with substance, though, because Venus won't hold them there. You'll have to rely on yourself for that. This is a good month for business or romantic liaisons, but don't expect much from them until next month.

Finance and Success

It's hard, but you need to wait a little longer. The climate isn't quite right yet to close the big deal. In the meantime, prepare—and work on those other, less-riveting projects to lay the groundwork for the coming period of focused effort. It's also better if you have more than one thing going at a time. Diversification is the key to flexibility and success.

Cosmic Insider Tip

Patience is still a virtue, and so is self-discipline. If you engage in your activities as if time is of the essence and you're preparing for something real and tangible, your unconscious mind will help you create it, too.

Rewarding Days 1, 4, 5, 6, 10, 11, 19, 20, 23, 24, 27, 28

Challenging Days 8, 9, 14, 15, 21, 22

Affirmation of the Month I work hard to create future success.

Aquarius/April

In the Spotlight

Your big plans can finally move forward this month as Jupiter goes direct on April 4. Still, don't push. Trust the universe to cooperate, and you'll fare better. Toward the end of the month you'll notice everyone's momentum will slow as Mercury turns retrograde. Don't worry—it's just in time to let you catch your breath.

Wellness and Keeping Fit

You may start seeing some results from your efforts this month as the new plan becomes a part of who you are. Don't let boredom toward the end of the month distract you from your goals.

Love and Life Connections

You are feeling more contented with life the way it is right now, including your relationships. In fact, you may be downright complacent. It's okay to rest and allow peace to fill you, but don't think that now you can just let things take care of themselves. A period of emotional challenge is just around the corner, and being receptive now can head off difficulties later. After April 21 don't let anger overcome your natural airy objectivity.

Finance and Success

The money's coming in now, and you'll be able to balance the budget. This may be a good time to liquefy some assets to make medium-sized purchases. The rest of your business affairs should start to rectify themselves after April 3, with a dip at the end of the month. Not to worry: It's just part of the flux and flow of life.

Cosmic Insider Tip

A time of relative ease is not the time to relax and expect things to take care of themselves. We can use these times to do noncritical tasks that will reduce the number of fires we have to put out in the future. This reduces stress and increases the quality of life.

Rewarding Days 1, 2, 6, 7, 15, 16, 19, 20, 23, 24, 28, 29

Challenging Days 3, 4, 5, 11, 12, 17, 18, 30

Affirmation of the Month I maintain balance in my activities.

Aquarius/May

In the Spotlight

Mercury retrograde until May 20 may take you deep into yourself to answer some questions about what makes you tick. This could also indicate a transition period in your home or with family relationships. Keep an eye on your anger level; it could ricochet against you.

Wellness and Keeping Fit

You may find impediments to your intended activities coming from within yourself. You may also need to focus more attention on your home, where cutting up a fallen tree may not be in the plan, but can still increase your calorie output.

Love and Life Connections

Taking part in some of your favorite pursuits may be one of the brief respites you enjoy in this eventful month. You may find that simple joys—going shopping with a friend or partner, meeting your sister for lunch, going to a museum—can be the lifeline that makes it all worthwhile. While relationships may be a little volatile, it doesn't hurt to set all the slights aside and normalize relations.

Finance and Success

With Mercury retrograde it is best not to make any big decisions until after May 20. This means avoiding buy-sell transactions and signing contracts. Misunderstandings at home can affect your ability to make good judgments at work, so give yourself time to figure things out. A feared change may seem necessary, and it may happen, but wait until you're comfortable with it.

Cosmic Insider Tip

You may need to open to those closest to you more than you like to. Emotions aren't really your cup of tea, yet you have them like everyone else. If you accept them as an essential part of life and give them time, you will find that many of the wrinkles smooth out.

Rewarding Days 3, 4, 12, 13, 16, 17, 21, 22, 25, 26, 27, 30, 31

Challenging Days 1, 2, 8, 9, 14, 15, 28, 29

Affirmation of the Month Sharing my inner self brings peace.

Aquarius/June

In the Spotlight

With the transiting Sun trining your natal Sun, everything flows. Use this time to enjoy life—entertain, vacation, or just relax. Once Saturn enters Cancer on June 4 you are likely to feel pressured to work harder. Moderate the urge to comply, since this could create health problems later on.

Wellness and Keeping Fit

Incorporating sports and social interaction into your plans will help you feel more fulfilled this month. When Saturn enters Cancer on June 4 you'll probably be more able to maintain the discipline required to get the results you want, no matter how you go about it.

Love and Life Connections

This month lends itself to romance and getting together with friends. This is the peak romantic month of the year for you, with Mercury, Venus, and the Sun all supporting love. There's never been a better time for it, especially after June 10. Bookstores, coffee shops, and sporting events are your erogenous zones.

Finance and Success

Although this is a time to invest, resist the urge to take it over the top. Once Saturn enters Cancer on June 4 you can look at your entire portfolio and rearrange your investments. You may be able to sell some of the stocks you've felt stuck with over the past two years, or jump into some that you've felt uneasy with in the short run. Business agreements should be flowing well now, too.

Cosmic Insider Tip

You're never better than when you're in a group, and this month it will be easy to find one. It's okay to be spontaneous—to decide to do things on the spur of the moment. It helps us to feel alive, and it's part of what defines "fun."

Rewarding Days 1, 9, 10, 13, 14, 17, 18, 21, 22, 23, 27, 28

Challenging Days 4, 5, 11, 12, 24, 25, 26

Affirmation of the Month I can have fun for its own sake.

Aquarius/July

In the Spotlight

The emphasis now shifts to work, organization, and the cares of daily life. There may be a growing stalemate in your income and expenses; being aware of it now may head off a problem at the end of the month when Mars turns retrograde.

Wellness and Keeping Fit

Much can be accomplished this month, but don't expect to see results right away. Moderate changes are best: They'll produce the most powerful results, and you'll be able to retain them.

Love and Life Connections

As your workload increases you may be spending more time with colleagues than those with whom you share more intimacy. Your personal relationships may suffer if they are new or there are confidence issues. By remembering to nourish your important relationships, you, your partner, and other loved ones will make it through without weakening them.

Finance and Success

This is a great time to engage in the work that feeds your revenue streams. Business partners will be especially open and pleasantly interactive, and coworkers will be easy companions. At the end of the month, Mars turning retrograde may bring up some strains in finances or other resources, but there should be sources of income to shore up the weak areas. Since Mars will be affecting this area for two months, be prepared to maintain these measures for that long.

Cosmic Insider Tip

There is no direct path to our goals. The way we get where we want to be is a winding road, and the planets reflect this universal truth. Be content if things seem to take a wrong turn at the end of the month. Sometimes a wrong turn brings an unexpected joy.

Rewarding Days 6, 7, 10, 11, 14, 15, 19, 20, 24, 25

Challenging Days 1, 2, 3, 8, 9, 21, 22, 23, 29, 30

Affirmation of the Month I accept income from unusual sources.

Aquarius/August

In the Spotlight

Jupiter, Mercury, Mars, and Uranus will be interacting in new ways at the end of the month to create a broad-based change in perspective. Since this will influence not only you but those around you, be prepared to shift course, and don't push to conclude things before then, because they could self-destruct.

Wellness and Keeping Fit

Exercise routines that reduce stress may be helpful now, such as yoga and Pilates. Meditation can be important to maintaining your inner health, since stress levels can climb toward the end of the month.

Love and Life Connections

Others are inclined to be generous with you this month, in spite of difficulties. Even though you may proclaim that you are a free spirit and don't need others, they will ignore that and lend you a hand, both emotionally and financially if necessary. Give yourself a break and let them help. It'll tighten the bonds between you in a good way.

Finance and Success

With Mars retrograde, you may experience cash-flow difficulties. While these are only of a temporary nature, they do require addressing. It's important to move forward—and not cry over milk that's already been spilled. Even if your past actions could have been better, you must deal with your situation as it is now, not dream about what it could be if only.

Cosmic Insider Tip

This situation won't last forever, but it may feel that way even to you by the time it's over at the end of September. Until then you'll see subtle shifts but no big release. Keep up your steady efforts, and if you have to be less than perfect for others, then so be it. It probably won't matter in the long run.

Rewarding Days 2, 3, 6, 7, 8, 11, 12, 15, 16, 17, 20, 21, 22, 29, 30, 31

Challenging Days 4, 5, 18, 19, 25, 26

Affirmation of the Month I can give and receive help from others.

🏺 Aquarius/September 🏺

In the Spotlight

Relief begins to arrive: New resources come in, especially after September 20. There'll be lots of movement, and you may begin to get some elbow room after September 15. The final and critical release point occurs on September 27, when Mars goes direct.

Wellness and Keeping Fit

With all that's going on in your external affairs, it's difficult to have the patience for something so mundane as your health. Don't forget to take your prescription medications, and do some gentle activities every day to get away from the stressors and keep your chi moving.

Love and Life Connections

You have never needed your loved ones more than you need them now. Although you are not at the center of the difficulties, you are affected. This is a time for interdependence, for relying on each other. Share with each other. Take time to communicate and enjoy the simple pleasures of peace in each other's company. If you can get away together, this is a good time to do so.

Finance and Success

External events are affecting everyone, and you are no exception. However, you will do well in the long run. Think long-range with the decisions you make now, as hard as that may be. Over the next year, Jupiter in your house of others' resources will make sure some come your way. You may catch a glimpse of that right now, but it will be easier to see after this month.

Cosmic Insider Tip

A new yearly cycle of Jupiter started August 21. This begins a year of reward and financial growth, but it is obscured by the planetary clashes of August and September. Allow yourself to look ahead in order to make the most of this cycle.

Rewarding Days 3, 4, 7, 8, 12, 13, 16, 17, 18, 26, 27, 30

Challenging Days 1, 2, 14, 15, 21, 22, 23, 28, 29

Affirmation of the Month I am thankful for what I have.

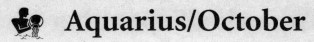 Aquarius/October

In the Spotlight

Your finances get back on the right track—you've even got the chance to travel! In the last half of the month your attention turns to a longer-term project you've been working with. It'll be time to dig in and do it after October 24.

Wellness and Keeping Fit

This is an ideal month to get away from it all and do something different. Relax in the country, or try a sport you've never tried before. You will benefit greatly by getting away from the daily cares of life.

Love and Life Connections

Now that the coast is clear, it's okay to get out and enjoy life with the partner or other companions of your choosing. Some of the gatherings may be work related, but what's wrong with that? As long as you don't cheat your partner of the attention he or she deserves, you can create a win-win. Harmonious interactions with parents may also be part of the month's undertakings.

Finance and Success

Financial success doesn't seem like such an oxymoron these days—in fact, things seem like they're on a straight trajectory up. Your main focus now is that new work initiative. You may be more in the background on this one, or you may be doing groundwork for a later, more visible effort. Either way, five months from now you'll begin to have something to show for it.

Cosmic Insider Tip

Old cycles are ending and new ones are beginning this month. It will be very busy as you make the transition. Don't forget to properly finish up old business in your eagerness to start new projects and develop new ideas. Otherwise, your new efforts will be less effective.

Rewarding Days 1, 4, 5, 9, 10, 14, 15, 23, 24, 27, 28, 31

Challenging Days 11, 12, 13, 19, 20, 25, 26

Affirmation of the Month I complete the old and start the new with ease and finesse.

🦐 Aquarius/November 🦐

In the Spotlight

Sparks are flying as you enter a very effective action period in November. As the year comes to a close, more old situations fall away and new ones develop out of them, especially with respect to your own self-transformation and improvement. Career and group undertakings gain the forefront, and finances continue to get better.

Wellness and Keeping Fit

You are feeling strong and healthy, unless you've been overworking. Although your focus is on your next success, don't shirk your responsibilities to your body. You may especially enjoy workouts with business colleagues—and find them both refreshing and fruitful.

Love and Life Connections

Although you are focused on career expansion right now, take care to include your loved ones in the picture. Share your joys and fears, breakthroughs and breakdowns. You've recently learned how valuable the people you love are to you. Don't forget to let them know.

Finance and Success

The new cycles are starting to take shape, and you can see real potential ahead. Although the fruition of your dreams and plans will come in 2004, it's time to build them now. You have the opportunity to make a larger than usual number of contacts this month, and this is where your extra effort should be expended. Don't forget that project waiting for you at the office.

Cosmic Insider Tip

You are in demand now, but there are limits to what you can do. It's okay to say no once in a while; practice graceful ways of saying it. Better to say no than to do a poor job because you're overwhelmed. By choosing the right tasks carefully, you lay the foundation for the successes of 2004.

Rewarding Days 1, 2, 5, 6, 7, 10, 11, 12, 20, 21, 24, 25

Challenging Days 8, 9, 13, 14, 22, 23, 28, 29

Affirmation of the Month I make the right choices for my career.

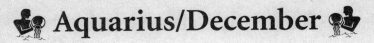 Aquarius/December

In the Spotlight

Right from the beginning of the month you may feel more like withdrawing into a restorative phase. The financial woes of the late summer are behind you as Mars finally leaves your house of resources.

Wellness and Keeping Fit

You're more likely to run on your own than to seek company as Mercury and Venus enter your solar Twelfth House. Your exercise time can be a reverie, since the endorphins that are released bring the same physiological responses as a meditative state.

Love and Life Connections

As Mercury enters (on December 2) and then retrogrades in (on December 17) your solar Twelfth House, it's time to reconnect with your inner self. You may take a few close others on a tour of the process, but it is something we each must experience alone. This retreat time will help you adjust to reality and make your relationships more genuine. Just take the time to reassure your loved ones that the need for retreat is temporary, lasting until mid-January.

Finance and Success

You finish the year with relative financial peace. Most of your energy right now is going toward the project you started working on at the end of October. As you immerse yourself into it you may find yourself lost to time until late at night as the holidays elapse. Keep your focus here; you will begin to see internal benefit and the prospect of success will take shape at the first of the new year.

Cosmic Insider Tip

The universe seems to fold in on itself as the year ends. You can consciously make use of that time by turning inward yourself and taking care of those background duties that others are only dimly aware of. Rest if you need to—you won't miss anything.

Rewarding Days 2, 3, 4, 7, 8, 9, 17, 18, 21, 22, 25, 26, 30, 31

Challenging Days 5, 6, 12, 13, 14, 19, 20

Affirmation of the Month My time alone replenishes me.

Aquarius Action Table

These dates reflect the best—but not the only—times for success and ease in these activities, according to your Sun sign.

	JAN	FEB	MAR	APR	MAY	JUN	JUL	AUG	SEPT	OCT	NOV	DEC
Move				6-25	20-31	1-12						
Start a class			22-31	1-5								
Join a club	8-31	1-3									3-30	1-2
Ask for a raise		14-28	1-27									22-31
Look for work						30	1-30			25-31	1-12	
Get pro advice		15, 16	14-16	11, 12	8, 9	4, 5	1-3, 29, 30	25, 26	21-23	19, 20	15-17	13, 14
Get a loan	21, 22	17, 18	16, 17	13, 14	10, 11	6-8	4, 5, 31			22, 23	17-19	15, 16
See a doctor	23-31	1-28	1-4			30	1-30					3-16
Start a diet	18					30	1-13					
End relationship		16										
Buy clothes						11-30	1-4					
Get a makeover		1, 14-28	1-4									
New romance					31	11-30	1-4					
Vacation	23, 24	19, 20	18, 19	15, 16	12, 13	9, 10	6, 7	2, 3, 29, 31	16-30	1-24	20, 21	18, 19

PISCES

The Fish
February 18 to March 20

♓

Element:	Water
Quality:	Mutable
Polarity:	Yin/Feminine
Planetary Ruler:	Neptune
Meditation:	I successfully navigate the seas of my emotions.
Gemstone:	Aquamarine
Power Stones:	Amethyst, bloodstone, tourmaline
Key Phrase:	I believe
Glyph:	Two fish, swimming in opposite directions
Anatomy:	Feet, lymphatic system
Color:	Sea green, violet
Animal:	Fish, sea mammals
Myths/Legends:	Aphrodite, Buddha, Jesus of Nazareth
House:	Twelfth
Opposite Sign:	Virgo
Flower:	Water lily
Key Word:	Transcendence

Positive Expression:	Misuse of Energy:
Idealistic	Gullible
Healing	Confused
Imaginative	Clinging
Forgiving	Unaware
Caring	Impenetrable
Spiritual	Over-emotional

Pisces

Your Ego's Strengths and Shortcomings

More than any other sign, Pisces, you know that you are spirit inhabiting physical form. This is because you, as the "gaseous water" sign, are more tuned in to the unseen levels of reality than any other. You know it's more than just "spiritual"—there are layers upon layers of reality that most people are not aware of. However, you can feel them: the other possible worlds that could exist, the alternate ways of interpreting what you see, and the other voices in your head.

It also means that you are more sensitive to energies than most people around you. You are innately attuned to the "ethers," often experiencing feelings, thoughts, impulses, fears, and sensations of others as if they were your own. This suggests that you may need time alone on a regular basis to sort yourself out from the other stimuli you've received in your daily activities.

In this rough-and-tumble world, you may find it necessary to treat yourself more gently (and ask the same of others) than the average. You may find yourself unhappy or less able to cope where high levels of stress and competitiveness prevail. The best way for you to deal with these feelings is to tap the strengths of the world with which you are most familiar—the world of spirit. When you feel imbued with a higher vision, an intention greater than yourself, you will find yourself strengthened and emboldened to act, and you will be impervious to others' criticisms and negative energies. As long as you are acting for the higher good, you will find yourself buoyed up by your experiences, not drained by them.

At the deepest levels, you dance to the song of the universe, fulfilling the role of the visionary in the zodiac. You are the music maker, dreaming the future into being. Learning to love in yourself what is not always valued in modern culture is the key to contentment and making the best use of your gifts.

Shining Your Love Light

You're looking for a spiritual love, a soul mate with whom you can share tender moments and deep communion. You are likely to have a vision of your ideal partner, but since the world very seldom gives us perfect people you have most likely found that you need to compromise. When you begin a relationship, you may find that you adapt quickly to the other person's needs and desires, so you lose yourself in the process. Even if this happens, gradually you must let your true self come out if you are to form a fulfilling relationship.

Your most harmonious partners may be found in the other water signs, Cancer and Scorpio. They share your experience of living in an ocean of emotion. Aries is a shock to your system, what with this sign's direct approach and fast action, but you also appreciate the sincerity. Taurus is easy on the heart and mind, and provides solid footing for building your dreams. Gemini's fountain of knowledge dazzles you, but you may find your partnership low on practicality and high on giddiness. Cancer's enfolding support is a balm for your tender heart and allows your true self to emerge. Leo can seem overbearing and brash, but you can learn from this sign's bold self-confidence and partake of a zeal for life. Virgo, your opposite sign, can bring into material form your wildest dreams—and can help you discern which of those dreams are worth realizing. Libra shares your joy in peace, harmony, and beauty, but may lack an attunement to the world of psychic sensations you inhabit. You understand Scorpio's intensity and admire this sign's protective nature and tenacity in the hardest circumstances. Sagittarius can be a little too blunt and casual at times, but you share ideals for life and compassion for the human condition. Capricorn provides structure and safety for you to express your deepest nature, and guides you through the world in savvy ways. Aquarius embraces the highest ideals you have for humanity, but your respective ways of pursuing it may be diametrically opposed. A fellow Pisces may help you create a space where you feel honored and completely understood, but it may be difficult to stay grounded.

Making Your Place in the World

Your most successful career is likely to be in an area to which you are led by belief, because you want very much to better the world. Your compassion could lead you to work in medicine as a nurse, physician, or medical technician, or to provide administrative support in a hospital or other medical environment. Or alternative healing may be your thing—especially reiki, energetic healing, faith healing, or auric cleansing.

You also have an artistic side, and you excel at anything visual: photography, film work, painting, or music. You may also find yourself drawn to theater or film directing, acting, or production. And then there are the spiritual pursuits: A vocation in religious ministry and counseling or spiritually based self-help writing could attract you. Your excellent psychic abilities could lead you into work as a clairvoyant, tarotist, or aura reader.

No matter what you do, you will suffer if you do not take measures to keep your energy field clear of others' thoughts and emotions. If you spiritually detox every day, you will travel a happy and fulfilled career path.

Power Plays

Your power is the power of surrender. Surrender does not mean giving in to opposing forces; it means having an absence of resistance. When you surrender, you open to an experience and let it flow through and around you. When you surrender, you are like a reed in the river. The force of the river is powerful, and it damages and destroys larger, stronger objects that offer more resistance. However, the reed bends and shifts, turning sideways to let the river pass. It retains its wholeness, its identity, even after overwhelming force has threatened it.

Just like the reed, surrender gives you the power to survive because you offer no resistance. You go with the flow until the flow recedes and you can free yourself. This year, as the planets create perhaps one of your greatest challenges to wholeness at the end of August, surrender may be your best power play. To do this is to take advantage of one of the universe's great truths. By surrendering to forces when they threaten to overwhelm you, they cannot attack you. Then, holding to your sense of what is inwardly correct, you can act when the forces have relaxed.

Famous Pisces

Erykah Badu, Juliette Binoche, Mary Chapin Carpenter, Charlayne Hunter-Gault, Dame Kiri Te Kanawa, Kyle MacLachlan, Sidney Poitier, Helena Sukova, Jennifer Warnes, Billy Zane

The Year Ahead for Pisces

We're all starting a new adventure this year, and you're in the forefront, Pisces! Uranus is entering your sign, and this means that it's time to walk through the door of that brave, new world and get to where you're meant to be.

In August, Jupiter moves into Virgo and your solar Seventh House. Until then Jupiter will inhabit your Sixth House and Leo, putting more emphasis than you like on lifestyle. You may feel like you're becoming a Virgo, what with all the new standards of discipline you've been setting for yourself in diet, exercise, and daily living. You're probably working hard, too, and for less reward than even your self-sacrificing soul is comfortable with. Once Jupiter enters Virgo the focus will shift: You'll be getting more rewards, your health will stabilize, and you'll be used to the new routines. This is your opportunity to delegate, to bring other people to you, and to enjoy the love of those around you. You'll probably find that you are suddenly gaining more natural respect from others, as if some dues-paying hurdle has been leaped. If you can accept it gracefully, you'll be laying the foundation for greater success in three years.

Saturn in Gemini may have made you feel as if you had lead in your boots. Getting started in the morning, feeling enthusiastic and energetic, takes more effort than in the past. You've also had to learn to be more effective, and serious, about what you do. More than at any other time in your life, you've probably been thinking about wasted time and energy. Even if you have regrets about the past, gazing backward is only going to make the present part of problem. It's best to move on and make a study of those around you who are good at manifesting their dreams. Saturn's move into Cancer and your solar Fifth House in June will bring welcome relief as it inhabits a more harmonious area for you over the next three years. Of course, Saturn isn't always unbridled joy, and in the Fifth House it can make you very serious and distinctly unplayful, but you'll feel like you have flubber in your shoes compared to the weight of the last three years. Ultimately, you will use this energy best if you focus on bringing your creative ideas into form, or nurturing those creative ideas into which you have already breathed life. Chiron in

Capricorn and your solar Eleventh House may draw you into groups with a healing theme. You may also want to support those who have a wound or disability.

If you like fresh air and new challenges, Uranus's move into Pisces in March is just what you're looking for. This is nothing to fear if you live an authentic life, because that's what Uranus creates for us. If there is anything artificial or unhealthy for you, you can look forward to having it "startled" out of your life. This doesn't always mean that something unpleasant is going to happen—Uranus is the planet of miracles as well as accidents—and ultimately you will grow from whatever you experience. Neptune is still bringing its blessings from the spirit world. There may even be a feeling of karma to some of your experiences. Things work best with Neptune when you surrender to the influences around you and wait for clarity before you act. While Pluto has been challenging you since 1995, it has brought about a necessary strengthening process. Now you really know when it's worthwhile to complain and when what happened is just a blip on the screen of reality. It's not over yet, but you've got the right idea, and your intuition will see you through.

Starting in the middle of 2002, the eclipses brought survival issues into your life. You may have been thinking about moving, or changing jobs or even careers. The eclipses this year will be more harmonious, taking you to a more intellectual focus. You may find yourself wanting to gain more education so that you can make the changes you have envisioned.

If you were born from February 18 to 22, Uranus will rejuvenate your life by conjoining the Sun starting March 11. This is likely to be one of the most invigorating and powerful times of your life, affecting your outlook and direction from this time forward. Uranus awakens us through shock. Not all shocks are unpleasant or the result of catastrophic events. Some shocks, especially for Pisces, occur at the mere suggestion of disaster. The intent of shock is to jar us out of our routinized, formulaic way of thinking and get us to look at the world as if we have never seen it before. Once you see what could possibly happen, your ego is shaken out of its habitual position of being in charge of your actions. You begin to respond from the true source of your being; the more this happens, the more we learn to stay in that state and live from it. This ensoulment process is what can result from Uranus's transit, and you may make far-reaching reforms in your life as a result of the insights you gain. This is about empowering yourself to do what feels right in the core of who you are, and it gives energy—it doesn't deplete it. You may make changes in your relationships out of a need for more freedom to express your individuality. You may not be as tied to what other people think of you, and become more enthralled by your own daemon. You will want to change whatever you think stands in your path, so conditions you have long accepted may no longer seem tolerable. This could extend to any area, but home, family, career, and partnerships are areas of common restriction and so are ripe for change. As long as you retain your natural compassion for others, you will find the right balance to making alterations in your life.

If you were born from February 19 to March 13, Saturn will trine your Sun from June 4, giving a helpful structure to your life for the following year. Ten years ago you began to seek new goals, new causes to champion. You have learned and worked and hit the wall and surmounted it. Now you reach a place of respite, a time when progress becomes visible and rewards accrue. You may find it a good time to relax and enjoy life more, but if you have the energy for it, new opportunities can arise at this time which will require renewed effort. These opportunities are likely to inspire your creativity and seem more like fun than work. If you are on the road to turning a hobby into gainful employment, this may be the time when your avocation begins to pay for itself. You may benefit from investing time and money into creative activities, since this aspect will provide you with the grounding needed to manifest your natural artistic side in visible ways. Part of being more creative is feeling more confident about yourself and your abilities, and your self-assurance will be augmented with Saturn's support. You will find your energies easier to sustain, your efforts less likely to tire you out. If you use this time of greater physical strength to gain fitness through a new exercise routine, you will be able to extend the benefits of this transit beyond its dates of influence.

If you were born from February 28 to March 3, you will want to make adjustments to your path as Neptune semisextiles your Sun. Neptune's formlessness makes this more a process than an event; there are unlikely to be discrete incidents to relate to Neptune's influence. Here, you are likely to feel drawn toward amending your life according to spiritual impulses. You may begin to feel a vivid inner life that draws you away from the public, away from the eyes of others. You may discover that work in service to others is appealing, or that immersing yourself in the undiscovered frontier of inner consciousness is your next oyster. As long as you retain a modicum of self-awareness and balance it with your life in the "real world," you will benefit from your explorations and surrender to the higher power to which you are now attuned.

If you were born from March 7 to 10, Pluto will transform your life as it squares your Sun during the coming year. This is the aspect you've been waiting for; you've felt it coming like a slow-moving earthquake. Like an earthquake, it will test your survival skills—and your ability to let go of the artificial, the mask, and to make your life real. This transit is likely to affect your career, business, livelihood, and relationship to authority figures—from your father to God. This will come from the deepest part of who you are, the seed of self-awareness that sprouts in all directions, forcing growth where stagnation existed before. You will challenge yourself to be greater, to take on more than you have before. You will have the power, if you want it, to effect great changes in your status in your community or profession by daring to think of the greatest possibility. You may suddenly feel that authority figures you've been happy enough with in the past are oppressive and controlling. You may also find that others place you in that role, and you must make sure that you are happy with the way you are wielding the power you have. This transit can be about power and power struggle, and it could be easy to get caught in a tug of war with someone else. While this can happen because we are changing our role with those around us, it is tricky to avoid such "king of the hill" competitions when we alter our persona. By being patient, consistent, and ethical in our behavior, others will come to see who we really are and accept us in our new role.

If you were born from March 12 to 21, Saturn will challenge you as it completes its square to your Sun from January to May this year. This transit, which began last June, has been asking you to take a good look at the foundation of your life and modify it to make sure that it will support you in the years to come as you engage in other endeavors. You may find yourself examining your home or family life and determining ways in which to make it work better for you, to make it more pleasant or serviceable. You may need to make improvements or repairs; you could decide to contact long-lost relations, or break away from some unhealthy family ties that have sapped you. You may retreat into your private space in order to generate more internal fire for the projects to come. You could also decide to curtail your time away from home in order to focus on what is needed there. Less happily, someone could require home care which takes you away from your regular activities and curtails new initiatives. Although Saturn usually requires hard work when it squares our Sun, there are always tangible benefits that we can bank on in the future if we are consistent and savvy in our efforts.

If you were born from March 16 to 21, your Sun will be semi-sextiled by Uranus before it leaves Aquarius. This is an aspect of gentle awakening that signals the beginning of a time when the universe, often experienced as "fate," will play a larger role in the fashioning of your life experiences. This is when you start to get impulses and insights from the inner realms, which, if you pay attention to them, will guide you through the ups and downs of life. You can, if you want, learn to make this listening a part of your habitual way of life. You may also find yourself wanting to withdraw from social interaction in favor of more private activities. You will value your aloneness during this transit. Your ability to visualize the future can be exceptional at this time, and your psychic abilities may develop further, especially if you cultivate them. You are likely also to be especially aware of the needs of others now and to want to serve them in some way. As long as you maintain your sense of self, and pursue some personal benefits, your efforts will not go amiss.

Tools for Change

With your Sun sign serving as the new home for Uranus, and Mars making itself known there, you will deal with some unaccustomed stresses this year, especially from July to September. If you don't let it get you down, you can find unequaled opportunity to grow personally and create new avenues for success.

The key to dealing with these forces is to prevent them from overwhelming you. There are many tools and techniques you can use to stay afloat. First and foremost, you must find and stay attuned to your center. You may find that daily meditation helps you to decompress—mentally and emotionally—and get in touch with the core of peace within. Because grounding is an issue for you, try a meditation where you draw silver energy up from the center of the Earth and gold energy down from the heavens high above you. Mingle them in your heart and allow them to radiate from there to fill your aura. Then send the energy back down into the earth to anchor you.

You may also benefit from energy work: energetic healing, polarity therapy, radiatory healing, awareness release technique. You may get useful energy shifts from the use of Bach and other flower essences, which heal the emotions and help us deal with fears and holding patterns. Homeopathic remedies shift symptoms profoundly, yet without side effects, and you will respond to them easily with your sensitivity.

Don't forget to maintain your fitness program, adjusting up or down depending on how you feel each day. You may want to double your exercise time with some alone time, since the endorphins released during physical activity induce a meditative state. Yoga, tai chi, chi gung, and martial arts—especially aikido—will help you blend your spirit into your body and keep you from feeling cut off from yourself. Astrology is also a useful tool as well, providing insights into timing and energetic peaks and valleys.

Perhaps most importantly, remember that multitasking adds extra stress, so you'll work more efficiently and avoid burn-out if you do one thing at a time. Although you may be working a little more slowly, at least you can sustain a stable level of activity day after day.

Sometimes this means avoiding distractions like radio or TV. Keeping your energy balanced also means eating regular meals, including fruits and vegetables and high-protein, low-sugar snacks.

♓

Affirmation for the Year

I flow gracefully with the changes and opportunities
that come my way.

Pisces/January

In the Spotlight

Your career is on the rise as the Sun, Mars, and Venus transit "reward territory" in your solar chart. The groups and organizations that you are affiliated with may be absorbing more of your time, especially January 2 through 23. It's important to watch your words carefully this month, no matter where you are.

Wellness and Keeping Fit

If you didn't catch a vacation last month, you still have until January 17. This can give you a much-needed breather to prepare for the transits coming this year. Get away to the ocean or some other liquid environment to soothe your watery soul.

Love and Life Connections

You can combine pleasure and work this month by taking your partner to business functions, as long as there's some enjoyment value for him or her. Don't let the mood from business or organizations carry over to your private life. There may be a lot to handle on the outside, and your home should be your solace. Talk to others about it when you need to and then forget it.

Finance and Success

You are in demand now as the projects you've been working on for the past nine months are coming to fruition. The groups you normally associate with may be particularly difficult, or at least unhelpful, right now. After January 23 the situation will improve, and you can benefit by re-establishing contact.

Cosmic Insider Tip

A new cycle of vision and insight begins on January 30. Use this time to re-connect with your true self and gain insight into what you for want the future. Getting in touch with the depths of your being will help you direct your efforts more efficiently.

Rewarding Days 2, 3, 6, 7, 8, 11, 12, 13, 16, 17, 25, 26, 29, 30

Challenging Days 1, 14, 15, 21, 22, 27, 28

Affirmation of the Month I listen to my inner self.

Pisces/February

In the Spotlight

This is a time for building your inner self, perhaps with some periods alone. Work-related opportunities arise around February 2; only you know if they're right for you. Creative activities you began last fall take on new momentum after February 22.

Wellness and Keeping Fit

Use this time to build your immune system by eating well and sleeping; then refine your skills at pacing yourself. Establishing a spiritual practice, breathing exercises, or doing yoga now will help you remain faithful to those routines when stress builds.

Love and Life Connections

A burden that has been placed on you with respect to family, home, and your private life will be lifted around February 22. You've been dealing with it since last October as part of a continuous process of growth and change you've been experiencing since 1995. Your perception of your relationships has changed as you've changed yourself, and you feel much more empowered now than ever before.

Finance and Success

Contacts made in groups and organizations this month can be extremely beneficial to future projects. You may find others to team with or people who have vital information or contacts you can use. Your network has never been more valuable. Career activities continue to keep you stepping lively, reaching a peak of intensity on February 16.

Cosmic Insider Tip

A new cycle begins on February 17 involving innovation and inspiration. Starting in March it will have its impact in your sense of self, your personality, and possibly your health. You may not see its influences now, but you may find some areas ripe for change.

Rewarding Days 3, 4, 8, 9, 13, 14, 21, 22, 25, 26, 27

Challenging Days 10, 11, 12, 17, 18, 23, 24

Affirmation of the Month I am building strength for the future.

Pisces/March

In the Spotlight

With the Sun and Mercury already in your sign, you'll be electrified when Uranus enters on March 11. You're likely to be brimming with ideas, itching to get out of the cage you've been in, ready to take off the mask and just be you. It's here to stay for seven years, so give yourself time to work it out.

Wellness and Keeping Fit

You may feel almost electrified over the next seven years as Uranus pulses electrical energy through you. To balance that, use your breath and soothing, stress-reducing activities, such as meditation, yoga, tai chi, chi gung, and so forth.

Love and Life Connections

Although you may prefer to languish in quiet solitude, circumstances will lead you out and about this month. Friends and colleagues may fill your social calendar more than those closest to you, but there's nothing to stop you including your partner in your plans. You are especially attractive to prospective partners (or your current one) after March 26.

Finance and Success

Work is not so demanding now, but the opportunities that exist through networking with colleagues continues. Conferences and profession-based parties, where masses of like-minded people gather, can provide a real boost to your career or business. This is a key time for you, when you are vivacious and charismatic.

Cosmic Insider Tip

Denying the need to change will bottle up Uranus's energy inside you, and you may bring unexpected, even cataclysmic, events upon yourself. By becoming aware of your instincts and moving in that general direction you assist Uranus in expressing itself through you.

Rewarding Days 2, 3, 7, 8, 12, 13, 21, 22, 25, 26, 29, 30, 31

Challenging Days 9, 10, 11, 16, 17, 23, 24

Affirmation of the Month I am in touch with new directions.

Pisces/April

In the Spotlight

Projects burst forth after April 4, and you're suddenly busy, perhaps uncomfortably so. Don't become frustrated or disillusioned when progress slows in spite of your best efforts after April 25. Mercury retrogrades once again, giving you time to catch up.

Wellness and Keeping Fit

A lingering health issue may suddenly begin to be a thing of the past this month. If you want to, you can keep yourself on the same trajectory of improvement and work on a few other subtle conditions that throw you off balance.

Love and Life Connections

Your magnetism is strong now, and you attract people to you. If you are looking for romance the time is right, but don't let the electricity of the attraction lead you to be indiscreet. Keep yourself safe and let the relationship build slowly. If the person is right for you, they'll stick around.

Finance and Success

Efforts you've put forth since last summer are now coming together. Rewards are coming your way as the planets energize your solar Second House. After April 5, emphasizing communication-related fields—such as marketing or advertising, commerce, or education—will be beneficial over the long run. As April 26 approaches, communications become less beneficial as Mercury slows to retrograde.

Cosmic Insider Tip

Jupiter's return to direct motion on April 4 allows your latest enterprises to move forward again, but Chiron and Mercury turning retrograde will slow things down to a standstill on April 25 and 26. Be alert to changes at this time, as these will be the issues to deal with in the coming weeks and months.

Rewarding Days 3, 4, 5, 8, 9, 10, 17, 18, 21, 22, 25, 26, 27, 30

Challenging Days 6, 7, 13, 14, 19, 20

Affirmation of the Month I flow with the planetary tides.

Pisces/May

In the Spotlight

You may be awash in paperwork as the month begins, your activity level far above normal, especially from May 12 through 20. The eclipse on May 15 adds to the excitement—and work burden—creating a crisis in information and communication.

Wellness and Keeping Fit

Prioritizing the tasks that vie for your time is your best health practice this month. It will reduce stress and keep you well. Be sure to grab a few minutes of recreation every day, even if it's just a walk around the block.

Love and Life Connections

It may be hard to keep track of what you say to others, you're in such a rush. It is important, however, to express yourself with care. At least until May 20, others could have a tendency to misunderstand. Brothers, sisters, and other members of your extended family could be part of the picture this month. The eclipse on May 30 brings up familiar issues at home, which will require renewed effort.

Finance and Success

Work or study may be overwhelming right now as Mercury retrogrades in your solar Third House. There will be a flurry of activity May 12 through 20, and a longer-term issue may arise that won't be resolved until October. Finances will be good this month as extra receipts come your way—especially through May 16.

Cosmic Insider Tip

You'll feel like you need some time to yourself this month, but you may not get it, what with all the demands on your time. Not having that alone time may wear on you as much as any work you do, since you naturally pick up others' energies as you move through your day. Keeping your aura clear is essential to your good health.

Rewarding Days 1, 2, 5, 6, 14, 15, 18, 19, 20, 23, 24, 28, 29

Challenging Days 3, 4, 10, 11, 16, 17, 30, 31

Affirmation of the Month I manage challenges easily.

Pisces/June

In the Spotlight

The Sun, Mercury, and Venus move through your solar Fourth House, leading you to develop new plans and projects for your home life. Saturn enters Cancer on June 4 and brings a breath of fresh air.

Wellness and Keeping Fit

Mars entering your Sun sign on June 17 lights a fire in your life. You could want to grab this new vitality and run with it. If you do, you will deplete it before it has a chance to build your chi. Let it fill and warm you, and it will sustain you in the coming months.

Love and Life Connections

You may feel as though your private life has been pulling you down the last couple of years, but this has just been an adjustment period everyone goes through periodically. It's important to make sure your foundation is strong. Now, as Saturn enters Cancer, it's time to move on. If you have more work to do on the foundation, keep up your efforts. The universe feels more supportive now.

Finance and Success

You've been putting in the work, but you may not have been getting all the rewards for it. As Saturn moves away from the bottom of your solar chart you'll start receiving more recognition, status, and reward for your efforts. Your days of being anonymous are over. You'll also receive more emotional support for your efforts.

Cosmic Insider Tip

As Mars conjoins Uranus and trines Saturn you may get a boost of insight for a few days after June 16. Pay attention to your intuition. Mars will return to this point in late August with challenging consequences. Your gift for prescience may warn you of what's coming and allow you to divert the trajectory of events somewhat.

Rewarding Days 2, 3, 11, 12, 15, 16, 19, 20, 24, 25, 29, 30

Challenging Days 1, 6, 7, 8, 13, 14, 26, 27, 28

Affirmation of the Month I am building an inner savings account of energy and inspiration.

Pisces/July

In the Spotlight

Now begins a period of "interesting times" for you. Mars will retrograde in Pisces starting on July 29 and have a profound influence on you as it interacts with several other planets during August and September. This month provides foreshadowing to what is to come.

Wellness and Keeping Fit

You have felt good, energized, as Mars makes its way through your Sun sign, but don't overdo it. Keep your fitness routine and meditative practices going as much as possible.

Love and Life Connections

It is okay to have fun this month, in spite of dire warnings. In fact, it is recommended. You'll do better with a light heart and the sense of brightness and optimism that comes when you've reaffirmed life through play. Play is spontaneous and breaks the usual rhythm of your daily or weekly activities. Making sure that you engage others in your play times will add to the pleasure you experience.

Finance and Success

After July 13, your workload may increase to daunting proportions as Mercury enters your solar Sixth House. There may be a deadline or performance assessment that you are working toward at the end of the month that could increase the pressure. Pacing yourself and making sure that you maintain your rhythm of healthy eating, sleeping, and exercise will help your efficiency and give your mind the keen edge it needs now.

Cosmic Insider Tip

An issue may arise in a family, social, or professional group. It's possible to steer clear of it—and it may be wise to do so. If you feel a need to provide support, go ahead, but resist the urge to rescue. You don't really need this now, as you have your own dragons to slay.

Rewarding Days 8, 9, 12, 13, 16, 17, 18, 21, 22, 23, 26, 27, 28

Challenging Days 4, 5, 10, 11, 24, 25, 31

Affirmation of the Month I can pace my response to obligations.

Pisces/August

In the Spotlight

The pressure at work is at its peak now, and your health could be in question. The planets make their most challenging contacts between August 22 and September 3, creating tension in your relationships as well as in your general response to the world.

Wellness and Keeping Fit

It's hard to ignore the energetic static of so much activity so that you can get your work done, but it will help you remain well if you can cocoon yourself during those times. Physical exercise keeps your immune cells working and your mind at rest.

Love and Life Connections

You could find yourself drawn into a conflict with others because someone wants you to side with them in a factional dispute. Although the manipulation will occur earlier in the month, the lines will be drawn after August 21, creating tensions which will take weeks to resolve. If at all possible, avoid taking sides; listen without offering opinions or advice.

Finance and Success

Others may try to draw you into agreements that are not in your best interest. There may be an unspoken agenda that may not be at all obvious to you, but beware of anyone offering you something for nothing. Generally, this is not a good time to sign contracts without careful consultation with those you have known and trusted for years. It is possible to solicit the help of others in projects.

Cosmic Insider Tip

Confusion may plague you this month as you try to make sense of what's really going on. The most effective way for you to gain clarity is to spend time alone so that no one's energies are commingled with yours. On your own, the right courses of action will emerge.

Rewarding Days 4, 5, 9, 10, 13, 14, 18, 19, 23, 24, 25

Challenging Days 1, 6, 7, 8, 20, 21, 28, 29

Affirmation of the Month I take the time to make myself whole.

Pisces/September

In the Spotlight

Mercury and Mars are still retrograde and relationships may be murky, but circumstances begin to improve in stages after September 3, 10, 15, 20, and 27, as each of the planets disengages. Gradually, those around you begin to understand each other—and you.

Wellness and Keeping Fit

By focusing on recovering lapsed rhythms and health routines, you can signal to your body that life is returning to normal. It is a good time to get additional health treatments also, such as acupuncture, massage, herbal therapy, or energetic healing.

Love and Life Connections

Long-buried difficulties in relationships have surfaced, and now you know how others identify the problems, but you may not yet be clear about your own role in creating them. You are more than likely chagrined as you see your actions from their point of view, but it is easy to lose yourself in someone else's perception and forget your own motives. Delay passing a verdict on your own behavior until you are clear, no matter how long it takes.

Finance and Success

Hidden agendas have emerged, and now you know whether it is a good idea to agree with those putting pressure on you. It is tempting, just because the pressure will stop; however, they will give up eventually if you keep saying no—sooner if you are firm. Wait until a new offer comes in after September 27. It may not come right away, but it will be easier to work out invisible factors and motivations.

Cosmic Insider Tip

Benefits will come to you as a result of the experiences of the past two months. If they have resulted in a clear understanding of how much you have yet to learn, then that is reward in itself.

Rewarding Days 1, 2, 5, 6, 9, 10, 11, 14, 15, 19, 20, 28, 29

Challenging Days 3, 4, 16, 17, 18, 24, 25, 30

Affirmation of the Month I give myself time to see clearly.

Pisces/October

In the Spotlight

A spiritual lesson you've been learning is clarified as an obstacle appears on the way to accomplishing a creative or family goal. Financial matters may require your attention and decisions between October 6 and 24, and new inspiration gives your heart flight.

Wellness and Keeping Fit

You can assist a physical cleansing by meditating or signing up for a few energetic healing sessions. Don't neglect your need to exercise. You may have gotten out of the habit over the past few weeks, but it's time to reaffirm your pledge to fitness before flu season sets in.

Love and Life Connections

You need time to explore the far-flung reaches of consciousness, so why not blend this with the joy of the companionship of those you love? A special bond is built when you create memories with a person, and there's no better time than now. Don't wait for life to pause—seize the day!

Finance and Success

The yearly cycle of events is reaching its culmination point, and you may wonder if the circumstances of the last few months will bring the rewards you've hoped for. It's true that there may be a muting, or possibly a delay, in some of the effects. Your dealings that concern other people's money (bequests, insurance, taxes, business receipts, etc.) will be in the forefront of your mind, and extra monies may come in, especially between October 6 and 24.

Cosmic Insider Tip

We are currently participating in cycles that last longer than a year. These longer cycles bring bigger returns for our efforts, provided we remain consistent in exerting ourselves. Results that do not come in the next four months may still develop in the coming year or two.

Rewarding Days 2, 3, 6, 7, 8, 11, 12, 13, 16, 17, 18, 26, 27, 30, 31

Challenging Days 1, 14, 15, 21, 22, 28, 29

Affirmation of the Month I return to my routines with grace.

Pisces/November

In the Spotlight

You get a boost in the intellectual development department from the eclipse on November 8. This may open a doorway for you in study or instruction, or perhaps publication. This, and the solar eclipse on November 23, is all part of a long-term process of fulfilling your highest potential that began in 1995.

Wellness and Keeping Fit

You still have another six weeks of higher energy levels while Mars is in Pisces. If you temper your efforts and don't push too hard, you will gain a higher level of fitness that will stay with you.

Love and Life Connections

Your relationships are going well on just about every front now, although there are perhaps a few associations that did not make it through the planetary challenges of the summer. You have done the best you can—and people can always change. Holding a vision of their perfections, while realizing who they are in the now, supports the time when a change of heart may bring reconciliation.

Finance and Success

Travel, career goals, advancement, and outreach receive more emphasis in your public life now. You may be traveling for business or working with faraway or foreign clients and companies. A new opportunity around November 8 suggests an abrupt change in direction that will work out in your favor if you pursue it carefully.

Cosmic Insider Tip

Just as your life seems to settle down, the eclipses urge a sharp change in focus. Try to look at them as opportunities, not obstacles, and it will be easier to see their potential and move with their thrust. They may seem to divert you away from what you have wanted, but they are actually leading you toward it.

Rewarding Days 3, 4, 7, 8, 9, 13, 14, 22, 23, 26, 27, 30

Challenging Days 10, 11, 12, 17, 18, 24, 25

Affirmation of the Month I will follow where opportunity leads.

Pisces/December

In the Spotlight
The Mercury retrograde on December 17 may increase your focus in groups and organizations. You are finally released from the self-development processes of the past six months, however, when Mars leaves Pisces on December 16.

Wellness and Keeping Fit
The level of career and social activity that you sustain this month may put your immune system to the test. Keep it moving with regular exercise, plenty of sleep, good nutrition, and time to yourself.

Love and Life Connections
This is a great time to connect with others—both infrequently seen acquaintances and perhaps even a long-lost friend. You may meet new people, a new exciting social group, or learn of an organization that may be beneficial for you. It is important to watch your words, especially around December 17, but this month's Mercury retrograde will only have a mild effect on you as long as you don't take on someone else's problems as your own.

Finance and Success
You're in a period when you'll naturally attract the right people, especially through December 16. You may also receive an award, bonus, or other type of recognition this month. Starting December 16 you may be concentrating on how to spend the money you've been bringing in, perhaps making big expenditures.

Cosmic Insider Tip
The pressure has been off since Uranus went back into Aquarius in mid-September. On December 31, however, it returns to Pisces to remain there for the next seven years. This is a time of golden opportunity for you, when you will be able to open new doorways of possibility and make changes you never thought possible.

Rewarding Days 1, 5, 6, 10, 11, 19, 20, 23, 24, 27, 28, 29

Challenging Days 7, 8, 9, 15, 16, 21, 22

Affirmation of the Month I am willing to change for the better.

PISCES ACTION TABLE

These dates reflect the best—but not the only—times for success and ease in these activities, according to your Sun sign.

	JAN	FEB	MAR	APR	MAY	JUN	JUL	AUG	SEPT	OCT	NOV	DEC
Move					31	14-29						
Start a class				6-25	1, 20-31	1-12						
Join a club	23-31	1-28	1-4									
Ask for a raise			3, 28-31	1-21								
Look for work							14-31	1-27	20-30	1-6	13-30	1, 2
Get pro advice	21, 22	17, 18	16, 17	13, 14	10, 11	6-8	4, 5, 31	1, 26, 27	24, 25	21, 22	17-19	15, 16
Get a loan	23, 24	19, 20	18, 19	15, 16	12, 13	9, 10	6, 7	2, 3	20-30	1-9, 23, 24	20, 21	18, 19
See a doctor		14-28	1-21				14-31	1-27	21-30	1-6		
Start a diet		16					14-30					
End relationship			18									
Buy clothes						30	1-28					
Get a makeover			3, 5-21									
New romance						29	5-28					
Vacation	25, 26	21, 22	20, 21	17, 18	14, 15	11, 12	8, 9	4, 5, 31	1, 2, 28, 29	10, 31	1-11, 22, 23	19, 20

The Twelve Houses of the Zodiac

You may run across mention of the houses of the zodiac while reading certain articles in the *Sun Sign Book*. These houses are the twelve divisions of the horoscope wheel. Each house has a specific meaning assigned to it. Below are the descriptions attributed to each house.

First House: Self-interest, physical appearance, basic character.

Second House: Personal values, monies earned and spent, moveable possessions, self-worth and esteem, resources for security needs.

Third House: Neighborhood, communications, siblings, schooling, buying and selling, busy activities, short trips.

Fourth House: Home, family, real estate, parent(s), one's private sector of life, childhood years, old age.

Fifth House: Creative endeavors, hobbies, pleasures, entertainments, children, speculative ventures, loved ones.

Sixth House: Health, working environment, coworkers, small pets, service to others, food, armed forces.

Seventh House: One-on-one encounters, business and personal partners, significant others, legal matters.

Eighth House: Values of others, joint finances, other people's money, death and rebirth, surgery, psychotherapy.

Ninth House: Higher education, religion, long trips, spirituality, languages, publishing.

Tenth House: Social status, reputation, career, public honors, parents, the limelight.

Eleventh House: Friends, social and community work, causes, surprises, luck, rewards from career, circumstances beyond your control.

Twelfth House: Hidden weaknesses and strengths, behind-the-scenes activities, institutions, confinement, government.

2003
Sun Sign Book
Articles

Contributors

Janet Bowman Johnson

Stephanie Clement

Alice DeVille

Sasha Fenton

Therese Francis

Jonathan Keyes

Dorothy Oja

Leeda Alleyn Pacotti

Bruce Scofield

Maria Simms

Joanne Wickenburg

The Cycles of the Sun

by Bruce Scofield

We owe our lives to our Sun. In fact, almost all life on Earth is fueled by the Sun. The Sun radiates energy that simple organisms feed on, and more complex organisms, such as ourselves, feed on them. Ultimately, energy must come from somewhere, and for us, it's the Sun.

The Sun has several cycles that scientists have observed and measured. First, the Sun rotates once every twenty-five days, but just at its equator. The regions above and below the solar equator rotate more slowly—about twenty-seven days. This is possible because the Sun is not solid; it's plasma. Solar rotation is an important solar cycle and one that affects the solar wind, as we will see below. A second important solar cycle is the sunspot cycle. Sunspots are large, disturbed, stormy areas on the Sun, so large in fact that many, many Earths could be placed over a large one before it became obstructed. They are made of elongated filament-like structures, and are intensely magnetic. Sunspots appear dark because they slow down the heat radiating outwards from the Sun's interior. The number of sunspots on the Sun at any given time varies over a roughly eleven-year cycle. This cycle has many implications for conditions on Earth, and (of interest to astrologers) it may be driven by the motions of the planets.

The Sun is the closest star. When we look at it, what we see is the solar atmosphere, the first layer of which is called the photosphere. It's from this region of the Sun that solar radiation (including light) escapes and ultimately "feeds" the Earth. Above the photosphere is the chromosphere. This layer of the Sun's atmosphere is less dense and its gases are transparent—they do not emit light. The chromosphere is observable during a solar eclipse, when the main disk of the Sun is blocked by the Moon. Beyond this layer is the corona, also observed most clearly during an eclipse. This "crown-like" part of the solar atmosphere extends well out into space and gradually thins into the solar wind that flows out into the solar system.

The Solar Wind

The solar wind is a stream of charged gas particles, mostly hydrogen, that are lost from the Sun. The solar wind is essentially very rarified gas, so thinned out that there are only two particles of the gas in each cubic centimeter. But it is very, very hot—in the neighborhood of 200,000 degrees Kelvin. As the solar wind extends from the Sun's corona, it moves through the solar system, passing the planets. Because the Sun rotates, the solar wind radiates out from the Sun like streams of water from a rotating lawn sprinkler. The solar wind also carries with it magnetic fields that spiral out into the solar system, creating what is called the interplanetary magnetic field, or IMF. If the Earth or another planet happens to be in the way of one of these waves of magnetically-charged solar wind, it gets blasted.

The charged particles of the solar wind blow right into the Earth's own magnetic field, bending it like the bow of a ship bends the water in front of it. When the solar wind is particularly active—right after a solar flare occurs, for instance—its collision with the Earth's magnetic field is more intense. This is what creates the aurora borealis, better known as the northern lights.

When the Sun is very active, coronal mass ejections (CMEs) occur. These are massive magnetic gas bubbles that are ejected from the Sun and disrupt the flow of the solar wind. Solar flares and prominence eruptions are other violent solar phenomena that can occur in conjunction with CMEs. Particles from flares and CMEs can cause major disturbances on Earth. Radio communications are disrupted, satellites can be damaged, and passengers in high-altitude airplanes may be subjected to radiation comparable to that of a medical X-ray. The frequency of CMEs is related to the sunspot cycle (see below) and their intensity varies. When the cycle is at minimum, about one CME per week is observed. Near solar maximum the number is more like two or three per day.

Sunspots and the Solar Cycle

The sunspot cycle measures the frequency of dark spots on the Sun. Galileo was one of the first to notice these "blemishes" when he trained his telescope on the Sun some four hundred years ago. He thought they were clouds in the Sun's atmosphere. Besides discovering the spots themselves, he also discovered that the Sun rotates. He came to this conclusion by recognizing that the number of sunspots and their location on the Sun changes daily. Over a sequence of days, Galileo had observed specific sunspots moving across the face of the Sun, which strongly suggested solar rotation.

By the middle of the nineteenth century, astronomers had determined that there was a sunspot cycle of eleven years (on average), during which the number of sunspots changes from a minimum to a maximum. It had also been determined that over the course of the sunspot cycle the region where the spots form on the Sun shifts. Spot formation begins well above and below the Sun's equator, but as the cycle progresses they move toward the equator. What all this means to us will be explained later. For now, keep in mind that the sunspot cycle is a key solar cycle, that it tracks the number of sunspots that exist on the Sun over a period of time, and that this period averages about eleven years.

The sunspot cycle is not only the best known of the solar cycles, but its correlations with other cycles are of special interest. First of all, the cycle of the Sun's brightness, or total energy output, is linked to this cycle. The Sun is brightest when sunspots are at their maximum. It does seem strange that the Sun would be brighter at precisely the time that it is most covered with dark spots, but it is. When the Sun is brighter it is emitting more energy. The sunspot cycle is a way to measure the Sun's total energy output. Why should we be concerned about this? It affects our climate.

I've already stated that the sunspot cycle averages about eleven years, but actually it can vary from as little as seven years to as many as seventeen. Further, the number of sunspots in each sunspot cycle vary. Between 1640 and 1720 there was a lull in the number of sunspots—even though records were being kept, none were reported. This period was a major low of solar magnetic activity, and guess what? The overall temperature of the Earth declined by about one degree Celsius. While this doesn't sound like much, it is substantial enough to affect climate. This period has even been named the "Little Ice Age," and the testimonies of those who lived through it in Europe and North America speak of some very cold winters. Rivers froze where they never did before, glaciers grew larger, and crops failed to grow as they used to.

In contrast, the last fifty years of the twentieth century have seen very high levels of energy from the Sun, and consequently we are experiencing a warming. For many years this fact has kept many scientists from stating categorically that global warming as the result of fossil fuel burning was occurring. However, since 2000, most agree that the global warming we are experiencing is a combination of both. While it is getting warmer because the Sun is putting out more energy, this is nothing like what happened in the eleventh and twelfth centuries. Back then, the global temperature was up a degree or so. Scandinavia had become a comfortable place to live. People were growing grapes in England. Vikings sailed to Greenland and set up colonies there that lasted for hundreds of years, but they collapsed when global temperatures dropped again in the thirteenth century.

The "Little Ice Age" and other world climate variations have been verified in ways other than sunspot counts and eyewitness accounts. Normally, the Earth is bombarded by cosmic rays from outer space, but during the peak of a sunspot cycle these rays are deflected. This slows down the formation of carbon 14 in plants. Therefore, carbon dating can describe the history of energy coming from the Sun. This method of dating does point to the period between 1640 and 1720 as being very different from what came before and after it. Carbon-dating studies have also shown that there are larger solar cycles that affect life on the planet, cycles of 80–90 years, a 200-year cycle, and even one of about 2,200 years.

Forecasting Sunspots

The number of sunspots on the Sun at any given time is a good indication of how active and energizing the Sun is. At the high point of a sunspot cycle, when the Sun is very active, the push of the solar wind on the Earth's magnetic field is strong. There is evidence that suggests this push affects life on Earth, causing disruptions and excitability. Low sunspot numbers indicate the reverse. Each sunspot cycle differs from the previous one, not only in terms of the number of spots but also in length. Predicting the exact peak or trough of the cycle is difficult as it can range from 7 to 17 years, though the average is 11.1. Readers interested in following the solar sunspot cycle may wish to visit http://www.spaceweather.com, one of NASA's websites, or http://dxlc.com/solar/. On these sites are articles, graphs, and links that may be of interest. Below is a listing of twentieth century sunspot cycles.

One of the ways that we know the sunspot cycle has reached maximum is by the reversing of the Sun's magnetic field. Every eleven or so years, the Sun's magnetic poles flip; that is, the north and south poles reverse. The solar magnetic poles are much like those of a bar magnet: The magnetic energy flows from each end, or pole, and loops back into its opposite. At sunspot maximum, the combined effects of numerous magnetically charged sunspots is apparently enough to upset the status quo, and the poles reverse. The most recent reversal of the poles was in February of 2001. This change is not limited to the Sun; it extends out into space, carried by the solar wind, which is subject to all the twists and turns produced by the Sun's rotation. The extended solar magnetic field, called the heliosphere, makes a complex, corkscrew-like pattern that envelopes the planets of the solar system.

Predicting sunspot maximum is not difficult once the cycle has been running for about three years from minimum. But forecasting the nature of the entire cycle has kept scientists busy. Their predictions have not been too impressive. For example, the most recent maximum was predicted for 2000, but at the time of this writing (October 2001), the sunspot numbers are still higher than during most of 2000. The best methods used by scientists analyze the cycle during the minimum take into account the nature of the previous cycle and extrapolate into the next one. One of the most reliable

---

Sunspot Minimum Years:

1901, 1913, 1923, 1933, 1944, 1954, 1964, 1976, 1986, 1996

Sunspot Maximum Years:

1907, 1918, 1928, 1938, 1948, 1958, 1970, 1980, 1990, 2000/2001

---

techniques has been to note changes in the Earth's magnetic field just before and at sunspot minimum. These are called "geomagnetic precursor" techniques, which basically analyze correlations between fluctuations and sunspots. The currently established, scientifically acceptable methods do not seek any extrasolar causes for the sunspot cycle.

There is, however, a long history of considering planetary influences on solar cycles. Galileo was the first to suggest such a possible explanation, and there was much research on this during the nineteenth and early twentieth century. Most of this work is ignored by modern scientists, but there is one body of alternative research that is worth reporting. By the middle of the twentieth century, the radio industry recognized that strong solar events could disrupt radio communications taking place on the side of the Earth facing the Sun. One radio company, RCA, realized it could manage its communication network more efficiently if these disturbing events could be predicted. Around 1950, one of RCA's radio engineers, John Nelson, perfected a method for forecasting disturbances by considering the influence of the planets on the Sun. Using the positions of the planets as indicators of solar activity, his techniques resembled astrology. First, he charted the planets on a grid that looked very much like an astrological chart; then, he tried to locate times when the planetary positions formed alignments with each other. When they did, he would predict a solar storm, and his forecasts proved to be up to 90 percent accurate. Nelson's heliocentric planetary alignment maps were so similar to astrological horo-scopes, and his interpretive skills so comparable to those of practic-ing astrologers, that for many years Nelson was a welcome speaker at astrology conferences.

What Nelson found was that sunspots were usually (but not always) associated with geo-magnetic storms and that certain plan-etary angles would predict such conditions. Disturbances would occur when the planets were in conjunction (0 degrees), square (90 degrees), or opposition (180 degrees) to each other. These are, of course, the "hard" aspects in astrology. He also found that solar weather was quieter when planets were connected by trines (120 degrees). This aspect is known to astrologers as a favorable and "soft" aspect. Nelson noticed other, more subtle angular separations that produce solar activity, based on multiples of fifteen and eigh-teen degrees.

Nelson's work with planetary aspects and sunspots was the work of a seasoned engineer. Others have not been as successful in fore-casting radio storms in this manner. Burl Payne has also researched possible connections between planetary alignments and sunspots, and he found that only some planetary conjunctions correlated with increased solar activity; other conjunctions did not. Heliocen-tric conjunctions between the Earth and Jupiter or Uranus were coincident with peak sunspot numbers, while conjunctions involv-ing Mercury and Earth showed a dramatic decrease in numbers. However, Mercury-Earth conjunctions correlated with an increase in storms in the Earth's magnetic field. Venus and the Earth in con-junction seemed to show an initial increase in sunspot numbers, then a decrease. Payne also draws attention to the fact that the counting of sunspots can only account for those that are visible to the Earth. Sunspots on the far side of the Sun may form during planetary alignments, but we won't see them until the Sun rotates them into view. And since the Sun's rotation takes twenty-five days, changes can occur within this period.

More recent work done by astronomer Percy Seymour has shown that there is a correlation between peaks of solar activity and the peaks of the combined tidal effects on the Sun that are generated by the Earth, Venus, and Jupiter. In other words, these particular plan-ets can combine to form tides on the Sun, and these tides make the

Sun active. Seymour has proposed a theory of magneto-tidal resonance, which states that the pull of two or more planets moving
together around the Sun will pull the plasma of the Sun just as the
Moon pulls the oceans of the Earth. However, their combined effect
is much greater than the simple sum of their gravitational influence.
Like Nelson, Seymour is suggesting that the aspect theory of the
ancient astrologers is not incredible at all; it simply has not been
measured quantitatively—until recently.

If you look closely at the listing of sunspot maximums and mini-
mums given above, you will notice that there is not a neat symmetry between these highs and lows. In recent years, it has only taken
three or four years from a sunspot minimum to reach a maximum,
and this is not half of eleven. Although the cycle length averages a
little over eleven years, the actual length is not consistent. What
may be going on here is that the Sun is responding to the gravitational pull of the giant planets Jupiter and Saturn. While the Sun
responds to alignments between each of these planets and the other
planets in the solar system, it responds even more strongly when
these two are in conjunction or opposition. For example, Jupiter and
Saturn were in conjunction in 1980 and 2000, both big years for
sunspots. But because there are other planets in the solar system that
have their own gravitational contribution, the pull of the planets on
the Sun, and the consequent solar activity, is not so easy to predict.
In addition to alignments, another factor is the distance between a
planet and the Sun. Nelson was a master of solar activity prediction
and learned how to take into account a wide range of planetary
influences—just as an astrologer does when reading a chart.

Solar Effects on the Earth

The Sun may have something to do with earthquakes. We know
that planetary positions relative to the Sun can affect it, causing it
to be more active or passive. When the Sun is active, the solar wind
pushing against the Earth's magnetic field can, in turn, cause
changes in the circulation of the Earth's upper atmosphere. This, in
turn, can cause the Earth to slow its rotation a very small amount.
This change in spin rate has been found to correlate with changes
in seismic activity. Theoretically, when the Sun is active and causing the solar wind to blow strongly against the Earth, the normal

rate of Earth rotation is altered and earthquakes are more likely to occur. Also, solar activity affects global temperature, which in turn affects the amount of ice or water on Earth. Changes in the weight of water and ice can result in increased pressure leading to seismic activity. The North American continent is still "rebounding" from the release of heavy ice sheets of the last Ice Age. Solar activity also affects changes in atmospheric pressure, which acts the same way as water and ice—the sudden release of millions of tons of air pressure can cause the Earth to rebound.

There are probably many other processes on Earth that are affected by the Sun. Most organisms are very responsive to magnetic fields. The nervous system is essentially electro-magnetic in design and in certain cases has evolved to take into consideration the magnetic field of the Earth. For example, it is known that many birds can navigate by using the Earth's magnetic field. Considering that the Earth's magnetic field is itself susceptible to the solar wind, it is very possible that solar storms stimulate the nervous systems of certain life forms on our planet. It appears that the Earth-Sun relationship in regard to magnetism is quite complex and needs to be understood as a system, not as two separate phenomena. There is much to be learned about the Sun, life, and magnetism, which might someday turn out to be concrete evidence for the validity of astrology.

For Further Reading

Brant, John C. *New Horizons in Astronomy*. San Francisco: W. H. Freeman & Co., 1972.

Hodge, Paul W. *Concepts of Contemporary Astronomy*. New York: McGraw-Hill, 1974.

Seymour, Percy. *Cosmic Magnetism*. Boston: Adam Hilger, 1986.

Vaughan, Valerie. *Earth Cycles: The Geocosmic Evidence for Natural Astrology*. Amherst, Mass.: One Reed Publications, 2002.

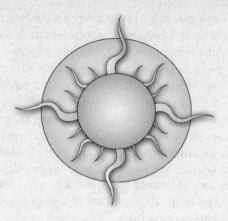

Catalysts for Career Change

by Alice DeVille

I n the ever-expanding world of the twenty-first century, you and
your career are likely to find unusual opportunities for growth. If
you are an astrology buff, you may have discovered that current
planetary movement has something to do with the shifting attitude
you have about your work, or the conditions that influence what
you do. As displayed in your personal astrology chart, it takes the
whole lineup of planets that appeared in the heavens at your
moment of birth to describe the unique qualities you possess. Your
natal chart zeroes in on factors that influence your career and the
reason why you wanted to be on the planet at this time.

Analyzing Your Career Zone

Career information appears in various "houses" or "departments of
life" in your chart. To understand what you really came here to do,.
you'll want to know more about the way the planets relate to one

another. The astrological chart features twelve different sectors that highlight your soul's unique path this time around. Planets appearing in certain houses at your time of birth form patterns that determine your creativity, drive, and expression. One career option alone is seldom your fate, although some individuals are reluctant to take advantage of new paths when they open up. I have seen clients use talents associated with the Moon's South Node, purportedly linked with the karmic past, because they relate via soul memory to talents used in previous incarnations. Once they get the wake-up call, these individuals find themselves pursuing new careers that stretch their current comfort zone. In many cases, it takes a natural disaster, layoff, merger, internal reorganization, act of war, or conflict of interest to influence the career transition.

Each of you has many talents and will experience opportunities to change careers at different stages of life. One day you'll just look in the mirror and say, "Is that all there is?" and acknowledge that you're bored with the status quo. That's when you usually find someone like me, and ask me to explore your chart for potential options. You have probably heard of individuals who leave one career and go in what seems to be a completely different direction from where they achieved recognition. The dormant expression hiding in the houses has been awakened by movement of planets via progression (movement of planets from their place at your birth) or via transits (current arrangement of planets in the heavens that trigger new action in your natal chart).

Where should you look for information about your career? I personally believe each house describes some aspect of what you find fulfilling in your career and work life. These planetary arrangements are your toolbox; so let's take a look at what they say. I'll describe conditions, attitudes, and careers related to each house. Later in the article I'll talk about current trends, and you'll learn more about career options members of your Sun sign may be considering. That way you'll gain insight about emerging fields of enterprise.

The First House

Planets in your First House mark you as a go-getter or self-starter type eager to get out of bed and move competitively ahead in your chosen field. You'll probably prefer leading the enterprise or supervising your team to taking orders from others. Colleagues would define you as a high-energy personality, ready to wield power by making timely, if not impulsive, decisions. Your pattern normally dislikes gobs of red tape that hold up action, but you would follow the rules as a military leader, corporate executive, or project director. All types of careers related to competitive sports that use hand equipment appeal to you—boxing, fencing, javelin throwing, or pitching. You might be interested in fire fighting or smoke jumping and other high-risk fields. A First House planetary grouping may produce graphologists or handwriting experts. Fields that require the use of tools are another option—mechanics, carpentry, or sculpting, for example.

The Second House

The Second House gives clues about how you want to earn your money and what talent you prefer to market. If several planets fall here you may be especially attuned to self-development, and eager to fulfill the career-change philosophy once you reach the pinnacle of success in your present employment arena. Depending upon the planetary array, some of you would be known in your circles as job hoppers. When the present employment environment no longer matches your picture, you roll out the red carpet and work your charm in another industry. While you're smiling and settling deals during core hours, you are in training during downtime in preparation for the next opportunity. Some individuals with Second House prominence excel in financial management, commercial enterprise, and industrial trades. The world of beauty may appeal to your fine-tuned aesthetic sense. It would be easy for you to picture yourself driving a pink Mary Kay Cadillac, the universal symbol of high-volume sales and success, if the cosmetics industry claims your passion. If hair is your thing, you cultivate the model of a sought-after hair designer and stylist, setting the stage for owning an upscale salon in a trendy high-rent district.

The Third House

In the Third House, planets beg for opportunities to sell products, communicate in diverse fields, take to the podium as an emcee, promote skills, and embark on a continuous education journey. With a flair for elocution, some of you are drawn to speech pathology, workshop presentation, giving acting lessons, or teaching languages. Transportation fields appeal to many of you with Third House dominance: The field of mechanics, driving all types of public vehicles or industry fleets, car care, and scheduling events that depend upon getting people where they need to be on time all appeal to you. Some of the best secretaries or support staff professionals reportedly are individuals with strong Third House placements. The entire realm of computers or office machinery and operation stimulates career options in the Third House. You may be hired in the training field as a systems installer, software demonstrator, program instructor, or corporate consultant charged with keeping an energized work force and a demanding client base educated in the latest products of twenty-first-century technology.

The Fourth House

When planets dominate your Fourth House, working from home appeals to you. Babysitting or child-care services give you the freedom to earn your income and set your own hours. Family matters play a role when this sector is highlighted, so interests for some of you may lie in operating a geriatric center, nursing home, or senior housing complex. You might also be attracted to the decorating industry, the real-estate field, environmental work, or the home-cleaning arena. When cooking appeals to you, the food services industry is a good bet, ranging from deli manager to proprietor of elegant dining facilities. With your often prominent green thumb, your forte may be in owning a nursery or florist shop, cultivating crops and excelling in agricultural fields, exploring anthropological and geological digs, or caring for the land through forestry management.

The Fifth House

Entrepreneurial, sports professional, and entertainment types have clusters of planets in the Fifth House of creative self-expression and children. Many individuals pursue careers in teaching, coaching, outdoor recreation, and guidance counseling. For those of you who love to travel, a tour guide or travel consultant fits the bill. Since the Fifth House rules your love life and people you date, you may be particularly fulfilled as a wedding planner, bridal consultant, professional matchmaker, or social secretary. Perhaps the Love Boat has better employment opportunities for you as a cruise director, steward, ship's officer, or chief purser. If your risk-taking desire is strong, you may find the perfect match in a gambling resort as a professional gambler, or get your thrills through watching the high rollers as a croupier.

The Sixth House

With dominance in the Sixth House of work, you favor a compatible environment in which to accomplish tasks, and feel attracted to service and healing industries. Fitness gurus and yoga instructors show their flair for toning the body and relaxing the mind when planets fill this house. Doctors, nurses, dentists, and medical researchers are good bets for those with an interest in health care. Expanding the options would be nutritionists, physical therapists, and medical insurance providers. A desire to serve your country appeals to those of you with key placements in this house. Here we'll find seekers of government and military careers. Since this house rules small pets and animals, areas like veterinary medicine, animal training, or pet sitting are good options. Individuals with many planets here often find it hard to separate their social lives from their work lives, especially those with Saturn in residence. Be careful you don't assume the life of a workaholic, who often uses work in place of emotional fulfillment and ignores the clock at the end of the workday.

The Seventh House

Partnerships, publics, and cooperative ventures mark your daily work life when planets dominate your Seventh House of business and personal relationships. You would excel in consulting, advising, public relations, and mediating fields. Gifted individuals with a Seventh House dominance would find employment success as astrologers or intuitives. Many of you run businesses with life partners or initiate multilevel marketing structures to keep wealth circulating via motivational techniques. Self-help practitioners shine with well-placed Seventh House planets. If politics is your niche, you could run for office or run the campaign of your chosen candidate. Be sure you have compatibility and clearly defined roles, or you could find your partnerships testing the profit margins. Get contracts in writing and look for the loopholes if you need to bail out.

The Eighth House

If your Eighth House of "other people's money" holds key planets, you really do like working in the counting house, lending money, and dispersing insurance claims. The stock market or mortgage industry may attract you even more when you help others evaluate their net worth as well as their buying power. If you choose more of a background influence on others' lives, you may excel in the funeral industry, depth psychology, estate law, or scientific research. Got a nose for crime solving? Many of you make crack detectives, mystery writers, or guards. This house in high gear has been known to breed its fair share of criminals, so you'll have your work cut out for you if you want to outwit the foxes. Don't overlook another compatible choice—the plumbing industry or waste management are both viable sources of income.

The Ninth House

The travel industry or fields that call for routine travel and long-distance moves appeal to you when planets fill your Ninth House of foreign relations, travel, and higher education. Writers and publishing industry affiliates usually have clusters of planets here, as do theologians, spiritual teachers and clergy, college professors, and individuals who relocate far from their place of birth. The Ninth House rules all aspects of the law, so you could be outfitted with judge's robes, become a clerk of the court, or argue cases before the bar. Metaphysician, mystic, seer, or swami could be your calling if you don't mind a diverse client base and a rash of phone calls in the middle of the night. If you like international relations, this is the house that offers the most options. Become a linguist, practice your skill in your foreign journeys, and bring home the flavor of each culture you integrate into your psyche. You could plan exotic getaways to purchase goods for your import/export business or add a safari hat to your list of personal collectibles. Finally, you could meet your mate on your dream vacation and live happily ever after, telling all your heirs about your first meeting aboard the luxury liner that changed the course of your life.

The Tenth House

With multiple planets in residence in your Tenth House, ambition and a desire for power in your chosen field are inevitable. A vice-presidency or higher could be in your future, since you easily see yourself running the show. You could probably shake hands with your Sixth House employees in terms of job commitment and a tendency to burn the midnight oil when the stakes are high. All manner of powerful positions are attractive to you when planets line up here—politician, business owner, head of an organization, authority figure or law enforcer, manager, high-ranking military person, or chairman of the board. As long as your career promises you the distinction of gaining fame or renown in your field you are happy. For those medically inclined, a draw to dentistry, geriatrics, osteopathy, or chiropractics appeals. If you like sports, you may earn your living taking vacationers mountain climbing or hiking.

The Eleventh House

If blessed with an Eleventh House stellium (array of three or more planets or the Sun and Moon located here), you select careers that advance humanity, intelligence, and technology on the planet. You have a broad range of interests, and some of them may seem controversial to others. Seldom do you waiver from your cause, and you put a great deal of analysis into your unfolding plans. If anyone can get a campaign going it is you, as you inspire others to join the ranks. For this reason you would do well in an elected office, with your zealous powers of persuasion and idealistic vision. Many of you would enjoy earning your living as a change agent, confidante, delegate, personal coach, or sociologist. Consulting appeals to you, and you would excel in various fields as a specialist or advisor because your credibility and expertise are valued. For those of you with wanderlust, the airline industry, international sales corporations, or the space program charge your batteries. Work that allows you to be a trendsetter and something of a maverick brings you career satisfaction. If you like working one-on-one with civic matters, advocacy or lobbyist groups may appeal to you, or your love of people would attract you to personnel management or industrial psychology. And if you really want to use your laser-like insight, try astrology—one of the fields that appeals to your sense of discovery.

The Twelfth House

Twelfth House clusters usually mark the talents of "night" people and industries that operate when others are home getting their eight hours of sleep. The sign of Pisces influences your career. Bartenders, hospital workers, prison or rehabilitation staff, shelf and supply stockers, wait staff, managers of all-night diners, or police officers are typical careers. A daring career such as espionage may appeal to you, or you may find intriguing work as an undercover agent or narcotics squad leader. If you're good with a pen, then mystery, romance (especially tearjerkers), poetry, and ghostwriting are favored topics. No one outdoes you as a charity organizer or fundraiser. You champion the underdog, and with your innate compassion would work tirelessly as a nurse, counselor, caseworker, or welfare advocate. Industries related to feet might be your niche: shoe buyer for a major department store chain, footwear designer, pedicurist, podiatrist, or shoemaker. If you have developed your talent with a camera you would make an excellent photographer. Your spectacular eye for spotting scenic backdrops or orchestrating poses gets raves. Perhaps lights, action, and drama are your forte. In that case, acting, casting, costume designing, directing, or producing films may be the runaway winner on your career wish list.

These examples of career choices merely scratch the surface of available fields of interest. Don't worry if your primary interest is not among them. You'll probably identify with at least a few career paths that may be on your dream sheet. If you haven't done so, be sure to have your astrology chart interpreted for career options so you can develop your talent to the fullest and maximize your opportunity for finding fulfillment.

The Age of Instant Career Ladders

In truth, the exciting era we're in represents a sweep of technological and societal transformations that no other generation has seen. Specialization and expertise in highly sought after fields make securing employment in emerging markets much easier. Being on top of the game means that firms stay competitive among the trendsetters and demand continuous improvement of critical resources—

the human kind. Your chart shows how you prefer to earn your money, carry out your work, and make yourself competitive for future assignments.

No doubt you have witnessed and experienced major changes in how you perform your job and where you do the actual work. Maybe you are a telecommuter and work all or part of the time from a remote site—or even from your home—and efficiently meet your employer's deadlines. The organization has probably installed state-of-the-art business, telephone, and computer equipment as well as system links that make you completely accessible to headquarters and your customers.

While far from accepted in all industries, this innovative work-place arrangement allows concentrated focus on tasks and uninter-rupted flow of work. Stern taskmasters (authoritarian types usually associated with the planet Saturn) refuse to trust employees to put in a good day's work, yet studies prove a high level of productivity occurs in off-site settings when the environment is harmonious to the task. Home-based employees often work far more clock hours than their on-site counterparts. What surprises many members of the labor force is that governments, including the Saturn-ruled fed-eral government, are strong supporters of telecommuting when the appropriate job classification permits it. Major initiatives are under-way to offer incentives to employers to cut down on traffic conges-tion and reduce vehicle-related smog and pollution levels by promoting alternative work sites for personnel. Telecommuting is a keeper that will affect over 50 percent of the workforce in the next few years.

Cosmic Career Travelers

Not since Pluto was in Gemini from 1883–1914 has the world of innovative communication and transportation been so revolution-ized. We have come a long way from the first crank-type telephones that appeared in general stores, the Model-T Fords that sputtered along the roads and byways, and the Wright brothers' first plane. Think of the industries that sprang up and the new career paths that appeared during this pivotal era in history. What would you have done if you were alive in such a restless yet inspiring time? Li of the population, you would you have been caught up in the Industrial Revolution and made a valuable contribution toward the modern conveniences and high-speed transportation we enjoy today. Perhaps your astrologer would have advised you to move to Detroit and find your niche in the hot new industry of the twentieth century—automobile manufacturing.

Let's examine your current routine. Are you a frequent business traveler in this Aquarian Age—an age known for its influence on invention and high-tech gadgets? If so you may be among the significant number of individuals who use Uranian products such as cell phones, palm pilots, and laptop computers to send e-mail from aircraft, trains, cars, hotel rooms, conference centers, and waiting lounges in global transportation centers. The staples in your brief case are sure to include a phone charger, a headset, and an auto adapter for your rental car. With your onboard "toolkit," you never miss a beat in completing your workload or assessing client needs. No one is ever really out of touch with you because of time zone changes, and you never have to keep your customer waiting with a reply to questions that come up in your absence. There is no reason to subject yourself to Mercury's memory lapse by waiting until you return to home base to write your trip report or return calls from important contacts. Regardless of where you are in the world, you have instant access to local or worldwide news and can get your credit approved within minutes for the loan application on your pending mortgage.

Evolution in the Jupiter-ruled world of big business is often instantaneous. Start-up companies with a novel edge do business just as soon as venture capitalists fund their enterprise. When consumers catch the wave, the infant companies hire resourceful staff with high energy levels (I'd bet these workers have Mars well aspected in their charts) and start making a profit. Before long, mercurial imitators flood the market with similar products and services. The original Mars-type companies, the real pioneer groups, must keep up the level of innovation or they fold just as soon as another rising star appears on the horizon.

Recall the flood of "dot com" companies in the last few years that came and went overnight, forcing thousands of personnel into the job market. Surely strong lunar influences were at work, sensing what the public was buying in the way of systems support and intelligence. Venture capitalists shelled out billions to support startup winners. Work place behavior changed, and the need for information became critical to doing business in global markets. Firms wanted access and ownership of websites that advertised their goods and services. First they had to learn the language or hire experts who could interpret and respond to the brand new dynamics that were emerging via the Internet.

Recruiting offices buzzed with activity, and online employment search engines could not meet the demand of prospering employers who wanted to fill new positions "yesterday." All they had to say was, "We have jobs," and qualified resumes flew back and forth across the world wide web. The corporate intellect—the domain of Mercury and Gemini—paved the way for techie types who set up control central and offered door-to-door service for budding entrepreneurs. Website designers and developers banked on hungry new customers who lacked the expertise to manage their networks or outfit their systems with the intellectual property they needed to be competitive. Everybody became the "new kid on the block." Rental markets soared, with fledgling companies begging for space that was leasing at premium rates after the sudden interest in available property emerged. Depending on their solvency, many of the "newbies" had to settle for modest square footage in trendy business enclaves to give their companies the prestigious location that spells success. The Cancer-ruled real-estate industry had to hire and train relocation specialists to handle the exploding housing demand created in hot market cities, especially those on the west coast and along the eastern seaboard. You could apply for a job anywhere in the world and relocate to one of these high-action zones. Competition for homes meant that available properties had multiple bids and often went for more than the asking price. Property values soared and so did tax assessments.

With the housing market accelerating, real-estate schools filled to their capacity and eager sales agents hung their shingles with high-volume brokerages as soon as they graduated. The need for educational and coaching skills that relate to the signs of Gemini (Mercury-ruled) and Sagittarius (Jupiter-ruled) emerged. Corporate rental markets attracted new clients and had to keep up with demand by locating experienced agents to move the properties. Many new sales professionals, eager for quick cash, climbed on board rather than waiting months to collect their commissions for selling their first home.

Commercial real-estate enterprises, the real big-ticket items that can leave the selling agent and often the brokerage solvent for a year when the deal settles, picked up on the pace set by developers who grabbed available land, and gave their building designs the flair and distinction that would make them the architectural look of the twenty-first century.

Now, why am I talking about these fields and their recent history? Because the pattern of world events has a constant, ever-changing effect on current and emerging careers—and keeps placement services and demanding publics looking for qualified talent. Measured economic evolution has something to do with that effect—as evidenced by recent "dot com" and real estate history—but more immediate, isolated events also have their impact. The terrorist attacks of September 11, 2001, an earthquake in Asia, the election of a foreign president—all of these events and more result in changes for the U.S. workforce.

Dealing with Change

What's it like in your life? Is the focus of your work and career ladder changing? Perhaps unexpected circumstances affected the financial outlook of your industry. If you are assessing the underlying current in your work environment and it has changed, you're probably ripe for a career move. Why not consider a new position in an emerging employment field? No one sign has a monopoly on each discipline—the variables in the planetary make-up of your chart show your particular inclinations. For those of you new to astrology, the twelve signs are divided by element (quality) into four types: fire, earth, water, and air. Let's explore a few of the newly in-demand choices in the job market.

Fire signs (Aries, Leo, and Sagittarius) favor pioneering, profit-generating fields and high-risk disciplines, including the military. If it is new and hot, this group wants in on the action. You'll find the fire element heeding a call to action when national security is at risk or their country goes to war. Satisfying career possibilities include: armed services, aviation, border surveillance, cable installation, diplomatic corps, firefighting, foreign relations or trade, translating and interpreting, law, motivational speaking, scouting, slogan and bumper sticker design, vehicle operation (aircraft, ambulances, jeeps, and tanks), weaponry manufacture or sales, or even USO coordination or entertaining.

Earth signs (Taurus, Virgo, and Capricorn) keep their eyes on the assets and people of nations as well as the cost of doing business. Members of this element pride themselves in being ready to protect the health and welfare of others, and gravitate toward positions as civil or military employees in all levels of government—federal, state, and local. They fill all layers of the hierarchy, ranging from file clerk to chief executive, or promote themselves as ambassadors of goodwill enjoying national celebrity. Emerging career paths include: account manager, administrator, biological warfare authority, financial analyst or planner, holistic health practitioner, law enforcer, mayor, member of congress, online banking specialist, realtor, security advisor, survival expert, and systems analyst.

New career paths for the probing yet sensitive water signs (Cancer, Scorpio, and Pisces) revolve around charities, fact-finding, forecasting, medical research, protective services functions, record-keeping, and new consumer products. This group explores the abyss of the human psyche to examine relationships, ferret out fears, and offer practical solutions to emotionally charged areas of conflict. When occupational wanderlust strikes, water signs often find themselves drawn to social science phenomena, the creative and intuitive arts, and industries that cater to the public. Career transition options include: disaster prevention and relief worker, estate planner, flag maker, food and drug inspector, historian, grief counselor, industrial psychologist, insurance agent, pathologist, personal coach, rental agent, sociologist, welfare worker, and writer of patriotic songs.

Intellect-stimulating interests attract the air signs (Gemini, Libra, and Aquarius), whose contributions in communications, education, and cooperative ventures raise the quality of life for people on the planet. Social choices or discontent with the status quo stimulate your emerging career paths. Diverse fields allow you to use analytical and interpersonal skills. Among the choices are: airport security tester, arbitrator, camouflage expert, change agent, freedom fighter, futurist, intelligence gatherer, linguist, marriage and family counselor, media personality, peacekeeper, political cartoonist, relocation specialist, software and data developer, Special Forces member, transportation specialist, war correspondent, and writer.

Ready, Set, Inspire

The times we are in call for flexibility. The key to success lies in "thinking outside the box" when new avenues for displaying your talent open up. Will you be ready? Be empowered by career challenges that close doors when the enterprise dries up. Expand your zone of possibilities and you will more easily find new opportunities to fulfill your career passion. Let astrology provide insight into how you embrace change gracefully. Boost your confidence with opportunities that support your enterprising spirit. May you remember 2003 as the year you catch the wave and launch a brilliant new career.

For Further Reading

Clement, Stephanie Jean. *Charting Your Career: The Horoscope Reveals Your Life Purpose*. St. Paul: Llewellyn, 1999.

Rathgeb, Marlene Masini. *Success Signs: A Practical Astrological Guide to Career Fulfillment*. New York: St. Martin's Press, 1999.

Townley, John. *Dynamic Astrology: Using Planetary Cycles to Make Personal and Career Choices*. Rochester, Vt.: Inner Traditions, 1996.

Your Spiritual Sun

by Stephanie Clement

The Sun in astrology represents your vitality and individuality. It also reflects the highest potential for your spiritual being. In a time in history when we are faced with challenges from all sides—economic change, terrorism, and an aging population to name a few—we seek deeper connections to spirit. These connections are not limited to religious beliefs. In fact, religion is but one of the many paths to spiritual health and well-being.

We are each born into a Sun sign that reflects our character. Small children act out the drama of the Sun sign very directly, showing the creative characteristics and the less constructive dynamics of the zodiac without modification. As we grow up, we learn, consciously or unconsciously, to modify our Sun sign expression to please the people around us. We sometimes leave our Sun sign birthright behind in search of a persona that fits into our family and social milieu more smoothly.

As we become adults, we often find that we are missing an essential connection to the divine in our lives. And we often find that the search for the divine leads us back to the best and highest expression of our Sun signs. In this search we face some challenges.

We must deal with social constructs that don't suit us. Parents, teachers, and peers expect us to fit into their patterns. In order to do this, we must suppress part of our individuality. Even some very strong, positive qualities must be abandoned in order to fit into certain situations. For example, in a strictly patriarchal family, girls are not encouraged to express personal ambition, but boys are.

We must deal with the darker side of our Sun sign—the things that we have abandoned. Once we realize that we are missing something, we have to work to regain Sun sign qualities that have been hidden or suppressed. Some of these are not very attractive qualities "in the raw," but are the essence of personal strength when we work to refine them. Coal is not as attractive as the diamond it may become, and the same is true of our personalities.

We discover our psychic and intuitive talents. Each Sun sign reflects unique ways to explore the psychic and intuitive realms. As we enter our thirties, if not before, we discover that we are tuned to the world around us in subtle ways, and we learn to listen to the messages of earth, air, fire and water.

We reclaim the creative, constructive facets of the jewel that is the Sun. As we pursue our spiritual nature, we discover that every talent has the spark of divinity within it. The more we work with the creative side, the more we become the kind of person we most admire. We experience less jealousy, less resentment, less fear, and we experience more confidence, more compassion, and more love.

Ultimately, we also develop an appreciation for the beauty and strength of other signs. We no longer demand of ourselves that we be exactly like anyone else, and we cooperate to bring out the best in our children, our friends, and our associates, even when that best is very different from our own personalities. Understanding the spiritual path of each sign can be helpful in working with ourselves and with others. The following interpretations include a re-evaluation of some of the difficult expressions of the sign, as well as ways to work toward re-integration and re-expression of the qualities of the sign that may have been forgotten or suppressed. Finally, there is an exploration of each Sun sign's spiritual expression.

Aries

The challenge for the Aries Sun is to moderate the tendency toward egotism. The headstrong nature of this Sun sign can lead to recklessness—even to violence—if it is not controlled. The temperamental nature of an Aries Sun can lead to resentment and jealousy. None of these are socially acceptable when they go to extremes. However, the energy of these thoughts and feelings can be used in more constructive ways.

When egotism is modified, it becomes confidence. Then the Aries individual can exert his or her will to take the initiative. When this happens, the true leader appears, overshadowing the willful side of the personality that only desires control. When Aries energy is mobilized in a constructive direction, the inner nature is expressed through resourcefulness, and intuition can become a powerful tool for forecasting the future outcome of today's decisions.

At the heart of the Aries sign's spiritual nature is the desire for freedom. This in itself is a positive spiritual value. We thrive when we are making our own decisions in every area of life, and spirituality is no different. We need to say yes in a positive way to spiritual values we encounter in life; otherwise we don't really take them seriously. This is one of the reasons that major faiths have rituals through which we "come of age" spiritually. At birth, infants are baptized or otherwise welcomed into the world. At about age twelve, around the time when Jupiter has made one full circuit of the zodiac, another ritual takes place in which the child becomes an adult in the spiritual sense. If this is a truly free choice, that is good. If it is not, then the individual faces another decision point at a later time, and may change his or her spiritual path dramatically. For Aries, the issue will be the freedom to choose the appropriate path. When the decision resonates with the inner being, the Aries Sun has found its proper path and can then act with greater confidence.

Taurus

For Taurus, the greatest challenge is to overcome a tendency toward stubbornness. Taurus can be every bit as dogmatic as Aries, but for different reasons. Taurus becomes enmeshed in habits that may not be to his or her best advantage. It is easier sometimes to indulge the self by following the familiar path, even if it is not leading in the most appropriate direction. Some would say that this is merely taking the path of least resistance. Others would say that it is a sign of a lazy mind. Regardless of the inner motivations, rigid adherence to the familiar can be a severe limitation to spiritual growth. What we have been doing is not right just because we have been doing it.

The same determined decision-making process can be turned to more positive goals. Taurus can be the ultimate patient, thorough practitioner. No one can stick to a worldly task like a Taurus, and the same can be said for spiritual tasks. The endurance of Taurus can get these signs through all sorts of trials, and will make them stronger through the process. Once Taurus has personally examined any life situation and made a personal decision about how to face it, a stable individuality is formed. An inner voice appears that speaks to all future decisions from a place of consistency—firm, but not unnecessarily stubborn any longer.

The persistence of Taurus can become a powerful tool on the spiritual path. To begin with, Taurus observes the material world from a position of practicality, and the spiritual path can benefit from a practical eye. Devotion to a religion, a teacher, or an ideal is all well and good—until it becomes obsession. The persistent ability to consider our ideas and ideals from the practical perspective helps us to avoid the trap of rigidity. If a spiritual belief brings only suffering to you and to everyone around you, perhaps it is time to ask whether that belief has merit. The true spiritual path may not be easy, but neither is it intended to be filled with suffering. The generous aspect of Taurus will resist actions that cause suffering for others.

Gemini

Gemini is a thinking sign. The Gemini mind is always working on one thing or another. Thinking becomes a challenge only when it leads to excessive worry about the details of life, or when it leads to indecision. When either of these occurs, then Gemini can become nervous, even impatient to get on with the process, only to find that worry and indecision prevent him or her from taking action. Thinking can also lead to a situation where Gemini tries many different things, but masters nothing in the process. Finally, any of these trends can lead to an unemotional expression, even though feelings may be seething just below the level of consciousness.

The more constructive path of thinking leads to an open-minded outlook on life. The willingness to explore many avenues of thought leads to versatility. Gemini can make use of the tools of one trade while exploring the values and requirements of another. Flexibility is an asset to the Gemini mediator, whether mediation is between individuals, groups, or facets of one's own personality. The capacity for tolerance is enhanced by the openness to different ideas. Gemini thrives by being active, communicating with the immediate environment, and storing information for future use.

On the spiritual path Gemini has several advantages. The capacity to talk with just about anyone exposes Gemini to the widest range of ideas in every area, including spirituality. The capacity to think things through allows Gemini to examine a spiritual belief or system and then make a decision about its significance. In the process of gathering together those ideas that form a meaningful package of beliefs, Gemini gradually overcomes any tendency toward superficiality. Over time, the central ideas call out to be examined on a more profound level, thereby deepening the spiritual conviction. Thus Gemini's active, thinking energy is a significant aid to spiritual development.

Cancer

The Cancer Sun has a deep-seated capacity for judgment. This is based on Cancer's ability to experience the world and to feel its impact in the physical body. One likely challenge to using this ability is that this Sun sign can become judgmental with regard to its relationships with people and the world in general. A possible outcome of this trend is to be possessive—holding on too tightly not only limits one's movement, but also prevents the flow of things to and from the self. This could bring spiritual development to a halt. The apparent causes could range from being too timid to reach out for the new idea to simple procrastination about making a change.

The capacity to feel is also the ground for developing sympathy for others. A natural intuitive connection can develop, based on the same kinds of bodily feelings mentioned above. Cancers are often inspirational lights for other people because they show that they truly understand and appreciate the feelings of others. They have the capacity for clear expression when they are allowing energy to flow to and through them. Instead of procrastinating to avoid a new contact, they are cautious, neither jumping in without thought nor holding back unnecessarily.

As Cancer travels the spiritual path, the sign learns the importance of taking care of the self, thereby overcoming a tendency toward self-indulgent behavior. Cancer often understands the value of different flavors and foods, and learns that a little bit of something adds spice, whereas too much only causes a stomachache later. Aimlessness and procrastination are often replaced with a sense of the natural flow of things. Water flows downhill at its own pace, and Cancer can use this as a metaphor for the spiritual flow of life. Relationships with others take on greater fluidity of interchange when Cancer learns to appreciate the other person's values and intention. This appreciation is part of the spiritual flow for this sign.

Leo

Leo is known as the fixed fire sign. "Fixed fire" is almost an oxymoron. Fire, by its nature, is movable. However, the fuel may not be so movable. The challenge for Leo is to resolve the paradox between solidity of intention and ultimate changeability. When Leo becomes too attached to his or her sense of self, the result is vanity—or even arrogance. Once Leo decides that he or she is better than other people, the result can be a snobbish attitude or a dictatorial nature. A selfishness may develop out of the belief that Leo deserves more because Leo is better than everyone else, possibly including other Leos. Such a person is unpleasant company.

The very fixity that can lead to unattractive personality traits can also be used to fuel a determined, courageous character. Powerful, effective leadership is born out of the dynamics of taking on a task and seeing it through. Think of pottery-making. Shaping the pot is only the first step. Patient application of heat is needed. Too much heat and the pot cracks. Too little and the clay never hardens. Leo's art lies in the steady application of just the right amount of energy for each of life's tasks. The honorable course includes both pushing others to succeed and refraining from singeing them in the process. Fueling the process is a Leo task.

Spiritual vanity is extremely unattractive. No one likes a snob, and because spiritual beliefs are such a personal thing, spiritual snobbery may be viewed as bigotry. Bigotry is the antithesis of true spirituality. None of us have a grip on the final word where spirit is concerned. By the same token, the leadership strength of this sign is to encourage others to accept and work with a set of spiritual values that are meaningful to them, even though they may not be a Leo. Leo presents spiritual concepts as positively as he or she can, without becoming attached to the outcome of the teaching. In this way Leo learns spiritually, too.

Virgo

The Leo contrast of fixed fire is reflected in Virgo—a mutable (changeable) earth sign. Here again we see a dichotomy that requires examination. The less-constructive expression of mutable earth is to be overly critical of oneself and of others. Virgo can take an idea apart with no goal except to destroy it—but to make a solid thing more flexible does not require that it be torn to bits. If Virgo feels inferior for some reason, one possible response is to become so straightlaced that any flexibility in thinking or feeling is stopped. By doing this Virgo hopes to maintain or regain a sense of solidity—a wishful thought that is unlikely to be fulfilled.

A more constructive use of the combination of energies is the development of dexterity. Virgo can move from one task to another with ease. A sense of fine discrimination does not thrive under an excessively critical nature. It does demand the capacity for critical examination of the details in order to understand them. When Virgo's high moral sense is built on critical thinking instead of criticism for its own sake, then spiritual progress is being made. The Virgo capacity to discriminate extends into every area of life. Such a person is perceived as being dependable precisely because he or she takes the time and effort to see individual differences before lumping people and things together.

On the spiritual path, discrimination is essential. Not all spiritual tasks suit all people, and some so-called spirituality is based on the personal needs and desires of the teacher. Faith is an important aspect of spiritual development, but a little bit of skeptical inquiry can save Virgo from wasting a lot of time and energy following a path ill-suited to his or her physical, social, and emotional situation. Because of the dichotomy of mutability and earth, perhaps, Virgo benefits from the exercise of caution in all areas of life, including spiritual matters.

Libra

The symbol for Libra is the scales of justice. Balance is an essential element of Libra's life. The knowledge that one can be out of balance leads Libra to be indecisive. Perhaps, if you don't move, you will not find yourself out of balance. The Libra challenge is to retain balance and at the same time experience the world of change. Without movement, however, Libra can become overly dependent on others for decisions. The opposite action is to jump into deep water without much thought, pursuing extravagant desires and engaging in extremes of behavior. Spiritually this can spell disaster, because spiritual extremes lead to friction within oneself and in one's environment. Alternately, Libra tries to remain balanced and aloof, only to fall into another set of extremes. Neither of these paths leads to spiritual development.

Libra needs to experience the things that happen when you step off the path. In fact, in order to choose your own path, you have to experiment, or at least experience other paths. In trying different ideas, Libra integrates those ideas and beliefs that resonate with the inner balance point. Impartial consideration does not require going full force in a new direction—a slightly aloof attitude may work very well when considering anything new: It allows time for careful thought. This attitude demonstrates consideration for the ideas being presented. The cooperative attitude wins friends and also provides balance in the personality.

Spiritual creativity is a huge advantage in every aspect of life. Making decisions and acting from the center of your values ensures a more balanced outcome. A huge advantage of finding the spiritual center is that all decisions become easier and smoother. Then you can be assertive in your life without going to emotional or physical extremes. The spiritual center is a bit like the axle on your car—you have the ability to go in every direction, yet you don't get jerked around by much of anything. Your energies are applied in a particular direction, and you stick to that path most of the time. You can allow yourself an occasional side trip to see what other people are doing without losing your sense of balance and spiritual direction.

Scorpio

Scorpio is the sign of fixed water. Fixed (or solid) water is ice, and there is no sign that can be colder emotionally than Scorpio. There is also no sign that can be hotter. Here again the challenge is to resolve a paradox, this time between the flow of life and the apparent solidity of the world. The cold side of this sign expresses itself through sarcasm and cruel truths. The hot sign expresses itself through jealousy, suspicion, and excessive emotions. It is through the negative expression of emotional traits that Scorpio has earned its name as the least-attractive sign of the zodiac. No one wants to be around a person who is hot and cold by turns, with no moderation in sight.

There is, however, a very positive expression of this Sun sign. Scorpio is the healer, the shaman who has been through a death experience and emerged to help others. The shaman can be cold, or at least emotionally balanced, and must be in order to do the work. The capacity to regenerate is strongest in Scorpio. It is through tenacity that Scorpios achieve anything, and their spiritual path requires a tenacious grip on life and on light. The constructive Scorpio is straightforward in speech and action, and seldom bothers to take the effort to lie.

The spiritual path of Scorpio includes rebellion against whatever is not working in your life. On the personal level there is a sometimes cruel edge to your actions, while on the interpersonal level there can be deep compassion. The contrast between what Scorpios do for themselves and what they do for others is visible. Moderation is something that every Scorpio can use along life's path, and this is even more true for spiritual pursuits. Still, an occasional excess is what reminds Scorpio of the benefits of the more balanced path. Rebirth is essential in the life of Scorpio.

Sagittarius

Sagittarius is challenged to pursue the highest spiritual aims without being led astray by one's supposed teachers. The sign of Sagittarius has, at its foundation, the capacity for transcendence. The spiritual basis of transcendence lies in the inspired idealism of this mutable fire sign. The less-constructive side of idealism is the pursuit of impractical aims that scatter one's energies. In addition, such a person can be gullible, taking in spiritual platitudes and treating them as profound truths. From this pool of so-called truths a self-righteous, dogmatic attitude can arise. At the same time, Sagittarius can be indulgent, both of self and of others, allowing people to take liberties with time and other resources.

Idealism in itself is a positive trait. Sagittarius holds up a spiritual light for others to follow, or at least shines light upon the realities of life so that higher values may be sorted out from less admirable thoughts and desires. The qualities of loyalty and honesty emerge from the inner idealism. After all, is it not idealistic to believe that honesty and loyalty are values worth having? Sooner or later, both are tested in the fire when friends or family need our support. In the bargain, Sagittarius upholds these values cheerfully and is generous with his or her resources.

Sagittarius aspires to the spiritual path naturally. Intuition is strong. What looks like almost frivolous idealism to others is often related to a clear vision of what the future can be, if one simply follows higher inspiration instead of ego-centered dogmatism. Thus Sagittarius on the spiritual path is definite without being dogmatic, and is willing to change direction if there is a good reason. This sign has the capacity for justice in all dealings, but it is justice mixed with wisdom and mercy. Because of the profound thought that has gone into past decisions, Sagittarius is no longer easily moved from a decision, yet is willing to listen to all sides of a spiritual discussion.

Capricorn

At its worst Capricorn energy is tinged—even permeated—with fear. The challenge is to trust instead of experiencing fear. If an inner distrust of other people and of the future has developed, Capricorn can become the miser, unwilling to share material, emotional, and spiritual resources with others. This materialistic stance comes across as unsympathetic in circumstances where it is clear the resources exist in reasonable abundance. Because these attitudes create distance between Capricorn and other people, a deepening sadness may develop. Others find it more and more difficult to be around Capricorn because of the emotional walls.

Capricorn is also capable of exercising prudence without succumbing to fear. Such a person is perceived to be dependable in every activity. You apply energy to the task at hand in an economical, even industrious, effort to achieve goals on the spiritual plane as well as on the material one. Capricorn tends to exact a harsh style of justice that other people may not like very much initially, but they eventually come to respect the consistency and efficiency of direct decisions. You know where you stand with Capricorn. Whether creative or less constructive in expression, Capricorn exercises a high level of self-control.

The practical side of Capricorn may never look as spiritual as some other signs, yet a practical spirituality has its advantages. Prudent action becomes completely natural. Conscientious behavior, while not necessarily the easiest choice, becomes the logical, practical, spiritual choice. If you learn to have faith in others and to exhibit this faith, the spiritual path becomes much less rocky. Overly restrictive self-control gives way to the expression of feelings in a more direct manner. Because Capricorn appreciates life's natural heights—of material success, intellectual achievement, and emotional expression—spiritual attainment is a natural, even expected, development.

Aquarius

The challenge for Aquarius is to think deeply and to establish a firm base from which to act. Aquarius is the fixed air sign. Here is another of those paradoxical combinations of energy. The fixed part of the sign would like to be stable, while the air part wants to move from one idea to the next—and from one human experience to the next as well. The outcome can be an intellectually informed rebellion that risks the destruction of whatever sound foundation has been laid in the past. An Aquarius who is willing to follow a fad without thinking may be unsympathetic to family and friends who demand more traditional behavior. Rebellion becomes eccentric behavior, and visionary ideals take the place of sound thought.

Any of these extremes are actually the expression of more moderate traits. Aquarius can be friendly with just about everyone. You see the light within others and are seldom fooled by appearances—at least not for long. Your interests extend to psychic and occult matters, and you are not afraid to look at both the dark and the light side of any topic. Aquarian persistence isn't like the practical Taurus stick-to-it attitude. Rather, the Aquarius can float several different boats at the same time, keeping all of them in sight and redirecting them as needed.

On the spiritual path Aquarius has the advantage of a deep and thorough memory. The capacity to link seemingly disparate ideas allows them to develop innovative new plans that use information already available. The ingenuity extends to the spiritual path as well. Aquarius is not likely to adopt entire bodies of spiritual practice. Instead, they will draw upon a variety of cultural and religious sources. They persist in developing a framework of beliefs that all fit logically with one another. Perhaps this is why Aquarius is considered to be the sign of the astrologer: Astrology offers an elegant system that considers all aspects of human experience.

Pisces

For Pisces there is an abundance of feeling. The challenge is to create a balanced flow from the inner life toward the social sphere. The sensitive Pisces can easily tip the balance, becoming hypersensitive on every level. Indulgent and fearful by turns, Pisces often finds that grounded security is an elusive goal. In fact, it is these utopian goals that prevent you from finding satisfaction in ordinary experience. A psychic negativity can develop in which you become mired in pessimistic thoughts and feelings toward other people and life in general. The tendency to withdraw from a world of perceived sharp edges causes some Pisces to become recluses who avoid contact whenever possible. Because life is sometimes too painful, you recede from it like the ebbing tide.

Like the tide, the Pisces sign's direction has to change. Profound sensitivity brings you back into contact with others. Your empathy urges a less-selfish attitude. Your intuition provides the content for inspirational speaking or writing. Your compassion connects you to other beings on a universal level. Yes, you may seek isolation again, especially if life has temporarily overwhelmed you. Yet, like the tide, you will come back. There is a mystical quality in Pisces that is sometimes reflected in the glamour of movie or music stars, but is found more often in the sensitivity of caring professions. Pisces naturally perceives and understands the feelings of others.

The Pisces spiritual path can involve martyrdom. While it is occasionally appropriate to pursue spirituality to the extreme, most Pisces will not be called upon to give up their lives for spiritual beliefs. However, the spiritual path may feel like it leads to a kind of death. If ideals cannot adapt to circumstances, something has to give. A major spiritual storm can cause severe damage, as the flood-waters of ideals smash against the barriers of familial and societal beliefs. A more balanced approach is to be receptive to others while remembering that all their beliefs are like one drop in one's own ocean of understanding, and cannot pollute it unless Pisces allows it.

Summary

The above descriptions of each Sun sign include both creative, positive expressions and less-constructive expressions of the potential energy. Your individual spiritual path may follow the path of your family in every respect. Or it may take rather different turnings on the path to becoming the spiritual being you wish to be. You probably can see yourself in the negative descriptions, or at least you probably will admit to having exhibited some of those traits in childhood. You also can no doubt relate to some of the more positive expressions of your Sun sign.

You will take a giant step along the spiritual path when you stop beating yourself up for the less constructive things you think and do, and start using those weaknesses as guideposts along the path. After all, without some human limitations we would have no way to understand or value our own spiritual progress. Remember, mistakes are just mistakes. You do the best you can all the time. And your best gets better with experience, until you find you are living, almost all the time, the spiritual life you aspire to. You can only move toward strength of character by experiencing life.

For Further Reading

Armstrong, Jeffrey. *God the Astrologer: Soul, Karma and Reincarnation*. Badger, Calif.: Torchlight Pub., 2001.

Clement, Stephanie Jean. *Charting Your Spiritual Path With Astrology*. St. Paul: Llewellyn, 2001.

Lake, Gina. *Symbols of the Soul: Discovering Your Karma Through Astrology*. St. Paul: Llewellyn, 2000.

Healing with Astrology
Twelve Signs, Twelve Herbs

by Jonathan Keyes

In the past thirty years we have experienced a revolution in health care. After years of experiencing the side effects of allopathic medicines and treatment plans, millions of people from the United States have sought alternative care for their health problems. Many have turned to naturopathic, Chinese, and ayurvedic medicine. All of these systems have the same fundamental philosophy: encourage the body to heal itself naturally through gentle and nourishing modalities. In all of these systems, healers look at the mind/body holistically and look to see the relationship between emotions, lifestyle choices, diet, and health. By looking at the underlying causes of illness, natural health-care practitioners seek to go to the root of the problem instead of suppressing the symptoms.

During this recent renaissance in natural health care, we have chosen primarily to seek out eastern systems of healing while ignoring a rich and powerful western tradition of our own. Dating back to the time of Hippocrates in the fourth century BC, the Western world has enjoyed a profound system of diagnosing and treating health-care problems from an energetic perspective. Physicians up through the Middle Ages used astrology as an integral part of their healing tools. By knowing a patient's astrological chart, a healer could ascertain the best treatment plan. For example, a client who had a predominance of fire in his chart (Aries, Leo, and Sagittarius) would have an increased likelihood of heat conditions such as rashes, heart problems, and hypertension, as well as emotional conditions such as mania and anger. Treating these problems would involve remedies that were cooling to the system, such as soothing herbs, hydrotherapy, and a new diet.

Around the time of Galileo in the seventeenth century, scientific thought became more prevalent and ancient traditions such as astrology and alchemy came to be regarded as outdated superstition. A few popular herbalist astrologers such as Nicholas Culpeper continued to thrive in England, writing numerous books on the relationship of herbs to astrology and the use of decumbiture (the ancient art of casting a horoscope to determine the outcome of a disease and the best course for healing). But by the end of the 1600s, the traditional alliance of healing and astrology slowly began to wane. As we veered away from energetic and holistic ways of seeing health, we moved further toward the very precise and scientific models of health that we see practiced today.

In these scientific models, disease and illness are seen as the same no matter who the patient is. The same drugs and surgery plans are prescribed for a wide variety of clients. Doctors rarely take into account the unique personality and constitutional factors that make up each individual person. In traditional holistic medicine, each person is seen as expressing a certain temperament or constitutional type. In ayurveda, one may be classified as predominantly vata (wiry and energetic), pitta (hot and fiery) or kapha (slow and steady). In traditional Western medicine, one may be classified as predominantly choleric (fiery and hot), phlegmatic (watery and heavy), sanguine (airy, quick, and buoyant) or melancholic (earthy and weighted). By understanding one's type, one can specifically tailor healing modalities specific to each client. This ancient Western form of medicine is a powerful traditional healing method and one that deserves to be studied along with the many other traditional healing systems.

In this article, I will write about herbs that are specifically tailored to each sign. Herbs have a long history of being used not only for their physically medicinal value but for their emotional and magical value as well. Herbs have been worn as talismans, used in rituals, and burned as incense to help ward off danger, strengthen vitality, and increase spiritual growth. The Roman herbalist Pliny once wrote that someone wearing mugwort would be protected from poisons and wild beasts. In ancient Russian folk tales elder blossoms were gathered to drive away evil spirits. And in ancient Greece a garland of rosemary was tucked in one's hair to strengthen the memory (this was often done by Greek students who needed to have good memory for their studies).

For each sign I will pick only one herb to represent it. This lets us concentrate on just a few herbs and their powers. Those who are strong in a particular sign may choose to work with just one herb, but we often have a number of signs strong in our chart and we may want to visit with several of the herbs listed below. By working with just a few herbs, we develop a powerful relationship to those plants. By spending time with them in their natural setting, watching them grow and die back, we gain a deep understanding of their energetic aspects as well as their medicinal ones. Take your time studying these herbs; make tea and drink their infusions. Wear the herbs in amulet pouches or dry them and leave them hanging around the house. This will help you get in touch with their magical abilities.

Aries

Those with Aries strong in their chart tend to be strong-willed, energetic, self-directed, and willful. Aries signs are often creative, inventive, and leaders in their field. This type can have a tendency toward impatience and needs to watch out for bursts of temper.

Physical Correspondences
Head, eyes, upper jaw

Herb
Yarrow—*Achillea millefolium*

Medicinal Properties

The Latin name *Achillea* comes from Achilles—a Greek warrior who used yarrow to help heal his soldier's wounds. A poultice of the herb helps staunch the flow of blood and has antiseptic qualities. Yarrow is one of the best herbs for reducing fevers by inducing sweating. Yarrow also helps lower blood pressure by bringing increased blood flow to the skin. Yarrow helps move and circulate the blood, and is a great herb to help regulate menstruation. Finally, yarrow is known for its ability as an anti-inflammatory agent, helping to heal rheumatic and arthritic conditions.

Spiritual Properties

Yarrow's tall, strong stalks remind one of the features of an Aries. Yarrow helps maintain strength and resiliency while also helping to reduce excess heat in the system. This is a perfect herb for those Aries signs who need to cool down and be more relaxed in life. In flower essence, yarrow is helpful as a protective herb, and can strengthen one's auric shield against negative emotional influences. It is truly a warrior's plant, and can help one to gain courage and strength in the face of adversity. In legend, Achilles was mortally wounded in his heel. Like Chiron, the centaur god who was also wounded in the heel, these myths describe the personality of a wounded warrior or wounded healer—a powerful person who has a deep emotional vulnerability often stemming from childhood. Yarrow helps us to work with these vulnerabilities and transform them into part of our strength and beauty.

Dose and Preparation

Steep one ounce of the flowers and leaves to one pint of hot water for thirty minutes and drink as a tea, or take ten to thirty drops of the tincture twice a day.

Taurus

The Taurus type is often steady and calm. They tend to be down to earth and usually more slow-paced. Taurus signs often have a relaxed and pleasant attitude toward life, but sometimes can be stuck in ruts and get bogged down. Taurus signs are often physical and sensual creatures who enjoy using their five senses.

Physical Correspondences
Neck, throat, mouth, tongue, lower jaw.

Herb
Sage—*Salvia officinalis*

Medicinal Properties
Sage is commonly used as a gargle for healing sore throats, laryngitis, and tonsillitis. Sage is also known for its positive effect on the digestive system, helping to calm and relax the stomach and increase better assimilation. Sage helps to strengthen the nervous system. It can also be helpful for mothers who need to lower their production of breast milk. Sage contains substances similar to the hormone estrogen, which helps to regulate the menstrual cycle. *Caution*: It should be avoided by pregnant mothers.

Spiritual Properties
The Latin name of the herb, *Salvia*, comes from the root verb *salvare*, meaning to save. Sage is a powerful herb for increasing self-expression. It seems to act powerfully on the throat chakra area, where it can help those who have a hard time saying what they feel, or singers having a hard time with their voices. This is a wonderful herb for Taurus signs who need to develop self-confidence. It can also be helpful for creative types who feel blocked in their ability to express themselves. Sage has an effect on those who are sexually inhibited due to emotional reasons: It helps transform intense feelings and aids in the process of healing these wounds. Finally, sage helps open the doorway to the inner guide, the wise inner voice who knows best. By drinking sage tea or taking sage flower essence we gain a better understanding of our direction and path.

Dose and Preparation
Steep one ounce of the leaves in one pint of hot water for thirty minutes and drink as a tea. Add sage to meals or take ten to thirty drops of the tincture twice a day.

Gemini

Geminis are often noted for their quick wit, friendliness, and talkative demeanor, as well as their varied interests and hobbies. They can be animated and intelligent, though sometimes they are prone to sarcasm. Geminis tend to have a heightened nervous system and can occasionally feel hyper and "wired."

Physical Correspondences
Lungs, arms, shoulders, hands

Herb
Peppermint—*Mentha piperita*

Medicinal Properties
Peppermint is commonly used as a digestive aid. One of its volatile oil constituents, menthol, has an antispasmodic effect that helps soothe and assist in the digestive process. Peppermint helps cool the system if one is running a fever, and is helpful for healing colds and the flu. It is also helpful in relaxing the nerves and alleviating tension due to stress and anxiety. Peppermint's antispasmodic effect can assist women who are having painful cramps and tension associated with premenstrual syndrome as well.

Spiritual Properties
Peppermint is a perfect herb for Geminis because it encourages their lively and buoyant personalities while also relaxing and strengthening their nervous systems. Peppermint is a friendly and likeable plant with a delightful aroma. Working with peppermint helps offset melancholy and moodiness. Peppermint lifts us up and energizes our spirits when we need a boost. It also helps keep negative people from coming into our lives.

Dose and Preparation
A handful of fresh leaves will make a good cup of tea when steeped for fifteen to thirty minutes (dried peppermint leaves tend to lose their medicinal effect due to the volatile oil evaporating). Or, you can take ten to thirty drops of the tincture twice a day.

Cancer

Cancer is a water sign, and water is associated with emotion and feeling. Cancers are sensitive, impressionable, and sometimes moody. Cancers can show a great degree of empathy and compassion and are often mothering to their friends and family. Cancers have a strong protective instinct and usually need a secure, private place to retreat to in order to recharge their batteries.

Physical Correspondences
Breasts, stomach

Herb
Lemon balm—*Melissa officinalis*

Medicinal Properties
Lemon balm has a number of uses. As a digestive aid, lemon balm helps alleviate stomach cramping and flatulence. It also helps strengthen assimilation when food is processed in the stomach. Lemon balm is noted for its ability to alleviate insomnia and anxiety. As a mild nervine, balm helps strengthen the nerves and offset nervous tension. Balm seems to help out when there is mild depression as well. Lemon balm has antiviral properties and also induces sweats—helpful in the treatment of colds and flu. The volatile oils found in balm have an antihistaminic effect which makes it a useful herb for those who suffer from hay fever and asthma. Finally, lemon balm has antispasmodic effects that can help alleviate cramping associated with menstruation.

Spiritual Properties
In Culpeper's *Complete Herbal*, the author writes that lemon balm "causeth the mind and heart to become merry, and reviveth the heart, faintings and swoonings, especially of such who are overtaken in sleep, and driveth away all troublesome cares and thoughts out of the mind." Indeed, this sweet little plant is helpful especially for the type of depression and anxiety that comes out of feeling insecure and unsafe. It is useful for those who feel cut off from others and need to receive and give love in a more equal manner. For Can-

cers who feel worried, confused, and helpless, balm helps to bring some peace and clarity to their lives. Balm brings one back to feelings of joy and serenity.

Dose and Preparation
The medicinal volatile oils evaporate when we dry this herb, so try to take it fresh as a tea once a day (steep one ounce in a pint of water for fifteen to thirty minutes) or take twenty to thirty drops of the tincture twice a day.

Leo

The characteristic Leo is charming, expressive, dynamic, and flirtatious. They are often somewhat regal in disposition and enjoy having a good time, and Leos often like to be the center of attention. On occasion they can seem pompous and arrogant, and they need to avoid being too self-centered. Leo rules the heart, and Leos have the ability to shine love and joy from their beings and help others to find their own sense of happiness.

Physical Correspondences
Heart, dorsal vertebrae, back

Herb
Marigold—*Calendula officinalis*

Medicinal Properties
As an external salve, marigold helps soothe and heal wounds. Marigold has antiseptic qualities that help to ward off infection as well. Internally, marigold is helpful for healing ulcerated gastric conditions. It aids in the process of digestion, since it stimulates the flow of bile. As a blood cleanser and liver tonic, marigold is useful for alleviating chronic skin conditions. It also seems to stimulate the lymphatic system and helps improve immune response to illness. Finally, marigold is noted for its ability to regulate menstrual cycles and alleviate the symptoms of tension associated with PMS.

Spiritual Properties

This beautiful garden herb is particularly helpful in bringing joy and cheer to the heart—the place ruled by Leo. Watch as this plant blooms into a delightful orange-yellow blossom. Like the Sun, marigolds help bring heat, warmth, and peace to one's life. For Leos who need more courage, a deeper sense of their own beauty and worth, or a sense of joy and creativity, marigold is a wonderful herb to work with. Marigold is a gentle herb and works subtly on the system, helping to alleviate the stress that the heart takes on during times of crisis. If you have experienced shock, trauma, or great grief lately, marigold will help alleviate these conditions and bring gentle, soothing contentment.

Dose and Preparation

This herb can be used in salves or taken internally as a tea once a day, steeping half an ounce in one quart of water for thirty minutes.

Virgo

Like a sweet maiden reaping corn from the fields, Virgos are able to draw the best from life and cull the parts that are not necessary for good living. Virgos tend to be analytical and are often tidy and organized. Sometimes Virgos can be too exacting, and may be overly critical of themselves and others. Virgos are often good with their hands and have an eye for detail. The sign of Virgo is associated with service, humility, and dedication.

Physical Correspondences

Intestines, spleen

Herb

Oats—*Avena sativa*

Medicinal Properties

Oats have a high source of vitamins, minerals, and proteins, which make them one of the most nourishing foods available to us. Oats also contain an alkaloid known as avenine, which helps relax the central nervous system. Oats are gentle and are a wonderful remedy for those who have been weakened and exhausted from stress, tension, and overwork. Oats can help to gently lift the spirits and strengthen the entire system. Anxiety and nervousness start to dissipate, and a greater degree of clarity, tranquility, and contentment develops in those who eat this grain regularly. Oats can also be used externally to heal skin conditions, due to a high level of silicic acid.

Spiritual Properties
If you ever have had a chance to go out into a field of oats you will notice the long stems—up to four feet tall—gently waving in the fields. This gentle herb seems to float along the wind and breathe in the sky as it bends and waves. Oats have long been associated with the goddesses of the land, and are a representation of the most nourishing qualities of Mother Earth. Through working with this plant, Virgos can alleviate any stress or tension they may be feeling. They can develop a stronger constitution and better digestion.

Dose and Preparation
Take oats as a daily part of your nutrition. I like to eat oats regularly in the morning with some raisins.

Libra

Playful and sociable, Libras often are able to glide through social gatherings and be charming and graceful. A little distant emotionally, Libras excel at drawing people together, and they often have a strong desire for romantic partnership. A partner helps act as a mirror to the Libran soul so they can grow spiritually. Libra is the sign of the scales, and often Libras need to learn the lesson of bringing balance into their lives.

Physical Correspondences
Kidneys, lower back, abdomen

Herb
Parsley—*Petroselinum crispum*

Medicinal Properties

Known primarily as a culinary herb, parsley has some wonderful medicinal uses as well. Parsley is helpful as a kidney and bladder tonic, helping to remove deposits and stones through the urinary system while also healing infections. Parsley is a galactagogue, meaning it increases the flow of mother's milk, and also acts as a uterine tonic. Finally, parsley helps soothe the digestive system and promote optimal absorption and assimilation. With a rich source of vitamin C, parsley is an underestimated gem in the world of herbs.

Spiritual Properties

Just as the herb helps to loosen stones in the urinary system, parsley helps to loosen us up as well and bring us a greater sense of ease and peace. In Chinese medicine, the kidneys are associated with the emotion of fear and holding on tight. Parsley helps us to relax and enjoy the ride, to let go and flow. With its friendly disposition, it does this in a gentle, nonthreatening manner. When we feel split in two and separated from our head and our heart, parsley helps bridge the gap and join the two in union. Parsley helps Libras to relax and feel at ease, and helps them to honor their own hearts as well as the needs of others.

Dose and Preparation

Steep one ounce in a pint of hot water for thirty minutes and drink as a tea, or take twenty to thirty drops of the tincture twice a day.

Scorpio

Those strong with this powerful sign are often magnetic, intense, sensitive, and protective, but also desire intimacy. There is often something hidden about Scorpios, as if they are only showing a part of what they are feeling. Scorpios have a capacity for deep, rich relationships when they decide to open up and be vulnerable. Scorpios can channel their powerful intensity into transforming their own and other's lives. They also can get stuck in emotionally charged ruts and need to periodically release deeply stored feelings.

Physical Correspondences

Sexual organs, reproductive organs, bladder, colon

Herb

Raspberry—*Rubus idaeus*

Medicinal Properties

In 1941, a study was published in the British medical journal *Lancet*, which issued findings that raspberry helped to relax the uterus. Raspberry leaf has long been used by herbalists to help strengthen, tone, and relieve spasms in the uterus during pregnancy. Raspberry also helps relieve the tension associated with menstrual cramps. Because the leaf contains tannins, it can be especially helpful for relieving diarrhea. Raspberry fruits are rich in antioxidants and are helpful for preventing heart disease, cancer, and degenerative eye conditions. Because of the high amount of nutrients in raspberry, this fruit strengthens the entire system, helps with anemia, and nourishes the kidneys.

Spiritual Properties

This twining, thorny member of the rose family goes deep and is a rich, powerful friend. Raspberry is helpful during childbirth—one of the most transforming events in life. It is in touch with the Earth, pulling up nutrients from the fertile soil to help strengthen and nourish itself. Raspberry is a Witch in touch with pleasure (her fruits) and pain (her thorns). This is a beautiful herb to work with when a person needs to move through emotional trauma and stress. A wonderful Scorpio herb, raspberry will help transform the emotions and move one through the pain of intense experiences. Raspberry will help fortify you when you are feeling low, and will also help you visit deep and powerful realms when you are floating on the surface.

Dose and Preparation

Steep half an ounce in one quart of hot water for thirty minutes and drink as a tea, or take twenty to thirty drops of the tincture twice a day. And don't forget to eat the fruits!

Sagittarius

This fiery sign is noted for its playfulness, exuberance, and extroversion. Sagittarians have a desire to explore life in all of its fullness—sometimes to an excessive degree. These are the travelers, the adventurers, and the partygoers. They like to take a bite out of life and live with joie de vivre. But there is also a quieter side to Sagittarius. They enjoy the philosophical realms and like to study the deeper meaning of life through higher education. Sometimes Sagittarians can feel scattered because of their many interests, and so they need to focus on one or two things in life.

Physical Correspondences
Liver, hips, thighs, sciatic nerve, buttocks

Herb
Dandelion—*Taraxacum officinale*

Medicinal Properties
This herb is a perfect antidote to the high-energy, occasionally excessive lifestyle Sagittarians like to lead. Too much alcohol and too many drugs, fatty foods, and rich meals can tax the liver; dandelion helps to cleanse and strengthen this organ optimally. The root of this herb helps increase the flow of bile and has a mild laxative effect. Dandelion also helps clear up skin diseases such as eczema and psoriasis—diseases often associated with a poorly functioning liver. In Chinese medicine, the liver is associated with the emotion of anger. Because of its liver-healing properties, dandelion also seems to be helpful for reducing symptoms of anger. Dandelion has a notable effect on the digestive system, helping one to assimilate and process food better. This wonder herb also has a diuretic effect and helps strengthen and tone the kidneys as well. Finally, dandelion is nutrient- and mineral-rich, and is helpful in cases of anemia and vitamin deficiency.

Spiritual Properties
This herb grows everywhere. Dandelion helps get you on the right track when you've wandered off. The root will help you get back

down to earth if you've been wandering aimlessly or feel lost and confused. Dandelion works on those who are too heated and are storing a lot of anger and frustration. Dandelion helps us move through these emotions and release them. The herb is also a mover and shaker, and can help those who are too quiet and meek to stand up for themselves and take life full-on. Dandelion instills courage and a powerful sense of self. Sagittarians can work with dandelion to help them stay grounded and on course—while also releasing negative mindframes.

Dose and Preparation

Steep one ounce of root in a pint of hot water. Let sit for two hours and drink throughout the day. Or, you can take twenty to thirty drops of the tincture twice a day.

Capricorn

This Earth sign is known for being powerful, industrious, direct, and ambitious. Capricorns set goals and meet them. These are the builders around us—helping to create lasting structures that work. Capricorns can sometimes overwork themselves and need to be able to relax. Capricorns also have a secret, sensitive side, and they can feel melancholy from time to time. They need to be around people who will make them feel light and playful so they can loosen up. Capricorns also have a sensual side and enjoy touch and massage.

Physical Correspondences

Knees, bones, skin, teeth, nails

Herb

Horsetail—*Equisetum arvense*

Medicinal Properties

Horsetail is one of the best sources of silica, a mineral which helps strengthen bones, nails, and teeth. Silica increases the absorption of calcium and decreases the deposits of fatty acids in the arteries. Horsetail is filled with minerals and nutrients, which makes it a great herb for strengthening someone who is weakened and debilitated. Because of its high levels of iron, horsetail helps to build up hemoglobin levels and counteract anemia. Because it is an astringent, horsetail is wonderful for healing stomach ulcers and diarrhea. Horsetail has a mild diuretic effect and helps to strengthen the kidneys and the prostate gland.

Spiritual Properties

Horsetail is an ancient prehistoric herb that once grew as tall as a tree. This herb likes to grow in damp, moist areas of the woodlands and along roadsides. Horsetail strengthens resolve, brings solidity, and nourishes our root chakra. When we need to be firm and focused, horsetail brings us iron-like resolve. Horsetail also helps us to adapt and flow with situations as they come, and helps relieve stress when we are taxed. Work with horsetail to contact your spiritual source. It helps to strengthen your core. Capricorns can work with it to help strengthen their inner selves and remain fluid and adaptable in their approach to life.

Dose and Preparation

Steep one ounce of herb in one pint of hot water for thirty minutes, or take twenty to thirty drops of the tincture twice a day.

Aquarius

Those who have this air sign prominent in their charts are often known for their unusual approach to life and their orientation toward the community—even as they maintain a unique vision of their own. This explains the problematic nature of Aquarians, for while they seek company and are usually able socialites, they are also often detached and a little cool or removed. Their rebellious nature helps them to be pioneers, free thinkers, and revolutionaries, even though they can also be sometimes dogmatic and stubborn in their ideas.

Physical Correspondences

Ankles, nervous system, blood circulation

Herb
Lavender—*Lavendula officinalis*

Medicinal Properties
With its sweet, unmistakable odor, this lovely herb can be used in oil form (in baths) and in incense form to relieve tension, anxiety, and insomnia. Lavender can also be taken internally and has an overall strengthening effect on the nerves. Lavender has an excellent effect on the digestive tract, helping us to process and assimilate food better. It primarily acts on the liver, stimulating it to clear stagnation and promote cleaner blood. Lavender lowers blood pressure for chronic hypertensive types and calms a heart prone to palpitations. Externally, lavender can be used as a remedy to heal burns and stings.

Spiritual Properties
This beautiful herb heals one through its taste, touch, scent, and appearance. Its beautiful purple flowers delight and stimulate the senses while its odor intoxicates. Spend some time with this herb and it will help lift depression, remove stagnancies, and enliven the heart. Lavender has an association with the third eye and clairvoyancy. It helps stimulate our mind and increases telepathic and extrasensory perception. For an Aquarian, it helps to develop mental acuity, and can relax and soothe the nerves that may be frayed from overstimulation.

Dose and Preparation
Steep one ounce of lavender in one pint of hot water for fifteen minutes and drink as a tea, or use as external oil or salve.

Pisces

This dreamy water sign is associated with imagination, romanticism, idealism, and the transcendence of the mundane. This desire for transcendence comes in many ways for Pisceans. For some it may mean religious and spiritual worship or the love of music, movies, and theater. For others it may mean a descent into the world of addiction to drugs and alcohol. Pisceans often have an "old soul" quality about them. Because it is the last sign of the zodiac, there is a sense of Pisceans wanting to return back to the beginning point—the source and center of all creation.

Physical Correspondences

Feet, immune system

Herb

Licorice—*Glycyrrhiza glabra*

Medicinal Properties

Licorice has a sweet taste that makes it a great harmonizing herb when added to more bitter or harsh-tasting herbs. Licorice contains glycyrrhizin, a chemical similar to hormones made in the adrenal glands. Because of this, licorice is said to have a strong effect on fortifying the kidneys and adrenals. Over prolonged periods of time this chemical can also lead to hypertension in some cases, and should not be consumed if you have a tendency toward this illness. Licorice has a wonderfully soothing effect on the mucous membranes of the throat, lungs, and stomach. It is a great herb to take if there are inflammations in these areas. Licorice reduces acid in the stomach and has an antispasmodic effect that helps soothe intestinal problems. Finally, licorice also reduces fevers if one has a cold or the flu.

Spiritual Properties

This soothing and harmonizing herb helps bring sweetness and nourishment when there is despair and anguish. Licorice helps ease feelings of stagnation and immobility. When you need to grease the wheels a little, or soothe inflamed emotions, work with licorice. For a Pisces, licorice is a wonderful ally. This herb also helps draw forth emotional energy, bringing out deep and hidden parts of ourselves and allowing those emotions to be processed and released. If one is feeling lost and confused, licorice root helps bring people back down to earth.

Dose and Preparation

Steep one ounce of root in one quart hot water for an hour and drink as a tea. Or take ten to twenty drops of the tincture three times a day.

For Further Reading

Dreyer, Ronnie Gale. *Healing Signs: The Astrological Guide to Wholeness and Well-Being.* Mansfield, Ohio: Main Street Books, 2000.

Reinhart, Melanie. *Chiron and the Healing Journey: An Astrological and Psychological Perspective.* London: Penguin, 1999.

Tyl, Noel. *Astrological Timing of Critical Illness: Early Warning Patterns in the Horoscope.* St. Paul: Llewellyn, 1998.

Sun Sign Attitudes
A Mental Health Checkup

by Joanne Wickenburg

How often have you heard someone say, "That really galls me," or, "Get off my back," or, "I wouldn't bend my knee to her," or any number of other clichés that refer to bodily functions or anatomical parts? It's important to realize that the subconscious mind is not always able to differentiate between the positive and negative data we feed it, nor does it always make distinctions between aphorisms and fact. Perhaps you once said, when referring to someone you didn't like, "She really makes me sick," and then within days you landed in bed with the flu. Thoughts are things.

Anatomical functions that relate to these age-old clichés are ruled by the signs of the zodiac. There is also a direct relationship between the psychological needs represented by the twelve signs and the physiological functions each rule. When the needs of the signs are suppressed or the physical functions they rule are referred to irreverently, the body often suffers the consequences.

Your Sun sign describes what you need in your life in order to feel vibrant and important. When the needs of your Sun sign are not met, personal energy is diminished or misdirected and physical dis-eases could occur. Here is a rule of thumb to follow when consider-ing how distressed signs manifest in illness: Dis-eases of internal bodily functions are induced by repressed needs and energy, while external dis-eases that are visible to others often occur as a result of excessive or aggressive behaviors.

For example, a broken ankle can result from careless action. Ulcers, on the other hand, are usually caused by pent-up emotional stress. What types of dis-eases are you prone to experience based on the Sun's sign position on the date of your birth?

Aries (Head)

Your personal fulfillment is dependent on your fearlessness to initi-ate new activity independently. You "shine" as you develop your potential for leadership and tap into the courage that is required to blaze new trails. Do you have the freedom you need to do your own thing without undue interference from others? If you fear taking the initiative to secure your independence, Aries discomforts could be the result.

Headaches are symptoms that your freedom is being compro-mised. Perhaps you feel trapped, unable to "be yourself." If your need for leadership (to be the "head") is threatened, headaches could result. When obstacles to freedom occur you feel as if you are "hitting your head against a brick wall" and getting nowhere fast.

When meeting others for the first time, your face is the first thing they see. What does your face tell them about who you are? Head or facial wounds may be your way of showing others that you have recently overextended boundaries by being excessively aggressive, or that you allow others to dominate you. Small burns or fevers, also Aries-ruled, can be your response to being "burned." Fever blisters can say the same thing.

Acne is another Aries-ruled disorder. How many adolescents suf-fer from an inability to be themselves? Frustration results when told to both grow up and act their age, all in the same breath. The result-ing frustration, if not handled outwardly, can erupt in facial welts.

In summary, Aries dis-eases are a result of "identity frustration."

Taurus (Neck)

While Aries is concerned with action for action's sake, Taurus needs to create something valuable that can be demonstrated in some tangible way. Productivity and practicality are key words that qualify your self-worth. When your value (material or otherwise) is compromised, dis-eases associated with the neck and throat could result.

Possessiveness and envy at one level, or lack of productivity and self worth at another, can lead to sore throats. Tonsillitis, for example, often corresponds to a period in a child's development when his or her "worth" is challenged. When sore throats interrupt your usual productive schedule, it might be wise to ask yourself, "What is it that I just can't swallow?" Or, "Who is challenging my values or self worth?" Or, "To what have I become overly attached?" Coughs and choking, on the other hand, can result from taking in too much or fear of letting go of what has no future value. Because Taurus is a fixed sign, change is seldom easy.

In summary, Taurus dis-eases are a result of misplaced values or low self-esteem.

Gemini (Arms, Hands, Shoulders, Lungs, Nervous System)

You need to gather information from a wide variety of sources in order to fulfill your innate curiosity. You learn by association, or by "connecting the dots." While these skills lead to a talent for multitasking, the potential to spread yourself too thin can lead to difficulty channeling or focusing your thoughts. Injuries to the hands and fingers are common signs that you have your "fingers in too many pies."

Likewise, when ideas are repressed or verbal communication is prohibited, nervous habits can result. Gemini is associated with smoking because of its rulership of the lungs. Geminis are particularly vulnerable to this habit because they tend to be high-strung.

Gemini also rules the shoulders. How many times have you sat over a computer and had your shoulders ache from muscle tension? Has your Gemini glow been extinguished by your lack of mobility or because your curiosity and need for variety are not being met?

In summary, Gemini dis-eases are a result of boredom or unfocused mental energy.

Cancer (Stomach and Breasts)

You are the great protector. You discover your own importance as a result of creating and enforcing safety zones, not only for your own protection but to assure the safety of those people and things you hold dear. However, when your need for strong emotional foundations is threatened in some way, the breasts or stomach could experience the resulting pain.

Upset stomachs or ulcers are two potential outcomes of excessive emotional stress. If you suffer from one of these discomforts, ask yourself: What is going on in your life that you can no longer "stomach?" Like the crab whose pincers hold on to its prey at the cost of its own life, it is important that you learn to let go when circumstances show the time is right to do so. Instead of nurturing the problems surrounding you and watching them grow, try releasing your hold with love.

Because Cancer is the most nurturing of all of the signs, it isn't surprising to find that it rules the breasts and ovaries. If you feel unable to nurture, or what you love has been "torn from your breast," physical difficulties in these areas could result.

In summary, Cancer dis-eases are the result of feeling unneeded or emotionally unsafe.

Leo (Heart and Spine)

Your sign is the "heart" of the zodiac, ruled by the Sun's brilliant splendor. You grow in self-awareness as you see your own personality reflected on everything that you touch and everything that you create. You need to shine and take pride in all that you do. You are not happy when someone else overshadows your role on center stage. It is not easy for you to ask for help when life presents heavy burdens. Perhaps this is why so many who share your Sun sign suffer from frequent back pain. If you fall into this category, ask yourself, "Have I taken on too great a load because I am too proud to ask for help?" Can you "bend" your will without feeling spineless?

You need to put your whole heart into what you are doing, and you want others to value your efforts. Heart patients often confess to a building fear of not being appreciated. Some literally fall victim to a "broken heart."

In summary, Leo-ruled dis-eases are a result of misplaced ego.

Virgo (Intestines)

Your purpose is to distinguish the difference between what is valuable and useful and what is superficial waste. You need to be efficient and productive, and you are discriminating in the techniques that you use to accomplish these ends. As information is accumulated, it must be analyzed to see the value contained within it. What proves to be superfluous is eliminated while what is deemed valuable is put to good use.

So it is with your body. Food is processed in the intestines. Part of its substance is absorbed through the intestinal walls while the rest is prepared to be eliminated. Failure to use discrimination in both what you eat and in what you do can result in intestinal distress.

If you suffer from such dis-ease, ask yourself: What is going on in your life that you are unable to "digest?" Is your life out of order in some way? Are you being discriminating without becoming excessively critical? Are you helping others by providing them with tools to help themselves?

In summary, Virgo dis-eases are a result of lack of discrimination or excessive criticism.

Libra (Kidneys)

Balance and harmony are your ultimate goals. You grow in consciousness as you learn to share experiences and ideas with others. Interaction leads to objectivity—an important ingredient for your success. By sharing with others you learn to understand contrasting points of view, which cultivates an awareness of the importance of polarity, equality, and justice for all.

Imbalances in your personal life that interfere with your need for a counterpart can create an imbalance in the body's functioning, particularly in the kidney function. The role of the kidneys is to purify the body of toxins and irritants. When relationships become "toxic" to the point that you lose your equilibrium, physical dis-ease can result.

An unfulfilled craving for a partner with whom to share your life can result in a craving for "sweets" which can exacerbate diabetes. Sharing, working side-by-side with others, and seeing the needs of others as equal in importance to your own without losing your identity in the process can help minimize Libra disorders.

In summary, Libra dis-eases are a result of imbalances between the self and others.

Scorpio (Sexuality and Elimination)

Scorpio is the sign of regeneration. You are intense and powerful and oh, so magnetic. Your purpose in life is to unite your power with the power of others in order to create something together that you alone could not. This requires trust; this requires passion; this requires sacrifice.

Regeneration and release are the major lessons involved with this sign. Resentments that hang on, a fear of letting go, or an excessive drive to control can easily lead to blockages in both the body's elimination process and in your sexual drive.

It is interesting to note that when we feel completely out of control, we tend to use clichés or profanities that refer to either the body's elimination process or the sexual function. These profanities are powerful symbols that can be used to intimidate or to frighten away the things we fear the most.

In summary, Scorpio dis-eases are a result of control issues.

Sagittarius (Liver, Hips, Thighs)

Life has no limits for you; your future seems always bright. Sagittarius is the sign of expansion, and you live out its purpose by always looking ahead and seldom looking back. "Don't fence me in" is your motto. Your sights are set on the promise of tomorrow, but often at the expense of the realities of today. The harder you try to avoid these realities, the more likely you will be to confront them. Like your symbol, the archer, you aim for the sky. Focus is your challenge. While it is important to be aware of the promises of the future, and to understand the larger, more philosophical point of view, you also need to bring your ideals down to earth so they can be used creatively in your daily life.

Sagittarius dis-eases are associated with excess. Obesity, liver malfunctions, and alcoholism are associated with this sign. Over-eating or over-drinking stem from either an inability to see the potential of how to attain your goals, or from dissatisfaction with the realities of everyday living. Learning to live one day at a time might be helpful in dealing with problems associated with excess.

Impatience, procrastination, and exaggeration are also ruled by Sagittarius. A broken leg or an arthritic hip will certainly bring you down to earth, where escape is no longer a choice.

In summary, Sagittarius dis-eases are a result of excess or fear of losing freedom.

Capricorn (Bones, Knees, Joints)

You need to know where you fit in the larger social structure. You are concerned with defining your territory, achieving success, and making sure you're recognized for your ability to respond to important life situations.

In order to find success within the social structure, you need to be aware of its rules and the boundaries that define your place within it. Yet, in the process of reaching your ambitions, it is easy to get caught up in the expectations, regulations, and limitations of society to the degree that you lose your individuality and flexibility both psychologically and physically.

If you hear yourself saying, "I wouldn't bend my knee to him," stop and ask yourself if you have become inflexible and unresponsive to the needs and rights of others in your quest for personal success. Likewise, if your bones are becoming brittle is it because of your age, or is it because you have become crystallized in an inflexible mindset? Humility is the keynote here. Can you find success within the social system without becoming excessively authoritative or judgmental?

In summary, Capricorn dis-eases are often a result of inflexibility and excessive ambition.

Aquarius (Ankles, Calves)

You are the oddball of the zodiac; to you, conformity is synonymous with suffering. Your self-awareness comes as a result of rebellion and demonstration of your originality as well as your eccentricity. Never satisfied with the status quo, your mission involves breaking the rules, changing outdated attitudes, and introducing a new way of viewing the world. Your originality can develop into true genius, or when left undirected it can lead to useless rebellion and foolish risks. For this reason, Aquarius has also been associated with accidents and unexpected, unpredictable events.

Aquarius rules the more highly geared nervous system. When your urge to be unique and to break out of a mold you no longer fit into is ignored, nervous disorders could result. This sign also rules the ankles and calves. How many times have you twisted an ankle shortly after having done something erratic without thinking about the consequences? Is your body punishing you for rebelling? Or is it punishing you for not standing up to your right to be a unique individual, with unique ideas that don't always conform to the norm?

In summary, Aquarius dis-eases are often a result of excess risk-taking and unpredictable behaviors.

Pisces (Feet)

Developing faith in an unknown future is your major lesson in life. You need to believe in something greater than yourself, and you need the security of knowing that you are safe even when the world feels like it's a scary place. You are a dreamer; you are creative; you are also a little naïve.

Life challenges you to make a commitment to something having value to others regardless of the material benefits this commitment offers you in return, or the level of recognition that is given to you as a result of your contributions. On the other hand, it is important that you don't invite people to "walk all over you" out of your sincere desire to serve the human race.

With faith as a foundation, you will stand tall. Lack of faith weakens the very foundation of who you are, as symbolized by the Pisces rulership of the feet. If you have problems with your feet, maybe its time to examine your faith and the strength of your spiritual foundations. Fear, doubt, or past failure, when left unattended, can fester until they weaken the strength of your base.

The sensitive, creative, yet evasive tendency of this sign can also result in a sensitivity to drugs or alcohol. Altering the psychic balance creates distortion and eventually dissolves the spiritual foundations upon which your life stands. Work to enhance your compassion without taking on the problems of the world. Learn to serve without losing your ego. Know in your heart that tomorrow's Sun will shine even if yesterday's weather was a little disappointing.

In summary, Pisces dis-eases are often a result of fear or lack of proper "grounding."

Learning to Create Ease

It is not my intention to imply that the simple concepts introduced in this article can, or should be, applied when evaluating serious physical diseases or handicaps. Some things won't change regardless of how we alter our attitudes and behaviors. We can, however, change the way we let these problems affect us. Likewise, no one should use astrology as a means of physical diagnosis unless she or he also has a medical background. I do believe, however, that there are health conditions that people can fix by making changes in lifestyle or attitude. In these cases, astrology can be very helpful by pointing out what energies can be used for self-healing.

Regardless of your Sun sign, pay attention to the clichés you commonly use. It is possible that when you tell your subconscious that someone is making you ill, it will take you literally and manifest your suggestions. For example, if you say (or feel) that someone is always "pulling your leg," don't be surprised if you lose your balance. If someone is a "pain in your backside," it might be more than coincidence that you find yourself at the local pharmacy counter purchasing Preparation H. Always remember, thoughts are things.

It is equally important to realize that all charts contain all twelve astrological signs. If you have a copy of your horoscope, and you are suffering from a physical "nuisance," find where the sign that rules the complaint is located in your chart. The house cusp it occupies will enlighten you to the specific experience in your life that is causing you physical distress. For example, if you suffer from frequent headaches, find the house cusp in your chart ruled by Aries and strive to function more independently in the area of life described by this house. Perhaps Aries is on your Tenth House of career. If you feel hemmed in or unable to function independently in your profession, headaches could be the result. Changing professions or taking on a more independent role could be your miraculous cure.

For Further Reading

Gibson, Mitchell E. *Signs of Mental Illness: An Astrological and Psychiatric Breakthrough*. St. Paul: Llewellyn, 1998.

Naumann, Eileen. *Medical Astrology*. Cottonwood, Ariz.: Blue Turtle Pub. Co., 1996.

Your Sun's Strongest Ally
Solar Aspects

by Dorothy Oja

Your Sun sign is the most widely known astrological position in popular culture. When people voice the overused phrase, "What's your sign?" they're always referring to the sign that your Sun was traveling through in the month of your birth. Most people never bother to learn more about astrology than this. But knowing your Sun sign is the merely the beginning of a journey through the planetary archetypes, and that's a good thing. The twelve signs of the zodiac are the foundation and the building blocks of a very complex and amazing study encompassing nine other planets and the endless variations and combinations formed between them.

For now, we will focus on the Sun's placement in your chart. The Sun holds great power and sway, and it is the primary expression of your ego—your will to live your life in a particular way, following your own unique lifestyle. The Sun represents your essential self and your overall purpose in all that you do. And it is at this point that simplicity quickly becomes complexity. After noting the sign the Sun occupies, the modifications begin, and these take you from the generalities to the specifics—and then to the rare human being only you can be.

In addition to its zodiacal sign, your Sun is also placed in one of twelve locations or houses, which modify its behavior through the natural environment it occupies. Although we can list many characteristics of Sun signs, the basic key words quickly become modified by the Sun's house location and its connection to any one of nine other planets, including the Moon (which, like the Sun, is technically known as a "light"). The basic key words of your Sun sign have now been modified by the location of your Sun and its aspects (mathematical relationships or connections) to one or more of the other planets. So now, not only do we need to consider the basic energy your Sun sign represents, and its house position, but also the inevitable energetic blending that is required when one planet reacts with another. There is not enough space here to describe all facets of this amazing combining of influences. However, we can discuss effectively some of the energies exchanged between your Sun and its strongest ally. This is the planet that makes the closest aspect to your Sun by degree.

The Sun is our greatest daytime light, providing warmth and light to Earth's activities and seasons. In your chart, it provides a central governing role and the energy necessary to express your vital life force. The Sun is literally where you shine, and represents the methods you employ to accomplish the will that seeks the strongest expression within you. The Sun represents your overall life goal and the requirements needed for your accomplishment and success. It is the essential means, mode, and energetic pattern that will be used to reach your goals. The other planets are in the employ of the Sun, the director of your life's theater. After assessing the Sun's sign and its location or house position in the chart, the next condition to consider is the closest aspect made by the Sun to another planet in the chart.

The closest aspect to the Sun gives an even stronger indication of the combined methods, means, and characteristics you will employ to achieve whatever you most seek to accomplish with your life. An aspect is simply the angle between two planets in a chart, expressed in degrees. The type of aspect that exists between any two planets will modify the flow of energy between them. For instance, the aspects of trine (120 degree angle) and sextile (60 degree angle) are a smooth blend and flow of energies, and generally indicate ease in expressing the planetary energies joined by these aspects. The aspect of square (90 degree angle) and the aspect of opposition (180 degree angle) are more challenging and may, at least initially, thwart you from getting what you want and need. By focusing on the essential principles of the two planets, however, you can ease the tension of conflicting energies and find ways to balance the needs of both planets' essence. When the Sun is conjunct (at the same degree or within a few degrees of) another planet in the chart, the two must blend their characteristics and work closely together as a team. Depending on the planets involved, this can be an easy process or a more strained one that will take time to integrate. In the following sections we will consider this kind of interaction by describing potential manifestations of the Sun in aspect to each of the other major planets.

The easiest way to determine which planet is closest to your Sun is to look at the degree number of your Sun and determine which of the other planets is at exactly the same numerical degree or within five to eight degrees on either side of that degree. For example, if your Sun is located at ten degrees Taurus, you may have Mars located at eight degrees Capricorn. These two planets are closely connected to each other by two degrees of exactitude. Often there is an even closer aspect, say another planet at ten degrees or one at eleven degrees. There are chart services you can contact that will calculate your birthchart. And, of course, you can always consult with a professional astrologer, who can explain your chart and all its aspects in thorough detail.

The Sun Aspecting the Moon

The Sun and Moon are opposites in many ways. The Sun is generally externally oriented and associated with the masculine energies of action, going out to achieve, and external visibility. The Moon governs the internal or emotional processes and the feminine energies of attracting or magnetizing things and people to oneself. The Sun and Moon, the two "lights" of the chart, provide a good basis for understanding the personality of a person.

If the strongest, closest aspect to the Sun in your chart is with that other lovely "light," the Moon, your life will have a strong emotional dimension. Your feelings will need to be seriously considered and acknowledged in the pursuit of your life purpose. In general, feelings will be closer to the surface of your daily activities. Compassion, protection, safety, and security—as well as individual, family, and community growth and development—are sure to be important in your career or life choices. Also, family ties will play an important role, whether that means family of origin or friends and companions along the way who become like family to you. There is a need to belong to and be part of a family, a group, a tribe, or a community. Security and protection issues become an integral part of your life expression.

The Moon softens the sometimes harsh rays of the Sun, tempers the ego, and adds a strong emotional quality to the overall expressions and events of your life. The ego is more aware not only of what it wants from life, but of what life wants from it. The Moon adds compassion, caring, and unconditional giving, and raises the issues of nurturing and developing. There is a greater focus on community, women, and women's issues, and all those in need of support and protection. The family will, for better or worse, in some way play an important role in the overall scheme of your life. Difficult angles (square or opposition) between these two planets can indicate conflicts between what you feel on an inner level and what you actually express or manifest on the outside. This conflict needs to be understood so that your life can be more fulfilling. Everyday creature comforts and a rhythm that allows for regular relaxed times will sustain this combination best.

The Sun Aspecting Mercury

If the closest aspect to the Sun in your chart is with Mercury, then reasoning, thinking, and the processes of communication will take on a primary role in your life. The Sun amplifies Mercury and increases mental activity. Mercury gets a boost from the Sun and consequently feels proud of its ability to express ideas and concepts. Language, learning, teaching, writing, speaking, and all forms and ways of communicating ideas and interacting with others are amplified by the Sun's strong contact with Mercury. Mercury, which naturally supports all forms of communication, accentuates language's many uses and forms and its role in social interaction. Because of the essential ability to speak on many different levels, working with youth and children can be a skill with this combination of planetary energies. Finely developed social and communication skills can lead you into teaching or into various forms of writing and computer-based technology.

The Sun's close connection to Mercury gives you the ability to remain curious all your life, and often conveys skill in several different areas of interest. In order to attain ego satisfaction (Sun), you must feel that you are recognized for the specialized skills you have. However, at times the Sun can overpower Mercury and create a strongly opinionated mind that holds on to its ideas or theories even in the face of conflicting information. Certainly, exploration of many topics and interests will be part of your life's adventures. Loquaciousness, wit, and an easy conversational style, as well as the ability to engage in social banter, will make you a much-requested guest in group gatherings. In some cases you can exhibit technical and mechanical skills, as the mind is likely to be quick, and can perceive both small and large concepts. Difficult angles between these two planets can bring about narcissistic tendencies and a mental inflexibility with a know-it-all attitude. Wit, awareness, and a quick study will develop with this combination, and at times the need to hear yourself talk in a steady stream of consciousness will alternately annoy or amuse your friends.

The Sun Aspecting Venus

If the closest aspect to the Sun in your chart is with Venus, you will enjoy the goodwill of others more often than not—much to the chagrin of your close friends, who feel you may be getting away with far too much. The blending of the Sun and the goddess of love creates a basically affectionate nature interested in issues of fairness, cooperation, and harmony. Venus seeks to establish relationships that are fruitful and beneficial to both parties involved. Because Venus has a natural proclivity toward generosity, gifts and favors given will return in equal measure to the sender.

When Venus is closely associated with the Sun, your relationship life will be in high focus. In fact, you may be identified primarily by the relationships you have, or you can grow dependent on your relationships—so much so that you may not feel quite right if there isn't a special significant other to share your life. Venus loves creature comforts and good feeling, and is therefore often willing to compromise for the sake of securing these maximum amounts of pleasant, happy encounters and environments. Typically, this combination creates a basic likability by developing a pleasing social manner, disposition, and appearance, which makes it easy for others to approach you. Other Venusian qualities such as music, the arts, literature, dancing, beauty, and appealing surroundings are also bound to play an integral role in your life. There are, of course, many ways to find a sense of beauty in life, but the point is to derive a sense of pleasure and emotional equanimity from something emotionally or physically beautiful.

Venus can cultivate quite an indulgent side and gravitates toward all sorts of sensual pleasures in food and drink. Difficult angles between the Sun and Venus often lead to overindulgence or feelings of being undesirable, undervalued, or unloved. Trying too hard to gain love and affection can then lead to excessive compromising of personal values and principles, leading to breaches of integrity. Indecisiveness is often accentuated because of the fear of displeasing a partner, or a habit of deferring decision-making to others. The Sun and Venus don't face confrontation well and are ever seeking to negotiate their way back to pleasure.

The Sun Aspecting Mars

If the closest aspect to the Sun in your chart is with Mars, you will have a bold streak in some area of your life. You are the type of person who will go where angels fear to tread—and this is something that can get you into hot water if you're not careful. Considering the potential consequences of action is not always your strong suit, and acting first and thinking about it later means you'll find yourself in an undesirable position at times. This is not necessarily a bad thing, but you need to consider what you're doing instead of letting the heat of the moment dictate your actions. At other times, your courage will make you the hero who saves the day. You will have said or done things that others could only imagine or entertain in their minds.

When the Sun and Mars team up, the personality takes on that of a warrior for a cause—not just a rebel without a good cause. A pioneer in some way, you tend to be the first to take action when others are simply content to stand on the sidelines and wait. This aspect of your character can mean that you are quite often impatient with the reluctance of others to move in the direction of their goals and dreams. You are a self-starter and a brave leader, especially when a cause has captured your interest. You are not likely to allow any circumstances to stop your progress or prevent you from reaching your desired goal. By the same token, if obstacles prove to be insurmountable, you could just as easily move on to a goal that is more attainable. You need to win the day and gain recognition for your achievements, and you don't particularly enjoy beating your head against the wall for a long period of time. It's important to remember that being impatient with others will not win you lots of friends. Instead, do what you must, break new ground, forge a new path, and go after your goals. Leading by the example of your actions is the best way to effect change in others. "Go for it" must have been written with you in mind.

The Sun Aspecting Jupiter
If the closest aspect to the Sun in your chart is with Jupiter, you will most often express optimism, generosity, and goodwill, and you appear to have an endless reserve of that energy. You can be positively hard to keep up with. It's a good thing that you have more energy than the average person at your disposal, because the Sun-Jupiter connection broadens your life, opens doors, and offers many opportunities—so many, in fact, that it's easy to exhaust yourself with activities. Having too much on your plate can make you inattentive and overloaded to the point of missing commitments and appointments. Your main job is to sort through all the goodies life offers you and determine which are worth the effort and, more importantly, what the consequences will be after the party is over. Your life will revolve around learning situations and the acquisition of information. In fact, you often feel as if life is one big classroom—and every situation teaches you something valuable. Not only that, but you want to share the wisdom you've gleaned with anyone who will listen to your endless stories. All those lucky things don't just

happen by themselves, though—it's your own generosity of spirit and enthusiasm that will inspire others to give you special perks and extend favors.

Although you have a certain amount of protection because the biggest planet in the solar system is cozying up to your Sun, you can easily get a swelled head or a know-it-all attitude, and then you will be very hard to take indeed. Make sure you leave some room in your life for a bit of humility and give others some credit for knowing things, too. Your greatest asset is to inspire others to take a chance on getting what they want out of life. Often you do it simply by showing them how it's done. They'll be amazed at your prolific abilities and wonder what in the world is holding them up from going after their own goals. Igniting the enthusiasm of others can be one of your greatest satisfactions in life, and one of the ways you meet your life purpose.

The Sun Aspecting Saturn

If the closest aspect to the Sun in your chart is with Saturn, you could feel a great sense of responsibility for just about anything that happens—and even things that don't happen. Feeling overly responsible for sins of ommission as well as those of comission can produce negative thinking, so lighten up! It is true you have a mission, and your life is about commitment and dedication. You may be tested on your conviction and integrity. At times you will be frustrated at how long it takes to get where you want to go, but when you really think about it you realize that all things worthwhile take longer to attain. Time is on your side. In other words, the older you get and the more experience you have under your belt, the more recognition and respect you are likely to earn, provided that you've done your homework.

Make sure you build a sturdy foundation, because you wouldn't want to get to the top and have it all blow away. You might be tempted to take a short cut to your goal, but I'd strongly advise against it. Others appear to be able to get away with that kind of thing, but since you have Saturn as the closest buddy of your Sun you'll have to prove your worth every step of the way. Aggravating, I know, but at least when you get there you'll be sure you're the real thing. One pattern that could set you back is being much too hard on yourself and taking the most negative view. Cut yourself some slack: As long as you've met your commitments, go ahead and take an hour off. You're likely to work hard and play hard, both.

Saturn expects you to carry some extra burdens and responsibilities, and there will be times when you just want to run away, but by then you will have built up the extra muscle those responsibilities require and, oddly, you won't feel comfortable just being a laggard. Saturn is funny that way—you wind up getting used to doing the best you can every time. Keep your eyes on the prize and on how important your reputation is in the long-term scheme of things. There is a sense of strength and community in you, and you may be surprised to find out that others depend on your resilience, determination, and strength of purpose. You are admired for your adherence to principle and ethical behavior.

The Sun Aspecting Uranus

If the closest aspect to the Sun in your chart is with Uranus, there is an element of rebellion somewhere in your life. Not even you may be fully aware what exactly will activate the rebel in you. What's for certain is that you dislike taking anyone's word for the truth. It's important that you find out for yourself what the fuss is all about. You are not easily impressed. Your life involves going beyond the socially acceptable paradigms, questioning authority, and inventing a better model in any area of life that captures your interest. Luckily, you usually foment rebellion with a sense of humor. In fact, you are charmed by the foibles and eccentricities of others and gravitate to those who have unusual or interesting slants on life's issues. It's those oddities that pique your interest.

Creative endeavors are vitally important to your overall health and well-being. Nine to five is typically not the best option for you. If you must work for someone other than yourself, you will need a great deal of freedom and leeway in your daily schedule to be content, or have work that is highly stimulating. Another option would be to work on a project that contributes to the development and evolution of humanity. That's likely to do the trick and keep you from the terrible fate of boredom. Being boxed in is definitely not your bag. Okay, so you're somewhat eccentric and often feel misunderstood. The antidote is to find others of like mind; then you won't stand out in the crowd as the odd one—or at least not as noticeably, because you'll be in good company. It's also best that your rebellion has good cause; otherwise you will quickly become persona non grata without any redeeming value, and that would be a grand waste of your precocious and stunning abilities.

There is an innovator and inventor either apparent in your lifestyle or lurking just beneath the surface, waiting to burst onto the scene. Your life can be like a wild roller-coaster ride at times—filled with unusual happenings that are meant to shock you out of your lethargy. Insights can come like the lightning bolts of Zeus and highlight the obvious truth of your life in unprecedented ways. These sudden bursts of revelation can mean that at times your life takes a sharp turn that will not only surprise you, but those who know you well.

The Sun Aspecting Neptune

If the closest aspect to the Sun in your chart is with Neptune, there is great desire for unity and an attraction to some form of spirituality—something to believe in. When the Sun's closest ally is Neptune, you will feel as if you are the proverbial mouse in the maze looking for the cheese. You are likely to run into many dead ends, experience endless detours, and hit yourself in the head as you bump into the walls of reality. In fact, your life is a continual "reality check." What appears to be real one day disappears just like a mirage the next. Sooner or later you will learn that although what you feel and sense so strongly is often invisible, this doesn't mitigate its value or its ultimate substance.

People may think that you have a split personality, but it's because you truly have one foot in the real world and another in the other one. And after much time experiencing the paradox, you cannot let either go. They are equally valid, and you are often caught between them. This is a disconcerting state of affairs and, if not handled properly, can be a difficult process. Music helps a great deal, as does art, dance, and any endeavor that allows your energies to flow without restriction. Expect to be misunderstood most of the time, unless you are fortunate enough to find others who are aliens like you. Yes, you inhabit a human body—but you also live in other dimensions. The key is to find ways to bring back some of the magic from those nonphysical realities. This is part of your redemptive process. Ignoring or denying the idea that you easily blend with the otherworldly will only make your life more confusing and frustrating. Trust what you feel and allow yourself to share those images with others. In this way you will be an inspiration. Once you acknowledge and accept the unity of all things, you can then look for the author of everything. This quest will lead you to a form of worship. But please do not mistake this quest for abuse of drink or drugs. Those habits will quickly bring depression and cut you loose on the vast seas of despair. You don't want to go there. Guard your delicate sensitivity by knowing your absorption limits for stimuli and retreat when you've had enough—of anything. Your greatest success comes when you have mastered the ability to choose wisely among the endless illusions and choices life bombards you with. In choosing wisely you will open the channels to the inner voices of your soul and act in concert with the purpose of your higher self. It is then that supreme happiness will be yours, and acceptance of what is becomes a daily prayer.

The Sun Aspecting Pluto

If the closest aspect to the Sun in your chart is with Pluto, you are probably intense and passionate. Your survival instincts are strong and your intensity can be off-putting to others at times. If you've lived this life for any length of time, doubtless you will have heard it said that you are too intense. You notice things: the way the wind moves the trees, the movements of birds, the magical shift of people's expressions, the energy of bodies as you stand next to various people. In other words, you notice many things that others simply let slide or miss in everyday interaction. This places a certain amount of consternation at your door. What do you do with the various forms of subliminal information you are picking up, and how do you react to the unspoken or unacknowledged? Often you will not be able to verify the truth of your feelings, and eventually you must rely on trusting your instinct or your gut reactions. Because of this, there will be times when you become silent as you seek to process the information that your antennae have received.

Others may consider you unapproachable, hard to read, or even threatening. It's quite a task holding the secrets of life and nature in the very cells of your being. After all, you didn't ask to be such a prime receiver. Take heart: There is a purpose and a pleasure to all of this. Once you accept what life has dealt you, your honed instincts will keep you safe and in the company of those whom you can trust. Your X-ray vision enables you to perceive patterns that work and patterns that will break down due to a glitch in the structure. This becomes valuable information with which to build the empire of your dreams – that is, the lifestyle that will support your fondest desires. Knowing what you desire becomes of primary importance, because your ability to focus your intentions and energies is so great that you will eventually get exactly what you want. Remember the old adage, "Be careful what you wish for." This applies perfectly to you with Pluto empowering your Sun. There's nothing wrong with getting what you want, as long at it's not at the expense of the next person. After all, the power you channel carries responsibility and, because you have the gift of influencing others, how you influence people, and why, becomes crucially important.

Conclusion

Learn as much as you can about your Sun's strongest ally. Your Sun's sign, house position, and the sign and house position of the planet most closely connected to it is a great source of strength. It will both test you and build your character. As others move past your obvious personality traits, they will discover the qualities of the planet closest to your Sun expressed in the plan of your life. It is this combination that describes your main purpose and the meaning you seek from life. The other planets will help or hinder you in achieving these primary goals.

For Further Reading

Arroyo, Stephen. *Chart Interpretation Handbook: Guidelines for Understanding the Essentials of the Birth Chart*. Sebastopol, Calif.: CRCS Publications, 1990.

Burk, Kevin. *Astrology: Understanding the Birth Chart*. St. Paul: Llewellyn, 2001.

The Astrology of Lady Luck

by Leeda Alleyn Pacotti

Regardless of country, culture, or ethnicity, humans simply don't like to feel controlled or out of control. Facing situations of the unknown, particularly the future, we feel lost and fretful. Our first reaction is to flee, removing ourselves from the fear. But what confronts us is a circumstance, not a thing. The intangibility of circumstances and situations actually heightens and expands fear. Our only other choice is to fight.

We fight nonphysical chance or possibility by creating a distraction—a diversion to dispel our qualms. We humans hold that man is the master of his fate. The idea that a circumstance or situation could best us challenges the notion that we make our own way against all odds. To fight or maneuver, we must do one of three things: take a risk, engage in speculation, or gamble.

No matter which choice we make, the winner's hallmark is confidence. Without spirit, without inner strength to withstand the unknown, we have little expectation of overcoming our fears, worries, or outright losses.

Confidence and Fire

Confidence means we keep faith with ourselves. But with what are we keeping faith? Modern man has placed faith in many different things or ideas, nearly all outside himself. When challenges arise, these things or ideas fall easily, providing little or no support in return. They are not reciprocal and have no more strength than the belief with which we endow them. If our belief fails, so do they.

To arrive at true confidence, we look inward and make an exacting examination of our abilities and strengths. Dissecting these, we find clues about the fiery dragon within: the soul. Confronting this archetype of spirit, we drop all the pretenses that get us through daily life. Even if modern society doesn't permit enough expression of our true natures, we can meld fiery spirit into our thoughts, activities, and judgments.

With confidence, we become generals, diplomats, leaders, and philanthropists. We recognize ourselves as caretakers of the earth, seas, and skies. Standing certain and straight with belief in our thoughts, schemes fail and attacks are foiled. Enemies tremble before our mighty stare.

Certainly, every day isn't that dramatic, but the things we do encounter carry enough drama for us to summon confidence and stave off defeat. Armed with faith in ourselves, chance and possibility become allies—tactical kinsmen wielded in our struggle against circumstance and situation. We regain our control and are no longer blown by the winds of fortune.

By association, spirit has affinity with the astrological element of fire. Fire burns with passion, enjoying adventure and a healthy challenge. Whether it roars in flames or glows as soft embers, fire sheds light on our deepest desires, impelling us to act and attain. When we observe fire in animals or people, we see them as courageous, defiant, proud, and joyful. They revel in victory and pick themselves up quickly from defeat. Their movements are sure, powerful, and responsive.

Everyone of us has spirit. Through astrology, we each have some contact with the fire signs of Aries, Leo, and Sagittarius. Intelligent and inquisitive, these signs embody daring and action. From these signs and their rulers—Mars, the Sun, and Jupiter—we gain an understanding of the differences of risk, speculation, and gambling, and we gain a determination to use them to our advantage.

Risk usually manifests as action. We plunge into a situation, putting cherished ideas or possessions on the line or our lives in harm's way. A part of risk is the all-or-nothing possibility, revealing itself as one-on-one competition as in sport, or man-to-man combat as in battle. Because survival is at stake, risk extends physical endurance with adrenaline to speed blood flow, physical reactions, and mental quickness. Impulsive Mars rules over risk, spreading its influence through its sign, Aries, and into the First House of self and the physical body.

Speculation manipulates, taking time to create security. A risk is still taken, but within limits. To produce a specific effect or outcome, we purposefully apply our resources. Using careful strategy and keeping private counsel, activities are concentrated within defined boundaries. We establish a territory with an aim to claim and rule it. The goal is security and the freedom it brings. Speculation involves a long process of puzzling and planning, requiring steadfast patience of heart and mind. Upon success, the winner basks undisturbed in complete comfort. The radiant, steady Sun rules speculation, imparting this activity to its sign Leo and its natural Fifth House of faith, loyalty, and recreation.

When confrontation and planning are ineffective, an outright gamble or chance becomes the final option. Gambling is the ultimate test of faith and confidence. To take this step, we must accept any consequence, because all possibilities are present. Although survival isn't usually involved, something cherished is put to the test. We mete out our energies, jockeying for advantage. Eventually, the moment presents itself, and we go for broke or withdraw completely. Gambling is fickle and unpredictable, requiring a strong mind and sense of humor. The power of humor cannot be underestimated, because it lets us carry on, even if we lose the car and house in a craps shoot. Jovial Jupiter rules the changeable nature of gambling, relating its activity to the sign of Sagittarius and the Ninth House of sport, beliefs, and good nature.

How the Signs Take a Chance

Life is full of chance and possibility. How we deal with thrown curves and the unanticipated lies in our individuality, astrologically associated with the Sun. Roughly every thirty days, the Sun passes through a different sign. Each sign draws its motivation from one of four astrological elements: fire, earth, air, or water. Each sign draws its style of action from one of three qualities: cardinal, fixed, or mutable. Cardinal signs are focused and active, meeting life with gusto. Fixed signs are reserved and cautious; their action is reasoned and maneuvered for effect. Mutable signs fluctuate over the broad spectrum; their actions change with circumstance and vary from bombastic to capricious.

The twelve houses of the horoscope divide among them different areas of life, which may be sympathetic with or contradictory to the expression of your Sun sign. For instance, if you are a Leo with the Sun in the Ninth House, you are inclined to take a recreational approach to gambling. If you are a Pisces with the Sun in the First House, you are intimidated by the amount of risk you encounter in life, even though you secretly want to act more forcefully.

The following descriptions explain the Sun by sign and house. Look to them for the description of your natal Sun. If you know the placement of your Sun by house, blend the two meanings to determine how effectively you deal with risk, speculation, and gambling. Remember that self-confidence plays a strong hand in the ability to deal with or manipulate chance. The values you received when young, and your own experiences, will color the way you let your Sun operate. Remember, too, that these Sun sign descriptions are only a guide, and not a guarantee. To get the most out of the planets and their luck, you should consult a professional astrologer.

Sun in Aries or First House

Aries is risk personified. You do very well in speculation and gambling, but only if you rely on yourself. Your enthusiasm is infectious and brings out your boisterous side. At the track, you'll yell at the horse from your jockey or turf club seat. When you win at gambling machines or tables, your laugh resounds throughout the room and seems to come up from your feet. Impulsiveness is your only enemy:

Don't be swayed by anyone else's winnings or drawn to a crowd. In fact, your independence can lead straight to the money. Make all your own decisions in stock investments; your broker or trader may not be as honest as you. You have good luck with manufacturers in fire and rescue equipment, meat packing, and surgical supplies. When you gamble on sporting events and races, place your own bets; never use a representative or go-between bookie. Commodities brokering, with its turnabouts, will keep you on your toes. Be prepared to get out quickly if you feel you are throwing good money after bad.

Sun in Taurus or Second House

Enduring, practical Taurus might go into a casino, but only to watch everyone else play. Greenbacks belong in the bank, and coins, inside the piggy. No high roller or one-hit wonder, you make your money the old-fashioned way: you earn it. Of all the signs, you are the least fazed by bright lights, twittering machines, or hawkers at the game tables. It's all too much like a carnival, which insults your refined mind-set and gentle manners. Stock risks don't usually get your nod either, although you probably have several thousand shares of blue-chip certificates squirreled away in a safe-deposit box. Investment banking and corporate strategy hold the highest appeal for you, where you can calculate expected returns and interest. Your best avenues of investment follow your preferred pleasures and the strength of your pocketbook. For instance, if you love football, invest in the equipment manufacturers until you have a bankroll that lets you buy a team. Stable commodities suit you well, particularly cattle, hogs, and poultry. Just remember to let your personal preferences and enjoyments be your guiding star.

Sun in Gemini or Third House

Quick and facile Gemini gets the ultimate thrill from games of chance. You use your mind, making fast decisions, and the results are immediate. The down side is that you don't know when to stop. When it comes to risk, particularly high finance, your changeable nature won't sustain the long term. Avoid signing investment papers of any kind, especially on the fly, without doing a thorough reading or asking an expert's advice. You, more than anyone, can fall heir to undisclosed obligations, or misunderstand the rules. If you gravitate to commodities and stocks, your electric swiftness suits you for the fast in-and-out, such as day-trading or short-term speculation on crops and livestock. Just beware of rules for forced contract sales in commodities and margin calls on stocks. These hefty requirements are also immediate, and you might lose your stake, plus your possessions, to meet the sale demand. At the gambling tables, if you make a nice win, walk away. Consider putting the winnings into a hobby or recreation that challenges your mind.

Sun in Cancer or Fourth House

With as much emphasis as Cancer places on the confines of its home and territory, it's surprising how inclined it is to gambling and risk. The fluctuating Moon rules Cancer, and fluctuation describes Cancer's approach to risk, speculation, and gambling, which are all short-term. Risk takes the form of entrepreneurship, which, if it doesn't pan out, is quickly dropped. Speculation is very enterprising and follows the flow of the public good or population at large. In ventures of commodities and futures you do well with cheese and silver; avoid crude oil. For stock issues choose companies, either new or old, dealing in infant foods and goods, home construction, milk products, and refined oil. When it comes to gambling you need to let your intuition have full rein. Somehow you tend to beat the odds, such as drawing on an inside straight or suddenly running a full bet on a multiline slot after playing single coins. Just remember it's short-lived, just like the Moon's changes. Be sure to cash out your winnings regularly; visit the cashier's cage to pocket some in folding money; and continually switch to different game machines or tables. If your intuition is off and you feel the urge, have a nice meal at the sports book, but don't bet.

Sun in Leo or Fifth House

Speculation is an old friend to you. You constantly look for an excellent buy with continuing returns. Leo is the most likely sign to understand the rules and machinations of the stock market and stay in for the long haul. Being careful, you wait until you have amassed a considerable financial portfolio before delving into speculative ventures. This way, the money you invest will not jeopardize or deplete your nest egg. Review every offering carefully, especially the company's profit record and history through recessions. In general, you do best with blue-chip companies. Of course, only preferred, voting shares will do. Commodities and futures are too volatile for your tastes, but, if you have the knack, stick to gold. Gambling and its easy losses have little appeal for Leo, who enjoys the confidence booster of return on investment. However, if you do go to a casino, dress to the hilt, take in a stage show, and have a meal you'd never get at home.

Sun in Virgo or Sixth House

There's no beating about the bush with direct Virgo. You work hard for your money. You understand insufficiency and its effect on your nervous system. Although you will always have an income, you won't jeopardize your savings or pension on schemes. Even if you only entertain the possibility in your thoughts, gambling is simply an annoyance and a waste. For you, the idea of putting coins into a slot machine is the equivalent of throwing them into a storm drain. The very idea of plunking fifty dollars down on a craps table, to be lost on one throw of dice, is enough to send you into a panic attack. For you, a gambling win is a cash prize in a dance contest, where you didn't pay an entry fee.

Sun in Libra or Seventh House

Libra loves theory and watching it work out. You won't be much of a gambler, because losses will erode your sense of comfort. Risk is not your forte; it involves too much physical effort. In speculation, you have a simple formula: Continuing, modest returns are a must. Understanding that government substantiates all legal tender, invest in U.S. Treasury bonds, municipal bonds, and special revenue bonds of state and local government. All these have guaranteed interest, plus you know your investment cannot be lost. Among all the signs, you are the most likely to master the rules of commodity trading. If so, stick with food basics, such as butter, grains, and sugar. In case you are lured to the gambling halls, stay with single-deck card games, with a low bet requirement per hand. Although the winnings are smaller, you'll enjoy the strategy of the game much more.

Sun in Scorpio or Eighth House

Scorpio and its ruler Pluto are the champions of extraordinary gain. Mystery rules here; no one knows exactly how it happens. One major clue comes from Pluto's rulership of legacies, inheritances, and gifts from other people. Add unique events and the one-in-a-million chance to the mix, and you have once-in-a-lifetime gambling odds. Pluto rules football pools, lotteries, sweepstakes, and nationwide progressive slot jackpots. Scorpio, which likes to make money and keep it, doesn't squander through speculation or gambling. However, this sign really understands this peculiarity of chance and doesn't shy from putting in forty dollars to get back sixty-five million, after taxes. In a way, the whole venture is Scorpionic: A huge number of people, each contributing a few dollars, amass a fortune, which Scorpio, by being at the right place at the right time, inherits. Whew! Fortunately, practical Scorpio knows this won't happen every day and continues to work or run a business after winning the big one.

Sun in Sagittarius or Ninth House

You'd think Sagittarius and its ruler Jupiter, the king of the Greek and Roman pantheons, would bestow a Midas touch. That would be true, except you don't like to labor at amassing wealth. The promise is there, though. Turning your good mind and extraordinary experiences to the task, you enjoy success from a variety of speculations and investments. However, you need to research, think, and judge before you plunk down your dollars. Never work in the company or field in which you invest: You'll have too much contact with day-to-day changes, which clouds your judgment. Aligned with Sagittarius, the Ninth House rules gambling. Gambling and gaming rest on strong mathematical principles of combinations and permutations. You might have one or two effortless, lucky hits, but don't delude yourself that you are a master. Instead, go to your favorite bookstore; purchase some texts on games you like and a hefty volume on the mathematical theory of probability. Let's face it, well-applied knowledge that produces a series of wins is mouth-watering sweetness for Sagittarius.

Sun in Capricorn or Tenth House

Have you ever seen a snowshoe rabbit freeze when it gets a whiff of a predator? Its entire body goes rigid; its little heart races and pounds; its luminous eyes glaze over. The same effect occurs when a Capricorn stands in front of a one-armed bandit. Everyone knows Capricorn pursues wealth and displays an incredibly frugal approach to spending. You have the first nickel you ever made, and the idea that you'd actually put into a slot machine is laughable. For you, taking chances is not an adventure; it's a calculated, researched maneuver to gain the best advantage. But, there is your drive for wealth. When it comes to investments, they are not risky, speculative, or full of unknowns. Instead, you stick to the tried-and-true, established concerns that have proven themselves over time. These will be companies with extensive customer bases or global markets, such as national grocery chains, IBM, Microsoft, or shipping lines. No matter how lucrative the short-term appeal, never get involved in industrial booms or boomtowns. You'll lose everything you put in, because you can't gauge the timing on when to get out.

Sun in Aquarius or Eleventh House

Windfall earnings, double and triple stock splits, turning catastrophe to gold—let's talk Aquarius! It's a good thing you prefer isolation and hand-crafting your own success. Aquarius isn't a victim of gambling compulsion, because time is too precious to waste standing around in casinos or lounging in trading rooms. Your intuition leads you to speculate and invest inconsistently, but these ventures pay out at odd moments or in unanticipated bounty. The way you win turns heads. You might be waiting in line at a casino restaurant and plunk five dollars in a slot machine and hit the jackpot. You tend to buy stock after a new discovery and then leave it for twenty years, while the company's research and development finds inventive, marketable applications that skyrocket profits, share values, and dividends. Only you would purchase cheap land in an earthquake zone—and then find a mother lode of gold after the earth heaves. You have no particular how-to when you risk, because you're guided by a different star—from a different galaxy.

Sun in Pisces or Twelfth House

Pisces wants to win and is swayed by ideas of hitting the "easy, big jackpot." In nearly every situation of risk, speculation, and gambling, you need to pull back anytime you hear or see those three words—especially "easy." Pisces understands that things are not as they seem. Unfortunately, your accepting, understanding viewpoint can be a weapon against you in the hands of confidence men, fraud masters, and scam artists. The second you hear of ballooned returns or wild odds, back off. You tend to think it discourteous to investigate claims, but you would benefit from checking information with the Better Business Bureau, your state's attorney general, and the Securities and Exchange Commission. Admittedly, gambling tables are your Lorelei, so never bet more than a dollar per hand.

Gambling Out in the Open

When Pluto entered Sagittarius in 1995, gambling came out of the shadows and was legalized into mainstream American culture. Long denounced as sin and the destruction of the family in strict religious circles, these activities quickly grabbed their share of the economy, proving they were no longer a pastime or an occasional dalliance with a personal demon.

So strong was the economic lure that within five years, forty-five states had instituted one or more forms of gambling. Soon, these states squabbled with independent Native American reservations, which instituted identical gambling venues—the only ones permissible under Department of Interior regulations.

With gambling legalized, the genie was out of the bottle and running rampant. Although the light of Sagittarius had dispelled the shadows, the extremism of Pluto prevailed and will continue through 2008, when it begins to switch into Capricorn. Pluto represents compulsion—that demand to act, even against better knowledge. The fears of religionists and family values proponents came true as major casinos swamped economically depressed states such as Mississippi and Michigan, or revived river boat gambling. Pluto was popping out all over with sweepstakes, lotteries, and the Powerball. Sagittarius chimed in with sports book betting and bigger, extravagant resort casinos. Together, the lord of the underworld and the sign of the lord of the skies conspired with statewide, then nationwide, Megabucks slots.

What came from the shadows, however, wasn't simply a new economic trend. Pluto also exposed the social issues that derive from gambling life. Compulsive gambling deprived families of incomes when wage earners cashed paychecks at casinos and tried for a quick jackpot, only to lose rent and food money. Casinos put out the red carpet during the first week of every month as Social Security recipients swarmed to the slots, hoping to double or triple their monthly government benefits.

As money for dependent families was lost, depression set in and alcohol consumption, used to offset the oppressive feeling, soared. Prostitution, loan-sharking, and drug dealing moved in or escalated with the new cashflow. Reactive rather than proactive, state governments which initially hailed gambling as a new revenue for higher education were flabbergasted when these funds couldn't pay for enough vice squads or crime investigators, let alone social workers to help despairing families.

The introduction of legalized gambling and its attendant social ills came to light during the transit of Pluto through the first half of Sagittarius. The mysterious planet moved into the second half at the beginning of 2002. Pluto's lesson is very simple: Anything that is repressed will erupt violently. Although it will take some time for the dust to settle, we can expect that gambling, like alcohol consumption, will find its place permanently in American society.

Through 2008, expect to see more governmental regulation of gambling, especially with regards to advertising and promises. As with smoking and drinking, our schools will have programs explaining responsible gambling and the problems of compulsive behavior. Eventually, governmental regulation will require that gambling staff, especially pit bosses and managers, will have to refuse play to compulsive gamblers, after the fashion of bartenders refusing drinks to intoxicated drivers.

Enhancing Your Luck

Of course, denouncing gambling has never deterred it. Many people enjoy the activity for the mental exercise, the thrill, and especially the winnings. Their disappointments usually stem from not winning or failing to find a workable method.

Let's dispel an important myth now. There is no trick or method that works 100 percent of the time in gambling. However, astrology provides clues for putting luck in your favor, if you are willing to have your horoscope prepared and analyzed.

In the natal chart, the conjunction or opposition of Jupiter and Pluto spells "winner." Jupiter or Pluto in the Fifth House of speculation or the Eighth House of legacies increases the willingness to wager. Either of these planets in the Ninth House of gambling actually makes Jupiter overoptimistic and Pluto compulsive: You'll still wager, but you won't be able to stop.

If Jupiter and Pluto weren't in conjunction or opposition at your birth, consider obtaining a transit report to discover when these two planets will temporarily make these aspects in the future with your natal positions. For instance, transiting Jupiter will need to be conjunct or opposite natal Pluto, or transiting Pluto will need to be conjunct or opposite natal Jupiter. With a transit report, you can find out if unpredictable Uranus throws in a surprise with a good aspect, too.

A recent analytical discovery is astrolocality mapping, which projects tracking lines onto the globe that follow the path of planets as observed from Earth. An important part of this mapping includes paran lines, which are the points where planetary paths cross. These "crossroads" appear to affect your natal chart. Consequently, if your birth place isn't propitious for gambling luck, somewhere else in the world might be. Of course, your lucky spot could be at the bottom of an oceanic trough or in the middle of an Antarctic shelf.

In astrolocality mapping, look for the lines of the Jupiter Midheaven and the Pluto Ascendant. Where these lines cross is your lucky point, but, as an added benefit, that luck reverberates all around the globe on the same latitude. At the lucky point, though, the strongest area is within a fifty-mile radius.

Given the fire element's sympathy with confidence and risk, two other astrolocality combinations work well for your lucky points throughout the world. Crossings of the Sun or Mars with Jupiter produce strong effects for success. From the Sun with Jupiter, expect optimism, enthusiasm, success, and good fortune. With Mars crossing Jupiter, you gain confidence, luck, courage, and high energy.

For many people, the main deterrent to winning is the feeling of being a loser—a deep-seated conditioning from unresolved childhood disappointment or repeated failures in adult life. Although astrology points out the problem, Bach flower remedies, available at health-food stores, may help you overcome emotional restrictions. Larch and Pine are two flower remedies that deal directly with lack of self-confidence, especially when competition and winning are involved. Take flower remedies at least one week prior to any gambling and immediately before entering a casino.

Larch helps people who believe they aren't as good as others, who expect failure, and who believe they will never have success. These people fail to venture forth or make a strong attempt to succeed. To regain your self-trust, Larch stimulates belief in your self-worth and instills confidence before competitive events and mental games of gambling such as backgammon, blackjack, and poker.

The flower remedy of Pine assists people who believe they don't deserve to win and who continually emphasize their worthlessness through self-blame. As children, they were ignored or given a model for success, which had nothing to do with their abilities. These people have low self-esteem and feel guilty over achievements. Self-sabotage inhibits their gambling efforts. Pine creates a winning attitude, dispels guilt, and creates acceptance of achievement. If you feel your only luck is bad luck, by all means take Pine.

Risk, speculation, and gambling involve chance—a natural part of living. With daring, great success is achieved. Except for risk, Marco Polo would never have left all behind in Italy for a caravan ride to the Orient. Without speculation, Columbus wouldn't have gone out on a limb and asked Queen Isabella for a loan.

Resources for Problem Gambling:

Gamblers Anonymous: Check your phonebook or visit the website at gamblersanonymous.org.

Texas Council on Problem and Compulsive Gambling: Call 1-800-522-4700. This state-funded agency serves as a referral for Gamblers Anonymous chapters, private counselors and therapists, and private rehabilitation facilities throughout the United States. TCPCG accepts both national and international calls.

A Closer Look
Sun Sign Decans

by Sasha Fenton

Decans, or decanates as many astrologers call them, are an ancient form of astrology that divides each sign of the zodiac into three equal parts. From our point of view, the Sun appear to make a circle (360 degrees) around the Earth. The twelve signs of the zodiac represent the twelve constellations in the night sky that lie along the apparent path that the Sun takes. Astrologers know that each sign of the zodiac contains 30 degrees (360 divided by 12), so when a sign is broken into the three segments that we call decans, each segment comprises ten degrees—hence the name decan, which comes from the Latin for "ten."

Decans influence the effect of Sun signs. As you will soon see, those whose birthdays fall in the earliest decan will be most typical of their Sun sign and probably the most like the descriptions that you see in this book and others like it. Those whose birthdays fall in the middle and later decans will be slightly different. This is one of a number of reasons for the diversity among people born under the same Sun sign.

For those of you who don't yet have your astrological data, the following instructions will give you the information you need to find your Sun sign decan. The list below starts with the first date for each decan, so you must select the date that precedes your birthday. For instance, if your birthday is April 4, use the decan that begins on March 30, because it runs from March 30 through April 10. Make a note of your Sun sign decan, and also those of your friends and loved ones (and even your enemies), so that you can discover the effect of the decans as you read this article.

The list shows the gender and element for each Sun sign, and these attributes also apply to each decan within that sign. The qualities (cardinal, fixed, and mutable) change with each decan, and you will find each quality noted in brackets beside the decan. Make a note of the gender, element, and quality of your sign and decan so that you can check these out in the interpretation section that appears later in this article.

The Sun doesn't enter each sign and decan at exactly the same time or even on the same day each year. The list of dates that you will find below is for the average situation. Those of you who are on the cusp of two signs or decans should read both until such time as you can have a formal birth chart drawn up and interpreted. If you have a horoscope chart drawn up, it will be easy to work out which decan your Sun sign occupies. Each Sun sign contains thirty degrees, beginning at zero and running through twenty-nine. The first decan runs from zero to nine degrees, the second from ten to nineteen degrees, and the third from twenty to twenty-nine degrees. Thus, if your Sun is at fourteen degrees of a sign, it is in the second decan.

Note: This book deals mainly with Sun sign astrology, but remember that everything on a chart falls into a decan. This is particularly interesting when looking at the Moon sign, rising sign, or the Midheaven—although you will need an accurate chart that shows the degrees and minutes for every feature that you wish to examine. Even twins, though they share very similar charts, may have ascendants or Midheavens that fall into different decans.

Dates for the Sun Sign Decans

Aries decans: masculine, fire element

March 21	Aries (cardinal)
March 30	Leo (fixed)
April 10	Sagittarius (mutable)

Taurus decans: feminine, earth element

April 20	Taurus (fixed)
April 30	Virgo (mutable)
May 10	Capricorn (cardinal)

Gemini decans: masculine, air element

May 21	Gemini (mutable)
May 31	Libra (cardinal)
June 11	Aquarius (fixed)

Cancer decans: feminine, water element

June 21	Cancer (cardinal)
July 2	Scorpio (fixed)
July 12	Pisces (mutable)

Leo decans: masculine, fire element

July 23	Leo (fixed)
August 2	Sagittarius (mutable)
August 12	Aries (cardinal)

Virgo decans: feminine, earth element

August 23	Virgo (mutable)
September 2	Capricorn (cardinal)
September 12	Taurus (fixed)

Dates for the Sun Sign Decans

Libra decans: masculine, air element

September 23	Libra (cardinal)
October 3	Aquarius (fixed)
October 13	Gemini (mutable)

Scorpio decans: feminine, water element

October 23	Scorpio (fixed)
November 2	Pisces (mutable)
November 12	Cancer (cardinal)

Sagittarius decans: masculine, fire element

November 22	Sagittarius (mutable)
December 2	Aries (cardinal)
December 12	Leo (fixed)

Capricorn decans: feminine, earth element

December 22	Capricorn (cardinal)
January 1	Taurus (fixed)
January 11	Virgo (mutable)

Aquarius decans: masculine, air element

January 21	Aquarius (fixed)
January 31	Gemini (mutable)
February 9	Libra (cardinal)

Pisces decans: feminine, water element

February 19	Pisces (mutable)
March 1	Cancer (cardinal)
March 10	Scorpio (fixed)

The Genders

Masculine signs belong to those who are extroverted and fairly assertive. These types are more likely to say what they mean rather than to beat around the bush. They may be more capable than the feminine signs in worldly matters, but they can also be arrogant and selfish. People with feminine signs tend to be shy, introverted, and more passive than those with masculine signs. These people learn to be assertive in time, and some may overcompensate and become aggressive and unpleasant as a result. Feminine sign people are more receptive to the ideas of others, more caring by nature, and they can often put up with more difficulties than masculine signs can. If your Sun sign is masculine, each of your decans will also be masculine— and if your Sun sign is feminine, then each of your decans will be feminine. All fire and air signs are masculine, and all earth and water signs are feminine; thus the gender will be the same for all three decans within your sign.

The Elements

As we have already seen, each sign belongs to an element and all three decans in that sign share the same element. When a sign is broken into decans, the first decan is a repeat of the sign itself, while the second and third decans belong to the two following signs of the same element. For instance, Scorpio is a water sign; its first decan is Scorpio, the second decan is Pisces, and the third is Cancer.

Fire: Aries, Leo, Sagittarius

These people are quick, clever, humorous, enthusiastic, adventurous, and sometimes impulsive. They can be irritable when tired, hungry, or when others stand in their way or disagree with them. They can make money, but they also love spending it. Relationships are important but changes of partner are fairly common, although less so for Leos. They work hard in any career that sparks and maintains their interest and which allows them to progress upward.

Earth: Taurus, Virgo, Capricorn

These people are sensible, practical, and reliable. They are shrewd, careful with money, and often clever business people. They all need a secure base and emotional security. Taurus and Virgo are sociable, but Capricorns are more interested in their family than in friendships and socializing. All earth sign people are hard workers, if for no other reason than that they fear debt and poverty.

Air: Gemini, Libra, Aquarius

Logical, analytical, and talkative, these people like to be in the know. They are intelligent, up-to-date, and very sociable. They are more attuned to liaison work, arbitration, and legal matters than business, although they are quick to spot trends. Where relationships are concerned, they can be fickle unless with the right partner. These people make friends easily, but they tend to lose touch when they move on.

Water: Cancer, Scorpio, Pisces

These people take time to get anything off the ground, but they can be very successful in sales or working for the public due to their intuition. Water people respond slowly when called or when asked a question because they filter everything that comes their way through their auras or intuitive faculties. Their moods can swing upward into excitement or down into depression quite quickly, and they can suffer from self-pity, but they are also extremely understanding and caring toward others. They are loyal to their friends and families.

Qualities

This is where radical changes can be seen, because while the element and gender will be the same, the quality will be different for each decan. For example, Libra is a cardinal sign, and since the first decan repeats the sign, it remains cardinal. However, the second decan belongs to the fixed sign of Aquarius and the last to the mutable sign of Gemini. There are three qualities, so each sign contains one decan of each quality.

Cardinal: Aries, Cancer, Libra, Capricorn

Cardinal-sign types tend to be self-motivated and prepared to go after what they want or need, whether it's for financial or emotional security. Aries is self-centered, Cancer centers on the family, Libra centers on maintaining partnerships at home and in business, and Capricorn will concentrate on the needs of a business in addition to keeping the family happy. Cardinal people initiate ideas, and they are often surprisingly ambitious and capable of pulling the coals out of the fire in an emergency. They are able to start new projects and set things in motion, but they may not see things through to the end. Cardinal signs can motivate and encourage others to take action, but they need to ally themselves to people who can finish the jobs they start.

Fixed: Taurus, Leo, Scorpio, Aquarius

Fixed-sign people maintain the status quo. They try to finish what they start and they stick to jobs and relationships to the bitter end if at all possible. They can be obstinate and determined, and it may be hard for them to see other ways of doing things. They are reliable in business matters and caring toward those they love. These people may not initiate projects, but they can plod their way through to the end. They often attach themselves to more dynamic partners or to those with a more flexible outlook.

Mutable: Gemini, Virgo, Sagittarius, Pisces

These people need variety in their working lives—and sometimes in their private lives as well. They often have some special skill that they can take from place to place or sell to a variety of buyers. They enjoy meeting different people and getting away from home for a change of scene. Mutable people often do a part of a project, moving on to allow others to complete it. A typical example is that of a carpenter or electrician who specializes in his part of a large project, or a writer who contributes to a publication rather than writing an entire book. Mutable people often ally themselves with those who can initiate ideas and concentrate on the overview, and also with those who can see things through to the end. Many mutable people are interested in health, alternative and spiritual healing, and psychic subjects.

Putting It All Together

Now let us look at each Sun sign and its decans. Remember that the first decan repeats the Sun sign itself, and, unless there are other features on the chart that strongly influence it, people born under the first decan should be the most typical of their Sun signs.

Aries

Aries Decan

Pure Aries. Being self-motivated, your natural instinct is to take charge of a situation and, being courageous and pioneering, you will try your hand at anything that is new. Active pursuits such as sport, dancing, or gymnastics help to sop up some of your excess energy. Although clever and capable, you may be too opinionated and you may sometimes lack common sense. Your greatest joy is shopping (especially for clothes) but you happily take on extra jobs to pay for your self-indulgence.

Leo Decan

You are more likely to maintain the status quo and to finish what you start than other Aries signs. Change and transformation are difficult for you, so you may stay in a relationship or a job longer than you should. Your standards are high, and you are generous and affectionate, but you may be snobbish and easily irritated. You need a high standard of living and you are happiest when in a relationship.

Sagittarius Decan

You accept change far more easily than either of the other two Aries types, and the need for freedom may be a powerful issue for you. You may become interested in spiritual matters, philosophy, or education, and you might choose to work in these fields. You will travel more than the other Aries signs, and you take less luggage when you do so. You enjoy meeting new people.

Taurus

Taurus Decan

Pure Taurus. You are creative, artistic, and musical, and you love to work with your hands. Sensible, cautious, and shrewd, you rarely allow yourself to get into a financial mess and you prefer a comfortable lifestyle. You are a true family person and are unlikely to experiment with relationships. Home, family, friends, and even your pets are important to you. Your chief fault is obstinacy.

Virgo Decan

Your mind is quicker, more flexible, and more active than the other two Taurus types, and you will choose work in a field that requires intelligence, competence, and an analytical mind. You are less obstinate and more able to go with the flow. You may earn less than the other two types because you tend to choose jobs that fulfill intellectual needs rather than financial ones.

Capricorn Decan

Family life is hugely important to you, and if there are older parents who need help you can be relied upon to give it to them. Shrewd and money-minded, you can become penny-pinching. But if this is not the case your business instincts will take you further than the other two Taurus types. Relationships may be difficult due to your tendency toward fussiness.

Gemini

Gemini Decan

Pure Gemini. You need a job and a lifestyle that offers variety, and you may actually prefer two part-time jobs that are quite different from each other so that you can switch gears when boredom strikes. Your overdeveloped sense of responsibility makes you the worrier of the zodiac. Despite your reputation for flirtatiousness, family life is extremely important—but you cannot cope with sick people or lame ducks. You love to spend money on clothes.

Libra Decan

You are more easy-going, self-indulgent, and less apt to overwork yourself than the pure Gemini type, but you have a knack for finding jobs that will support your lifestyle. You can live alone if necessary, but you prefer to be in a relationship as your sex drive is rather high. Jobs that involve agency work, arbitration, and communication appeal to you, but so does anything artistic or beautiful.

Aquarius Decan

More intellectual than the other two types, you may choose a lifestyle that offers you an opportunity to use your academic ability. Writing, teaching, and providing the public with information are career possibilities. You need a partner who is practical and capable in order to offset your occasional lapses in common sense. Your interest in motives and behavior can take you into the fields of psychology and astrology.

Cancer

Cancer Decan

Pure Cancer. Your family is the most important factor in your life, and you are prepared to make sacrifices on their behalf. It is essential that you have a home that you can call your own, but you also need to escape from the home and go on short trips to see new faces and places. There are times when you are extremely kind-hearted, sympathetic, and a good listener. However, you can suddenly switch moods, becoming angry, resentful, and cantankerous.

Scorpio Decan

It is true that you see the faults of others very clearly, but you are not immune from faults either. Try switching your critical faculties off and instead turn on your wonderful intuition and your uncanny ability to understand and sympathize with others. If necessary, you can make an excellent living in some form of house refurbishment or real estate.

Pisces Decan

This is the real earth mother, but you need to guard against sacrificing too much of your time and energy for family members or lame ducks. Intuitive to the point of being psychic, you see through people in an instant and you can often feel the future before it happens. Artistic, creative, and talented in many ways, your lack of confidence can hold you back.

Leo

Leo Decan

Pure Leo. Proud and hard working, your standards are probably too high. You can't tolerate laziness or failure in yourself or in others, which means that you put more pressure on yourself than is healthy. A true family person, and especially attached to your children, you will even put up with a bad marriage rather than allow someone else to muscle in on your kids. You need a high income to support the requirements of your lifestyle.

Sagittarius Decan

You are more interested in travel and exploration than the other two Leo types, and you are more prepared to take chances on life as well. Your belief system is important to you and you may explore a variety of ideas until you find one that is meaningful. In practical matters you can make or mend anything, while in relationships you are less constant than other Leos.

Aries Decan

You enjoy travel and adventure, and you need plenty of money to support the comfortable lifestyle you enjoy. However, you are also a hard worker, so you succeed in providing this for yourself. Your family (especially your children) are vitally important to you. You can be vain or snobbish at times, but your kindness and generosity are wonderful, as is your sense of humor.

Virgo

Virgo Decan

Pure Virgo. You are practical, capable, and efficient, so work comes easily to you. However, you may prefer a less high-pressure job than that of running an organization because you quickly become nervous and stressed out. Relationships may be less important to you than friendships, partly because you find family life restricting or disappointing. You can succeed in the fields of health, healing, research, and writing.

Capricorn Decan

This decan endows you with far more ambition and business ability than the other two Virgo types, so you should go far. The problem is that you might become so wrapped up in work that you neglect family life or love relationships. You can be fussy and a worrier, but your intelligence and sense of humor saves you from being too cold, dour, or difficult to know.

Taurus Decan

You are far more comfort-loving than either of the other two Virgo types, and you have the instincts of a real family person. This means that you may be less successful in business matters but far happier in personal life. The arts, craft work, and dressmaking might appeal to you, and you could have real musical talent. Your communication skills can take you far, as long as you find a creative outlet.

Libra

Libra Decan

Pure Libra. What a mixture you are! Clever and capable, an intelligent air sign and also an artist—especially in cooking and homemaking. Yet you may be too independent for a permanent relationship and family life. Sociable and friendly, you also enjoy your own company. Your symbol, the scales, allows you to see both sides of an argument and often to argue with everyone—even sometimes yourself. Laziness may be your downfall.

Aquarius Decan

Your intellect is deeper than the other two Libra types, but you may spend so much time thinking that you find it hard to get anything practical done. Your flair and originality can take you far in the world of design, and if politics grabs you, you can become extremely successful—as long as you can maintain a grip on reality. You fare better in relationships than the other two types.

Gemini Decan

You can put your nose to the grindstone, and this helps you to achieve more than the other two Libra types, especially in business. This is even more true if you have a practical and less-idealistic partner alongside you. Versatile and capable, you can be a high earner, which is just as well because you love to spend money. You need a secure relationship that anchors you to reality and prevents paranoia from creeping in.

Scorpio

Scorpio Decan

Pure Scorpio. You don't like being kept in the dark, so psychology and research are your forte. Careers with importance attract you, and you might find yourself working in a hospital, law enforcement, the armed forces, in engineering, or as a career advisor. You hate wasting money or watching others waste their talents, so motivating others is important to you.

Pisces Decan

Surprisingly ambitious and somewhat bossy, you can be a wonderful leader or helpmeet as long as you keep your critical tongue inside your head. Your desire to see what's beyond the end of your nose and to help humanity can take you into the fields of medicine, research, or even law enforcement. You are reliable, capable, and very sexy.

Cancer Decan

You are a real family person and in many ways easier to get along with than the other two Scorpio types, but your moodiness is a real problem, as are your sudden rages or fits of resentment or depression. Hard working and ambitious for your partner and your children, you can go far and take them onward and upward with you. You have a magic touch when it comes to money and business.

Sagittarius

Sagittarius Decan

Pure Sagittarius. You are amazingly capable and, given the tools and a how-to book, you could probably build a house single-handed. However, your restless nature and quick descent into boredom make it hard for you to stick to anything. If you can find a lifestyle that offers you freedom and the chance of meeting new people, you can make a success of yourself. Even when hard times come along your lucky streak ensures that you survive.

Aries Decan

You have more get-up-and-go than the other two Sagittarius types and also more personal ambition. Studying and teaching is your forte, but you also have a strong drive to discover a belief system or a form of spirituality that makes sense to you. You travel far and wide in order to discover what the world has to offer. Broadminded and humorous, you are great company for a while and then move on, leaving friends and relatives behind.

Leo Decan

Less restless than the other two Sagittarius types, you are more inclined to stick to a job and cope with family life. Humorous, generous, and great fun, you can be the life and soul of the party as long as you are in the right mood. Travel and exploration appeal to you, but you prefer to do this in comfort. You could be drawn to youth work, teaching, broadcasting, and show business.

Capricorn

Capricorn Decan

Pure Capricorn. Whether shy or outgoing, it takes you a long time to trust others and open up to them. Indeed, your suspicious nature may make you distrust others too much to rely on them. The most important areas of your life are your career and your parents. If you find the right partner who can give you the emotional security you require, you can become relaxed and happy. Ambition and hard work inevitably take you to the top.

Taurus Decan

More creative and artistic than the other two decans, you may aspire to a career in the arts or show business. You certainly manage to look good, and you remain young-looking long after everyone else has gone to seed. Family life is easier for you than it is for the other types and you enjoy such home-based projects as cooking and gardening. However, your ambition and attraction to careers in finance exert a strong pull.

Virgo Decan

More intellectual than the other two Capricorn types and quicker to grasp ideas and possibilities, you may opt for a career in business or sales. Your outlook is slightly unconventional, and you may choose an independent lifestyle that allows you the freedom to concentrate on your career. Something in your childhood or background makes you afraid of commitment and worried about being short of money, which can make you unnecessarily tight-fisted.

Aquarius

Aquarius Decan

Pure Aquarius. Your head is filled with wonderfully original ideas and it may be way up in the clouds. Unfortunately, your feet may also be up in the clouds as well, because it is hard for you to deal with practicalities or harsh reality. A humanitarian idealist, you spend your life trying to set the world to rights and, who knows, you may even succeed! If you find the right kind of oddball partner, you can be happy in a settled relationship.

Gemini Decan

You are more businesslike and practical than the other two Aquarius types, but even so your head is filled with original and creative ideas. Your career choice leads you to communicate ideas to others—either face-to-face through teaching or by writing or designing computer software. A secure relationship helps to settle and relax your tense nervous system. You are surprisingly sexy.

Libra Decan

Far more laid-back and less tense and moody than the other two Aquarius types, you are easier in many ways to get along with. However, you may be argumentative and picky, which can make you a bit of a pain in personal relationships. You have an artistic streak and you are also more creative than the other two types, but you may be hopeless with money, and be a big spender even when you don't have it to spend!

Pisces

Pisces Decan

Pure Pisces. You have a reputation for being dreamy and otherworldly, but the two fishes in your symbol suggest that this is not all there is to you. Creative, musical, and artistic, you can find fulfillment by working in these fields; while you are unlikely to become rich, you will always ensure that you and your family have the necessities in life. Being sensitive, intuitive, and probably psychic, the world of spirit, prediction, and mystery calls you.

Cancer Decan

You are a great homemaker and family person, and your children mean a great deal to you despite the fact that love relationships and jobs may come and go. If you can find work in a caring profession such as medicine or teaching you will be happy. You may be too prepared to sacrifice your own needs for those of others. You may be prone to a kind of nervous moodiness, disorganization, and a touch of miserliness.

Scorpio Decan

It is almost inevitable that you will wish to investigate the spirit world, and you could become an excellent medium. You may find work in a hospital or pursue a field that deals with the boundaries between life and death. Emotional security is essential to your well being, but it may be hard for you to find. Guard against being too critical and allowing resentment to make you hurtful or bossy.

For Further Reading

Burk, Kevin. *Astrology: Understanding the Birth Chart.* St. Paul: Llewellyn, 2001.

Fenton, Sasha. *The Hidden Zodiac.* New York: Sterling Publishing, Inc., 2002.

Humanity and Conflict
World Predictions for 2003

by Leeda Alleyn Pacotti

During the last fourteen years, astrologers have observed an orbital waltz between two gas giants of the solar system, Uranus and Neptune. This year, the Titan and the oceanic god deliver once again, creating a potent astrological portent at the cusp of the ages of Pisces and Aquarius.

In late 1988 Uranus joined Neptune in Capricorn, a sign with which Uranus has some affinity because of its saturnine trait of establishment. For Neptune, Capricorn was nearly a strangulation of its watery emotional expression. By 1998 both planets resided in Aquarius, where that sign's ruler Uranus frolicked while Neptune languished. In fact, for the last seven years Uranus has dominated the entire astrological landscape.

In March this year Uranus moves into Pisces, where it remains through 2011, while Neptune stays in Aquarius, causing the two planets to reside in each other's signs—a cordial astrological phenomenon known as "mutual reception." With Neptune in Aquarius and Uranus in Pisces neither planet has an advantage over the other. Instead, a sympathetic relationship of blended identity permits each planet to express itself through the other's sign—so much so that both planets act as if they were one and the same. Rather than being mutually weakened, Uranus and Neptune will both be strongly expressive, but the expression will not be more attributable to one than the other. They will act as supportive neighbors.

The Dynamics of the Duo

For most of the next nine years Uranus and Neptune will resolve Piscean Age issues—which have been cloaked in Aquarian Age circumstances and with which we have become familiar during the last half of the twentieth century. The majority of these concerns gained prominence during the 1990s while Uranus held the astrological upper hand and created challenges for the resolution of the situation by promoting overintellectualization. Not to be completely outdone or undone, Neptune ballooned the universality of these issues by introducing an uneasy, gnawing sense of overload and dehumanization.

As an astrological refresher, Neptune signifies people who are outcast or disadvantaged—particularly prisoners or others in forced confinement, the homeless, the indigent, widows, and orphans. Extending itself into the rulership of Pisces, Neptune colors this sign to include prisons, hospitals, pharmaceuticals, welfare programs and institutions, and songs of lamentation.

As an example, the horoscope of the U.S. Constitution, which officially organizes the nation, places the Sun in Pisces. This casts a hopeful beacon to the downtrodden around the world. It is no small significance that the bronze plaque formerly inside the base of the Statue of Liberty bears the compassionate inscription: "Give me your tired, your poor, / Your huddled masses yearning to breathe free, / The wretched refuse of your teeming shore; / Send these, the homeless, tempest-tossed to me,..." (*The New Colossus*, by Emma Lazarus, 1883).

Through witnessing the desperate plights of fellow humans we recognize travail, usually expressed distantly as "there but for fortune go I." By internalizing our feelings we gain compassion and sympathy—two of Neptune's finer gifts. Eventually, we confront the knowledge that the vagaries of life can touch anyone, as understanding reaches beyond you, me, and her to encompass all humanity. We have earned universal consciousness, which is the ultimate Neptunian, Piscean reward.

Some of us are awed by and withdraw from universal consciousness, cowed into a sense of impossible, unimaginable responsibility toward humanity. For these people, Neptune and Pisces show different faces, manifesting as escapism, isolation, and withdrawal: three facets of self-imposed confinement from society. Here the god of the deeps reigns over drugs, liquor, and tobacco—substances that blunt the mind from emotional onslaught.

Uranus, the ruler of Aquarius, bears a sharp contrast to Neptune by distancing itself from humanity for a broad perspective. Generally, it doesn't signify specific types of people, except for friends, legislators, and allies. Despite its preference for estrangement and aloofness Uranus provides closely cherished, unquestionably loyal benefactors through these relationships, who are so few they can be counted on one hand. Uranus creates a group apart, its members sure of themselves and sharing a like mind, which is why it often includes aristocratic or superior attitudes. Clearly, the sign of Aquarius, which expresses brotherhood, draws from this idea of groups formed from mental attunement, rather than blood relationship.

Because the mind and ideas are so important to Uranus, it celebrates the different viewpoint or approach, which we observe as reform and invention. Uranus is the planetary influence of ingenuity, which must not be confused with creativity. Ingenuity takes existing objects or methods and remolds them into something more usable ("Necessity is the mother of invention"), giving us varieties of gadgets and legislation meant to resolve life's confusions. On the other hand, creativity draws from an imaginative reservoir of perceptions and ideas to introduce wholly new or unheard-of answers to problems that often resist being broken apart and manipulated toward resolution. Consequently, Uranus frequently gives us fads—which seem novel but are actually ingenious derivations or combinations of less-glamorous appliances, styles, or thinking. Friendly amalgamation best describes Uranian ingenuity.

However, Uranus and Aquarius, it must be remembered, definitely prefer distance. Under their rulership are all types of "tele-" (far away or distant) sciences, such as telecommunications, telescopes, and television. These pursuits commonly permit the user to have sensory input without the cumbersome annoyance of immediacy or proximity. Uranus and Aquarius will never be accused of being overly intimate or personally hands-on.

While none of us was alive to witness the movement of Neptune through Aquarius in the middle of the nineteenth century, a number of people are still living who were young adults or children during the passage of Uranus through Pisces in the 1920s. At that time, a prohibition against alcohol and drinking establishments was instituted; the Jazz Age evolved into the Blues; and gangster economics with a gun to the head generated protection scams, racketeering, and smuggling. Although an exact repeat of history is unlikely, the next nine years could easily bring new prohibitions on tobacco and gasoline; more harmonious and sympathetic music combinations, with lyrics specifically intended to comfort personal economic losses; and the overall health of the nation held up by the wealth of drug companies.

Enamored with Our Own Ingenuity

Keeping in mind the portraits of Uranus and Neptune and applying them to social issues, the likely developments of the next nine years find their foundation in the programs and ideas prevalent during the 1990s. For instance, during the sojourn of Uranus and Neptune through Capricorn in the late 80s and early 90s legislators fancied the idea that no one needed any more than two years in a lifetime to collect any type of welfare benefits. These attitudes targeted what were considered welfare "generations," particularly young unwed mothers, who obviously wouldn't be on welfare if they were working. Unfortunately, because of higher costs of living the idea of limited welfare did not account for many seniors whose social security and limited pensions barely covered housing, let alone provided them food. They, too, became dependent on food stamps and food surpluses. After 2003, Congress and state legislators, now removed by ten years from this limited welfare concept, will encounter the specter of welfare within their own family ranks and realize that its solution must be a communal effort of society to take care of all its members. Administrative measurements using statistics and expenditure histories will evaporate when people find their elderly mothers can't buy food.

While Uranus was in Aquarius and Neptune in Capricorn, prisons were privatized, resulting in lucrative and exclusive contracts with state and local governments. During the next nine years the idea of prison as the appropriate solution for poor or different social development simply fails. Too many people are incarcerated, while governmental programs for readjustment are too narrow. Expect a greater tolerance for community programs and halfway houses, which keep young and first-time lawbreakers productive and provide for social mentoring.

Long fretted over, the burgeoning costs of social security overtook most legislative discussions in 1998. By 2000, an employment law was enacted permitting seniors to work without loss of benefits. While this approach does solve the problem of a wider income base for social security revenue, expect a sense of disenfranchisement among younger workers during the next nine years as they crash into a "gray ceiling," preventing upward career mobility. As well, salary and wage increases will be paced further apart, which creates a static revenue collection, while the population ages and more individuals begin to receive their benefits.

In 1998 and 1999 Uranus launched a couple of salvos in the direction of Neptune. First, the tobacco industry buckled under public outcry, legislative scrutiny, and class-action lawsuits from various states. Always thrilled with the changes it makes, while forgetting to look too far into the future, Uranus failed to account for the many incremental federal, state, and local taxes that are tagged on to the sale of tobacco and earmarked as special revenues. Many of these apply directly to parks and recreation. In 2001 the National Park Service introduced new entrance fees. While smoking, chewing, and lung or mouth cancers are not to be condoned, the future of our parks requires replenishment of the lost tax base through some other frequently purchased item or commodity. Given the elemental natures of Uranus and Neptune, the most likely tax attachments may be on electricity, natural gas, fuel oils, or water.

Another wide-ranging tax base comes from the sale of gasoline, which began to see huge increases in 1999. Independence from fossil fuels has been thirty years in the making, from the first energy crisis in 1972. Rising fuel costs for private vehicles have precipitated the introduction of electric-gas hybrid passenger cars and the design of silent electric mass transit. These solutions smack of Uranian ingenuity, but again the incremental add-on taxes, which often fund social or welfare programs, are ignored. At some point during the next nine years outrageous prices for electric batteries and portable electric packs will force research into cheaper, more accessible electrical devices, relying on the conductivity in salinated water.

As the centuries turned, Uranian influence gained force, swooping down on a variety of social and health issues directly related to Neptune. The flurry of ideas for solving the nation's ills emanated from a society drawing ever more into disparate groups, seeming to eliminate those who were not participants.

First came the rise of pharmaceutical companies as multinational businesses with escalating revenues. Gone was the humanitarian thrust of a life saved, as drug companies scrambled to patent the next generation of symptom-specific compounds. In the melee, several problems surfaced. Corporations paid private physicians handsomely for "observations," rather than test conclusions. Research on rare illnesses ground to a halt. Suspicions about price-fixing soared when costs for prescriptions doubled, tripled, or quadrupled from one month to the next, forcing many patients to abandon their prescriptions. Profit, rather than health, has become the question, especially with the governmentally sanctioned use of about sixty groups of stem cells, franchised for limited private research. By 2011 stem cell research is likely to be a thing of the past, once the narrow results from a minutely limited genetic pool fail to indicate benefits for the population at large. As for pharmaceutical revenues, progressively deteriorating health in six living generations of the populace, caused by accumulations of chemical concentrations in food, will fuel the demand for antidotal medicines rather than an overhaul of the food industry—for at least the next twenty-two years or until after Neptune passes out of its own sign, Pisces.

The same problem of revenues over health concerns became apparent in 2001 when legislators in some states discussed passing costs of indigent hospital care along to local populations in the form of taxes. A little earlier in the year decreases in Medicare coverage were discussed. Indigent health care has its roots in the New Deal of the 1930s, when Neptune was in Virgo; Medicare springs from the Great Society of the 1960s, when Uranus moved through the same sign. Through the mutual reception of these two planets, particularly while Uranus is in Pisces, which is Virgo's opposite, more than curing physical ills will be on the minds of people and their legislative representatives. Health isn't just a physical condition or ability to be productive; it is an encompassing sense of well-being, pervading the body and mind. Depression often accompanies physical illness. Expect this emotionally cancerous illness to become epidemic, affecting family members who must assume the responsibility of home health care and gradually lose enthusiasm for careers and jobs as they buckle under the strain of being home psychologists, caregivers, and breadwinners. As much as tax increases are vilified, expect a hefty new base, most likely levied on the telecommunications industry, to fund far-reaching governmental health programs tailored to supplement individual households.

Finally, destitution, another face of Neptune and Pisces, is a publicly known problem, unaddressed since the 1930s. At one time, those who had no homes were thought to be only shiftless men, called hoboes. For twenty years now whole families have lived in tents, cars, and shelters. They are a reminder of how fragile our economic structures can be. When Neptune was in Virgo through the 1930s music echoed the blues lament for lost titan economics, "Once I had a railroad, made it run . . . Brother, can you spare a dime?" At the turn of the new century, booming Internet companies fell hard, reducing the marketability of newer and better software. Software giants, too, sank or withdrew their resources, leaving their entourages of well-paid developers adrift. As a new tide of young families find themselves displaced, expect a rising sense of community to come to the rescue. Communes, or shared communities with common ownership and activities, play a large role in shaping a new social order in which the family is held inviolable, while the community surrounding it sees that common needs are adequately met. This socially constructed community, in which all age groups participate, will be the new planning model, rather than walled, segregated developments based on economic income.

The Nations in Focus

As this article is written, the United States has sustained its first attack with casualties within its national boundaries. The attack on Pearl Harbor, not to be dismissed, occurred when the Hawaiian Islands were still a strategic territory. In a departure from the usual list of nations, this focus discusses the global effects of the event horoscope for the terrorism attacks, beginning in New York City on September 11, 2001; the national condition of the United States; the true nature of its enemy; its allies; and two observing nations.

Attack on the United States

Within three weeks after the attack, much that was learned from the event horoscope had been confirmed by President Bush. However, the attacks occurred during a void-of-course Moon, which creates a situation without an outcome. At the same time, Mars represented the United States, and was held besieged between internal confusion over lack of electronic surveillance and the threat of hasty, decimating nuclear retaliation. The United States was prevented from reacting, while its population was horrifically exposed. Although the event horoscope seems to "come to naught," it actually sets the stage for an ideologically based conflict, waged covertly, that will continue throughout the next forty-five years. On the positive side, the United States military is forced to respond slowly and methodically. Several placements in this horoscope show that the war of minds has karmic associations. The United States will learn that the exercise of freedom and liberty, short of permitting the destruction of fellow man, is the birthright of every human and not just those endowed with its citizenship. The anger, hatred, and intolerance toward minorities and differing religious and social groups within its own population have become personified by an enemy that eludes conquest.

United States

Initially considered weak, President Bush carries two extreme burdens as he leads the nation. On one hand, he bears an incredible guilt that the attacks on New York and the Pentagon were a karmic retribution for his father's war on Iraq. From an astrological perspective, this is correct. For several years the United States has been affected by an important progressive aspect of stress, which will not resolve except through a deep incision into the nation's psyche. Besides the Iraqi war, the infighting throughout Congress for nearly eight years, the impeachment proceedings against President Clinton, and the confused 2000 presidential election all indicated serious internal strife. While nations are not usually thought of as people, the United States has been dealing with extreme emotional conflict. The population itself, confused over what the nation symbolizes, retreated into technological and commercial pursuits that have estranged it from the rest of the world. This divisiveness between domestic and national images sets the stage for an open attack. As for President Bush, his other burden is severely diminished health, precipitated by the shock of the attack on his neurological system. The gradual weakening and eventual illness may not be publicly, or even privately, known.

Whether the President knows of his illness or senses it intuitively, he will not seek reelection. By the winter of 2003 the population has become more vocal in its demands to go to war. However, the economy is restricted and businesses are again floundering. The president prefers not to repeat the cycle of war as a rescue for economic woes. Military readiness abroad is high on the agenda, but the time to act openly has not come. The nation is focused on cementing its alliances for the long haul. With the spring, the nation takes a last look at the good old days: An economic surge coincides with a return to enjoyment of pastimes. It is a season of remembering, although short-lived, as financial relations with other countries become strained. The burden of covert war is beginning to take its toll. By 2005 an open war is declared, with the United States launching attacks overseas. By this time the population is psychologically ready and the military is fully prepared for domestic protection. Although the war activity is attributed to the new president, these plans were formulated three years earlier. From a strategic standpoint, one of the greatest advantages of the United States is its diverse population: Recruits from throughout the country can easily infiltrate any other ethnically concentrated population.

The Enemy

The horoscope of the terrorist attack on New York provides many clues about the enemy of the United States. Primarily, the enemy is a group of men from prominent families who have no possibility of attaining rulership through birthright. Essentially, they are men without a country. Therein lies the problem of going to war. Nations declare war on other nations. For a powerful nation to declare war on a person is a hideous concept. Further, the United States will not vanquish unnecessarily a less-influential nation that might temporarily aid the enemy; it is not the harbinger of genocide. Although the men of the terrorist regime are from wealthy families, this wealth does not completely sustain the group's activities. What has not been divulged is that Osama bin Laden has set the stage for a continuing revenue by enticing underdeveloped countries that want global influence with the sale of nuclear weapons and plutonium. His prices are extravagant, but the payments are plentiful. As long as any nation wants this technology, the terrorist groups will have ready revenues.

The Allies

The two strongest allies of the United States are the European nations of Great Britain and Germany. Among these three powers an incredible storehouse of economic, intellectual, military, and technological capability is brought to the stage of war.

Great Britain

Despite the separation through revolution in their mutual history, Great Britain and the United States are economically and militarily interdependent. Britain realizes that its position within the European Community is jeopardized if the United States is lost, while other European nations continue to jockey for control of the continent. For the United States, Britain represents the threshold and introduction to the European Community, which is its only technological equal worldwide. Similar to the United States, Great Britain, too, is headed for an internal showdown, which had its beginnings with the royal scandals of the 1990s. While those stories increased tabloid revenues, the real stress on Britain is the shifting identity of its citizenry away from royal leadership. Gradually, the population has consciously realized that it gives the monarch power. This year, the focus is on local governments. The economy of the nation is strong. Like the United States, the British have been overwhelmed with the prospect of war and need some better days. People are upbeat, although casting a wary eye to the future, knowing good times can't go on forever. Great Britain is strong militarily, and its population is in agreement for any active clash.

Germany

Since the reunification of the nation Germany has finally hit its stride domestically. Its population is comfortable; communications are good; food is plentiful. The country has capably harnessed nuclear power, adding to the pervasive good feelings of security and advancement. The possibility of governmental overexpenditures looms on the horizon, but much of this is due to sponsorship of research in health and medicine. In the past Germany has also been the recipient of terrorist attack, but has moved forward in spite of the attempt to undermine its population. It stands as a model for the United States to follow. During the first half of the year Germany focuses on its treaties and alliances, tightening up relationships and dismissing any countries that will not commit. As the summer begins, this nation, too, may be experiencing some problems with electrical shortages or self-imposed rationing of power consumption. In the second half of the year Germany deals with communication problems, which are electronic in origin. The entire population wants full electronic access, but the infrastructure is not available to carry the demand. Although it has not previously discussed its military involvement in any global conflict, Germany has worked extensively within the alliance to develop scatter-disrupt laser weaponry.

The Observing Nations

Initially committed to the United States as allies, the two nations of China and Russia have much to gain strategically and geographically in the event of a prolonged, undeclared conflict.

China

This most populous nation, although outwardly backing efforts of the United States against terrorist attacks, is hiding its real intentions. China, the primary weapon provider and strategic advisor to what was then North Vietnam, still maintains a secret agenda. The collapse of Afghanistan will make that territory ripe for the pickings. For most of the twentieth century China has sought annexation of the entire Asian land mass, including India. If it acquired Afghanistan it would hold the Indian subcontinent in a pincer grasp. Despite the amount of poverty and subsequent poor health throughout the two nations, China is the stronger. China's bargaining chip on the global scene is its proliferation of nuclear power, which forces technologically advanced nations to tip their hats politely to keep it at bay. However, the nation's population is growing ill; there are simply too many to feed. China will not use nuclear weaponry to take India; it needs additional land for its population and extended agriculture. In the latter half of this year famine reaches crisis proportions within the nation, with reports of new strains of auto-immune disease that the rest of the world wants confined at China's borders. The grip of death is so severe that the nation's domestic economy begins to falter. As long as the United States is willing to fight a war and take the losses, China will be right by its side.

Russia

Reborn in a social and economic climate of insufficiency, the Russian Federation has a cold axe to grind. While still the Soviet Union, this Eurasian giant was weakened by its prolonged armed conflict in Afghanistan. The economic losses through military expenditures directly led to the break-up of the united republics—a demotion in global influence over which Russia still smarts. Had the former Soviet Union succeeding in taking Afghanistan it would also have moved to absorb fragile Pakistan. The annexation of these two countries, as republics, would have given the Soviet Union a direct port or pipeline to the Arabian Sea, simplifying delivery of accessible crude or refined oil. Although Russia's military viewpoint aligns with the U.S. reaction to the domestic attack in New York, it has lost its fire. Currently, Russia is suffering unimaginable losses. The nation's dream to return to global grandeur has devolved into a list of hardships. Sugar staples are gone; the military is antiquated; communications systems are faulty beyond local areas. The very soul of the nation is colder than its tundra. A land giant with incredible reserves in natural resources, Russia is held at gunpoint by a lack of intermediate technology. Throughout this year Russia suffers in its financial relations with other countries. As much as the nation says it is self-supporting, it cannot repay its debts. In fact, the only military resource Russia can give to any action, domestic or foreign, are the lives of its soldiers. The Russian people will not permit a hopeless future as a result of the death of another generation. Now in its tenth national year, the Russian Federation is ready to erupt in nationwide civil war. This hungry wolf of the north deserves a careful watch.

For Further Reading

Hamaker-Zondag, Karen. *Handbook of Horary Astrology*. Boston: Weiser, 1993.

Louis, Anthony. *Horary Astrology Plain and Simple: Fast and Accurate Answers to Real World Questions*. St. Paul: Llewellyn, 1998.

Rushman, Carol. *The Art of Predictive Astrology: Forecasting Your Life Events*. St. Paul: Llewellyn, 2002.

Mundane Natalogy

Germany
May 23, 1949, 00:00:00 am EET, Berlin

Great Britain
December 25, 1066, 12:00:40 pm GMT, London

People's Republic of China
September 20, 1954, 00:00:00 am CCT, Beijing

Russian Federation
December 24, 1993, 00:00:00 am BGT, Moscow

United States of America
March 4, 1789, 12:13:12 am LMT, New York City

Terrorism Attack on the United States
September 11, 2001, 8:48:00 am EDT, New York City

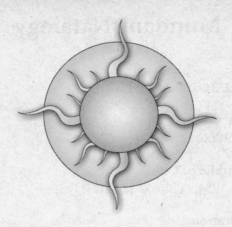

Astrology and Magic
Spells for the Seasons

by Maria K. Simms

Editor's note: One of the main uses for astrology is the timing of events. Astrology can help choose the best time to plant herbs, see a doctor, buy a house, or even get married. In Wiccan and Pagan communities, astrological timing is often taken into consideration when casting spells. We have included the article that follows as an example of this kind of timing.

Whatever the future may bring, this I believe: The power to prevail, to initiate action or effectively respond to the actions of others, is most highly influenced not by the planets but by our own choices. Astrological factors can give us clues to future trends, but these trends must be placed within context of the environment. How planetary themes manifest in each life varies greatly depending on individual attitude.

The choice of an appropriate time to initiate an action while the planets support your intent is the point at which astrology most becomes magic. There are essentially two ways this can work. You can scan for when planetary themes fit your purpose (either magical or mundane). Or, you can look at the astrology of a particular time and design a spell, or plan an action, that takes advantage of the astrological factors in play. Either way, you are choosing to be "in the flow," moving with the current of natural energy rather than fighting against it.

No matter what the astrological factors may indicate at any given time, you have a choice! Don't wait to see what will happen, or fear upcoming transits of the planets. Take charge by choosing the ways to manifest those transits in a manner most supportive of your goals and intentions. Of course there will be times when events of regional or worldwide import influence your life in ways you cannot control—no matter how focused you may be. You will always have control over how you respond to crises and challenges. Meditation and magic, along with the understanding that astrology brings, will assist you in your response.

For ideas about the state of the world in general, astrologers often turn to charts set for the entrance (ingress) of the Sun into each of the cardinal signs. Each of the seasonal spells to follow is created from astrological phenomena at or near each equinox and solstice of 2003. The spells may be worked as solitary ritual or incorporated into group ritual.

Winter Spell for the Solstice

December 22—Astrological Indicators

The Sun at 0° Capricorn applies to a square with Mars at 3° Aries. Mercury in Capricorn, which retrograded five days ago, is now exactly opposite Saturn in Cancer. The symbolism of this planetary combination at the beginning of winter is one of serious, deep thinking. In challenging aspect, it can mean you may find yourself dwelling on the gloomy side of things and feeling alone. Mercury retrograde is often looked upon as a time when all things having to do with communication are likely to go wrong, but you may also choose to seek the advantages of this retrograde period—this is a very good time to review, reflect, and remember. These energies will continue until January 6, when Mercury turns direct.

Ideal Timing

The Capricorn Ingress at 2:05 am EST, December 22, is in the nocturnal hours of a Sunday. Earlier that day or evening is when you may best work this ritual, which I encourage you to do with a small group or with friends and family. People who are night owls may begin late in the evening closer to the actual ingress. This may help encourage quiet personal reflection, but beware that a potential tendency of the Mercury-Saturn opposition can be negative thinking. For this reason, I recommend sharing this ritual with others. Choose a Mercury hour, or, if that is a bit too late in the evening, the Venus hour just prior would also be good. Check with a planetary hour table for accuracy of times for your location.

Preparation

Plan a project you can do with a group. (Or, if you will be alone, work with magical intent to make something you can later share with others.) Choose a project that will keep hands busy, but not one so complex that it interferes with conversation—the sharing of personal reflections and memories. (If you are working alone, keep a journal handy to jot down thoughts that come to you.)

Possible projects: Baking holiday cookies or making other holiday treats might work well for a small group. A roomful of people could make simple toys, fix up old ones, or prepare small packets of treats to donate to a charity. Compiling shared activity photographs into album pages would go well with the talk, especially for a family group, and everyone can have copies of the resulting pages to keep (that is, once you take them to a copy shop later for color copies). Collect fresh pine, other evergreens, fresh herbs, and perhaps dried fruits to make potpourri: This activity is very conducive to conversation. Have cheesecloth or net bags ready to tie with ribbons so everyone can take some potpourri home.

Whatever project you choose, you must organize it in advance. Coordinate everyone to bring something to contribute to the project, and plan a workspace and supplies that will allow the activity to proceed smoothly. If you are working with family and friends, including those of other faiths, this might be presented as a simple holiday gathering, and a simple statement of intent preceding this working should set a tone that is comfortable for all.

The working itself is essentially the same either way, so use statements of intent and of closure appropriate for a mixed-faith group. Those of you using it within a Sabbat celebration or working alone should be easily able to modify my words below with deity names or magical terms appropriate to your tradition. With a group, you need some way to make sure everyone is heard, and a traditional talking stick may not work well while hands are busy. A fun alternative could be to pass a hat for the speaker to wear. You could make a paper hat or crown with a star perhaps, or buy one of the many novelty headbands or Santa hats that are available this time of year.

Beginning Instructions

Before beginning, the group leader should explain the intent, the supplies, and the activity. As an example of intent, you might say:

> We have a special project to share with our hands. While hands are busy, let's also share our thoughts and feelings, and listen well to whomever is speaking. So that everyone will be heard, let's observe the rule that the speaker is he or she who wears this hat. If you have a burning question for the speaker, state it now rather than waiting your turn. Raise your hand and allow the speaker to invite your question. When you, as the speaker, have had your say, pass the hat to the person sitting clockwise from you. Can we all agree on these ground rules? Good! Let's begin.

Your very important task, as in any group magic, is to monitor the flow of energy. This activity is rather spontaneous, and will require quite a bit of sensitivity. Your task: Keep things on track so that each individual has the chance to speak in turn and be heard by the others within an atmosphere that is friendly, warm, fun in some moments, serious in others, and always trusting. Inevitably some spontaneous interruptions will occur. Be gently firm about returning to the ground rules, but flexible if the conversation takes a differing direction than you may have previously planned. Just as long as interruptions are appropriate to the intent of the evening, allow for serendipity.

Some possible topics for the conversation include: my favorite holiday memory, my main wish for the new year, a little but special wish, my worries or fears, what's happened in my life since the last time we were together, if I could change the world, I'd . . . , what I can do to help (this family, circle, our community, country, Mother Earth), I'm most thankful for . . . , and so on. You'll think of alternative topics, I'm sure, and ideas may come spontaneously from the group as well.

The Working of the Ritual

After initial instructions have been given and everyone is settled into the work area, the ritual continues as follow.

> (Opening) *We gather this evening at the time of Winter Solstice, also called Yule, the darkest time of the year, the longest night. In the most ancient of times our ancestors huddled together and prayed for the return of light, and their prayers were granted. So the traditions of Sun were reborn. Though we know the Sun will soon wax again, we still find special warmth in winter's darkest and coldest times through our companionship with each other. Tonight is an especially good time for us to be together, work together, and share our thoughts, our memories, our hopes and intentions for the future, as we reflect on that which binds us together in friendship, in love, and in Spirit. May the results of our work this night be charged with the magic of our sharing. May this magic stay with us as we go back to our separate lives, and be extended also to anyone not present who receives a gift that we create this night.*

Let the work begin. Put on the hat, and let the sharing begin with you. When the work project is completed, say:

> *Let's all join hands. Feel the energy of our magical evening of sharing pass from hand to hand, and see it in the eyes of others in our circle. Feel the warmth of our energy, the beautiful light of peace and love. May it surround and fill us all and permeate what we have created, so that it will be carried out into the world. Though we now go our separate ways, hold in your hearts the unity of sharing and love we have experienced, and take that energy with you to call upon when you have need of it, and to share with others. Let's share a moment of silent thanksgiving to the divine Spirit of Oneness, for our many blessings. (Pause.) As light returns to Earth, let Light be rekindled in our hearts and minds, filling them with the peace of Spirit. Know that our hopes for our world begin with the*

light each of us carries within. May those points of light be shared with others and grow ever more brightly, that peace may spread throughout the Earth. Until we meet again, blessed be.

A Spell for Spring

This spring, as the Sun enters Aries, Saturn has finally begun to move forward in Gemini and away from its three confrontational oppositions with Pluto over the past two years. The Saturn-Pluto theme reflected a major transformative crisis in our world. Structures have been torn down or changed—sometimes drastically—over these two years, forcing all of us to adjust. Though it may seem a little strange to do a ritual for the two Dark Lords on the Spring Equinox, in the eightfold cycle of the year this is the time to "spring forward" into the light. We'll call on Venus to mediate between Saturn and Pluto, and so help us "spring forward" with renewed purpose.

The Spring Equinox occurs on March 20, at 8 p.m. Eastern Standard Time, Saturn's hour on Jupiter's day, Thursday. Our Saturn selves most need Venus now, and we will call on her in her stronger position of applying aspect to Saturn. Ideally, if you are working alone or your group can meet on weeknights, perform your ritual on Thursday evening in the hour of Venus (check planetary hour tables to find when that is). If the Venus hour is too late in your region, choose the Jupiter or Sun hour.

Preparation

The first part of this spell can be an active meditation if you are working alone. Within a group ritual, three people enact the dialogue in invocation of Pluto, Saturn, and Venus. Have the following ready on your altar: a candle for each deity (deep red for Pluto, black or brown for Saturn, white or pink for Venus); a red working candle in a holder; an open incense burner and charcoal; patchouli (for Saturn), dragon's blood resin (for Pluto), and a mixture of crushed, dried thyme and rose petals (for Venus).

The Working

Cast a circle as usual, cleanse and consecrate the tools to be used.

Then, invoke as follows, lighting the corresponding candle.

Pluto, God of the Underworld, Lord of Death and Rebirth, Bringer of Great Change, I call you to this rite. Hear me, I am waiting to receive you. Flow within me and within this sacred circle. So mote it be.

Saturn, Kronos, Father of Time, you who set Limits and Structure, I call you to this rite. Hear me, I am waiting to receive you. Flow within me and within this sacred circle. So mote it be.

Venus, lovely Goddess of Peace and Love, you who are Queen of All that is Fair and Just and Balanced, I call you to this rite. Hear me, I am waiting to receive you. Flow within me and this sacred circle. So mote it be.

The gods speak:

Pluto: Ha! Pathetic humans, open your minds to how much you have yet to learn.

Saturn: (to Pluto) You lawless one. How dare you upset my people's stability.

Pluto: Be still old one! It is high time for a shake-up; they've brought it on themselves. (The two face off and give each other a shove.)

Saturn: But the chaos! All for the sake of your amusement!

Pluto: It's a whole new world—get used to it.

Venus: My lords, aren't you weary of this power struggle yet? Won't you help your people learn reconciliation rather than conflict?

Pluto: I challenge them to look deep within and find a center. I only ask them to pledge to seek and live your Truth.

Each person puts a pinch of dragon's blood resin on the brazier, saying: "Lady, I pledge to live by your Truth."

Saturn: I assist them to organize into workable structures. I call upon them to forge the peace and help others whenever you can. And to pledge to your Goddess an offering.

Put a pinch of patchouli on the brazier, saying: "Lady, I pledge to do my share and more."

Venus: May they find the peace that comes from understanding and the grace of Spirit.

Put a pinch of Venus' incense on the brazier, saying: "Great Mother, to you I pledge my love and sacred honor."

Sit silently for a moment or, if with a group, stand in a circle and begin to hum until everyone blends into a vibrating tone. Thank Pluto for his challenge to see and live your truth. Thank Saturn for inspiring you to do your share responsibly. Thank Venus for her wisdom and grace.

Extinguish the candle of each with a bow, after you have thanked them. If you are able, close your rite by planting a rose bush in honor of the goddess. Care for it as you go forward into the future to carry out the pledges made in this magical working.

A Spell for Summer

This summer, the Moon in Aries has just separated from waning square to the Sun in Cancer. This symbolized a looming "crisis in consciousness" just as the Sun is conjunct Saturn and trining to a Mars-Uranus conjunction in Pisces. This culminating planetary cluster of Sun, Moon, Mercury, Venus, and Saturn occurs on June 30 in Cancer. At the center of the cluster is Saturn.

Therefore, now is a perfect opportunity to bring about creative innovation in our lives, especially where the Cancerian emphasis relates to taking responsibility for home and family.

Ideal Timing

The Summer Solstice occurs in the United States on June 21 at 3:11 pm Eastern Standard Time. That is a Saturday, and if you are doing a group Midsummer ritual you'll likely be doing it that day. You could also choose to perform this ritual during the June 30 Monday planetary cluster mentioned above. On either date, I recommend beginning your working in an hour of the Moon.

Preparation

Have ready a broom, water, salt, incense, athame, and white candle. My house-cleansing incense is composed of frankincense, myrrh, dragon's blood, dill, wood betony, and rose geranium. Grind your incense with mortar and pestle, and burn on charcoal.

The Working

Before you begin the ceremonial part of this ritual, very practical magic is called for. Walk through your home and take a good honest look at it. Any area that is sadly cluttered or disorganized likely reflects such a part of your mind or life. No amount of magic will be as effective in uncluttering these spots than your physically removing the clutter and organizing the space. As you clean up the mess, you also clear your mind. Now you are ready to begin.

Center yourself by breathing deeply and drawing on the energy of the cosmos above and Earth below. Face each of the four directions and call the guardians, asking for the assistance of the four elements. Ask the Goddess and the God for assistance in your work.

With your broom, sweep all around your home, beginning with the front door and working clockwise. Visualize all unwanted thoughts and energies being swept up, controlled, and directed just ahead of your sweeping motion. When you return to the door, sweep them firmly out. If possible, and if it fits your situation, you may want to proceed outdoors and sweep all around your property, as well. Direct what you are sweeping away from yourself into a safe place to return it to the Mother for cleansing and renewal, with harm to none. Afterward, return to your altar.

Ritually blend the water and salt, visualizing the earth/water blend of the Earth Mother's womb. Circle the home and property once more, sprinkling water as you go, cleansing and purifying everything. Think, and state aloud if you wish, the things you are cleansing from your life. Return to your altar and set your incense burning, ritually creating the fire/air essence of spirit. Circle all around your home and property again, purifying and charging everything as you waft the incense smoke. This time think or state aloud all the things you wish to charge into your life.

On your final circuit, ask the Goddess and God to protect and bless your home and family. Carry a lighted white candle in a holder that will protect hands and household furnishings from drips. With the candle scribe a clockwise circle of light energy around your entire home. This is a shield that will welcome those people and situations you want in your life, while protecting against harmful influences. If you are including your property, also scribe as closely as possible around its entire perimeter. Keeping always in mind your visualization of the protective shield, pause at each point of entry to your property—indoor doors and windows; outdoors at each direction, and also at driveways or pathways. Draw a solar cross with the candle, saying: "With the light of the God (*downward motion*) and the love of the Goddess (*horizontal motion*), I seal and protect this passage from all harm. So mote it be!"

When you are finished, return to your altar and thank the Goddess and God for their assistance and blessing. Once again, face each direction and thank the guardians for their assistance. Your rite is complete.

A Spell for Fall

At the beginning of fall the Sun is in Libra, exactly quincunx Mars in Pisces. Mars is conjunct Uranus, and both are retrograde. The quincunx symbolizes any adjustments that need to be made. Mars, retrograde since late July, will turn direct within the week following the Autumnal Equinox. If you have been experiencing frustrating slowdowns, now is the time to charge your Mars energy. Much work needs to be done in this season, including anything involving the spiritual—so it's time to get moving.

Ideal Timing

The Libra Ingress is at 6:48 am, Eastern Standard Time, just before sunrise, which means that in the planetary hour system it occurs in the last nocturnal hour of Monday. By the calendar, this occurs on Tuesday, a day of Mars. I'd choose Tuesday for this working, in an hour of Mars. If that hour just won't work for you, choose an hour of the Sun or Jupiter. If you want to adapt this for your Autumnal Equinox coven ritual and need to work on a weekend, opt for the one after the equinox rather than the one before, when the New

Moon is in Libra and Mars is just turning direct. This will be a stronger time for a Mars working.

Preparation

Before you begin the ritual, have drums and rhythm instruments ready. You and your group can effectively trance by drumming, or by dancing to recorded drumming. Or you can do both, playing at first as part of your centering, and then continuing with recorded drumming in the background as you work with your candles.

Next, assemble the following: a red candle and a metal holder in which it will be safe to burn the candle, a knife for carving the candle, fire oil (cinnamon or dragon's blood), fire incense (dragon's blood mixed with crushed basil, pine, and allspice), an incense burner, small bowls of water and of salt, an eight-inch square piece of paper, and a red pen or pencil.

Cast sacred space in your usual manner and consecrate the tools to be used in the spell. Within this rite you'll be calling on Mars as god of fire, or if you prefer on Artemis or Brighid as fire goddesses.

The Working

Center by stretching tall, with feet firmly planted on the ground. Feel the energy of the Earth coming up into your body from her molten core. Now visualize the planet Mars shining above you, a shining reddish point of light. Call down a red ray of light from it, and feel it enter your body through your head. Allow this ray to flow throughout you, glowing and building within as you begin to slowly drum. Keep a consistent rhythm and slowly build it as you feel the energy build within you. Think about what it is that you need to get moving in your life. Feel it, want it, desire it, demand it as you drum ever faster. When your intent is fully clear and the energy peaks, culminate with a flourish and then drop to the floor, grounding a measure of the energy while you take time for a few breaths and focus your intent into action. Hold your intent through all the actions that follow.

Cleanse the candle by rubbing it with your fingers dipped in salted water, and say, "As I cleanse and purify this tool with the power of earth and water, I cleanse myself of fear and self-doubt and make pure my heart with compassion for myself and others."

Charge the candle by passing it through incense smoke, saying, "As I charge this tool with the power of fire and air, I charge myself with the will, courage, passion, and faith of a warrior of Spirit." With oil on your fingertips, touch your forehead and your heart, and then rub oil on the candle, saying, "With this oil of Mars fire, I anoint myself and this tool to my desire and my purpose." Now, carve the astrological glyph for Mars (♂) all around the candle, at least eight times.

Draw a large Mars glyph in the center of your paper square. Then begin writing around the outside edges, over and over again, a short phrase that identifies to you what you will. Fold the paper in an eightfold manner as follows. Fold in half, then half again, then into a triangle, thus creating eight triangles. Sprinkle it with water, pass it though the incense smoke, and anoint it with oil, using the same words as for the candle. Place it under the candleholder.

Cleanse and charge a length of red thread in the same manner as you did the candle (about a yard will do). Wrap the thread tightly around the candle, spiraling from top to bottom, saying, "As I bind this candle, I bind myself to persist with courage and honor to the fulfillment of my purpose." Put the bound candle into its holder. Take a deep breath, focus, and light your candle.

Begin slowly drumming or dancing again, once again building the energy until it peaks, then ground some of it into the earth, and offer thanks for the energy and focus you have received. The candle should be burned all the way down. Keep the paper in a safe place until you have achieved your intent, and then, once again giving thanks to Mars, burn it, returning it to Spirit.

For Further Reading

Cunningham, Scott. *Wicca: A Guide for the Solitary Practitioner*. St. Paul: Llewellyn, 1998.

McCoy, Edain. *Inside a Witch's Coven*. St. Paul: Llewellyn, 1997.

———. *Magick & Rituals of the Moon*. St. Paul: Llewellyn, 2001.

Sun Sign Selling
The Astrology of Sales

By Janet Bowman Johnson

Sold anything lately? Even if you say no, you probably have. Think about it. If you persuade your date to go to the movie of your choice . . . when you talk your lover into giving you a back rub . . . when you talk your kids into eating Cheerios instead of Coco Puffs . . . when you convince your spouse to eat at KFC instead of McDonalds. . . . You've just "sold" them. We all sell things. Persuasion is a skill everyone has, and everyone uses. Kids are really good at it. It's a natural skill that is needed for survival, so we have to have it.

While none of us are totally typical of our Sun sign alone (which is based on the month and day of birth) the core characteristics of that sign will still be present in our character. And character is, well, character.

And each of us characters has our own style of selling things. Do you think an Aries has the same style of persuasion as a Taurus? No way. They both do it, but they do it very differently.

Aries (March 20 – April 18)

How might you expect a Ram to approach sales? Aggressively? You're right. This Mars-ruled sign is very straightforward, often no-nonsense, and wants action now. Mars is the god of war and strife: He rules action, not patience, and Aries signs are known for their impatience. Yet, they can be charming, too. Aries is assertive, but also playful, childlike, and compulsively optimistic. They are in perpetual fast-forward motion, and rarely look back—so follow-up is not their strong suit.

The Aries selling style is assertive: They're the first ones out the door, and the first ones to go through a potential client's door. The problem is, due to their headlong rush they don't always plan well, so the door they burst through may be the wrong one. This may cause some confusion, and it certainly creates wasted time, but their natural optimism helps them to maintain their drive. And they are driven. Remember that need for action? Aries signs need to have ongoing challenges to keep their attention. Boredom is a dangerous state for an Aries to visit. Active Aries signs will always find some trouble to get into.

Their selling style is to get directly to the point. It might go something like this: "This-gizmo-is-the-best-one-made-and-your-life-will-never-be-complete-without-it-so-let-me-show-you-how-it-works-and-then-we-can-decide-how-you-want-to-pay-for-it." You may feel breathless when they're through with you, but you'll own the best damn gizmo ever made.

Aries women can seem especially aggressive, since their direct style is in stark contrast to our cultural expectations for women in this country (although that is changing). The dynamic Mars energy is very masculine, and it can be a challenging thing for the Aries gal to handle smoothly. If she doesn't have a strong and feminine Venus influence to balance her Mars, she may seem pretty coarse and quarrelsome. She'll also be effective. Most Aries signs are effective at sales. All you have to do is keep them pointed in the right direction. If you need someone driven to action, Aries is the one.

Taurus (April 19 – May 19)

Taurus, the gentle Bull, has a different tactic altogether. Taurus signs may be the last ones out of the office, but that's because they took the time to plan out which sales targets to pursue, and then made calls to those targets to set appointments. Taurus is a builder by nature: slow and patient, but very thorough. Taurus people finish what they start. They prefer to qualify their leads because they hate to waste time chasing something that takes them nowhere. Ruled by social and comfort-loving Venus, Taurus signs will approach more gently than assertive Aries. And they'll be sure they have all their documentation in place before they go. Taurus is a fixed sign—and that means controlling. Taureans like things to stay where they put them, and they need to feel confident about where they're going and what they're doing before they start. They don't do "last minute" very well. But they don't give up either. Once they've set a target (and they don't choose their targets randomly—they will do their research) they'll continue to pursue until they win. In fact, even being asked not to come back may not deter them from a target. They'll just change their tactics and try it from a different angle. Taureans are very persistent.

Unlike some other signs, Taurus is motivated by money—they like nice things; quality things. As a Venus-ruled earth sign, Taurus loves things that are both beautiful and serviceable; high quality things that last. And Taurus signs are willing to do what it takes to get them—no matter how long it takes. They do tend to be a little slow by nature. (Taureans march to their own measured beat, and will not be hurried. Ever try to push a Bull?) People born under Taurus build lasting and profitable relationships with clients and customers. And their follow-up is excellent. With the same thoroughness used to plan their sales calls and appointments, they'll also make those follow-up calls, send those (hand-written) notes, and stay in touch with their customers. So be patient with your tenacious Taurus. Give him the tools he needs and watch him build the business. If you need a dependable and tenacious person, one who never gives up, Taurus is it.

Gemini (May 20 – June 20)

Gemini loves to talk. This Mercury-ruled sign of the Twins is intellectually and verbally based. Have you ever been around two Geminis at the same time? It's an incredible experience. Of course, you can't get a word in edge-wise, but it doesn't really matter. Just being there is rewarding for the sheer audacity of it—so long as you don't have to experience it twice. These two talk at the same time and understand each other. It's amazing. A Gemini's approach to sales is to talk a lot and listen a little and talk some more. Geminis love to meet people and learn about them, and they can talk to just about anyone about almost anything, so gaining rapport is pretty easy for them. Closing the sale may be problematical, however, since they eventually have to shut up to do it. Geminis really can do two things at once, too. So, just because they're talking don't assume they can't hear you, or don't know what you're doing. They do. And it's often easier for them to get through a door because they get acquainted so quickly and gain rapport so readily. That's a tremendous skill in any business, but especially in sales.

Geminis make natural telemarketers. They love to talk on the telephone—but you may have to keep an eye on them to be sure they're still talking business. Even if they're not, however, they'll probably close the sale anyway. Geminis are awfully easy to get to know—and they seem to know so much. Geminis are really skilled at capturing buzzwords and learning just enough about something to sound more knowledgeable than they are. It's a gift and a curse—a gift because it's what makes it so easy to talk with anyone, whether it's the president or the janitor, and a curse because, since they sound like they know what they're talking about, assumptions can be made that don't work out well. So Geminis need to be encouraged to get all the facts before they close the deal—and they need to learn to listen more, and take notes. But when you need someone to break the ice and gain rapport quickly, Gemini's the one.

Cancer (June 21– July 21)

Moon-ruled Cancer (the Crab) is the first real caretaker in the group. It is the Cancer nature to nurture and protect others. Great customer service is the motto here. Cancer is a water sign, and that means they are emotionally based, not rationally based. The way you feel is what's most important to Cancer. So, as a salesperson, a Cancer is more concerned with customer service than with sales goals. Cancers want to know that your needs are met and that you feel good about doing business with them.

Cancer rules the stomach (as well as the breasts) so these signs often want to feed or nurture their clients in some way. Client lunches or dinners are a natural part of the Cancer agenda. Cancer's selling style takes a little longer than Aries and Gemini, because Cancer approaches things in a round-about manner, which goes something like this: "How are you today? How's the family? Is soccer season done yet? How did the kids do? . . ." Now you see why Cancer takes a little longer to close the sale.

A typical Cancer manager often has food at his or her desk—food to offer employees, clients, and themselves. Cancers can be assertive, and they are very protective—of both their clients and their turf. Home and family is always first priority, even if they live alone. The lone Cancer creates family wherever she is—so the sales team or the office staff becomes "family," whom she needs to nurture and protect. Cancers do exceptionally well selling insurance, home protection systems, or residential real estate. Their follow-up is good, too. Once a relationship is established with the customer, Cancer will be sure that the customer's needs are met to the best of his or her ability, and service will be at the top of the list in his or her sales skills.

Cancer excels in management—not leadership, per se, but management; taking care of things, people, situations, etc. If you need a natural organizer who will take excellent care of your clients, Cancer's the right choice.

Leo (July 22 – August 21)

The Lion is a team player, so long as it's his team and he gets to be the coach. Leo loves to be the boss. And Leos want to deal with other bosses, so these are the people to send in when you need to reach the CEO, COO, CFO or the prez. Leo loves to play with the big dogs. Even if a Leo isn't a big dog himself, he'll try to sound like one. Remember in the movie *The Lion King*, when the cub is learning to roar? He lets out a squeaky attempt and everyone in the audience giggles. That's how a Leo starts out—expecting to make a big noise (or a big splash) right away. But even a Leo has to earn it. The point is, Leos expect to be king or queen of the hill. So, a Leo will talk big even if she or he isn't. But any size Leo loves a challenge, and as part of a sales team, he or she really wants to win.

Sun-ruled Leo has a knack for seeing the "big picture" versus getting tangled up in the details. So give them the vision and they'll hold it for you. Just as the Sun is the overlord of our solar system, so Leo is the lord of . . . well, whatever they're involved in. Leos will go after a goal with heart and soul set on winning through. As with all fixed signs, Leos won't quit, won't give up, won't fail. They have great stamina and determination once a goal is set. And, as the Sun unfailingly shines, so Leo will pursue sales goals with unfailing warmth and enthusiasm.

Leos love to play. Make the sales goal look like a game for them to win and they'll throw themselves into it with everything they've got. Ever watch a big cat play? Cats have the natural killer instinct. Whether it's a dangling ball of yarn or a field mouse, the cat will stalk and pounce. They're very successful hunters. Leos are very successful players in the sales game. They'll stalk their sales target, wait till just the right moment, and pounce for the close of the sale. Then they'll proudly return to the office with their "kill" to await your worthy praise. Don't forget the praise part. To encourage continuing success, be sure to honor the king and queen for their accomplishments—and do it in front of the sales team. Leo needs recognition and attention. Fame, more than fortune, is what motivates Leo. If you need someone who can play with the big boys, Leo's it.

Virgo (August 22 – September 21)

If any Virgo (Maiden or Server) has a choice, she probably won't choose sales as a career. But if she does, here's how she'll handle it: with great attention to the little things. Virgos sweat the small stuff every day of their natural lives. Virgos don't miss the forest for the trees, they miss the trees for the veins on the leaves of the trees. Discernment is their natural gift. As an earth sign, Virgos are grounded in practicalities, and since they are ruled by Mercury those practicalities always involve a lot of details. Mercury is the planet of rational thoughts. Earth signs have to do with tangible, rational things. Virgo is both thought-based and an earth sign, so Virgos have to apply what they know in rational ways. In sales, they'll pay attention to the details and apply what they know in practical ways to solve their customers' problems and concerns. They'll also do the necessary research to accomplish that, which means they'll ask the right questions and, determined to serve their clients well, they'll find a way to fix whatever's broken—be it systems, products, or concepts. Virgos are also notoriously cost-conscious, so they'll do it cheaper, too.

A Virgo's natural arena is customer service, and due to a natural tendency to hypochondria (since Virgos pay so close attention to details, they feel every little ache or pain as if it were a big deal) they do well in health- or nutrition-related sales.

Virgos tend to be pretty observant, often picking up on things other sales people miss. Because of their intense awareness of innuendo, body language, and other subtle details, Virgos won't miss a single thing.

They do have to watch their humor, however. Virgos have a very dry wit and tend to say things in jest with such a straight face that they are taken seriously. More likely they're just trying to see if you really are paying attention.

Overall, due to their attention to details, Virgo is another sales person who does selling through service. If you need someone who is rational, articulate, and gets the job done, Virgo's the one.

Libra (September 22 – October 22)

Now here's a natural sales person. Libras are known for their charm, finesse, and persuasiveness. Remember all that hype about Libras being indecisive? Well, it's true, they are—but in this case it works in their favor. Here's how: Libras are indecisive because they weigh and balance everything (their symbol is the Scales)—wanting to please everyone and create win-win solutions. Since Venus-ruled Libras want everyone to love them and be happy with their decisions, that weighing and balancing can go on incessantly. Since they're always looking at things from so many different perspectives, it's just natural for them to have already considered just about every angle you can think of. Therefore, no argument can hold water with a Libra because he's already come up with a solution for it. Libras are absolutely the best at playing devil's advocate. They think of all the arguments ahead of time, come up with plausible answers to your concerns, and just wait for an opening. Therefore, no rational argument will deter them.

These air signs are thinkers and talkers. There's not much that will slow them down once they're on a roll. Also, since they're ruled by Venus, Libras use their natural charm to win you over. It can be very difficult to say no to a Libra who's done her sales homework.

Actually, that need to weigh and balance is based on a desire to be fair and just to everyone involved. A natural facilitator and negotiator, Libra's the one to send in when you have a problem with a client. They'll find a way to get things moving again. Libras have a better handle on negotiating than all the other signs put together. So, if you need s negotiator on your sales team, a Libra sign is the one to hire.

Libras want people to feel good about doing business with them, and they treat their customers accordingly, both before and after the sale. Once in a while you'll run into a Libra who's truly "slick" (ugh) but more often you'll come away from the deal feeling pretty good about it all. And since Libras have a strong need to be liked, you can usually negotiate with them—at least a little. If you need someone who is sophisticated, fair, and client-friendly, Libra's the right choice.

Scorpio (October 23 – November 20)

Shrewd: that's Scorpio. Alternately represented by the Scorpion or the Eagle, Scorpio is intensely driven, whether in sales or any other line of work. Scorpio wants to win—at (almost) any cost. Of all the signs, Scorpios are the most passionate about what they do. Once involved, Scorpio tends to stay involved. A fixed sign, Scorpio can be very tenacious. Also a water sign, Scorpio is compassionate and nurturing, wanting to assure the well-being of all client relationships. But Scorpios are the least likely to show their emotions in their facial expressions. In fact, they can have quite the poker face. The client will never know exactly what Scorpio is thinking, unless for some reason Scorpio chooses to tell them. Scorpios play their cards close to their chests—an important skill when it comes to negotiating the close on an major deal.

Scorpio is very loyal by nature (it's a fixed sign) so you don't see a typical Scorpio job-hopping. They like to establish themselves with a company or within an industry and become very knowledgeable in their field. Scorpios have a naturally investigative nature, and they seem to get information no one else has access to. They're willing to do the research necessary to gather enough information to close those big accounts. Leave the smaller accounts to Gemini or Virgo—give the big boys to Leo and Scorpio. Scorpio will be the better customer-service person—a Scorpio tends to take his customer commitments very seriously. And Scorpios expect their customers to also be loyal to them. Scorpios can be aggressive when necessary to close a deal, which is not a quality all the other signs share. So for that hard-to-close business, Scorpio's the one.

Sagittarius (November 21 – December 20)

This highly enthusiastic Archer goes into sales for the freedom. They hate a boring desk job. Sagittarius is Jupiter-ruled, and Jupiter, the largest planet in our solar system, represents Sagittarius's need to have room to explore, expand, and roam. Sagittarius is the original trader—the one who travels the world in search of truth, trading along the way to finance the voyage. Sagittarians also have a tendency to tell the (usually very blunt) truth, so, unlike Scorpios (who will take a secret to the grave) Sagittarians can't be trusted not to speak out. So, even if it isn't prudent to say something, they'll probably say it anyway. But don't worry too much—a Sagittarius's clients will love him. They appreciate the refreshing honesty with which Sagittarius approaches sales. You know what to expect when you deal with a Sagittarius, because she or he will tell you exactly what's going on.

Jupiter is also the planet of royalty and riches, and Sagittarius signs tend to expect to be well paid for their time and efforts—by their company, and by their clients. So don't expect a Sagittarius to offer clients a discount: They'll pay full price, and like it.

Much less suave than Libra, a little less dependable than Taurus, and not as customer-service oriented as Cancer or Scorpio, Sagittarius is all about the next frontier. They're the ones to hire when you're ready to take your business to the next level, or open new offices overseas, or on the opposite coast. Fire-sign Sagittarius gets excited about checking out a new territory, breaking into a new area, exploring future possibilities with clients and prospects, and learning something new. If you want someone to expand your business, Sagittarius is the one.

Capricorn (December 21 – January 18)

Industrious, hardworking, honest Capricorn is a responsible sales-person. This sign does things the hard way, the traditional way, the-way-it's-always-been-done way. Capricorn is a traditionalist in every sense of the word. Capricorn is also very reliable. When Capricorns have firm goals, they'll reach them; if it takes a lifetime, they'll get the job done.

Capricorn is an earth sign: practical, rational, grounded. Capricorns need things to make sense to them. They need to see results—tangible, I-can-see-feel-taste-and-touch-it results. So don't make dreamy promises to a Capricorn: Lay out the cash value for their efforts. Remember, though, that a typical Capricorn tends to under-value his worth. And if you pay him more than he thinks he's worth, it may sabotage his performance. So make sure you pay Capricorns fair market value for their services—no more, no less—and be sure it's on time.

Capricorn is ruled by Saturn—the planet of serious, the planet of dour, the planet of answerable. Saturn sits on you and weights you down until you do what you know you should have done in the first place. Saturn is heavy. And Capricorn is used to heavy. Capricorns will take on more than most, and handle it effectively. They're used to doing the hard work and they are determined to go the whole road. Capricorns will get where they're going . . . they just don't have a lot of fun getting there.

Capricorns are ambitious—always looking to go one more notch up the corporate ladder. So if you want someone who will stick to business, work hard, do it by the book, and be on time, get a Capricorn. They make good team leaders—not because they inspire, but because they're responsible and hard working, and will demand the same of their sales teams. If you need a responsible, dependable, and ambitious person, Capricorn's the one.

Aquarius (January 19 – February 17)

Aquarius knows everybody. A natural networker, these signs just seem to meet people wherever they go, and they use those connections. Water Bearers don't care so much about selling, per se. They care about making connections, finding out how things work, and solving problems. They make great sales people because, ultimately, that's what sales people do. They solve problems. To be able to solve problems, you must first ask appropriate questions and then listen in order to understand what the problems might be. Aquarians are great listeners. It's one of the things customers love about them. They listen, and they remember what you've said. Their customers feel as though they've been heard and acknowledged, which is something they will always appreciate.

Aquarius is an air sign, which means that communication is vital. Aquarians are great information gatherers, and, since they're always gathering information from a wide variety of sources, they're frequently able to accurately predict future trends well before anyone else sees it happening. So if your Aquarian sales rep says she sees a trend toward an increased need for pork bellies, now is the time to invest. Also, if an Aquarius sees a new trend that may affect your business, it should be noted and, if possible, acted upon.

Unlike Gemini (frequently) and Sagittarius (sometimes), both of whom may forget an appointment, Aquarius is always on time for meetings. If you have a luncheon appointment with an Aquarian, even if it's two months from now, the Aquarian will be there at that time, on that date, in that restaurant. The restaurant may not still be there, but the Aquarian will be, and she'll expect you to be there as well.

Aquarians are very skilled at remaining detached and objective about what's happening around them. They observe and analyze before moving forward. If you need someone who is rational, dependable, a skilled listener, and able to talk with anyone about anything, Aquarius is the one.

Pisces (February 18 – March 19)

Pisces is not a "natural" sales person, but if these signs are in sales, they'll serve their customers well. Unlike rational Aquarius, Pisces is emotionally based rather than intellectually based. These signs are much more likely to dismiss their own needs and desires in favor of yours. They need to establish their own boundaries before they will be effective in sales; otherwise they may become emotionally tangled in their clients' affairs, and business will suffer because of it. Typical Pisceans always have boundary issues. It is difficult for them to define where they leave off and you begin.

Pisces is the most intuitive and sensitive of all the signs and can use that skill during sales calls to sense what is really going on with the client, as opposed to what the client says is going on. I have a Pisces client who uses this skill in an exciting way: Her clients hire her to sit in unobtrusively on important meetings and then report back on some of the undercurrents and "unsaid" things that happened during the meeting. If Pisces signs are negotiating an important deal, or working with a foreign culture where language or cultural differences may be problematic, this insight can substantially assist them in knowing what is really going on.

It's an interesting skill, and Pisceans use it well, provided they stay grounded and know how to separate themselves from the client's problems. They're so remarkably sensitive to the feelings and emotions of others that it may at times interfere with their sales work. However, they truly want to serve their customers, and will suffer emotionally when unable to do so.

Pisceans are people who truly need to believe in what they're selling to be effective. Otherwise they're using their skills for deception instead of service, and ultimately that does not serve them, their company, or their clients. If you need someone who is truly service-oriented and intuitively sensitive to client needs, Pisces is the one.

For Further Reading

Bowman Johnson, Janet. *Sun Sign Selling: Increase Your Success by Understanding the 12 Styles of Selling and Buying!* Tempe, Ariz.: American Federation of Astrologers, 2002.

How Loki Saved the Sun and the Moon

by Therese Francis

After hearing the Sibyl's prophecy about Ragnarok and the fate of the gods of Aesir, Odin and Thor decided that Asgaard needed a defensive wall. So they contacted the Master Smith and had him build an impregnable wall around Asgaard to keep the giants out. In payment, the Master Smith demanded the Sun and the Moon as his servants. He would keep them in his forge and be able to melt any metal with their assistance.

Pressured by a great need to get the wall built, Odin agreed to the Master Smith's terms, upon the condition that the Master Smith must complete the wall within three days or forfeit his claims to the Sun and the Moon. Odin didn't think this would be possible, and therefore the Sun and the Moon would be safe. The Master Smith agreed and started work the next day.

By sunset on the first day, the Master Smith had finished a third of the wall. This made the gods of the Aesir nervous, to say the least. It looked as though the Master Smith would make good on his end of the bargain. And, out of honor, there was nothing the gods of the Aesir could do to back out of the pledge. Plus, they needed the wall to protect Asgaard. Things did not look good, and so Thor decided to spy on the Master Smith at his work the next day to determine if there was any way to stall the construction of the wall.

The next day, so as not to be noticed, Thor watched the Master Smith from a distance. He discovered that the Master Smith's secret was an incredible horse that could pull a sleigh ten times heavier than what an ordinary horse could pull, and at five times the speed. It was no wonder, Thor mused, that the Master Smith was already finished with two-thirds of the wall by sunset the second day. At this rate, the Master Smith would easily finish the remaining third by sundown the next day.

Thor brought his news to the council that night. No one could think of anything to do to prevent the Master Smith from finishing the wall on time. In desperation, everyone turned to Loki, the trickster god.

"Do something, or I'll bind you to the center of the Earth forever," threatened Odin.

"Do something, or I'll strike you down with my great hammer, Mjollnir," roared Thor.

Loki wasn't sure what he would do, but he agreed that the Master Smith's wall needed to be stalled to protect the Sun and the Moon. For without the Sun and the Moon, everyone would live in total darkness, and Loki, like the rest of the gods, did not want that.

Therefore, on the morning of the third day, Thor took Loki to his spying place to watch the Master Smith and develop a plan. Watching the great steed pulling the sleigh loaded with materials for finishing the wall, Loki got an idea. If the horse could be distracted before he reached the wall, the Master Smith would need to pull the sleigh himself. Although the Master Smith was incredibly strong, he was not as strong as the great stallion, and could not finish the wall himself.

So Loki shapeshifted into a beautiful mare that could run at the speed of the wind. In this form, Loki galloped out onto the plains surrounding Asgaard. When she got just within hearing distance, she neighed loudly, challenging the stallion to come to her. The stallion stopped in his tracks and perked up his ears. Again he heard the mare out on the plateau. Rearing up, he turned in his tracks and galloped out onto the plains, looking for the mare. Meanwhile, the Master Smith yelled after him and cursed, knowing there was no way for him to retrieve the stallion in time to finish the wall.

Loki, in the guise of the mare, was able to lure the stallion away from the Master Smith for several hours. Although the Master Smith made a gallant effort to finish the wall without the assistance of the stallion, he was unable to complete it. As the Sun set in the west, an area the size of the Master Smith's thumb was unfinished. Thus he forfeited his claims to the Sun and the Moon.

For Further Reading

Nibelungenlied. A. T. Hatto, translator. New York: Penguin, 1965.

The Poetic Edda. Carolyne Larrington, translator. New York: Oxford University Press, 1999.

Planetary Associations

Sun: Authority figures, favors, advancement, health, success, display, drama, promotion, fun, matters related to Leo and the Fifth House.

Moon: Short trips, women, children, the public, domestic concerns, emotions, fluids, matters related to Cancer and the Fourth House.

Mercury: Communications, correspondence, phone calls, computers, messages, education, students, travel, merchants, editing, writing, advertising, signing contracts, siblings, neighbors, kin, matters related to Gemini, Virgo, and the Third and Sixth Houses.

Venus: Affection, relationships, partnerships, alliances, grace, beauty, harmony, luxury, love, art, music, social activity, marriage, decorating, cosmetics, gifts, income, matters related to Taurus, Libra, and the Second and Seventh Houses.

Mars: Strife, aggression, sex, physical energy, muscular activity, guns, tools, metals, cutting, surgery, police, soldiers, combat, confrontation, matters related to Aries, Scorpio, and the First and Eighth Houses.

Jupiter: Publishing, college education, long-distance travel, foreign interests, religion, philosophy, forecasting, broadcasting, publicity, expansion, luck, growth, sports, horses, the law, matters related to Sagittarius, Pisces, and the Ninth and Twelfth Houses.

Saturn: Structure, reality, the laws of society, limits, obstacles, tests, hard work, endurance, real estate, dentists, bones, teeth, matters related to Capricorn, Aquarius, and the Tenth and Eleventh Houses.

Uranus: Astrology, the New Age, technology, computers, modern gadgets, lecturing, advising, counseling, inventions, reforms, electricity, new methods, originality, sudden events, matters related to Aquarius and the Eleventh House.

Neptune: Mysticism, music, creative imagination, dance, illusion, sacrifice, service oil, chemicals, paint, drugs, anesthesia, sleep, religious experience, matters related to Pisces and the Twelfth House.

Pluto: Probing, penetration, goods of the dead, investigation, insurance, taxes, other people's money, loans, the masses, the underworld, transformation, death, matters related to Scorpio and the Eighth House.

Activities Ruled by the Planets

To check aspects for the activity you have in mind, find the planet that rules it.

Sun: Advertising, buying, selling, speculating, short trips, meeting people, anything involving groups or showmanship, putting up exhibits, running fairs and raffles, growing crops, health matters.

Moon: Any small change in routine, asking favors, borrowing or lending money, household activities such as baking, canning, cooking, washing, ironing, cleaning, and taking care of small children.

Mercury: Bargaining, bookkeeping, dealing with literary agents, publishing, filing, hiring employees, learning languages, literary work, placing ads, preparing accounts, studying, telephoning, visiting friends.

Venus: Amusement, beauty care, courtship, dating, decorating homes, designing, getting together with friends, household improvements, planning parties, shopping.

Mars: Good for all business matters, mechanical affairs, buying or selling animals, dealing with contractors, hunting, studying.

Jupiter: Activities involving charity, education, or science, correspondence courses, self-improvement, reading, researching, studying.

Saturn: Anything involving family ties or legal matters such as wills and estates, taking care of debts, dealing with lawyers, financing, joint money matters, real estate, relations with older people.

Uranus: Air travel, all partnerships, changes and adjustment, civil rights, new contacts, new ideas, new rules, patenting inventions, progress, social action, starting journeys.

Neptune: Advertising, dealing with psychological upsets, health foods and resorts, large social affairs, nightclubs, psychic healing, travel by water, restaurants, visits, welfare, working with institutions.

Pluto: Anything dealing with energy and enthusiasm, skill and alertness, personal relationships, original thought.

Planetary Business Guide

Collections: Try to make collections on days when your Sun is well aspected. Avoid days when Mars or Saturn are aspected. If possible, the Moon should be in a cardinal sign: Aries, Cancer, Libra, or Capricorn. It is more difficult to collect when the Moon is in Taurus or Scorpio.

Employment, Promotion: Choose a day when your Sun is favorably aspected or the Moon is in your Tenth House. Good aspects of Venus or Jupiter to your Tenth House are also beneficial.

Loans: Moon in the first and second quarters favors the lender; Moon in the third and fourth quarters favors the borrower. Good aspects of Jupiter or Venus to the Moon are favorable to both, as is Moon in Leo, Sagittarius, Aquarius, or Pisces.

New Ventures: Things usually get off to a better start during the increase of the Moon. If there is impatience, anxiety, or deadlock, it can often be broken at the Full Moon. Agreements can soon be reached then.

Partnerships: Agreements and partnerships should be made on a day that is favorable to both parties. Mars, Neptune, Pluto, and Saturn should not be square or opposite the Moon. It is best to make an agreement or partnership when the Moon is in a mutable sign, especially Gemini or Virgo. The other signs are not favorable, with the possible exception of Leo or Capricorn. Begin partnerships when the Moon is increasing in light, as this is a favorable time for starting new ventures.

Public Relations: The Moon rules the public, so this must be well aspected, particularly by the Sun, Mercury, Uranus, or Neptune.

Selling: In general, selling is favored by good aspects of Venus, Jupiter, or Mercury to the Moon. Afflictions of Saturn retard. If you know the planetary ruler of your product, try to get this well aspected by Venus, Jupiter, or the Moon. Your product will be more highly valued then.

Signing Important Papers: Sign contracts or agreements when the Moon is increasing in a fruitful sign. Avoid days when Mars, Saturn, Neptune, or Pluto are afflicting the Moon. Don't sign anything if your Sun is badly afflicted.

About the Authors

Janet Bowman Johnson is an accredited professional astrologer with more than thirty years of experience. She provides personal and business forecasting for an international clientele. She is past vice president of Professional Astrologers, Inc., and serves on the Board of Directors for the American Federation of Astrologers. You can visit her website at http://www.astro-insights.com.

Stephanie Clement is an accomplished astrologer with twenty-five years of professional experience. She has written numerous magazine articles and several books, including *Charting Your Career* and *Charting Your Spiritual Path With Astrology*.

Alice DeVille, an internationally known astrologer and writer, has a busy consulting practice in Virginia. Her specialties include relationships, career and change management, government affairs, real estate, and business advice. She has developed and presented nearly one hundred workshops and seminars related to astrological, metaphysical, motivational, and business themes. Alice also writes astrology articles for the StarIQ.com website.

Marguerite Elsbeth, also known as Senihele (Sparrowhawk), is a hereditary Sicilian strega, and is also proud of her Lenni Lenape (Delaware) Indian ancestry. She is a professional astrologer, tarot reader, and spiritual healer. Marguerite is the author of *Crystal Medicine*, and co-author of *The Silver Wheel: Women's Myths and Mysteries in the Celtic Tradition*. You can visit her website at http://practical SPIRITkeeping.com.

Sasha Fenton has been reading hands, cards, and horoscopes since childhood, and she eventually teamed her talents with her writing ability to become the author of twenty-three books and five years worth of annual horoscope guides—with more in the pipeline. You can visit her website at http://www.sashafenton.com.

Therese Francis is an author, astrologer, folklorist, herbalist, and public speaker. Her most recent books are *The Mercury Retrograde Book* and *20 Herbs to Take Outdoors*. She is also author of numerous articles on herbs, astrology, and New Age topics, and has written for Llewellyn for several years. An active member of the Santa Fe Astrology Forum, she teaches astrology, psychic and intuitive development, self defense, and integration of body, mind, and spirit.

Jonathan Keyes writes a regular "lunar health" column for StarIQ.com and has written for the *Mountain Astrologer*. Jonathan is a health astrologer who works with herbs, diet, and animal totems to help harmonize planetary influences for health and well-being.

Dorothy Oja is a certified astrological professional and career astrologer offering complete astrological consulting through her practice, MINDWORKS. Dorothy writes a free weekly e-zine, *Planet Weather*, which includes social and cultural commentary. She is the author of *Relationship Compatibility & Conflict*—a computer interpretive report that analyzes romantic relationships. You can visit her website at http://www.planetweather.net.

Leeda Alleyn Pacotti practices as a naturopathic physician, nutritional counselor, and master herbalist, incorporating specialized diagnostics of dream language, health astrology, observations from Chinese medicine, and the resurrected science of personology. Recently her investigations have extended into neural and brain dysfunctions, particularly ADHD and the emotional signals of physical illness.

Bruce Scofield is a professional astrological consultant who works with clients in the United States and abroad. As a consulting astrologer he specializes in both psychological astrology and electional astrology. His special interest is the astrology of ancient civilizations, especially that of the Maya and Aztecs. He is the author of thirteen books and numerous magazine and journal articles and is on the faculty of Kepler College.

Maria K. Simms, author of *A Time for Magick* and *The Witch's Circle*, has been an astrologer for nearly thirty years. She has also written numerous astrology books, articles, and computer texts. Maria is Chair of the National Council for Geocosmic Research. A Wiccan high priestess, Maria is credentialed as clergy by Covenant of the Goddess. Her Circle of the Cosmic Muse is active in the seacoast area of New Hampshire.

Joanne Wickenburg has been a practicing astrologer for over thirty years. She is the author of six books and a comprehensive correspondence course on astrology. Joanne has lectured extensively throughout the U.S. and Canada and is a regular speaker at numerous national and international conferences. Joanne is the Chair of the Board of Trustees of Kepler College of Astrological Arts & Sciences.

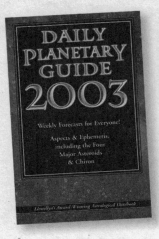

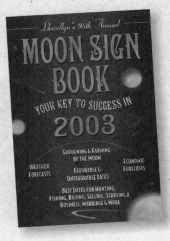

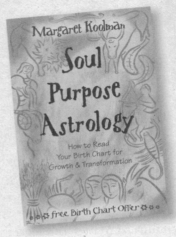